Woman Abuse
FACTS REPLACING MYTHS _____

Woman Abuse
FACTS REPLACING MYTHS _____

Lewis Okun

State University of New York Press _____

Published by
State University of New York Press Albany

© 1986 State University of New York

For information, address State University of New York
Press, State University Plaza, Albany, N.Y., 12246

Library of Congress Cataloging in Publication Data

Okum, Lewis, 1954—

Woman abuse.

(SUNY series in transpersonal and humanistic psychology)

Bibliography: p.

Includes index.

1. Family violence—United States. 2. Wife abuse—
United States. I. Title. II. Series.

HQ809.3.U5037 1985   362.8'3   84-26912

ISBN 0-88706-077-3

ISBN 0-88706-079-X (pbk.)

10 9 8 7 6 5 4 3 2 1

CONTENTS _____

v

vi

Assailant's Alcohol Abuse
Batterer's Criminal Record of Violent Offenses

Factors Relating to the Level of Violence
Predictors of Batterers' Counseling Outcomes

Discussion
Indications for Future Research

LIST OF TABLES _____

ACKNOWLEDGMENTS

No one has played a greater role in the writing of this book than the battered women and their families whose lives are reflected in Part II. I wish I could thank them all by name, but ethical principles of confidentiality and safety prohibit me from doing so. Anyone who knows anything about woman-battering has learned her or his knowledge either through direct subjection to abuse or—directly or secondhand—from battered women. Therefore, I wish to express my humble thanks and my respectful admiration to my most important teachers, the former residents of SAFE House whom I had the privilege to meet and to attempt to serve.

Much has been written about the low self-esteem and fear experienced by battered women. The public stereotype of the battered woman tends to portray her as weak, or as shrewishly provocative, or both. Yet as I recall the battered women whom I have counseled, and those of my social acquaintance, I am impressed by their display of courage, strength, devotion to their children and families, their practicality and common sense, charm, and friendliness. As I reflect on the enormous hardships these women have faced, their ability to continue to display such fine human qualities moves me to genuine awe. I hope that I manage to convey the utmost respect for battered women on the pages that follow, for certainly that is what I feel.

I would also like to thank the women's advocates with whom I worked at SAFE House: Marlene Atkins, Susan Smith, Susan McGee, Michele Guthrie, Janice McKinnon, Carole McCabe, Jane Conrad, Michelle Wood, Bernadine Williams, Ann Thomas, Elva Williams, Viki Quibell, Barbara Warrington, Nancy Ralph, Lorraine Lafata, Karen Yinger, Susan Huff, Beverly Fish, Lois Carr, Lynn Couey, Maureen Fitzsimons, Leannah Llewellyn, Sue Howard, Susan Hodgson, Jill Kind, Vicky Lewis, Jane Ramsey, Kimhoa Granville, Lori Weinberg, Wendy Siegel, and the numerous others whom I may have overlooked here or whose names I have forgotten. I have never seen such dedicated workers anywhere. Their decency, good humor, practicality, strength, and creativity have inspired, uplifted, and taught me. While few of the above women's advocates had professional training prior to working with battered women, they displayed counseling and advocacy skills in working with battered women that were on a par with, or better than, those of professional therapists I have known.

I would like to acknowledge my great debt to the National Coalition Against Domestic Violence, its membership, and its publications—*Aegis* and *The NCADV Voice*—for their invaluable guidance in thinking about battering and assisting battered women. I intend to contribute the major portion of any personal financial gains from this book to the NCADV and its member women's shelters. I am deeply grateful to Camella Serum for first enlightening me to the parallels between battered women and concentration camp inmates and to the understanding of woman abuse as a coercive control situation. I would also like to thank my colleagues who counsel male batterers and who have shared their insights with me, particularly the members of EMERGE and RAVEN (Rape And Violence End Now).

I wish to thank those who have guided me through the writing and publishing of this work: Richard Mann, Eric Bermann, Irene Butter, Susan Contratto, and Robert Gunn. I am especially grateful to Richard Mann, who has been a friend, a mentor, and an important human model to me. I would also like to thank Eric Bermann and Robert Gunn for their guidance throughout my training as a clinical psychologist, and Susan Contratto for her rare gift for giving strong—but truly constructive—criticism.

Michelle Wood and Karen Pernick deserve special thanks for assisting me in the data collection for the study that appears in Part II. By keypunching, checking raw data printouts, researching divorce records, and tracking down census information, they also made an invaluable contribution to this study. I am very grateful to Susan Schechter for her helpful comments and suggestions on an earlier draft of this work.

The Board of Directors of the Domestic Violence Project, Inc., was generous in permitting me the use of the shelter records. I could not have written this work so easily without the assistance of the University of Michigan Statistical Laboratory, particularly David Smith and Kenneth Guire. Peggy Gifford has earned my thanks for her competent and meticulous editorial assistance.

Finally, I would like to express my love and deep gratitude to my parents for bringing me up in a home that was always loving, virtually free of violence, and largely free of verbal abuse. That is no easy accomplishment, nor a common one. I would like to congratulate my brother Matthew for being a successful househusband and father, my brother Steven for his humane creativity, and my mother for her strength and independence in surviving my father's untimely death. Last and certainly not least, I want to express my gratitude to my partner in life, Michelle Okun, for her emotional and financial support, her patience and understanding.

INTRODUCTION _____

Thanks to the work of the women's liberation movement, the issue of woman-battering has gained considerable, long-overdue attention in the past dozen years. More and more, members of our society are realizing that woman abuse is not an isolated aberration best ignored and kept secret, but a national epidemic in need of effective social redress. It is conservatively estimated that 1.8 million women are seriously battered each year by their husbands or cohabitant male partners. Since the founding of America's first battered women's shelter in 1974 through the end of 1983, well over 19,000 Americans have died in incidents of woman abuse or other forms of conjugal violence.[1] During that same time, the number of women's shelters in our nation has multiplied geometrically, to over an estimated 600 shelters for battered women today.

Despite the encouraging signs of increased social concern about battering and the spread of shelters to accommodate battered women and their children, we still have a long way to go. There are still nowhere near enough women's shelters to provide refuge to every woman seeking a safe temporary dwelling. Destructive myths and misconceptions about battering persist throughout the greater portion of our society. As a culture, we apparently do not yet recognize the importance of battering as a potentially lethal health and crime problem. Government funding for battered women's shelters is extremely scarce, and federal funding for shelters is virtually nonexistent at present. In comparison, the level of government expenditures for many health problems causing fewer fatalities than conjugal battering is far greater. Efforts to prevent battering and research on the problem are still in their very infancy.

PURPOSE OF THE PRESENT WORK

In the wake of the battered women's movement, research on battering has burgeoned. This research increasingly permits us to replace old myths about conjugal abuse with recently discovered facts. In this book, I seek both to summarize and to advance the current state of knowledge about woman abuse in particular and conjugal battering in general. Part I of the book begins with the historical context of woman-battering and then proceeds to a thorough review and critique of the existing empirical and theoretical literature on conjugal abuse. To my knowledge, this contribution represents the most extensive summary of the literature on conjugal violence published to date. This should be a useful resource for battered women, those who work with battered women and their families, researchers, people in legal and law-enforcement occupations, theoreticians, activists opposing violence against women, or any interested students of this problem. At the end of Part I is a theoretical chapter, portraying woman abuse as a coercive control situation similar to the brainwashing or torture of political prisoners. Important ramifications of coercive control theory for our notions about marriage and family will be discussed.

Part II of this book reports the method and results of a study that I conducted, using records on 300 battered women taking shelter and on 119 woman-battering men in a shelter-affiliated program for counseling batterers. This study has some especially valuable characteristics. It is still among the earliest studies in the field to use statistical tests of hypotheses generated in the existing literature in order to analyze its empirical results. It reports on unusually large numbers of battered women seeking refuge at a shelter, and also of woman batterers seeking the specialized services of a batterers' counseling program. A rather unique portion of the study results compares the reports by battered women and their respective violent male partners on the violence that they have endured/perpetrated.

AUTHOR'S INTEREST AND EXPERIENCE

My interest in woman abuse and my opportunity to undertake this work stem from over five years' personal involvement as a counselor and activist serving battered women and their families. In May 1979, I had the great good fortune to be hired by the Domestic Violence Project, Inc.—operator of SAFE House, the battered women's shelter in Washtenaw County, MI—to be the first counselor employed in their program of services for spouse abusers. My job was to design and execute a program of counseling to promote nonviolence in conjugal abusers. It was expected that the great majority of clients of the program would be men who had assaulted their wives or girlfriends. However, at the inception of the batterers' counseling program, my mandate also included provision of counseling services to lesbians and gay men who abused their partners, to women who abused their husbands or boyfriends, and to battered men. While a few of my counseling clients over the ensuing five years did come from these rarer types of conjugal abuse situations, the vast preponderance of my counseling clientele, as expected, consisted of woman-battering men.

While I began providing counseling to batterers in my second week on the job, I spent most of my first seven months with Domestic Violence Project in orientation at the battered women's shelter, SAFE House. My supervisors had wisely decided that I should learn about battering first from the perspective of battered women and their children, and that only after in-shelter experience should I begin concentrating my efforts on counseling batterers. Thus, I was trained as a shelter worker—or woman's advocate, to use the official role title. I learned a model emphasizing the empowerment of battered women in a safe environment, peer counseling, and advocacy with relevant agencies and the community on behalf of battered women and their children. Working with battered women and their children, I soon discovered to my horror—as does any shelter worker—that many familial homes are in effect nothing more nor less than places of imprisonment and torture. I had spent nearly a quarter-century of my life blissfully unaware of a holocaust being perpetrated against American women and children in the privacy of their dwellings, perpetrated by the men who are supposed to love and care for their mates and children. This startling discovery compelled me to dedicate myself to working against woman-battering.

I spent seven months working primarily at SAFE House. Like most of the shelter workers, my role varied according to the needs of the shelter and its residents. Mostly I acted as a woman's advocate or as a child advocate. This meant cooking, caring for children, cleaning, first aid, janitoring, chauffeuring, heavy lifting, carrying, community relations work, a great deal of crisis phone counseling, as much or more in-person peer counseling and problem-solving, listening, listening, and listening—usually with sorrow, outrage, shock, admiration, fear for the victimized women and children, and, at times, fear for myself. This is all routine for a shelter worker.

In January 1980, I cut back drastically on my direct involvement at the shelter in order to concentrate on providing counseling to batterers at the downtown office of Domestic Violence Project (DVP). From this time until Spring 1983, I remained in close communication with the shelter staff. I also occasionally worked at the shelter as a fill-in for vacationing or ill staff members, and was a guest speaker on about a monthly basis at the shelter's women's support group.

As a result of my orientation at the shelter, I remained a shelter worker throughout my employment at DVP, both in the perceptions of the shelter staff and in my own mind. This meant that as a batterers' counselor, I still placed the highest priority on the safety and liberty of the victim of battering. More relevant to my subsequent role as researcher, I had earned—or at least gained—the trust of the shelter staff. Consequently, I encountered no hesitation in 1982 when I asked to use information in the shelter files for research purposes. In summation, I write from direct personal experience in a variety of roles working against woman abuse, from library research, and from statistical research on a portion of the people served at DVP. I appear in this book not only as author and researcher, but also as the batterers' counselor who worked with all of the violent men in the study. I also interviewed some of the battered women in the study.

VALUES ASSUMPTIONS

One of the crucial contributions of the battered women's movement to the analysis of battering is the emphasis on violence as behavior so unacceptable and avoidable that the violent person must be held solely responsible for the violence. The present book shares this value assumption. From this standpoint, initiating violent behavior cannot be attributed as the responsibility of the assaulted party, nor as the joint responsibility of the batterer and the battered partner. Consequently, neither victim provocation nor interpersonal processes can properly explain violence.

The only person ever responsible for violence is the person who commits violent behavior. If a person chooses to become violent, whether the choice is made consciously or unconsciously, *only* that person is responsible for the violence. I consider the decision to commit conjugal violence justified only when used to the minimum extent necessary in certain rare and extreme situations: to prevent the partner's suicide, to prevent grave physical harm to someone else, or to defend oneself from grave physical danger. If nonviolent tactics can be used effectively in the above situations, they are always to be preferred.

A second value assumption in this work concerns the battered woman and her decision whether or not to attempt to dissolve the violent relationship. I do not view battered women—or battered men, either—as obliged to attempt to terminate their relationships. I believe that abused mates have the right to make an informed choice free of coercion as to whether to attempt to continue or to dissolve the battering relationship. Providing the opportunity for free choice is a major function of battered women's shelters, second only to providing safe refuge. It is remarkable how common the opposite view is in our culture—that battered women must attempt to break off with their abusers in order to merit assistance or even sympathy. Continued cohabitation with a batterer, however, is not the same as looking for, wanting, or deserving abuse; abuse is by definition something no one can deserve.

TERMINOLOGY

The terminology of this book will be complicated by the lack of good or simple terms that include both marital and unmarried-cohabitant relationships. One way I will approach this will be with "slash" words such as *marriage/relationship, husband/partner,* or *wife/partner.* Most commonly, the term *conjugal* will include both sorts of relationships. A member of a conjugal relationship will most often be referred to as a *partner, mate, woman,* or *man,* in the attempt to avoid matrimonial terms. At times, however, I will use terms usually connoting marriage to represent both married and "living-together" relationships. To avoid confusion, when referring specifically to marriage and not to other types of intimate relationships, I will use terms that may seem redundant, such as *legal marriage* or *legally married.*

To define battering, I will borrow Ganley's definition: "assaultive behavior between adults in an intimate, sexual, theoretically peer, and usually cohabiting, relationship." In this definition, *assaultive behavior* includes verbal threats of assault and behavioral threats such as the destruction of property or pets.[2] This definition is improved for my purposes by adding the observation that the relationship in which violence occurs need not be cohabitant and will often be formerly cohabitant rather than currently or actively cohabitant. Further, the sexual aspect of the relationship is a typical feature, but is not important as a criterion for the definition of battering. Also, the term *intimate* in the above definition refers to physical intimacy and not necessarily to psychological intimacy: *proximal* would be a better term here if it did not sound so unusual.

Woman-battering and *woman abuse* would refer strictly to violence by men against their women partners. *Conjugal violence, conjugal abuse,* and *battering* are all gender-unspecific synonyms. My use of gender-unspecific terms such as *conjugal violence* and *battering* is not intended to imply equal implication of both genders in the commission of battering. Rather, as shall be demonstrated later, I believe that the empirical evidence shows that well over 90% of conjugal violence is woman abuse. I intend gender-unspecific terms for conjugal violence in this work to denote a phenomenon mostly perpetrated by males. Consequently, as used in this work, nouns such as *conjugal violence* or *battering* are similar to many other nouns of violence—e.g., *combat, war, rape, bombing, murder, kidnapping, armed robbery.* That is, all of these terms refer to violent acts usually committed by men and only rarely, if ever, by women. When expressing my own ideas, I will tend to avoid the term *spouse abuse* because it has come to connote a belief in equal numbers of battered women and battered men. When reviewing the previous publications on battering, I will tend for the most part to use the same terminology as the original source. Thus, the term *spouse abuse* will appear in this work mostly in passages quoting or paraphrasing sources who prefer that term. *Child-battering* will be referred to as such, or as *child abuse.*

Abuse as a term has an advantage over the terms *violence* and *battering* in that its connotation captures the fact that violence is but one technique in a repertoire of abusive tactics. Thus, *conjugal abuse* will at times be used here to include psychological and emotional levels of abuse, and economic and social deprivation, as well as physical and sexual violence. Nevertheless, *conjugal abuse, battering*, and *conjugal violence* will most often be used interchangeably, as synonyms.

Conjugally abusive behavior is characterized by the motive to dominate or to control the conjugal partner, to treat the partner as a thing or a possession. This work will evade the issue of the threshold levels at which assaultive or manipulative behaviors become defined as abusive. While this issue is of philosophical interest, it is convenient to set it aside for now. Throughout this work, the threshold question will be largely irrelevant— fortunately for research purposes, but most tragically for the people from whose lives the study derives.

Ganley's definition of battering, as quoted above, is sufficiently broad to include homosexual and bisexual, as well as heterosexual, relationships. It is not even limited to couples, but could also apply to three or more adults in one relationship. Her definition applies both to relationships where one member of the relationship is typically the assailant or where more than one member are the typical initiating assailants. This book shall deal almost exclusively with heterosexual couples where the male partner is either the sole or typical initiator of conjugally assaultive behavior. A bit of the literature review, however, will survey works that refer to couples where the male partner is battered by an assaultive woman partner or where the two partners are reciprocally assaultive. Due to the lack of available information, very little reference will be made in this book to violence in either gay or lesbian relationships.

Throughout this work, *woman abuse* will mean conjugal abuse of a woman by her male partner. The male terminological complement of *woman abuse, man abuse*, sounds strained, due to the unfortunate denotative equation of *man* with *mankind* or *human beings*. Therefore, the term *husband abuse* will be applied in this work to conjugal violence by women against their male partners. Note in particular that *woman abuse* in this work will denote conjugal violence by a man against a wife or female partner only, although the term logically could include the situations of battered daughters, battered mothers, assaulted female strangers, or battered lesbians.

Terms synonymous with *battered woman* are fairly self-explanatory. Note that *victim* will in general be used as a synonym for battered woman, with rare exceptions that will be clear in context. As a term with active and competent connotations, I heartily recommend *survivor* as a preferred synonym for *victim*. Terms for the violent male partner will include: *batterer, woman batterer, assailant, abuser, woman abuser, violent mate, violent partner, abusive mate, assailant partner, assaultive partner*. Thus, an *assailant partner* here will not mean "the partner of an assailant," but will mean "assaultive conjugal partner." Terms such as *battered woman* and *batterer* will generally imply involvement in chronic or repetitive conjugal violence, but not always. Some of the battered women and batterers to be discussed in this book were apparently involved in only one conjugal assault.

Terms like *violent couples, battering relationships, violent relationships*, etc., are far more semantically convenient than such synonyms as "couples who have experienced conjugal violence," "relationships involving a batterer and a battered woman," or "couples where battering occurs/has occurred." In this work, terms like *violent couples* will usually refer to relationships between a male batterer and a battered woman, although occasionally *violent couples* will be intended to include heterosexual couples involved in any permutation of conjugal violence.

My use of terms such as *violent couples* is reluctant because these terms carry an unintended and unwanted connotation of mutual assault or equal violence by each member of the couple. *Violent couples* or *battering relationships* as terms may seem to imply beliefs in victim-precipitation of assaults, or in the equal implication of both assailant and victim in the initiation of an assault, or in a view of conjugal violence as a product of the marriage/relationship which transcends the members of the couple. As should be clear by now, I intend none of these meanings because they are contrary to my values and assumptions.

OUTLINE OF THE BOOK

This book consists of two main parts—a review and critique of the literature on battering, and a second part reporting on a study that I conducted of battered women and woman batterers seeking help at DVP. Part I is composed of five chapters. Chapter 1 presents an historical context for battering. Chapter 2 gives an overview of the empirical literature, concentrating on the methodologies of studies published to date. Chapter 3 reports the results gathered and reported in the existing empirical literature. Chapter 4 surveys and critiques important theoretical perspectives on conjugal violence. Chapter 5 is a theoretical chapter on woman abuse as a coercive control situation.

Part II, consisting of Chapters 6 through 11, presents results of a study that I conducted concerning 300 battered women taking shelter at SAFE House, and 119 woman batterers whom I counseled at the affiliated DVP batterers' counseling program. Chapter 6 reports the method of the study. Chapters 7 through 10 report on the five main categories of results derived in this study. Chapter 11 summarizes the study results and discusses some of their implications for social policy, intervention, and future research.

PART I

REVIEW AND CRITIQUE OF THE LITERATURE ON BATTERING

Chapter 1

HISTORY

The following history of woman-battering will concentrate particularly upon the legal status of wife-beating over the course of Euro-American history. This is the focus not because it is necessarily the most important historical issue in woman abuse, but, rather, because these facts are readily available and document very well the status of woman abuse as a legal and formally accepted institution in Western society. Seen in historical context, it becomes evident that woman-battering has always been epidemic and is not the symptom of a modern breakdown in a formerly nonviolent family structure.

Before proceeding with the history of woman-battering, I will first digress briefly to review the published history of violent abuse by women against their male partners. Husband abuse is much harder to trace than woman abuse. Unlike woman abuse, husband abuse was not written into law throughout Western history. Furthermore, it is probable that battered husbands/male partners have always been quite rare, compared to battered women. Apart from isolated case histories, the only allusions to husband-beating occur in the literature on the charivari and the "conduct of misrule."

The charivari was a process of public ritualistic shaming and mockery popular in France during the latter Middle Ages. It served to impose sanctions on those committing various domestic transgressions such as adultery, cuckoldry, scolding, hen-pecking, as well as conjugal abuse. Transgressors might be forced to ride through town seated backwards on an ass, to the jeers and taunts of their fellow citizens. Other similar types of humiliations were also conducted in charivari. In cases of husband-beating, the victimized husband would generally be the one subjected to public derision, apparently because he was perceived as tolerating the abuse he received from his wife.[1]

WOMAN ABUSE IN HISTORICAL PERSPECTIVE

The history of woman abuse begins with the tradition of the laws of chastisement. This tradition dates back to 753 B.C., the time of the reign of Romulus in Rome, and continues in custom to the present. Under the laws of chastisement, a husband had the right to discipline his wife physically for various offenses, often unspecified. Laws of chastisement are best exemplified by the "rule of thumb" of English common law, which stated that a man could beat his wife with a rod or switch, so long as its circumference was no greater than the girth of the base of the man's right thumb. No reciprocal right of chastisement was ever accorded to wives.[2]

Soon after he founded Rome in 753 B.C., Romulus set forth laws governing domestic relations which consolidated authority in the husband as sole head of each household. Wives were viewed as necessary and inseparable possessions of their respective husbands; a wife did not exist as a legal individual in her own right. This afforded the rationale for the law of chastisement. Since a man and his wife were one person under the law, the husband could be held liable for his wife's crimes. Ostensibly in order to protect themselves from prosecution, husbands were given the right to use physical punishment to prevent their wives from engaging in criminal activities. These laws established a tradition perpetuated in English common law and in most of Europe.[3]

The fact that husbands had the right of chastisement, while wives did not, was only one aspect of the Roman double standard for men and women. Wives faced the death penalty for offenses such as adultery and drinking wine, while husbands risked no punishment at all for these same activities. Women also had no property rights, even as widows.[4] There were few legal roles for women outside of that of wife and mother. The major alternative roles for women were those of priestess, prostitute, or concubine.

The Punic Wars, ending in 202 B.C., brought about conditions resulting in many changes in the family, including some increased freedom for women. For example widows could by this time be legally recognized as property owners. Laws against infidelity by wives were somewhat less severe at this time, and women could sue their husbands for monetary compensation for unjustified beating. By the fourth century A.D., excessive violence by either spouse was legally recognized as sufficient grounds for divorce.[5] It remains unknown, however, how often women were able in practice to have these new rights enforced.

Just as Roman law was liberalizing its treatment of women, the rise of Christianity reestablished the traditional extent of husbands' patriarchal authority. Although the teachings of Jesus Christ can be interpreted as supporting the equality of marriage partners, the early Church fathers soon left no doubt that the older Roman and Jewish patriarchal values would persist under Christianity.[6] Thus the apostle Peter said, "ye wives, *be* in subjection to your own husbands" (Peter I 3:1). Saint Paul receives the most criticism in the woman abuse literature for propagating an especially patriarchal outlook on marriage among early Christians.[7] Constantine the Great, the first Christian emperor of Rome, had his young wife boiled alive when she became inconvenient to him.[8]

From the time of Saint Paul, the Church played an ambivalent role regarding wife abuse, at times supporting it and at times encouraging husbands to moderation in punishing their wives. Support for woman abuse is exemplified in the *Rules of Marriage* by Friar Cherubino of Siena, dating to the second half of the fifteenth century:

> When you see your wife commit an offense, don't rush at her with insults and violent blows. . . . Scold her sharply, bully and terrify her. And if this still doesn't work . . . take up a stick and beat her soundly, for it is better to punish the body and correct the soul. . . . Readily beat her, not in rage but out of charity. . . . for [her] soul, so that the beating will redound to your merit and her good.[9]

On the other hand, Bernard of Siena, a predecessor of Cherubino, had exhorted his male parishioners to exercise more compassion for their wives by treating them with as much mercy as they would their hens and pigs.[10] Bernard's remarks presage the fact that the Society for the Prevention of Cruelty to Animals would predate the Society for the Prevention of Cruelty to Children, which in turn would long predate any organizations aimed at helping battered women. In the sixteenth century, the Abbé de Brantôme decried the husband's right to kill his wife. This right would persist *de jure*, however, until at least the 1660s in Russia and even until the twentieth century in some localities.[11] Husbands *de facto* could murder their wives without punishment in England in the nineteenth century.[12]

The advent of Protestantism did not alter Christianity's perpetuation of the laws of chastisement. Martin Luther apparently considered himself an indulgent husband because his wife received "no more than a box on the ear" when she was "saucy."[13] The rise of Puritanism in England led to "the golden age of the rod" in its use against wives and children. As a concomitant of this, women were taught it was their sacred duty to obey their husbands, who were vested with great authority to control the wives.[14]

As the foregoing discussion of Christianity has implied, violence against wives by husbands was permitted and often encouraged throughout the Middle Ages and thereafter. The Roman double standard continued; a medieval wife could be burned at the stake for such offenses as adultery, prostitution, permitting sodomy, masturbation, lesbianism, child neglect, miscarrying a pregnancy, or talking back to or refusing a priest.[15] Lest we assume that the age of chivalry brought better treatment to women, a quotation from a fifteenth century ballad should disabuse us of such a conception. From the "Knight of La Tour Landry" comes this example of proper punishment for a scolding wife:

> He smote her with his fist down to the earth, and then. . .he struck her in the visage and broke her nose, and all her life she had her nose crooked that she might not for shame show her visage it was so foul blemished.[16]

It has also been noted that raping and/or abducting a virgin of noble birth was an effective and fairly common method for a knight of low status to gain a marriage above his station.[17]

Through the seventeenth, eighteenth, and nineteenth centuries, men could continue to beat their wives with the tolerance and approval of the community. They could do so in public without fear of interference by others. Some norms did develop during this period against the use of sharp or crushing weapons, against violence during pregnancy, and against assaults on vital or sensitive organs. Still, the husband who violated such norms rarely faced stronger sanctions than expressions of disapproval. The usual English form of expressing disapproval was "rough music," a descendant of the charivari which was in practice until at least 1862.[18]

Throughout the period already discussed, the wife's status as her husband's property was interpreted to mean that she had no right either to consent or to refuse to engage in sex with her husband. John Stuart Mill noted that the conjugal right of husbands to marital sex at their command, regardless of their wives' desires, meant that English wives had fewer *de jure* rights than English slaves. Slaves, after all, technically had the legal right to refuse their masters "the final familiarity."[19] It would not be until the middle of the 1970s that invoking conjugal privilege would begin to be redefined as marital rape.

The latter nineteenth century saw the beginning of reforms in the treatment of women and wives in England and America. John Stuart Mill helped to foreshadow this movement when he wrote *The Subjection of Women* in 1861. Mill waited eight years until he thought the public ready for his essay to be published, and even then it caused intense controversy. His words have lost little of their relevance:

> When we consider how vast is the number of men, in any great country, who are little higher than brutes, and that this never prevents them from being able, through the law of marriage, to obtain a victim, the breadth and depth of human misery caused in this shape alone by the abuse of the institution swells to something appalling.[20]

> The vilest malefactor has some wretched woman tied to him, against whom he can commit any atrocity except killing her, and if tolerably cautious, can do that without much danger of the legal penalty.[21]

Soon after Mill, Frances Cobbe wrote "Wife Torture in England" (1878), in which she decried the brutality of husbands in working-class areas such as Liverpool's "kicking district."[22]

Spurred on perhaps by the writings of Mill and Cobbe, and no doubt influenced by the ascension of Queen Victoria to the throne, English lawmakers enacted various reforms in laws regarding women during the 1880s. This decade saw a return to recognizing life-threatening beatings as suitable grounds for a wife to be granted a divorce. Also, Englishmen could no longer legally keep their wives under lock and key, nor could they legally sell their wives and daughters into prostitution. Wife-beating was at this time an issue of vital interest to the women's suffrage movement, but apparently diminished as a priority once women were accorded the vote.[23]

In the United States, the writers of the Constitution did not directly address issues of domestic relations, with the possible exception of the Fourth Amendment securing the privacy of the home. It was therefore left to case law to decide whether America would uphold the tradition of the laws of chastisement. In 1824 a Mississippi court set the precedent allowing for corporal punishment of wives by their husbands. This precedent continued for four decades, until 1864 when a North Carolina court overturned the "finger-switch rule." The court was cautious about the implications of this ruling for the tradition that "a man's home is his castle," however, and so it advised that it was still best to "draw the curtain" on domestic interactions so that the parties could "forget and forgive."[24] Alabama and Massachusetts followed with similar decisions in 1871, overturning the husband's right to chastise his wife.

The Massachusetts ruling is chilling in its description of husbands' previous rights over their wives:

And the privilege, ancient though it be, to beat her with a stick, to pull her hair, to choke her, spit in her face or kick her about the floor, or to inflict upon her other like indignities, is not now recognized by our law.[25]

Maryland was the first state to outlaw wife-beating by legislation, in 1883.[26] In 1894, the Mississippi court repudiated the "revolting precedent" it had set seven decades earlier.[27] By 1910, 35 of 46 states allowed absolute divorce on grounds of physical cruelty, and many states had joined Maryland in making wife-beating prosecutable as an illegal assault.

De jure reform, however, must not be confused with *de facto* reform resulting in vigorous enforcement of assault laws in domestic situations. Recent history in New York demonstrates this fact. While the latter nineteenth century saw woman abuse technically defined as illegal and as sufficient grounds for divorce, it was not until 1976 that New York courts accepted the principle that one assault upon a wife was sufficient grounds for her to be granted a divorce.[28] Also in 1976, public service attorneys representing battered women in the city of New York were obliged to file a class action lawsuit (*Bruno et al.* vs. *Codd et al.*) in order to obtain equitable police and family court policies in domestic assault situations, so that batterers would be arrested and battered women would be informed of their rights and permitted access to judges.[29] Unfortunately, New York represents a typical case rather than an extreme one for battered women and the law.

The plight of battered women seems to have faded from attention in America for 50 years after the inception of women's suffrage in 1920. During this time, the customs of the double standard and chastisement continued to hold sway in the courts, on the police beat, and in the home. The following two legal cases form a vivid modern example of the judicial double standard. In 1953, a Nebraska woman sued her husband for depriving her and their children of vital necessities, demanding he provide food, clothing, etc. The judge ruled in favor of the husband:

As long as the home is maintained and the parties are living as husband and wife, it may be said that the husband is legally supporting his wife.[30]

Conversely, in 1962 a Connecticut wife attempted to respond in kind to her husband's inadequate support by refusing her domestic services. The court rules, however, that she was obligated:

. . .to be his helpmeet, to love and care for him. . ., to afford him her society and her person. . .and to labor faithfully to advance his interests. . .

[performing] her household and domestic duties without compensation therefore. A husband is entitled to benefit of his wife's industry and economy.[31]

Finally, it should be noted that conjugal assault remained legal in some states through the early 1970s, although it is currently recognized in all states as a criminal assault.[32]

Only in the 1970s were battered wives rediscovered. Three factors seem to have moved battered women back into public attention in the last decade. First, the work of Kempe and Helfer on the battered child syndrome, published in 1963, renewed overt public awareness of family violence. Second, the nation as a whole became more sensitive to issues of violence as a result of the civil strife of the latter 1960s and early 1970s, and perhaps also as a result of the war in Vietnam. Third, and by far the most important, the emergence of the women's liberation movement made the public aware of the injustices women faced in the home and in the workplace.

Woman abuse was not initially a priority concern as feminism was reborn in the late 1960s. Apparently, the tradition of domestic privacy and the resulting conspiracy of silence had effectively kept feminists—like other Americans—ignorant of the prevalence of woman abuse. Therefore, initial feminist efforts to oppose violence against women focused on prosecuting rape and establishing support services for survivors of rape. This in turn led to the founding of hundreds of rape crisis centers across the nation.

The problem of woman abuse was soon to surface, though, through the sharing of experiences by women in consciousness-raising groups bred by the women's movement. Thus, the first battered women's shelter— Chiswick Women's Aid in London, England—began in 1971 as a meeting place for functions of the women's movement. NOW chapters around the country established task forces on wife assault by the mid-1970s, and the first American shelters for battered women—Women's Advocates and Haven House—opened in 1974. Currently, there are over 600 shelters for battered women in the United States, as well as numerous programs providing refuge in volunteers' homes.

The mushrooming growth of the battered women's movement by no means signifies the end of the traditional acceptance of woman abuse. At best it marks the beginning of the end of values tolerating woman abuse. The laws of chastisement live on de facto—though they have been repealed de jure—in the form of police and judicial procedures which are inadequate to handle battering in the first place, and the tendency of the police and courts to avoid intervening anyway.

In keeping with the traditional husbandly right to beat his mate, police and prosecutors still in general view conjugal assault as a "noncrime." Police training has emphasized the undesirability of arrest in suspected conjugal assaults.[33] Police behavior reflects their training: available studies show that police arrest batterers for assault in less than 10% of police calls for woman-battering.[34] Despite the fact that a sizeable proportion of murders and felonious assaults arise from battering relationships, police fail to treat battering as a crime like any other assault. One example of this is the existence of so-called "stitch rules"—police policies applied exclusively to domestic violence that use the severity and visibility of injuries to the victim as criteria for whether or not to arrest.[35]

Like police, prosecutors also fail to treat woman-battering like they treat other illegal assaults. Prosecution is carried out completely in only a pitifully small number of cases. Field and Field found that less than 3% of 7500 women seeking assault warrants against their husbands succeeded in obtaining them.[36] Prosecutors also often fail to prosecute the most severe possible charges in an alleged incident of marital violence; instead, what would be felonious offenses between strangers are prosecuted as misdemeanors because they occurred between conjugal partners.[37]

Prosecutors generally rationalize that battered women drop charges so often that work on these cases becomes a waste of time. This assertion is open to question on its empirical accuracy, and it reflects an attitude that demands that battered women prove themselves to be "worthy victims" in order to obtain protection under criminal law.[38] Further, prosecutors are not obliged to drop charges at the crime victim's request, but they do this especially often in cases of conjugal violence. As Field and Field state: "Almost uniquely among crimes, these cases are brought, processed, and terminated at the whim of the victim."[39]

Of course, the battered woman is a crucial witness for the prosecution of these cases. Sometimes she is the only witness, and, more frequently, she is the only adult witness. Despite this, exceptionally resourceful and dedicated prosecutors have found ways of convicting assailant partners in some cases where the victim was a reluctant or even hostile witness.[40] The general failure of prosecutors to prosecute conjugal assault cases vigorously is another vestige of the laws of chastisement.

In those rare cases where a batterer is prosecuted and convicted for his violent crime, the sentence he receives is usually very light. This is often true even in cases where this is a repeat offense of grave proportions.[41]

The most common sentences seem to be probation and/or judicial admonish-ment not to do it any more—again, even in cases where this is a repeat offense resulting in severe injuries. Many shocking travesties of sentencing occur. A Kansas case in 1982 saw a convicted woman batterer sentenced to buy his battered wife a box of chocolates.[42] The usual judicial responses to woman-battering again reflect the attitude bred by tradition that woman abuse is a noncrime.

The legal profession is hardly alone in ignoring or disserving the battered woman. The fields of medicine, mental health, religion, and social services have all failed battered women in various and myriad ways, the enumeration of which goes beyond the scope of this work. Other published sources have done excellent jobs of exposing and critiquing the failure of traditional human service professions to halt or to diminish woman abuse.[43] The immediate sources of this failure have been professional ignorance of the problem or denial of the problem. There has also been refusal to place a high priority upon opposing woman-battering even where professionals have acknowledged its existence. Instead, higher priorities have traditionally been placed upon preserving families intact, upon treating substance abuse, reducing stress, tranquilizing anxiety, and minimizing social service expendi-tures by taxpayers.

The professional refusal both to acknowledge woman abuse and to treat it as a serious, high-priority social problem again can be traced to the tradition of the rule of thumb. The laws of chastisement both trivialized woman abuse and placed it in the context of a private family matter. The privatization of woman-battering served to hide it from public view, "behind closed doors," and thus promoted widespread ignorance of the epidemic prevalence and intermittent lethality of woman abuse.

As another consequence, the public continues to uphold the tradi-tional tolerance of woman-battering. People tend to view battered women—and battered men, too, for that matter—as deserving of their beatings, and/or as masochistically seeking a beating for unconscious thrills. Instead of receiving sympathetic assistance or support, survivors of battering are blamed for not terminating their relationships.

As most horribly demonstrated in the Kitty Genovese rape-slaying, outsiders tend not to intervene in assaults on women by men.[44] This phe-nomenon apparently occurs because observers infer that male assaults upon women are private, conjugal problems. Few neighbors will assist the battered woman by calling the police to stop a beating.[45] The tradition of husbands' right to beat their wives, in general no longer written into law, still holds sway in modern custom, as do many other aspects of the double standard dating back to ancient Rome. With the possible exception of the latter portion of the nineteenth century, it is only since the 1970s that civilizing trends opposing conjugal abuse have begun to emerge.

Reviewing the legal status of woman-battering in Western history, it should be obvious that what is now called woman abuse was not traditionally viewed as outside the bounds of ordinary use (*ab-usive*). Rather, woman-battering was legal throughout Western society for over two-and-a-half millennia. Woman abuse was acceptable, and at times outright encouraged, during this period. Consequently, we can deduce that woman abuse was not a rarity, but has instead been epidemic for centuries. This contradicts the contemporary popular belief that woman-battering developed recently as a symptom of a modern breakdown in the family. The record of history also contradicts another popular myth that the epidemic of woman-battering has broken out only recently, as a backlash against feminism.

The historical acceptance of woman abuse calls into question the common clinical assumption that battering is abnormal and/or aberrant behavior. It seems rather that battering may be all too normal, and not statistically aberrant at all. Against the backdrop of over 2600 years of the laws of chastisement, it is modern feminist values absolutely opposed to conjugal violence that must be viewed as the historical aberration—a most welcome aberration, indeed! While the public rarely intends this meaning of "breakdown in the family," it is true that the modern movement against woman abuse is a revolt against the rule-of-thumb tradition that was the keystone of marital and family relations for centuries. In this way, the demand for domestic nonviolence does represent a breakdown in traditional family life, a breakdown that is better termed a breakthrough.

Chapter 2

THE EMPIRICAL LITERATURE

HISTORY

The vast majority of written works on battering have been written since the 1970s. After Mrs. Cobbe's writings in 1878, there is a hiatus of nearly a century until the next work to address the issue of woman abuse as an urgent social problem. As far as I can discover, there are only four works in psychology during the period prior to 1970 that directly address conjugal violence: those of Mowrer and Mowrer,[1] Schultz,[2] Komarovsky,[3] and Snell et al.[4] Battering is also indirectly covered in other works from 1878 to 1970. In psychological literature, it appears most often under the topics of morbid or paranoid jealousy, homicide,[5] or sado-masochistic couples[6] (so-called, but not necessarily consensually or sexually sado-masochistic). There are also legal records and opinions from this period and, unfortunately, plentiful newspaper items relating crimes of conjugal violence, especially murders.

The other major vein of information prior to 1970 is criminological literature. FBI Uniform Crime Reports carry annual statistics on the number of homicides by relationship category, documenting murders between legal marrieds or ex-marrieds. Wolfgang's work on criminal behavior revealed that a large proportion of homicides and assaults take place between family members. Other works dealing with conjugal homicide appeared by

1962, including Schultz's work.[7] The appearance of Komarovsky's *Blue Collar Marriage* in 1963 marked the first study since 1928 alluding to the prevalence of non-fatal conjugal assault.[8] *Violence* had never appeared in a title of an article in the *Journal of Marriage and the Family* until that journal published a special issue on family violence in November 1971.[9] From this edition came many of the essays published in the first major anthology on family violence, Steinmetz and Straus' *Violence in the Family*.[10] Finally, the year 1976 saw the publication of Del Martin's *Battered Wives*, the first American book entirely devoted to discussion of woman abuse.[11]

Since battering has been with us for at least 2700 years, the question arises as to why it took so long to become an object of keen professional and scientific interest. Many authors answer this question by laying the blame on selective inattention by professionals and social scientists related to the almost sacred tradition of domestic privacy and to the myth of the happy family.[12] Martin cites no less than Maccoby and Jacklin's *Psychology of Sex Differences* as an example of social scientists' blissful ignorance of conjugal violence: "There can be little doubt that direct force is rare in modern marriage."[13] Within the next dozen years after the above quote appeared, Walker[14] and Straus[15] would speculate that the *majority* of contemporary American marriages experience conjugal violence.

PROBLEMS WITH THE LITERATURE

Another reason for the scientific neglect of conjugal abuse is that it has been, and continues to be, a greatly underreported phenomenon. Victims of battering—both women and men—are very reluctant to report their victimization to the police, doctors, therapists, and other helpers due to shame and embarrassment, both for themselves and their assailants; fear of retribution by their assailants if the abuse is revealed; and fear of unsympathetic responses from third parties. Outsiders who suspect battering tend not to approach battered victims to discuss their suspicions because of the attitude that battering is a private conjugal matter. A conspiracy of silence is thus enacted between assailants, victims, and those who could conceivably intervene to halt abuse. The primary support for maintaining this conspiracy of silence appears to be social attitudes that blame the victim.

Other factors also contribute to underreporting, such as medical and police categorizations of problems that obscure whether the source is conjugal violence. Doctors treat head injuries, facial cuts, broken ribs, etc., of "accidental," "traumatic," or "unspecified" origin. Police respond to "domestic disturbances," "family trouble," "assaults," "homicides," very often without recording victim-perpetrator relationships at all. Therapists treat "depression," "paranoia," "morbid jealousy," "anxiety neuroses," "explosive" or "psychopathic" character disorders, as well as children's psychological problems brought on wholly or largely by their parents' violent relationships. Whether the source of all these problems is in woman abuse (or other forms of battering) is hard, if not impossible, to discover as a consequence of these labeling conventions.

Another serious problem of studying battering concerns difficulties in obtaining subjects, especially for controlled or random populations. The literature relies heavily on clinical and quasi-clinical populations: women seeking refuge, applicants for divorce and/or restraining orders, police callers, volunteer subjects who consider themselves battered women, and psychotherapy clients. Of these studies of help seekers, only three have any kind of control group.[16] Of these three, one utilizes an internal control group—i.e., nonbattered women seeking divorce at the same agency as the battered group[17], while one uses control groups whose representativeness as controls is questionable.[18]

Only Straus and his collaborators, Komarovsky, and the National Crime Survey (discussed by Gaquin in *Victimology*) have attempted studies of nonclinical survey samples to determine the incidence and prevalence of conjugal assault. Most of these samples use university students, sometimes including the students' families.[19] Only Straus, Gelles, and Steinmetz, Owens and Straus, Steinmetz, and the National Crime Survey have used random samples to study the occurrence of conjugal violence.[20]

There are disadvantages with clinical and quasi-clinical samples. First, these samples are almost without exception reliant upon battered women seeking intervention of some sort. Consequently, such samples represent the specific subgroup of woman abuse victims—quite likely a minority of all battered women—who do seek intervention in such a way as to be identified as battered women. This subgroup may also be skewed towards representing the most extremely severe forms of woman abuse, rather than the entire range of conjugal abuse.[21] Thus, generalizing from studies of clinical samples to the entire universe of battering relationships is highly problematic. For obvious reasons, clinical samples are also suspect as a source for imputing prevalence and incidence of battering in the population at large. Relationships that need police intervention, or intervention by therapists or divorce lawyers, are likely not random representatives of America's roughly 50,000,000 couples and could well have higher incidence rates of violence.

A final major problem of the field is the scarcity of data concerning men, whether as abusers or as victims. Very few studies to be discussed here contain a majority of male respondents, and in most studies men compose insignificant minorities or are entirely absent. For example, Gelles wanted equal gender representation in his study, but found he had to settle for 17.5% men;[22] Snell et al. were commissioned to study wife beaters, but found it far more feasible instead to study and report on "the wife-beater's wife."[23] Most information available on woman abusers is related to investigators by battered women, not by the batterers themselves. Battered husbands appear in the literature almost strictly as ciphers in statistical accounts. There are case histories of husband-beating in only one work, and these may be fictionalized.[24] The sole analysis of the battered husband's situation is merely a rather forced and unsatisfying attempt to generalize from findings relating to battered women.[25]

OVERALL TRENDS

The empirical literature on battering has thus far aimed at five main goals: 1) documenting incidence and prevalence of woman-battering and/or conjugal violence; 2) discovering and relating patterns in conjugal abuse and factors contributing to its occurrence and/or cessation; 3) the influence of social factors such as cultural norms and helping agencies; 4) presenting psychological analyses or profiles of the abuser and victim; and 5) answering the question that has traditionally been in the forefront of the public's interest—why does the battered woman remain in her violent relationship. This question is usually rendered simply as "Why does she stay?" The recent literature on conjugal abuse—especially on battered women—uniformly repudiates the explanation that victims remain in their relationships due to unconscious masochism, with one exception.[25½] Apart from this, the latest study that invoked masochism as a promising explanation appears to have been undertaken in 1964.[26]

Since the 1970's, the vast preponderance of writers in this field have exerted themselves to refute what is often referred to as "the myth of masochism,"[27] a myth which clearly has prevailed in the public's beliefs about battered mates. To my knowledge, Shainess remains the sole writer since Snell et al. who has seriously entertained the masochism hypothesis as an important explanation of why victims remain involved with their conjugal abusers.[27½] Current debate in the field is mostly confined to whether masochism is entirely nonexistent,[28] or whether it exists in only an infinitesimal fraction of violent relationships.

Similar to its treatment of masochism, the recent literature on conjugal violence generally avoids viewing the victim as provocative of the assault. Many authors in this field critique the very concept of victim precipitation of assaults,[29] while others emphasize that the *assailant* provokes assaults because he seeks pretexts to stage them.[30] In part, this entails a change in value judgments from the traditional support for the chastisement of wives. Like the current author, the great majority of authors in this field reject nonviolent activities as sufficient provocation to justify a physically violent reaction.

How does the recent literature answer "Why does she stay?" Currently, authors concentrate on battered women's alternatives in order to explain this question. Inadequacies in helping and law-enforcement agency practices are exposed, not to mention indifference and at times outright antipathy towards the victim. The battered woman is described as trapped "behind closed doors," having "no place to go," and in a "catch-22" situation.[31] The battered woman's low self-esteem, her lack of self-confidence and assertiveness, and her failure to achieve independent control of her life are viewed not as results of innately female masochism, but as having other determinants entirely.[32] Pfouts acts as spokesperson for the literature when she reverses the earlier analysis of the battered woman's continued victimization:

> Given that most coping decisions are made in the grip of self-doubt and terror, on inadequate information and insufficient community support, it is surprising, not that many of these decisions fail to solve the problem, but that some of them do.[33]

Walker summarizes the double bind battered women face as follows:

> They [are] both beaten and blamed for not ending their beatings. Told they have the freedom to leave a violent situation, they are blamed for the destruction of their family life. Free to live alone, they cannot expect equal pay for equal work. Encouraged to express their feelings, they are beaten when they express anger. They have the same inalienable right to the pursuit of happiness as men do, but they must make sure their men's and children's rights are met first. They are blamed for not seeking help, yet when they do, they are advised to go home and stop the inappropriate behavior which causes their men to hurt them. . .If they were only better persons,. . .they would find a way to prevent their own victimization.[34]

It will be convenient to have a term by which to refer to the bulk of the literature on woman abuse, which represents a consensus on several key points. I will employ the term *woman abuse literature* for those works that operate under a unified, or at least similar, paradigm of investigation. Two of the essential criteria that characterize this paradigm have just been presented. The first is attention to the very constricted alternatives to abuse that battered women have, usually including acknowledgment these alternatives may even be nonexistent for some victims. The second is rejection of the concept of victim provocation in favor of defining conjugal violence as unacceptable behavior by the violent person and for which the violent party is responsible. The third distinguishing feature of the woman abuse literature is the belief that the vast majority of conjugal abuse is woman abuse. When including works on conjugal violence that do not fit the definition of the woman abuse literature, I will refer to this as the *conjugal violence literature*.

While existing literature engages in very little controversy about discrediting masochism, the are some heated controversies in the conjugal violence literature. Two of these issues concern the prevalence of battered husbands, and whether to conceptualize conjugal abuse as violence against women or as a type of intrafamily violence. The two issues are related in that the lower the prevalence of battered husbands the more *spouse abuse* becomes synonymous with *woman abuse*, which is obviously a form of violence by men against women. Conversely, if men are battered by women as often as women are battered by men, then feminist concepts about violence against women and woman abuse are of less relevance than a theory of conjugal and/or family violence in general.

Dobash and Dobash mention battered husbands only to question their existence and dismiss them as an issue.[35] They advocate an analysis in terms of woman abuse and violence against women, as does Martin.[36] Steinmetz, on the other hand, proclaims that women are as violent in conjugal relationships as men are, if not more so.[37] Straus takes a middle position, emphasizing the contribution of sexist cultural attitudes and norms to the predominance of woman-battering, while preferring—on a theoretical level at least—to term his subject *intrafamily violence*.[38] These controversies will be further discussed later in this work. Another important controversy pertains to whether lower-class status is associated with an increased prevalence of battering.

The entire field of literature concentrating on conjugal violence can be divided into six areas: 1) surveys of the subject; 2) anthologies; 3) theoretical formulations; 4) social analyses; 5) works concerning therapeutic and preventive interventions; 6) empirical studies. Of course, many books and articles cover more than one of the above categories. It is worthwhile to mention here the important surveys and anthologies of the literature. Del Martin's *Battered Wives* was the first book-length overview of woman abuse published in America and is highly recommended as an introductory reading. Terry Davidson's *Conjugal Crime* combines publication references, interviews, and moving first-person journalism about her childhood and her experiences working in a women's refuge. The works of Dobash and Dobash are invaluable resources in finding references and historical information. There is also a helpful article by Lystad,[39] surveying the literature. The overview by Langley and Levy is unsatisfactory because of their tendency to parrot interview and published sources uncritically without any evaluation or analysis of their own, even when their sources contradict each other on an issue.[40]

There are three important anthologies in the field. Steinmetz and Straus' *Violence in the Family* collects articles covering child abuse and the family as a training ground for societal violence, as well as conjugal violence. In the introduction, they state the major lesson of their work: "the potential for violence in the family [is]. . .as fundamental as the potential for love."[41] *Battered Women*, edited by Maria Roy, combines statistical and descriptive clinical studies, discussions of legal and police issues in woman abuse, and a fine section on prevention, highlighted by an essay by Straus.[42]

The special "Spouse Abuse" edition of *Victimology* is probably the finest collection of essays on conjugal violence to appear thus far.[43] This work collects book reviews and notes on research and intervention projects, is the best available source on cross-cultural and anthropological studies of conjugal violence, and covers all the major topics in the field. It is highlighted by a preliminary report by Straus on his national sample of 2143 families that is as useful for studying conjugal violence as the later book-length presentation of the same study in *Behind Closed Doors*; Steinmetz's controversial essay on battered husbands, and a critique rebutting her essay; essays by Dobash and Dobash that synopsize much of their later book; and Lenore Walker's presentation of her theory of learned helplessness. This *Victimology* issue certainly vies for the distinction of the single best published work available so far on conjugal abuse.

The empirical literature can be divided into two categories: 1) statistical presentations, and 2) descriptive, nonquantitative works—although some publications fall into both categories. The bulk of the statistical works do not utilize analytical statistics yielding probabilities of the significance of the data analysis. Rather, most works that are here called statistical merely present percentages of occurrences of various phenomena among woman-battering relationships. More studies utilizing tests of significance are desperately needed, and those which have been published so far are to be applauded for the use of these methods.

The variables presented in most conjugal abuse studies overlap to a very great extent. Therefore, it will be much more convenient and clear to report findings on a variable-by-variable basis, instead of a more conventional, study-by-study discussion. Before turning to the results of the empirical studies, the sampling methods, sample characteristics, and methodologies of existing empirical works related to conjugal violence will be examined.

THE EMPIRICAL LITERATURE — METHODS AND DESIGNS

Studies with Shelter Samples

Carlson reports on 101 battered women served by the Domestic Violence Project of Ann Arbor, Michigan, between January 1976, and July 1977. It is not stated if this sample is a random or exhaustive selection of the agency's caseload during this period. Data apparently are derived from intake information, but this is unclear. All 101 women received refuge in volunteer homes.[44]

Gayford interviewed the first 148 women sheltered at Chiswick Women's Aid in London.[45] From this group, he derived 100 useable questionnaires. Unfortunately, he does not state his reasons for discarding nearly a third of the original sample. The sample is English, which raises some question as to its generalizability to America. From other discussions of Chiswick, it is clear that the sample must be predominantly urban working class,[46] although Gayford does not address this question himself.

Roy presents data for 150 cases sampled at random from the first 1000 battered women calling the hotline at Abused Women's Aid in Crisis (AWAIC) in New York City. Socioeconomic, racial, age, and other identifying characteristics of the battered women are not mentioned. Reasons for previously staying with the batterer and pretexts for violent incidents are listed in rank-order of frequency, with vague references to the actual percentage distributions. Data apparently are gathered from telephone intake forms.[47]

Dobash and Dobash conducted semistructured interviews, usually lasting about two-and-a-half hours each, with 109 battered women at shelters in Scotland, mostly in Edinburgh and Glasgow. Interviews took place over an 18-month period beginning in June 1975. Presumably, the study represents only a portion of Scotland's shelter residents during the period. No woman asked for an interview refused. The subjects are mostly working class. Data presented are mostly qualitative and case historical, although percentage-type statistics were also gathered for some variables. One very unusual and valuable statistic gathered concerns the women's account of the couple's social life before and after marriage.[48] Similar to Gayford, it is ambiguous how easily the Scots sample generalizes to American battered women.

Star et al. gathered data on 57 battered women, 80% of whom were in shelters in California or Arizona. The rest were outpatients in psychotherapy. Subjects were administered a test battery consisting of five instruments: a questionnaire concerning personal data; another regarding exposure to violence; a third concerning the women's self-perceptions; and two tests devised by Cattell—the 16PF and the Clinical Analysis Questionnaire. Fifty of the 57 subjects completed all of the test battery.[49]

Pagelow sampled 350 battered women, 91% of whom were in one of at least seven shelters at the time of the interview. The other 9% were formerly battered women who volunteered to be interviewed in response to advertisements. It cannot be determined from her report how Pagelow chose the women's shelters in which she would conduct interviews. Her shelter samples may or may not be random samples of the women's shelters from which the interviewed battered women came.[50]

A far greater disadvantage than the probably nonrandom nature of Pagelow's sample is in her definition of the variable of greatest interest to her. Approaching the question of "Why does she stay?" Pagelow correlated various factors with a criterion variable—the length of time the woman had cohabited with her husband/partner since the first conjugal assault. This is highly problematic in two respects. First, it means that in Pagelow's work, women who took shelter soon after the initial assault are counted more or less as leaving or terminating their relationships—even if they subsequently recohabited with their violent mates. Conversely, in Pagelow's sample, women who successfully terminated cohabitation with the batterer after long periods of abuse are treated statistically as though they returned to live with the batterer. Thus, Pagelow's methods do not necessarily address the question of "Why do they stay?" at all.

Another serious problem is that the length of cohabitation since the initial assault is apparently derived from the question, "When was the first time you saw him behave violently?"[51] As far as I can decipher, the answer to this question is treated as the date of the first conjugal assault. It seems, however, that this question would often yield results pertaining to other forms of violence, including legitimate ones such as football or boxing or self-defense. A great strength of Pagelow's work is its theoretical elegance, which enabled her to conduct statistically sophisticated hypothesis-testing.

Prescott and Letko's study does not deal with a women's shelter population, but is included here because it is similar in methodology and its respondents resemble a hotline clientele in that they labeled themselves battered women. Subjects were solicited by means of an advertisement in *Ms.* magazine, thus resulting in a nonrandom sample. Sixty-six prospective subjects responded to the ad and were sent questionnaires, which 43 returned. Five of these 43 were excluded either because they were not conjugal abuse victims or because they failed to respond adequately to the questionnaire. This reduced the sample size to 38. Subjects reflect the *Ms.* readership in that they were as a group well educated and mostly middle and upper class. Seventy-six percent of the women were employed, 56% in white-collar jobs. Half of the subjects were still married or cohabiting with their abusers.[52]

Mental Health and Social Services Client Populations

Ball reports on 109 cases involving family violence intaken between December 1975 and February 1976 at an outpatient mental health agency. At least half of the cases involve conjugal abuse, while a third are child abuse cases. Nothing is said about socioeconomic characteristics of either the overall agency clientele or the violent subpopulation. Data is apparently derived from agency case files and clearly extends beyond the initial intake session.[53]

Flynn reports findings based on 33 subjects from the Kalamazoo, Michigan, area. Only 14 battered women were interviewed firsthand by Flynn. The other 19 cases come from Flynn's interviews with 54 local professionals in 42 community agencies. Hopefully, data for these 19 cases of woman abuse are derived from agency records rather than anecdotes, but Flynn is not explicit on this. Flynn states that there is more representation of higher educational and economic levels among his subjects, but, unfortunately, this is not quantified.[54]

Geller reports on 4600 hotline calls placed to the Victims Information Bureau of Suffolk County, Long Island, New York, during its first year of operation and on 465 counseling cases at the same agency. Her clientele is decidedly middle class and well educated, with a median income of about $12,000 and a median education of 12.3 years. Data are drawn from case files.[55]

Mowrer and Mowrer's study is exceptional because it was published in 1928, yet it alluded to physical abuse in marriage. They collected information on 1573 marriage counseling cases, 636 from Jewish Social Serv-

ices in Chicago and 937 from United Charities of Chicago. Data on physical abuse refer to the couples' presenting problems, apparently as recorded
at their initial intake appointment.[56]

Hilberman and Munson studied 60 battered women referred over a
year's time from a health clinic in rural North Carolina to an outpatient
psychiatry department. These 60 women comprised half of all women
referred by medical staff at the clinic for psychiatric evaluations. The population is two-thirds black and educationally and socially deprived. Most
families of these women are said to have poverty-level incomes. Much of
the report of the study consists of fine descriptive clinical information
concerning the women, but quantitative data are also presented.[57]

Pfouts collected information about 35 battered women from the records
of the Welfare Department of Orange County, North Carolina. The sample is consequently biased towards poverty. Blacks comprise almost half of
the sample (17 out of 35). She divides the 35 women into four groups,
according to whether or not they retaliated violently when assaulted, and
according to how long they remained in their abusive relationships. Substantial differences in certain behavior patterns and characteristics of the
four groups are discovered. Unlike most other samples discussed in this
section, this sample does not consist primarily of help-seekers. Rather,
about 80% of these cases were initiated by the agency or another third
party because of child abuse by one or both parents.[58]

Rounsaville discusses a sample of 37 battered women who presented
themselves for treatment at a hospital emergency room in New Haven,
Connecticut, over a 30-day period. Of these 37 women, 28 were referred
for psychiatric evaluations and 13 kept their appointments with the
psychiatrist. The bulk of the report concerns differences between the group
that did not follow through on their mental health referral, and the group
that did. These differences unfortunately are not quantified, but verbally
described.[59]

Snell et al. began with a sample of 37 husbands referred for psychiatric evaluation after being charged by their wives with assault and battery.
Finding the wives much more willing to be interviewed, Snell et al. shifted
the focus of study to the "wife-beater's wife." In particular, Snell et al.
concentrate on the question of why these women, after years of domestic
assaults, chose to file charges against their husbands at the time of the
study. The reason they find in most cases is that the eldest son had either
begun to intervene in the fights or was viewed by the mother as now old
enough to be negatively affected by the marital violence he witnessed.[60]

Snell et al. were able to conduct three or more interviews with each
member of the couple in less than one-third of the original sample of 37.

They opted to report solely about this self-selected subsample. They do not account for this decision, nor do they qualify their remarks as reflecting a self-selected minority of the original group. The report consists primarily of value-laden clinical inferences—e.g., the wives were "masculine, efficient, aggressive, and frigid" while the husbands were "sexually ineffectual, reasonably hard-working 'mother's boys,' passive, and indecisive, with a tendency to drink excessively."[61] There is no way to know what raw data developed into these evaluations. Quite possibly the "masculine" women and passive, tippling men represent couples where the husband has shirked his responsibilities in favor of drink, leaving the wife to try to manage the finances and household responsibilities. This is a common pattern in violent couples, and it need not be viewed as displaying masculinity on the part of the women. There is no way to tell for certain what really went on in these couples.

The study by Snell et al. is infamous in the woman abuse literature as an example of a study built on psychoanalytic foundations assuming female masochism. This criticism is quite justified, at the very least because the authors do not adequately support their inferences with raw data or case examples. Their empirical case for viewing the battered woman as a masochist is unknown. More likely than not, their assumptions directly determined their conclusions.

Walker reports on 120 battered women from the Denver, Colorado, area whom she and her co-workers have interviewed. The middle and upper classes predominate in this sample, according to Walker, but—as with all too many of her findings—she does not give quantitative data on this. This lack of quantitative data, combined with a vocabulary implying the existence of statistical data describing her sample, is her work's chief weakness.[62]

For example, Walker reports a "significantly frequent mention" of unusual sex acts perpetrated by the batterer, without any numerical allusion to this frequency. She then gives three case histories which clearly illustrate abusers coercing very bizarre sexual activity. Still, one is left with questions as to whether this exhausts her sample of weird sex. If so, is one out of 40 "a significantly frequent mention" of such activities? If not, why not allude to how many such cases exist in the sample?

In Walker's favor, her work is one of the best in the field at conveying the experience of the battered woman, chiefly because of Walker's judicious and frequent use of case historical examples. Her inferences seem well justified in relation to the case examples. Her analyses are very insightful, and her theoretical concepts are important, challenging, humane, and educational.

Four sources present descriptive empirical information based upon their clinical experience, as well as theoretical formulations and discussions of therapeutic intervention in battering cases.[63] Three of these authorities speak from experience with large clienteles involving woman abuse — Serum, Saunders, and Ganley and Harris. Singer's clinical experience relates more to ex-hostages and ex-members of totalitarian religious cults. She then draws analogies between these "coercive control" situations and the violent conjugal relationship. Walker's work in many ways resembles the works of this group of four.

Controlled Studies Including Mental Health Samples

There are two studies in this category — one by Gelles and one by Carroll. Carroll uses a sample involving 96 couples: 23 violent couples in therapy at a community guidance clinic and 73 nonviolent couples comprising a nonclinic control group. He then divides his sample according to how much physical punishment they received as children, and uses chi-square statistics to test for differences between these two groups in marital happiness and in the warmth of interpersonal relations in the families of origin. He also looks at violence incidences for the two groups by gender and by which parent conducted the punishment. He finds significant associations between the amount of punishment experienced and both current marital happiness and warmth in the family of origin. He finds a nonsignificant trend for the experience of conjugal violence to be linked to punishment by the same-sex parent. His division of the sample according to amount of punishment experienced in childhood cancels out the original control group design of the study, however. Thus, this study's results are only pseudocontrolled.[64]

Gelles' *The Violent Home* is his study of incidence and patterns of conjugal violence in 80 families. It is a landmark in the field because of its early publication date (1972) and its attempt to use a control group. Gelles derived his sample of 80 from 20 couples who had called the Portsmouth, New Hampshire, police in on conjugal assaults, 20 violent couples in therapy at Child and Family Services of Manchester, New Hampshire, and 40 married neighbors of the above couples. The neighbors functioned as a control group.[65]

The study began with 27 violent couples at the Manchester family agency, of whom 20 consented to Gelles' interviews. Lack of cooperation by the Manchester police then forced Gelles — who was bent on obtaining a police sample — to turn to the Portsmouth police. Conjoint couple interviews were initially attempted, but dropped because altercations almost arose in some of these interviews. Husbands were much more difficult to obtain for individual interviews, and consequently 66/80 of the respondents (82.5%) are wives. Interviews were unstructured, but "funnelled" by the interviewer towards topics of marital violence. Results based on this sample have also appeared in several spin-off papers by Gelles.[66]

The strengths of the study are that it has a good range of families representing the lower through middle classes; a good range also for education, income, and age; and its attempt at deriving a control group. Gelles noted these limitations of the study: 1) the different cities—with very different overall characteristics, unfortunately—for police and agency samples; 2) the disproportionate amount of working women in the agency group relative to the other three groups; 3) the skew in representation of the two sexes among respondents; and 4) the absence of upper-middle and upper-class families from the sample. Gelles fails to use tests of the statistical significance of his findings, in part because his sample subgroups are not very conducive to such statistical procedures. Additionally, it is open to question whether Gelles' use of neighbors of families known to be violent can derive controls really representing the overall married populations of the two cities involved.

Samples of Legal Clients

Levinger paved the way in this category when he surveyed 600 couples applying for divorce in Cuyahoga County, Ohio, as to the sources of dissatisfaction in their marriages. He broke his results down by gender and by class, using Hollingshead's index to define the latter, and tested for the statistical significance of differences between these categories. His study is to be commended for explicitly stating his method for defining class status, something done by pathetically few studies in this field. Levinger's main findings are a highly significant (p<.001) tendency for wives to report enduring more physical and verbal abuse than husbands, and a significant tendency (p<.01) for more lower-class wives than upper-class wives to mention physical abuse. His findings on the incidence of complaints of abuse are also important.[67] Fields later imitated Levinger's gathering of incidence data in a study of divorce applicants during 1976 at Brooklyn Legal Services Corporation and MFY Legal Services in Manhattan.[68] Her sample population—all users of free legal aid—tends to be indigent.

O'Brien sampled 150 couples applying for divorce in Madison, Wisconsin, during the first nine months of 1969. He excluded couples married from six to 12 years as a means of looking at differences between brief and long-standing marriages ending in divorce. Husbands comprise 48% of his sample, the highest male representation in the literature. His couples were 24% middle class, 29% lower-middle class, and 47% working class. What O'Brien terms the "lower-lower class" is not represented at all.[69] The definitions of class status used are quite vague.

One-sixth of the 150 couples mentioned the occurrence of conjugal abuse. O'Brien compares the violent and nonviolent couples for percentage distributions of various factors, for marital satisfaction regarding five selected behaviors, and for marital conflict over the same behaviors. His main conclusion is that marital violence is associated with underachievement by the husband. O'Brien views the violent husband as using coercive physical force to reestablish or reaffirm his ascribed superior sex role when his superiority is threatened by his underachieving.

Eisenberg and Micklow interviewed 20 battered wives applying for divorce, referred to them by Washtenaw County, Michigan, legal aid offices. While the women surveyed were poor or indigent at the time of the interview, 25% of their husbands held white-collar jobs and 50% of the husbands had middle incomes. The statistical data in Eisenberg and Micklow's study resembles most shelter studies already described in their listing of percentage distributions of characteristics of the victims and assailants, types and frequency of violent incidents, problems in leaving, and interventions sought. The main strength of Eisenberg and Micklow's work is not in these data, however, but in their shocking interviews with doctors, lawyers, and law enforcement officials, and in their perceptive analysis of the battered woman's catch-22 situation.[70] Similarly, the article by Field and Field is strongest in its analysis of how the criminal justice and civil legal systems promote "neither justice nor peace" in battering relationships. They also present a statistical result on the sad infrequency (less than 3%) with which women in Washington, DC, in 1966 were able to obtain warrants against their male partners for assault.[71]

Controlled Study with Legal Clients

Parker and Schumacher conducted the third of the three controlled studies of conjugal battering. Their study makes by far the best use of control groups to appear so far. They surveyed 50 of 51 women consecutively applying for divorce and/or restraining orders to the Domestic Relations Bureau of the Baltimore, Maryland, legal aid offices. The sample consequently may have a lower-class bias. They divided their 50 subjects according to whether or not they had been battered at least three times by their husbands, resulting in a group of 20 battered women and a control group of 30 women. They found significant differences between the two groups for whether the women's mothers had been battered, and for whether the husband had at least graduated from high school. Of the 30 women not repeatedly battered, 13 had still been assaulted once each by their mates. These 13 were found to be significantly different from the 20 battered women in terms of the amount of violence in their families of origin (p<.02, battered women's families more violent).[72]

This study excels in its sophisticated use of statistical tests of significance. Parker and Schumacher also develop an interesting issue with their study of a differentiating factor between women who manage to avoid further physical abuse after the first conjugal assault, and those who are battered on repeated occasions by the same assailant. It is often stated in the literature that many women walk out or break off with the batterer after one or two beatings. It may be useful to identify these "violence syndrome averters"—as Parker and Schumacher term them—in order to investigate the factors enabling some women to interdict effectively the abuse directed at them. On the other hand, studies differentiating between battered women who remain with the abuser and those who succeed in leaving the batterer need to be careful to avoid blaming the victim for the batterer's maltreatment of her.

Police Intervention Samples

Bard was instrumental in establishing and training a pilot project Family Crisis Intervention Unit for the New York City police. The unit operated for 22 months in the western part of Harlem, a predominantly poor and black area. In all, 1388 calls by 962 different families were recorded in the period. Bard and his collaborators published three accounts of this project, discussing police behavior compared to a neighboring control precinct, incidence of violence, effect of the unit, and what callers sought from the police. Another study result calls into question the important role usually attributed to alcohol in family violence.[73]

Other studies based on police samples are all of the same basic design. They involve the use of police or court records to analyze the relationship of victim and offender in crimes such as murder and assault. These include the works of Wolfgang, Pittman and Handy, and Pokorny—all cited by Gelles—as well as reports by Boudouris, Dobash and Dobash, Stephens, and Ward et al.[74]

Studies with Sample Populations Not Previously Labeled as Violent

Komarovsky surveyed 58 families from a midwestern town. She obtained a homogeneous sample by establishing criteria for inclusion in her sample. All couples studied had to be Caucasian, blue collar, and at least second-generation American-born, Protestant, and with at least one child, both members no more than 40 years old, and both members with no more education than a high school diploma. Among many other factors studied, she investigated the incidence of violent quarrels associated with beatings and/or the destruction of objects. She found conjugal violence to be more common among respondents who had not graduated from high school. Apart from Mowrer and Mowrer's neglected work, Komarovsky's stands as the earliest study deriving an estimate of the prevalence of conjugal abuse.[75]

College Student Samples

Steinmetz surveyed 78 college students in order to derive a correlation statistic for husband-wife and parent-child violence. Incidence figures are given for verbal and physical aggression between spouses, between siblings, and between parent and child.[76] In order to obtain these figures, she used a portion of the conflict resolution techniques scales (CRT) developed by Straus et al., which will soon be discussed in detail.

Straus sampled 583 University of New Hampshire students, of whom 555 completed his questionnaire based on the CRT. This sample was in turn reduced to 385 students coming from intact families. As a result, the sample is biased towards more stable and better-functioning families than a true cross section of American families. Consequently, figures from this sample on the incidence of spouse abuse are probably conservative relative to the true incidence of conjugal abuse in America.[77] In one allusion to this study, Straus reports on the effect of the wife's satisfaction with the family income on the incidence of marital violence.[78]

The main focus of Straus' study using this sample, however, was to test the catharsis theory. This theory postulates that verbal aggression and aggression against objects release pent-up aggressive tensions and, therefore, should each be negatively correlated with physical aggression. Straus' study obtained results contradicting these hypotheses derived from the catharsis theory.

Bulcroft and Straus administered the CRT to 110 students in their Family Sociology class, of whom 105 completed the questionnaire. Identical questionnaires were then sent to the 180 parents of the 90 students who were offspring of families still intact at the time. Of the 180 parents, 121 completed and return the questionnaire. Bulcroft and Straus thus obtained a sample of 55 families for whom they had data from both parents, as well as from the child.[79]

The reports of violence from the student group were correlated with the fathers' reports of violence, and the mothers' reports. These correlations are analogous to inter-rater reliability statistics. The figures are also broken down by class status of the family of origin. Incidence rates reported by each of the three family members are also presented, also broken down by class status. The main findings are that students report almost twice as much wife assault as their fathers admit to perpetrating, but far less husband assault than their mothers admit committing. This study has tremendous implications for the results of Straus, Gelles, and Steinmetz's national study, as will be further discussed below.

Studies with Random Samples

The National Crime Survey used a random sample of 72,000 American households, of which about 60,000 consented to join the study. Household members were interviewed seven times, at six-month intervals between 1973 and 1975, about whether they had been subjected to assaults of any kind, and about the consequences of the assaults that did occur. Incidence rates for conjugal assault are determined, broken down by age, gender, and marital status of the victim, and by household income. Also studied were injuries suffered and whether the victim sought police intervention.[80]

Owens and Straus derived correlations between adults' expressed approval of violence and each of three variables: violence committed as a child, violence observed as a child, and violence subjected to as a child. They found positive correlations with violence approval for all three variables; these were consistently higher for men than for women. The results are based on a random national sample of 1176 adults aged at least 18 years. The poll was conducted by the Louis Harris organization in October 1968.[81]

Steinmetz conducted a survey of 57 families sampled at random in New Castle County, Delaware. Families had to meet certain criteria to be included in the study, however, which subtracts from the actual randomness of the sample. They had to be intact white families with at least two children between ages three and eighteen. These criteria probably diminish the incidence rates of marital violence derived. The main finding was that 7% of the families experienced severe and repetitive conjugal assaults, compared to under 0.03% of the county's 94,000 families who reported a conjugal assault to the police in 1975.[82] This implies that less than one out of every 250 battering incidents in New Castle County are reported to the local police.

Straus, Gelles, and Steinmetz's study interviewed a random national sample of 2143 members of intact couples, 98% of whom were legally married. This work stands out as the most important existing study of the incidence of battering and of factors contributing to conjugal abuse. This is mainly because of the very accurate representation in the sample of the overall population of American couples and the sophisticated methodology of the study. The results of the study are thoroughly described in

Behind Closed Doors.[83] Several spin-off papers and studies based on this sample have also been written: Straus' fine preliminary report on the incidence of conjugal violence,[84] discussions of battered husbands by Steinmetz[85] and by Gelles,[86] and Yllo and Straus' comparison of violence rates among married and unmarried cohabiting couples.[87]

The study was designed by Straus et al. and interviews were conducted by a national polling organization. The 2143 subjects represent 65% of persons asked to participate in the study. Forty-five percent of respondents are men—the greatest divergence in the sample from the general population, but a very high level of male involvement for a study of conjugal violence.

The study was designed in hopes of countering the expected tendency of respondents to underreport the frequency and severity of conjugal violence. This was accomplished by first asking the subjects a host of questions pertaining to identifying characteristics such as gender, race, age, number of children, employment and occupational status, income, religion, and education attained. Then, hopefully after rapport was established between subject and interviewer, the final set of questions which constitute the CRT was administered.

The CRT itself is designed to mitigate against underreporting of violence. It is presented as a series of questions regarding strategies for resolving the conflicts that arise in any normal family. Eighteen behaviors which a spouse/partner may employ to resolve conflicts are presented, beginning with a calm discussion and gradually escalating until the eighteenth—use of a lethal weapon. Subjects are asked to indicate which of these behaviors they employed in the year prior to the interview, which behaviors they have ever employed in their marriage/relationship, and which behaviors their mate performed, for the target year and ever, in order to resolve conjugal conflicts. Responses concerning the frequency of each behavior in the prior year are also gathered. As a result of the design of the scale, subjects are not much, if at all, aware of when they have crossed the threshold of admitting to assaultive behavior or to violent victimization.

The 18 behaviors, referred to as Items A through R, are:

A) discussed the issue calmly
B) got information to back up his/her side of things
C) brought in or tried to bring in someone to help settle things
D) insulted or swore at the other
E) sulked and/or refused to talk about it
F) stomped out of the room, house, or yard
G) cried
H) did or said something to spite the spouse
I) threatened to hit or throw something at spouse

J) threw, smashed, hit or kicked something
K) threw something at spouse
L) pushed, grabbed or shoved spouse
M) slapped or spanked spouse
N) kicked, bit, or hit with a fist
O) hit or tried to hit with something
P) beat up spouse
Q) threatened with a knife or gun
R) used a knife or gun

Items K through R are often referred to as the Violence Index, Item K being the threshold at which violence is said to begin. Items N through R are the Severe Violence Index, also known as the Wife-beating or Husband-beating Index. A Reasoning Index and a Verbal Aggression Index account for the ten "nonviolent" items. Analogous protocols and indexes were devised to measure parent-child violence and administered in the same study, but are not relevant to the present purpose. The main findings of the study are that 16% of couples experienced a violent conjugal incident in the target year, 28% ever; and that 5.3% of couples admitted to the occurrence of spouse-beating in the target year, 12.6% ever.[88]

I note the following problems with the design of this study. First, despite measures taken to prevent it, underreporting remains a problem. Straus attributes this to two factors: 1) the less violent acts may not be noteworthy enough to be recalled and reported, while 2) the most violent acts will be underreported due to shame and guilt about these activities.[89] For the latter factor, I would note also fear by perpetrators of possible prosecution, and fear by victims of reprisals by their assailants should their disclosures be discovered. Underreporting is indicated in the study results by the fact that perpetrators of both genders consistently report more of the lesser forms of violence than their victims, while for severe violence the pattern is reversed, with victims of both sexes reporting more acts of violence than perpetrators. Furthermore, Straus points out that, since conjugal violence is a major cause of divorce and separation, limiting the sample to intact couples and to information only about their current relationships causes the study results to underestimate the overall prevalence of conjugal violence.[90]

Several features of the study function to inflate the incidence of conjugal violence committed by women, relative to conjugal violence committed by men. The study does not look at the context of violence, in particular whether it is in self-defense.[91] It fails to compensate for Bulcroft and Straus' validity study finding that men tend to underreport conjugal violence that they have perpetrated far more than women underreport.[92]

Also, the violence is recorded by behavior without regard for the effect of the behavior. Thus, when a husband slaps his wife, it is scored the same as when the reverse occurs, despite the fact that the usual male weight advantage and anatomical sex differences make it much more likely that the man's violence, rather than the woman's, will result in serious physical injury. Along these lines, the items for which women most predominate over men in violent behavior—"hit or attempted to hit with something" and "threw something at spouse"—include ineffectual and physically harmless attacks. The use of an object to strike the mate may reflect the woman's disadvantage in weight and in the physical force she can muster.

Another important issue arising out of Straus, Gelles, and Steinmetz's neglect of the effect of violent behavior can be called the "Godzilla effect." The Godzilla effect is named for the Japanese monster movie in which the Japanese army turns out in full force to destroy the monster Godzilla, only to find that their weapons do him absolutely no harm. They subsequently retreat in terror. Similarly, a conjugal partner—usually the woman—can assault or retaliate against her mate, attacking heatedly, only to find she has done no physical harm to him whatsoever. In this manner, the person scored as assailant can be intimidated or even terrorized by the inconsequential effects of executing an assault, while the so-called victim emerges dominant, victorious, and unscathed—this is the Godzilla effect.

The choice of behaviors to be scored on the CRT, like the problems discussed in the preceding two paragraphs, also tends to escalate the derived incidence of conjugal violence by women relative to that committed by men. As Straus speculates, striking with or throwing objects may be forms of conjugal violence that are especially common among women.[93] Many forms of violence especially germane to male behavior, however, are not scored here, including abducting, carrying, or physically restraining the mate; rape; choking and suffocating, among others. Certainly some women perform these behaviors also—except rape—but most of the latter set of behaviors are strongly related to the usual male advantage in weight and strength. This section of the critique pertains equally to Steinmetz's studies of battered husbands, reported in *Victimology*.[94] Threats of beating—a particularly male behavior[95]—are also defined by Straus et al. as less than violent despite their documented effectiveness in coercion.[96]

Finally, placing conjugal violence in the context of conjugal conflict overlooks the fact that many conjugal assaults are not carried out in the context of conjugal conflict. This last factor may not be as likely to promote skewing of results by gender as those just discussed, although this part of the discussion still pertains more to male behavior. The main point here is that conjugal assault is not always a strategy of resolving conjugal conflict.

It can be a means of discharging conflict and aggression that have arisen entirely in relationships other than the conjugal relationship—e.g., on the job, in church, with friends, or in the family of origin. Battering can also be a means of expressing intrapsychic conflicts, as Serum[97] and Elbow[98] point out. Serum states that woman-battering can act as an antidepressant agent, an antipsychotic, a tranquilizer, or a suicide preventative.[99] Presumably this applies to some husband-beating as well. Marital rape also need not occur in the context of marital conflict.[100]

Having critiqued the Straus et al. study at such length, it is time to reiterate its strengths. First and foremost, it is a large random sample, reflecting a fantastically accurate cross section of intact American couples. The findings are thus easily generalized with confidence to the general population, especially since they remain conservative estimates. Men are relatively well represented in the sample. Finally, the elegant design of the study does seem likely to reduce somewhat the effect of subjects' tendency to underreport violent conjugal behavior.

Gelles used a modified version of the CRT in order to study the relationship between battered women's decisions whether to leave their abusers and the severity of conjugal violence they had endured.[101] This modified CRT scale will be referred to as the Gelles scale in the present work. For the most part, the Gelles scale has the same limitations as those just described for the CRT. A full enumeration of the Gelles scale appears in item 29 of Appendix A.

The Gelles scale has two advantages relative to the CRT and one disadvantage. Unlike the CRT, the Gelles scale includes one item—"pushed down"—that registers the effect of violence and, thus, prevents to an increased extent the respondents' euphemistically downgrading the level of violence committed. The other advantage of the Gelles scale is that it includes choking, which is more typically perpetrated by males, and is experienced by victims as a very threatening form of abuse. The main disadvantage of the Gelles scale relative to the CRT is that it fails to account for threats of violence—both verbal threats and weapons threats such as pointing a knife or gun.

CRITIQUE OF THE EMPIRICAL LITERATURE

The primary shortcoming of the conjugal violence literature is the dearth of hypothesis-testing and of references to the statistical significance of reported results. When a shelter study records such simple statistics as incidence of unemployment among batterers and racial distribution of batterers and battered women, these could easily be tested against local or regional census figures in order to derive a probability of significance. It is harder to gather local or regional statistics on rates of alcoholism or service in the military, but with some effort these could be obtained, again for use in a test of statistical significance. Null hypotheses to be tested are a tremendous rarity in the literature despite the myriad possible null hypotheses to test. Studies which do use these statistical methods, such as Parker and Schumacher's, demonstrate the relative ease with which this is accomplished and, thus, blaze the trail for future studies.

Another problem which has already been noted is that studies using help seeker samples are not representative of the entire range of woman abuse victims, but instead necessarily focus upon those battered women who seek various forms of intervention. As will be discussed later, intervention-seeking by victims appears to be associated with other factors such as the woman's material resources, or greater severity and frequency of violence suffered. Consequently, these help seeker studies may be skewed towards more severe forms of violence, and/or towards battered women with a greater level of material resources.[102]

As must be clear by now, studies of help seekers make up the bulk of the available literature. This is because of the simplicity of collecting such samples; the people to be studied are there, knocking on a shelter's door or in the waiting room of a lawyer or therapist. In many cases, it would be valuable to look at the same variables derived for a control group matched to the help-seeking group. Thus, one might compare sources of marital dissatisfaction in 600 control couples from Cuyahoga County who were not seeking divorce, with Levinger's sample of divorce applicants.[103] This does not assume that control samples will be entirely nonviolent; in fact, it should be assumed that many controls will have experienced conjugal violence.

Random samples such as Straus et al.'s are very desirable because such samples accurately represent the general population and are thus more easily generalized to all couples. The problem with random samples and control-group studies is the difficulty and extra expense, time, and effort involved in executing such research designs compared to studies of help seekers. These are major considerations hindering the appearance of further studies with more sophisticated designs. Also, in all fairness, many of the earlier studies sought only to document the existence of woman abuse as a common and serious social problem. This function has now been performed more than adequately. It is time for research in the field to move on to more ambitious investigations of factors which contribute to the occurrence, perpetuation, and/or halting of conjugal abuse.

The authors who have published thus far could have been more conscientious in specifying in their reports factors such as the characteristics of their samples, and the definitions employed to determine such variables as class status, child abuse, and alcoholism. This is done quite rarely—e.g., only Levinger is very explicit about his definition of class.[104] It has been noted already that the types of behaviors inquired about as physical abuse, or scored for incidence and/or frequency of abuse, can have great impact on the results derived.[105] This pertains not only to Straus et al. and to Steinmetz, but to the many studies of shelter residents that ask about frequency of abuse.[106] Open-ended interviews are better at avoiding this problem than are structured interviews and questionnaires, but no method is invulnerable to this issue. There is a tremendous gap in the literature regarding measuring relative severities of abuse situations. No one has attempted to define the concept of severity, except for the CRT's flawed, commonsense definition of a hierarchy of severity.

Another epidemic problem in the field is underreporting. There is really no way to eradicate underreporting of conjugal abuse (unless it were to become a matter of pride susceptible to overreports, which will hopefully never occur). There are means to neutralize underreporting somewhat such as the use of sophisticated methods to gain subjects' trust or to distract them from the researcher's intentions. Still, it seems underreporting is here to stay in the research in this field. Even victims tend to minimize or to forget the full extent of abuse.[107]

A final problem, and another pesky one, is the lack of male respondents. Batterers are notorious for their reluctance and unreliability as subjects. Still, researchers must not depend so much upon secondhand accounts of woman abusers by their partners and children. The field is in a double bind on this issue. Random samples, especially large ones, can somewhat compensate for the problem of the abusive man's reluctance to be studied, but will fail to provide the rich descriptions available from clinical studies. However, it is questionable if clinical studies can provide an accurate cross section of batterers, since the abuser voluntarily in therapy is an exceptional type of batterer. Protective services and other legally mandated cases still are probably not truly representative of all woman abusers.

The battered husband is thus far even more elusive than the battering husband, absent from clinical studies and secondhand accounts, a mere cipher in some incidence studies. This is probably due to the rarity of husband-battering. Still, it may be that studying battered men will yield results with important consequences—only time will tell.

Chapter 3

RESULTS OF EMPIRICAL WORKS

INCIDENCE AND PREVALENCE

Criminological Incidence

Studies show that from 11% to 52% of all assaults occur within the family.[1] Conjugal assaults comprise from 5% to 11% of reported assaults in America, and an even greater proportion of total attacks (as opposed to reported assaults), due to the greater tendency for spouse assaults to be repeated.[2] In the Dobashes' Scots sample, wife assaults comprised 26% of all violent crimes recorded, the second most common category of violent crime in Scotland.[3] The higher Scots proportion is probably a reflection of Scotland's being a less violent society, at least as far as nonconjugal violence is concerned.

There is little doubt that conjugal assaults are underreported to the police. Dobash and Dobash's sample of 109 battered women reported to the police an average of 4.75 assaults apiece, while reporting over 290 assaults apiece to the researchers, a reporting rate of 1.6%.[4] The National Crime Survey found 45% of battered women reported at least one assault to the police, accounting for one-fourth of the total attacks they experienced. Extrapolating from her Delaware sample, Steinmetz estimates that less than one out of every 250 spouse assaults are reported.[5] Conjugal assaults tend to have more serious consequences than other types; while finding conjugal assaults to be 5% of total assaults, the National Crime Survey found they accounted for 12% of assaults ending in serious injury, 16% of those requiring medical care, and 18% of assaults causing the victim to miss at least one day's work.[6]

Spouse murders constitute from 12% to 18% of murders in America,[7] and an even higher proportion of murders in less violent societies—e.g., about one-third of British murders.[8] Over 40% of all female murder victims are the wives of their murderers, both in the United States[9] and in England and Wales together.[10] Since men are more often killed by other relatives and strangers, the proportion of husbands murdered by wives is "only" 10% of male victims.[11] Beatings are the most common method of wife murder.[12] These figures do not even include murders involving unmarried cohabitants and noncohabitant lovers, and also exclude many so-called love triangle murders.

Wives make up 52% of spouses murdered, husbands 48%.[13] Husbands are six to seven times more likely than wives to have initiated the violence in the incident leading to their eventual death; Wolfgang found that nearly 60% of husbands murdered were killed after they had initiated violence, compared to 9% of wives killed in "victim-precipitated" murders.[14] Ward found that 22% of female murderers claimed they killed in self-defense,[15] while Meyers reports that 40% of women accused of murder held in the Cook County, Illinois, jail had killed husbands or boyfriends who had regularly battered them.[16]

Murder-suicides account for 4% to 6% of murders in America and are even more often family-related murders than are murders where the killer does not immediately take his own life.[17] In Boudouris' study, 50% to 60% of murderous couples were still living together at the time of the murder, had not filed for divorce or separation, or shown other signs of estrangement.[18] Noting that about 15% each of assaults and murders take place between legal spouses, Gelles estimates conservatively that a similar proportion of all rapes occur within legal marriage.[19] Since marital rape is much more likely to occur on repeated occasions than other forms of rape, much more than 15% of rape incidents should be expected to occur in conjugal relationships. Consequently, Gelles' estimate applies better as an estimate of the proportion of rape victims who suffer marital (or conjugal) rape than it does as an estimate of the proportion of all rape incidents that involve conjugal rape.

Domestic disturbance calls are among the most dangerous types of call for police officers, resulting in 22% of murders of police officers in 1974—the leading type of call ending in police death for that year—and 28% of assaults on police that year.[20] In a sample of 300 police calls, Bard found that 80% of domestic disturbance calls involved legal marrieds, and that 32% of all domestic disturbance calls involved alleged assaults.[20½] Based upon this, an estimate can be derived that over 25% of domestic disturbance calls, family trouble calls, etc., to Bard's police unit involved alleged assaults between legal spouses.

Divorcing Couples

Levinger found that 36.8% of wives and 3.3% of husbands seeking divorce alleged physical abuse by their spouse.[21] Fields found that 51% and 57.4%, respectively, of wives applying for divorce at two legal aid clinics complained of physical abuse.[22] O'Brien found that 16.7% of his sample of divorce applicants spontaneously complained of physical abuse,[23] which means that this represents a minimum for the actual rate of conjugal violence in his sample. Parker and Schumacher found that 40% of their sample of wives seeking divorce said they had been conjugally assaulted three or more times, and that 66% had been assaulted at least once by their husbands.[24]

Clinical Samples

Ball found that 7% of all cases in her clinic involved family violence, over half of which was conjugal violence.[25] Saunders cites a study of over 1600 couples seeking help from American family agencies, 15.6% of whom complained of conjugal abuse.[26] Mowrer and Mowrer found conjugal abuse was a presenting complaint in 41% of their sample of 1573 couples seeking counseling services in the 1920s.[27] In medical and psychiatric samples, Rounsaville found that about 3.5% of women over 15 years of age presenting themselves to the surgical and psychiatric emergency rooms were battered by their mates.[28] Hilberman and Munson found that half of all women referred by their rural medical clinic for psychiatric evaluations were battered women.[29] Other studies indicate that from 50% to 80% of all battered women seek medical or psychiatric help for injuries and symptoms associated with their abuse.[30]

Estimates of Overall Incidence and Prevalence

In the study that he wrote up in *The Violent Home*, Gelles found that 55% of his sample of couples had experienced at least one violent incident, and that 47% of husbands and 32% of wives had ever been violent. Violence occurred at least twice per year in 26% of couples, while 25% of husbands and 11% of wives were violent at least six times a year. His control group couples had experienced violence at least once in 37% of the group, and at least twice per year for 12%. The lowest prevalence rate for husbands that Gelles found was that 20% of male neighbors of family guidance agency couples had ever hit their wives.[31] Komarovsky found that 24% of husbands and 21% of wives in her sample mentioned violent quarrels.[32] It is very unlikely, however, that these two studies can be generalized to the public at large due to the special nature of their sample groups. Steinmetz found that 7% of her random sample of Delaware couples experienced severe, repetitive beatings in the course of one year.[33]

Turning to studies of college students, Straus reports that 16% of a sample of 385 students reported violence between their parents during the students' senior year of high school.[34] Steinmetz found that 30% of a student sample said their parents had ever engaged in marital violence.[35] Bulcroft and Straus' sample of students reported that 16.7% of their fathers and 10% of their mothers had assaulted the other parent during the subjects' senior year of high school.[36]

The findings from Straus, Gelles, and Steinmetz's sample of 2143 members of heterosexual couples are presented in Table 1. The table is taken from Straus' preliminary report on the sample.[37] Figures in the first two columns represent percentage incidence rates for each behavior by husbands/male partners in the column headed M and by wives/female partners in the column headed F. The mean and median frequencies of each behavior, by gender, for those who did engage in each behavior are presented in the next four columns.

Table 1   Comparison of Male and Female Conjugal Violence Rates

| CRT Violence Item | Incidence Rate | | Frequency* | | | |
| | M | F | Mean | | Median | |
			M	F	M	F
Wife-Beating and Husband-Beating (N to R)	3.8	4.6	8.0	8.9	2.4	3.0
Overall Violence Index (K to R)	12.1	11.6	8.8	10.1	2.5	3.0
K. Threw something at spouse	2.8	5.2	5.5	4.5	2.2	2.0
L. Pushed, grabbed, shoved spouse	10.7	8.3	4.2	4.6	2.0	2.1
M. Slapped spouse	5.1	4.6	4.2	3.5	1.6	1.9
N. Kicked, bit, or hit with fist	2.4	3.1	4.8	4.6	1.9	2.3
O. Hit or tried to hit with something	2.2	3.0	4.5	7.4	2.0	3.8
P. Beat up spouse	1.1	0.6	5.5	3.9	1.7	1.4
Q. Threatened with a knife or gun	0.4	0.6	4.6	3.1	1.8	2.0
R. Used a knife or gun	0.3	0.2	5.3	1.8	1.5	1.5

*For those who engaged in each act—i.e., omits those with scores of zero. Source: Straus, "Wife-beating: how common and why?" *Victimology* 2, Nos. 3-4: 443-459.

Overall, Straus et al. found that 16% of all couples had experienced violence at least as serious as Item K—threw something at spouse—in the year studied, and that 28% had ever experienced such behaviors.[38] These findings are very reminiscent of the results from college samples mentioned above, derived by Straus[39] and by Steinmetz.[40] In the target year, 5.3% of the couples had encountered at least one of the behaviors listed in Items N to R, and 12.6% of the couples had ever experienced such severe conjugal violence. Straus estimates in his preliminary report that the actual rate of couples ever experiencing conjugal violence—Items K through R—is double the results of the study, or 55 to 60 percent.[41]

Based on these figures and an estimate that there are 45 million couples in America, Straus concludes that at least 1.8 million American women are battered each year, and possibly twice as many as that.[42] Steinmetz estimates elsewhere that there are 3.5 million battered women in America.[43] In similar fashion, one can conclude that at least 5.6 million American couples—perhaps many more—will ever experience battering (12.6% of 45 million). The National Crime Survey estimates that there are 1.06 million spouse assaults annually. Straus et al.'s figures imply that there are 6100 conjugal assaults annually per 50,000 couples, from which can be derived an estimate of nearly five and one-half million conjugal assaults per year.[44] The implications of Straus et al.'s belief that their study's estimates remain conservative are staggering.

In summation, these studies show that the members of 5% to 7% of American couples will admit that in a year's time they have experienced conjugal violence involving kicking, biting, punching, or worse. Slightly over one out of eight intact couples have a member who admits she or he has ever experienced this serious level of marital violence. One out of six couples have members who will report that one mate threw objects at the other—or worse—in the course of a year, while 28% of couples (nearly two out of every seven) will report this milder level of conjugal violence ever taking place in their relationship.

RELATIVE INCIDENCE OF BATTERED WIVES AND BATTERED HUSBANDS

Police records indicate that complaints of conjugal abuse by wives/women outnumber similar complaints by husbands/men by a ratio of about 12:1.[45] The National Crime Survey found a similar rate of 13 assaulted wives for every husband assaulted, while Levinger's sample yielded a ratio of 11:1.[46] Martin cites percentages of female complainants from court records of conjugal assault cases ranging from 75% to 95% (from 3:1 to 19:1, in ratio terms).[47] In O'Brien's sample, women reported 84% of the marital violence despite comprising only 52% of the sample.[48] Dobash and Dobash find the highest predominance of wife-beating over husband-beating, nearly 66:1 in 803 Scots cases of spouse assault.[49]

Conversely, Straus, Gelles, and Steinmetz find nearly equal aggregate conjugal violence rates for men and women, with women committing more severe violence than men. They find mutual assault in 49% of violent couples, exclusively male violence in 27%, and violence committed solely by the woman in 24%.[50] Steinmetz insists that wives and women partners are at least as violent as husbands/male partners, based on these results and the results of three other studies she conducted. She believes the heavy predominance of battered women in other reports can largely be explained by the extreme stigma men would receive for admitting to being victimized by their wives/partners.[51] I am quite skeptical of this argument, since it is clear that battered women also encounter a great deal of victim-blaming and opprobrium when they reveal their plight. Certainly it has not been proved that this effect applies even more strongly in the case of battered husbands. In fact, in another work of hers, Steinmetz mysteriously seems to change her mind, estimating that there are 14 battered women each year for every battered husband/male partner.[52]

It has been shown by Bulcroft and Straus that husbands seem to underreport the conjugal violence that they commit far more than wives underreport theirs. Fathers in the Bulcroft and Straus study reported committing only 52.7% as much violence as their children claimed to have witnessed them commit, while mothers confessed to 64% *more* violence than their children claim to have witnessed. Straus attributes this greater reporting by wives to the effect of violence behind closed doors which the children could not witness.[53] He does not explain why this effect would only apply to wives, however. It could be that these differences in reporting may represent the children exonerating their mothers and not counting when the women acted in self-defense, while the women themselves admitted which behaviors they performed abstracted from the context of the incident as requested by the study.

My own clinical experience has clearly demonstrated that men seriously underreport their violence. I have rarely seen a batterer who admits to perpetrating as much violence as his wife/partner recounts sustaining to shelter workers on her intake. To illustrate:

> Robbie was very resentful about coming to counseling. He said, "I'm not any wife-beater. This happens once, at most twice, a year." In the course of further questioning, he recounted five violent incidents from the past four months. There is good reason to believe that he had committed even more assaults during this period.

Sam's wife had left him a dozen times, all after beatings. Her bones had been fractured on many of these occasions. This last separation, however, occurred after he began drinking and before he could assault her. Regarding his request for a beer as a prelude to another assault, she threw a beer mug at him. It cut his arm badly, requiring 37 stitches. While Sam would admit in counseling that he was more violent than his wife, this remains the only violent incident that he reported.

John's wife, Lisa, returned to him after a week in the shelter. John called the DVP office, demanding to know where Lisa had received the bruises she still bore from his assault on her. The counselor told John that John had done it himself, and that Lisa had looked much worse upon arrival at the shelter. John denied all violence on his part, accused the counselor and other shelter staff of beating Lisa and holding her hostage. Ironically, this accurately describes John's behavior: not only did he beat Lisa with near-fatal results, he kept her under lock and key, with the windows nailed down as well.[54]

Presumably, an interviewer working for Straus et al. would have fared no better in eliciting candor from these men than I did. In Sam's case, however, the wife would undoubtedly have been scored as violent using Straus et al.'s methods.

Other factors were discussed earlier which escalate the derived rates of violence by wives/female partners relative to the rates of violence by male partners in Straus, Gelles, and Steinmetz's study. These are, briefly, no compensating for self-defense as a source of violence, neglect of the various implications of the male weight advantage, and a choice of behaviors to score as violent that appears skewed more towards female behavior. Their methodology also overlooks the Godzilla effect that has been described earlier in this work and neglects the effect of what Gelles calls protective-reaction violence, which appears to be a type of conjugal violence committed only by battered mates.[55] Protective-reaction violence is preemptive violence by the person who is usually victimized, as exemplified by Sam's wife, who hurled the beer mug at Sam when she believed—with good reason— that he would soon attack her.

Finally, there is one study of national attitudes toward conjugal violence which shows that wives slapping their husbands are viewed as somewhat less deviant than husbands who slap wives.[56] This effect is almost undoubt- edly a corollary of the female's lesser weight and strength, which means her slap generally does far less injury than his. Similarly, comic media are said to portray more conjugal violence by wives than by husbands. If violence by wives is in general perceived as less deviant, then logically it would also be more readily reported, inflating the apparent level of violence by women derived by Straus et al.

Another phenomenon in Straus et al.'s results is that, of the woman abusers in the sample, there is a subgroup who are violent with much greater frequency than other violent mates, especially compared to violent female partners. While Straus takes note of this result, Steinmetz overlooks it entirely.[57] This effect can be discovered from the almost uniformly greater discrepancies between median and mean frequencies of violence for husbands as opposed to wives. This applies especially to threats of, and actual use of, weapons—the most intimidating and lethal forms of violence.

For now, I remain unconvinced that the police-based estimate that 92% of battered mates are women is inaccurately high (this comes to 12 battered women for every battered husband/male partner in ratio terms). If anything, it seems that the proportion of battered mates who are women would be even higher than 92%. Clearly, more information would be useful and necessary in order to make more confident and accurate judgments on this issue. As mentioned, this issue has crucial implications for the validity of the feminist analysis of conjugal abuse as violence against women. It also has critical policy and service implications, since few if any refuges exist that accept battered husbands. Fortunately for battered male partners, old forms of transient, low-cost shelter have traditionally been oriented towards men instead of women in such institutions as the Salvation Army, the YMCA, and church-run hostels.[58]

AGE

Average ages in five studies of battered women range from 26.8 to 37 years.[59] The aggregate mean age of the 539 women in the five studies is 30 years old. The age range noted in the literature runs from 17 in Star et al. to 69 in Walker.[60] Age of woman batterers in three studies averages from 32 to 34 years, 34 in aggregate for 177 cases, and ranges from 18 to 81.[61] In the literature, the abusive men on the average are 3.4 years older than their female partners. The average length of the marriage/relationship prior to interview is 8.8 years, ranging from mere months to 31 years.[62]

The relative youth of the samples may or may not indicate the actual highest risk age for battering. The sample age is probably lowered by the effects of changing values among younger women concerning divorce and sex roles. Also, younger women may be more aware of the existence of hotlines and shelters. Still, both Straus et al. and the National Crime Survey found conjugal assault rates highest among people under 30.[63] If this effect holds true, it could reflect developmental factors in adult life and marriage, or it could reflect a trend that American society is be increasingly violent, or both.

Contradictory findings are also present in the literature. Gelles fo the most violence among couples in the 41 to 50 decade, and O'Bri obtained 64% of his reports of abuse from those married 13 to 37 years who are presumably 30 years and older.[64] Several authors argue on observational grounds that violence escalates in frequency and intensity as the battering relationship continues,[65] perhaps thus victimizing to a greater extent those 40 years and older.

Age discrepancy between mates has also been investigated for its relation to conjugal violence rates. Gelles found a higher proportion of violence in legal marriages where husbands were older than wives and the most nonviolence among couples where the woman was older. An older wife seemed to polarize the effect of age discrepancy in Gelles' study since these same couples also had the highest rate of frequent violence. Husbands and wives of equal age had the lowest rate of frequent violence, but equaled older husband couples in the rate of infrequent violence.[66]

MARITAL STATUS

The National Crime Survey found that 26% of perpetrators of spouse assaults "had no right to be in the victim's home at the time"—i.e., were either legally separated spouses or divorced ex-spouses. The overwhelming majority of these must have been men assaulting their wives or ex-wives, since 94% of conjugal assaults in this study involved men assaulting women.[67] It is very important to remember that a victim's breaking off an abusive relationship does not necessarily mean the halting of her victimization. It only means that she has done all she can to halt the violence. Both gunpoint incidents in O'Brien's study occurred after separation of the partners, and Serum considers the batterer to be most dangerous when facing actual or threatened separation from the partner.[68] One important answer to "Why does she stay?" is that even if she doesn't stay, he may keep showing up.

A surprising result related to marital status is that thus far unmarried cohabitants appear to be more violent than legally married couples. Yllo and Straus found this result to obtain with statistical significance in Straus, Gelles, and Steinmetz's sample of 2143 couples, 1.9% of whom were unmarried cohabitants.[69] "Living-together" couples seem to be disproportionately represented in several studies, at rates of 15% to 21% of the sample, compared to an estimated 3% of cohabiting American couples.[70]

Yllo and Straus expected unmarried cohabitants to be less violent than marrieds because "living-togethers" were thought to be free of the legal constraints of the marriage contract and to represent a nontraditional lifestyle.[71] The results so far refute this hypothesis. These results raise the possibility that traditional marriage provides a model which is adopted to a great extent by unmarried cohabitant couples. Also, the decision to cohabitate unmarried instead of marrying may be related to a perceived need of one or both partners for the potential for a quick exit from the relationship, if necessary.

RACE

Race is routinely reported in the literature, but without any context for its significance or triviality as a finding. The only study reporting racial rates of violence in a somewhat sophisticated way is, as might be expected, Straus et al. They found the rate of woman abuse to be triple and the rate of husband abuse to be double for blacks relative to whites. Judging from Straus et al.'s results, husband abuse seems even more common among other minority races in America.[72] Still, these findings could also result from more candid responses by minorities than by whites.

It is important to be cautious with findings related to race. Higher violence rates among blacks do not represent biological racial differences, nor are they likely to represent cultural or racial attitudes. Rather, they probably have more to do with the implications of being black in America for social status and for the amount of frustration encountered in life.[73] Further, there are few, if any, policy implications of racial results. In summation, one must be very careful about the study of race in relation to conjugal abuse due to the possibility of racist misinterpretations. On the other hand, the data is easily gathered and any datum can have important, unforeseen implications. Certainly it would shock many people if whites could be shown to be overrepresented among conjugal batterers.

RELIGION

Gelles and Straus et al. are the only authors to study whether religion plays a role in conjugal abuse. Both studies find mild tendencies for violence to occur more in couples where the members are of different religions than in couples with the same religion. Both studies also find conjugal assault most common among couples where at least one member professes no religious affiliation.[74] Straus et al. find that minority religions labeled as "Other"—i.e., not Protestant, Catholic, Jewish, or none— are the next highest religious category in conjugal assault. Jews studied by

Straus et al. had the lowest incidence of woman abuse of any religion, while Protestants were lowest in husband abuse.[75]

SOCIOECONOMIC VARIABLES

This topic vies as one of the hottest disputes in the field. Unfortunately, studies of socioeconomic status and conjugal violence are usually vaguely commonsensical in their definition of class. Through no inclination of my own, the ensuing discussion will reflect this problem. This discussion will break socioeconomic status down into its component variables: class status, income, occupational status, employment status, and educational attainment.

It is certain that conjugal violence occurs at all levels of social and occupational status, education, income, and employment. In order to support this point, case histories of abusive and abused professionals, academics, and political leaders are regularly recounted in the woman abuse literature. It is necessary not to overlook this fact, no matter what generalizations one draws about the relationship of class status and income to conjugal violence. Generalizations are just that; they only hold in general, not always. The public can be very quick to excuse the upper classes, the educated, and whites if they hear that these groups may be less involved—again, not *un*involved—in conjugal abuse.

Class Status Per Se

Both Flynn, and Owens and Straus, find no class effect whatsoever on the prevalence of conjugal violence.[76] Komarovsky's findings among working-class couples do not diverge from Straus et al.'s national rates.[77] Eisenberg and Micklow, Walker, and Geller all have predominantly middle- and upper-class samples.[78] Walker holds staunchly that woman abuse is more common among the middle class and higher income groups. Davidson is of the same opinion.[79]

Steinmetz and Straus, Whitehurst, and Goode are all of the opposite opinion, associating spouse abuse with lower- and working-class status.[80] There is more empirical evidence thus far to support this side of the question. Levinger found a significant class difference ($p<.01$) in the rate with which divorcing wives reported physical abuse—lower-class women reported more conjugal violence. The trend for husbands in Levinger's study was in the same direction.[81] (As mentioned earlier, Levinger is the only source who clearly states his definition of class.) Bulcroft and Straus also report consistently more violence by both genders in the working class than in the middle class.[82] This effect is far more pronounced for violence by husbands.

Perhaps even more important are the implications of Bulcroft and Straus' results for reliability and underreporting by class. First, there is consistently less reliability between parent and child reports of violence for middle-class families. This lack of reliability seems to have much to do with a more pronounced tendency by middle-class parents, relative to working-class parents, to underreport violence.

While working-class fathers report committing 64% of the violence that their children report on them, middle-class fathers only confess to 30% of the conjugal violence that their children say they witnessed their fathers commit. Middle-class children witnessed their fathers commit 49% as much violence as working-class offspring witnessed done by their fathers. Middle-class fathers confess to less than 23% as much violence as working-class fathers.

Similar class effects apply to mothers and offspring. Working-class mothers report committing 132% *more* violence than their children witnessed them do. Middle-class mothers report their commission of violence only 10% more than their children, and middle-class wives report 20% *fewer* acts of serious violence—Items N through R on the CRT—than their children report. This study thus seems to demonstrate clearly an association between higher class status and greater withholding of information about incidents of conjugal violence. It also continues to support the hypothesis that the incidence of conjugal violence is inversely associated with class status. The tendency to report less violence as social status gets higher may indeed reflect less middle- and upper-class acceptance of conjugal violence, which some authors believe to be the case.[83] This remains a hypothesis about class attitudes, however, not an established effect.

Income

The two largest samples reveal a lower incidence of conjugal violence to be associated with higher income,[84] as is widely believed. Gelles' study shows an inexplicable drop in the violence rate of the second lowest income group. Gelles also found no tendency for 22 violent families to have less income than their 22 nonviolent neighbors. Further, Gelles' wealthiest couple was also probably the most violent of the sample.[85]

The attitude of the partners to the family income may be even more important than the quantity of income. O'Brien found that the wife was seriously dissatisfied with the husband's income in 84% of violent marriages in his sample, but in only 24% of the nonviolent couples.[86] Straus found that as his student sample reported their mothers more satisfied with the family income, the rate of conjugal violence diminished.[87]

Occupational Status

Straus, Gelles, and Steinmetz find that the rate of severe violence in the couple is double for blue-collar workers of both genders relative to white-collar workers.[88] Gelles found violence rates for men peaked in the middle of the spectrum of occupational status, while the rate of violence by women was highest for both low-status and highest-status female occupational levels. Gelles also found that 82% of violent husbands were of lower occupational status than their nonviolent male neighbor.[89] O'Brien discovered trends for violent husbands, relative to nonviolent ones, to be more dissatisfied with their jobs and more often of lower occupational status than their fathers-in-law.[90]

Gelles investigated intracouple differences in occupational status. He found the greatest rates of nonviolence among couples where the man's job was more prestigious than the woman's. The greatest rates of both overall violence and frequent violence occurred in couples where the man's occupational status was lower than the woman's.[91]

Employment Status

Straus et al. find severe violence rates two to three times higher among families where the male partner is unemployed or employed part time, relative to families where he is employed full time. They find severe violence is also more common where the male partner is disabled (relative to full-time employed) and that violence is least common among couples with retired male partners.[92] Many authors find apparently high unemployment rates among woman abusers.[93] Geller, however, reports on a group of abusive men who were "all steadily employed."[94]

Education

Gelles found rates of woman abuse were highest among men with some high school education (short of graduating), then steadily decreased at higher levels of education. He found a trend for violent male partners to be less educated than their nonviolent male neighbors. Women who had graduated college were the most violent wives of Gelles' sample.[95]

Straus et al. found somewhat different results, with the most violent male partners being high school graduates, the least violent men either having less than eight years' education or some college short of a bachelor's degree. People of both sexes who had not graduated high school were most likely within their gender to be victims of conjugal abuse, while women with bachelor's degrees were most likely to avoid being subjected to woman abuse.[96] Unlike Straus et al., Parker and Schumacher found a significant tendency in their sample (p<.05) for nonviolent husbands to have graduated high school more often than had violent husbands.[97] O'Brien found that 44% of violent husbands—compared to 18% of nonviolent ones—had dropped out of either high school or college.[98] Two studies, by Erlanger, and by Stark and McEvoy, show that college-educated individuals express more conceptual approval of marital violence than the less educated,[99] but it remains unknown whether these groups act according to these beliefs.

Data on interpartner differences in education show much more uniform effects than the foregoing. O'Brien found 56% of violent and 14% of nonviolent husbands were less educated than the wives they were divorcing.[100] The lowest rate of conjugal violence in Gelles' study occurred where the husband was more educated; the greatest violence rate among couples where the husband was less educated.[101] Carlson found that in almost 45% of 58 couples experiencing woman abuse, the man was less educated than the woman, while the men were more educated than the female partners in 29% of these couples.[102] This result is derived from a sample where husbands/male partners on the overall average were slightly more educated than wives/female partners.

Socioeconomic Status in Summary

The implications of the data available on socioeconomic status variables and the incidence of conjugal violence remain extremely controversial. Whatever conclusions are drawn from the data, it must be recalled that no social group—however prestigious and affluent—is immune to severe conjugal abuse. Case studies in the literature corroborate my own counseling experience in establishing this last assertion as uncontestable fact.

The most sophisticated studies do seem to establish a relationship between lower-class status and a greater tendency to report conjugal violence. The "tendency to report" should be emphasized in analysis of these results because higher class groups show higher rates of underreporting of violence. It still must be granted, however, that even if one corrects for underreporting in such studies as Bulcroft and Straus, there remains a higher resultant rate of conjugal violence among the lower classes in the available studies. This effect remains highly controversial, and requires further study before a final judgment is made. Rather than a reflection of lower-class attitudes or norms, any positive relationship established between higher incidence rates of conjugal violence and lower socioeconomic status could be interpreted theoretically into terms of frustration, low self-esteem, or oppression. The literature thus far uncontroversially establishes that full-time employment of the male partner is related to decreased rates of conjugal violence, and that increased rates of conjugal violence are associated with women having more education and/or higher occupational status than their mates.

PATTERNS IN WOMAN ABUSE

Onset

Premarital beating occurs in 23% of Dobash's sample and 25% of Gayford's group.[103] Star et al. report that before marriage 49% of their sample of battered women saw the husband-to-be acting violently with others or were assaulted by him.[104] By the end of the first year of marriage or cohabitation, the proportion of women who had already experienced conjugal assault is 59% in Dobash and Dobash, 67% in Star, and 90% in Eisenberg and Micklow.[105] Walker says that battering begins within six months of cohabitation.[106] Only 8% of Dobash and Dobash's group could cohabitate five years without abuse, but Roy states that about 30% of her group started their relationships with five or more years of peace.[107] Star et al. state 84% of their sample had been battered within the first three years of the marriage/relationship.[108]

Related to onset is the cessation of woman abuse, which should not be blithely mistaken for the same event as divorce or separation. In 26% of spouse assaults reported to the National Crime Survey, the partners were separated or divorced.[109] Forty percent to 50% of Boudouris' spouse murderers were estranged from their victims.[110]

Frequency of Assault

The majority of battered women studied experienced multiple assaults each year, and daily conjugal assaults are often documented. Assaults occurred at least weekly for 55% of Eisenberg and Micklow's sample and 25% of Roy's group.[111] Few battered women present themselves to outsiders for help after the first conjugal assault ever to occur; when they do, they generally seek a doctor or the police.[112] Rounsaville found that only 6% of his battered women patients had been conjugally assaulted on only one occasion.[113]

Precipitating Factors

Factors precipitating, or argued about before, an assault are not to be confused with the cause of assault. Often the victim will be assaulted no matter what, so the pretext of the assault is not a cause in any sense, but rather a matter of expediency to the assailant.[114] Even where the above is not the case, the pretext of the assault is never a necessary or sufficient cause in Aristotelian terms, but a proximal cause. Many assaults are not at all preceded by verbal argument or conjugal conflict. Gayford found that 77% of assaults were not preceded by verbal arguments.[115] Eisenberg and Micklow found that 10% of their subjects were beaten while asleep,[116] a phenomenon I have frequently encountered in my counseling practice. The topics precipitating an assault can still be instructive, provided one still bears in mind the foregoing discussion. Financial problems and sexual jealousy are the two issues most commonly associated with conjugal assaults.[117] Disputes about housework and sexual relations appear to be next most common.[118] The man's alcoholism, ill temper, and unemployment also figure prominently, as do disputes about children.[119] The woman's pregnancy was noted as precipitating 4% of assaults in Carlson's sample,[120] and is ranked by Roy as the eighth most common precipitator of conjugal assault.[121]

Types of Violence and Injuries Sustained

Verbal abuse from the assailant is virtually always present in battering relationships.[122] This includes threats of murder against 20% to 40% of victims.[123] Threats of beatings are also common and appear to be a strictly male behavior.[124] Despite his finding that 33% of wives sampled were violent at times, Gelles found not a single instance where these women threatened violence. Threats of violence were quite common among violent husbands in Gelles' sample, and one physically nonviolent man in the sample also made serious threats against his wife.[125]

The vast majority of battered women are punched, ranging from 63% to 100% of samples studied.[126] Thirty-five percent of Eisenberg and Micklow's sample stated that punches were generally aimed at their abdomens while they were pregnant, shifting from the usual target area of the head and face; Gelles notes the same effect.[127] About a third of victims are pushed or thrown around, while about half are kicked.[128] Attempts to drown, smother, or strangle the victim were made against 15% to 20% of battered women studied. Weapons—including blunt instruments—have been employed against 15% to 42% of shelter resident samples.[129] Nationally, Straus et al. found that 3.7% of their sample couples had ever experienced conjugal violence using a gun or knife.[130] If this is true for the whole population, it means that over 1.5 million Americans have been shot at, stabbed at, or cut by their current spouse or cohabitant lover!

Beatings, both barehanded and with blunt instruments, are the most frequent method of wife murder in Mowat's and in Wolfgang's studies.[131] From 10% to 32% of victims studied suffer bone fractures at least once; from 5% to 10% are knocked unconscious at least once.[132] Cuts and lacerations are even more common; bruises are ubiquitous. Epilepsy, burns, blindings, disfigurement, miscarriages, various internal injuries, broken teeth, and torn-out hair are also reported as results of woman-battering.[133]

In Prescott and Letko's sample, 43% of respondents were perman.
physically scarred by the batterers' assaults.

Self-defense by the Victim

Self-defense was already mentioned in the earlier discussion of criminology data. The most dramatic of those findings was Wolfgang's observation that a majority of husbands murdered by their wives had initiated the
violence in the incident resulting in their death.[134] Despite this and related
findings, the popular conception is that battered women do not retaliate
but passively submit under attack. The literature leaves this belief open to
question.

Five studies show that 50% to 71% of battered women fought back at
least one time. Conversely, in the same studies, 29% to 50% of victims
never did.[135] The National Crime Survey found that victims of spouse
assault claimed to resist the attack at least as often as victims of other
forms of assault.[136] Most battered women who did fight back later abandoned this strategy, however, because it made matters worse or had no
noticeable helpful effect. In Carlson's sample, 77% of the women who
fought back found that their husbands/partners escalated their assaulting
in response to the women's retaliation.[137] Research findings showing that
more aggression is committed against victims who do not retaliate[138] may
not apply to woman abuse situations. Still, in two studies, 8% and 24% of
battered women generally fought back when attacked.[139]

SEXUAL ISSUES IN WOMAN ABUSE

Both Gelles and Gayford note that pregnancy tends to increase the
frequency of woman abuse.[140] Gelles found that 23% of wives in his sample who were ever assaulted were attacked while pregnant.[141] Other studies record a range of from 9% to 50% of battered women assaulted while
pregnant, with an aggregate rate of 20.5% of 234 abused women assaulted
while pregnant.[142] Gelles also notes that the only three descriptions of
wife-beating in the major American novels that he surveyed all refer to
assaults on pregnant women (in *Gone with the Wind, The Group,* and
The Godfather).[143]

Gelles offers five factors to explain the increase in woman abuse during pregnancy. First is sexual frustration due to many couples' abstinence
from sex during this period. Second, he speculates that biochemical changes
in the pregnant woman leading to greater irritability and dependency on
her part contribute to this effect by angering the husband. Third is the
defenselessness of the pregnant woman.

The fourth factor is related to family transition, stress, and strain brought on by pregnancy. Pregnancy, in Gelles' view, may mark the end of the honeymoon and impel a too rapid transition to parenthood. This is especially true for couples who marry to legitimize a child conceived premaritally.[144] In this connection, it is important to note that 67% of Gayford's sample and 17% of Star et al.'s were pregnant before marriage or cohabitation with their abuser.[145] As an indicator of stress, Gelles points out that half of his assailants who beat pregnant wives had poverty incomes, while 70% were not full-time employed.[146]

Fifth and finally, beatings during pregnancy can represent prenatal child abuse and/or filicide, or abortion attempts. Violence during pregnancy is associated with subsequent abuse of the child. In connection with abortion, Gelles states, "For many families, violence which brings about a miscarriage is a more acceptable way of terminating an unwanted pregnancy than is abortion."[147] Looking at women beaten during pregnancy, 30% in Gelles' study and 56% in Eisenberg and Micklow's experienced at least one miscarriage.[148] The unborn child in this situation is also at high risk for birth defects and mental retardation. Gelles documents one such case in his sample.[149]

Rape and Sexual Abuse

Marital rape has just begun to exist legally. The traditional marriage contract held that husbands had sexual access to their wives at will. Given this premise, marital rape was viewed in the past as legally impossible and was therefore not susceptible to prosecution. It was not until 1974 that a case of marital rape was prosecuted in the United States. Today, only ten states do not allow prosecution of estranged or divorced husbands for raping their wives, while 24 states have laws permitting prosecution of actively cohabiting husbands for marital rape.[150] Of course, de jure legal prohibition of marital rape does not guarantee reliable or vigorous prosecution of sexual offenses occurring within marriage or other conjugal relationships.

When I refer here to marital or conjugal rape, I mean forcible or coerced sex between conjugal partners that would always be recognized as rape were they unmarried or noncohabitant. In discussing marital rape in this way, I make a value judgment which contradicts the sexual arrangement under the traditional marriage contract. Not only does the law often not recognize marital rape, but the victim herself may not recognize the possibility of rape in a conjugal relationship. One-third of the battered women studied by Star et al. believed that they did not have a right to refuse sex with their husbands/mates.[151]

Another problem in defining and detecting marital rape arises from the longstanding intimate relationship between rapist and rape victim, unique to the marital or conjugal form of rape. If the woman has been beaten in the past for refusing sex and/or expressing her feelings, she may opt to ignore her own sexual inclinations and to submit quietly to her mate's wishes in order to avoid another beating. Thus, no force may be used for the man to achieve his goal of sexual intercourse, so that their sex does not superficially resemble forcible rape. Despite this, this kind of sex is still experienced as coerced and unwanted by the woman. In such cases, the man may honestly be unaware that he is committing rape.

There are numerous references to marital rape in the literature. Gelles estimates that marriage accounts for the same proportion of rapes as it does for assaults and murders—that is, 10% to 20%. He cites Bart's finding from a sample of 1070 women, in which she found that 0.4% had been raped by their husband, 1% by a lover, and 3% by an ex-lover. In his own sample, Gelles found that in his judgment four of the 38 assaulted wives (10.5%) had been maritally raped.[152] Walker says that most of her sample of 120 were raped by their male partners at least once, usually on repeated occasions.[153] Hiberman and Munson term the experience of conjugal sexual assaults *common* among their sample, mentioning that the women were often beaten and raped by their mates in full view of the children.[154] Prescott and Letko found that over 31% of the sample had been sexually abused by their mates.[155]

The contemporary consensus on rape is that "rape is a power trip, not a passion trip."[156] A case vignette from Dobash and Dobash documents a marital rape that definitely was not motivated by sexual deprivation:

> It was just really terrible, the thought of my husband raping me. I mean, if he wanted sex I always gave him sex. You see, there was no need for rape. I didn't know why he did it.[157]

The same book shows that at least sometimes the batterer experiences himself as a rapist and not as a husband deserving of conjugal privileges: "He phoned up his sister and says, 'I've just battered and raped Jane.' And he actually told his sister that."[158]

Rape in the above discussion carries the connotation of coerced genital intercourse with the coercer. Closely related to this definition of rape are various forms of sexual abuse, involving forced sex acts of other sorts. Most common of these are forced oral or anal sex. Also prominently mentioned is a tendency for batterers to force their mates to have unwanted sex with other men, either in full view of the husband/partner for his voyeuristic pleasure or for his purely commercial purposes of pimping.[159]

With one of my former clients, this even took the form of a gang rape that the husband organized and watched, without himself participating in intercourse. So-called "swinging" or "wife swapping" are other practices which often involve men coercing their female partners to have unwanted sexual contacts. Walker also describes two cases of forced bestiality.[160]

Some authors posit an association between woman-battering and father-child incest.[161] Beatings can effectively thwart the battered woman's attempts to halt or to object to incest, which usually involves father-daughter relations. Herman believes that physical coercion or its threat is frequently used to stop the woman's attempts at intervening to halt incest.[162]

Sadism and Assaultive Behavior During Sex

Sadistic sex practices are also mentioned in the literature.[163] I am distinguishing here between sadism and sado-masochism. The latter denotes a form of sex practiced by consenting adults. Sadism, on the other hand, here means sex between a sadist and an unwilling partner who is victimized. Sadism resembles sado-masochism behaviorally; the crucial difference is in the participants' attitudes. For example, the woman reported by Walker, who is tied against her will, forced to perform oral and anal sex for her husband, and to have intercourse with a dog,[163½] is not a sexual masochist in the present view. "Masochism" denotes the enjoyment of pain or humiliation, not the experience of pain and humiliation irrespective of the individual's feelings or preferences.

Related to sadism is assaultive behavior during sexual activities. This is hard to define in all instances, because mainstream sexuality involves some license to pinch, bite, scratch, and spank. This is one reason why Straus et al. decided to contextualize the CRT's behaviors; a bite during sex can have a very different meaning than in other contexts. The ordinary license for aggressiveness in the name of sexual abandon is of course susceptible to abuse, and assaultiveness during sex can be readily perceived in more extreme behaviors. Faulk notes the occurrence of choking, suffocating, and punching during foreplay and intercourse as examples of this.[164]

Jealousy

Woman batterers are often described as jealous or as morbidly jealous. This work noted earlier that jealousy is heavily implicated as a trigger to conjugal assaults. Jealousy is also widely recognized as a motive for murder. Mowat's sample of morbidly jealous murderers represents about 4% of English murders occurring between 1936 and 1955. He cites a study by East in which 23% of 200 murderers were motivated by jealousy. According to Mowat, usually the woman is killed, not her supposed paramour.[165]

Jealous murder has traditionally been legal under certain circumstances. For example, a husband traditionally was viewed as having the right to murder his wife and/or her lover if he caught them engaging in sex. This practice remained legal in Texas and Italy within the past 20 years.[166] Whitehurst remarks that one effect of the double standard of sexual fidelity is that men are socialized to become irate over infidelity while women have been encouraged to take the alternative approach of tolerance and forgiveness for a mate who has extramarital sex. Women can say, "Men are like that," while men are supposed to deny the possibility that women also are "like that."[167]

Faulk and others believe that beatings can serve as sexually arousing foreplay for some abusers. They observe that batterers frequently demand sex after completing a beating.[168] This was true of 47% of the violent male partners in Gelles' sample.[169] Sexual demands after a violent incident may be more a matter of power dynamics than sexual ones, however. The batterer may also desire sex as a gesture of forgiveness and making-up in order to appease his remorseful feelings after an assault. He may also demand sex as legal protection from prosecution for a conjugal assault, under the legal doctrine of condonation.[170]

NOT SEPARATING, SEPARATING, AND RETURNING

From 67% to 88% of battered women in five studies had left their mates for a day's time or more on at least one occasion.[171] In Gayford's group, 36% had fled four or more times, while a third of the Dobashes' sample had experienced six or more separations. The majority of these separation periods are brief, lasting two weeks or less.[172]

Gayford lists the following reasons the women returned (when they did): 1) husband's promise to reform, 27%; 2) husband's threats and/or continued violence, 17%; 3) nowhere else to go, 14%; 4) concern for children still at home, 13%; 5) felt love or sorrow for husband, 8%.[173] Roy also finds hope for reform, nowhere to go, fear of reprisals, and concern for the children to be the four most common reasons victims go back.[174] Hilberman and Munson emphasize reasons of financial dependence, which Roy found to be the fifth most common reason.[175] Pagelow similarly found in her study that hope for reform, continued violence, nowhere to go, and inadequate resources were the four most common reasons for recohabiting with the batterer.[176]

Often, there are enormous tactical and logistical problems in leaving. Eisenberg and Micklow remark that 20% of their sample of battered women were locked out of their house or car, without either their wallet or keys or money or adequate clothing. One-fourth of this group were at times in no physical condition to leave, as a result of beatings.[177] Serum remarks that attempting to leave is in the short run the most dangerous thing a battered woman can do; if any behavior could accurately be called provocative, says Serum, it would be this one.[178] In light of this analysis, it is remarkable how large a majority of the abused women studied thus far do leave.

Women rarely quit their violent relationship after the first separation. It generally takes repeated beatings, preceded and followed by repeated promises to reform, before the victim becomes disappointed and scared enough to give up on the relationship. Walker believes a woman will generally flee her abuser three to five times before finally severing their relationship.[179] The women in Hilberman and Munson's group who left permanently averaged four to five previous separations apiece.[180] There really is no good argument in support of expecting women to leave early on in an abusive relationship. Women are, after all, primarily socialized to be wives, and there is great social encouragement for them to "try everything" and keep working at improving their marriage. A nonbattered person's assertion that "I'd leave after only one time" is more an attempt at self-reassurance than a reflection of ordinary expectations about whether couples should persist at "working out" their marriages/relationships.

Conjugal relationships where battering takes place force the victims into various patterns of staying, leaving, and returning to their relationships. This description of her behavior may be entirely irrelevant to the battered woman, but it has been a key concept in the public's perspective. Speakers and writers on woman abuse are obliged repeatedly to field the question, "Why does she stay?" As Dobash and Dobash reply:

> The twin questions of why women stay in or fail to leave violent relationships to a large extent miss the point: they [assume]. . .that a woman engages in either one behavior or the other. Most women engage in both. . .Some women leave quite frequently but do so with varying intentions about the permanency of that act.[181]

Moreover, the figures cited above on separating, plus the higher incidence of abuse among divorcing couples,[182] justify a simple retort, "Who says she does stay?"

SEEKING INTERVENTION

Gelles finds that the best single predictor of whether a battered woman seeks intervention is the severity and frequency of the violence endured.[183]

The eight most severely battered women in his study all sought third-party intervention. He also finds that intervention-seeking survivors, relative to those not seeking intervention, are more likely to be employed, and to have had childhoods free of violence.[184] Similarly, Carlson finds a positive association between seeking outside help and having greater material resources.[185] Walker, however, believes that abused women already on welfare are more likely to leave because they have less to lose economically. She uses this argument to buttress her assertion that middle- and upper-class women are more often abused than lower-class women.[186]

Parties contacted by battered women for help include the police, family and friends, doctors, social services, women's groups, neighbors, and ministers. Women seeking no intervention comprise 27% of beaten women in Gelles' study. This figure is diminished by Gelles' sampling methods since half the families sampled are known to the police or a family service agency, but somewhat reinflated by Gelles' not defining friends and family as intervenors.[187] The majority of women in Dobash and Dobash's sample never sought aid from their friends.[188]

ASSAILANTS' CRIMINAL RECORDS

Four authors note that woman abusers frequently commit other crimes as well. One-third of the abusers of Gayford's group had been imprisoned for a previous violent offense and 52% had criminal records.[189] In Carlson's group, over 60% of batterers had criminal records, while Eisenberg and Micklow found 40%, and Flynn at least one-third, with criminal records.[190]

MILITARY SERVICE

Military service is also mentioned as a factor contributing to woman-battering. A surprising 90% of abusers of Eisenberg and Micklow's study group were military veterans.[191] Gelles found 10% of violent men in his study were on active military duty.[192] Straus has spoken of unpublished data demonstrating a higher rate of conjugal violence committed by persons employed in weapons-carrying occupations—i.e., the military, police, and security guards. Straus believes that for these occupations the permission to use lethal force on the job is partly generalized to the worker's domestic life to permit conjugal assaults.[193]

ALCOHOL AND CONJUGAL VIOLENCE

Alcohol is widely implicated in woman abuse. Gelles found alcohol abuse in 48% of his violent couples, Gayford in 52% of his cases, Carlson in 60% of her sample of couples, and Eisenberg and Micklow in 70%.[194] Roy found 85% of batterers in her sample were also substance abusers.[195] Abusive incidents where one or both parties were said to be drunk accounted for 67% of assaults recorded by Carlson and 44% of assaults in Gayford's sample.[196] Wolfgang found beating murders were most associated with alcohol abuse, relative to other forms of killing.[197] Eisenberg and Micklow state that 60% of batterers were always drunk at the time of assaults.[198]

Bard and Zacker, in their essay on assaultiveness and alcohol abuse, question the generally high rates in the battering literature of association between conjugal assaults and alcohol intoxication. Their experimental police unit found that 26% of complainants and 30% of the accused parties in domestic disturbance calls appeared to have been drinking. The complainant alleged that the accused was inebriated in only 10% of these police calls, and the police officers on the scene concurred with 43% of these allegations. That is, in only 4.3% of Bard's 1388 police calls did both the complainant and police officer agree that the accused was intoxicated. Police officers believed alcohol to be the cause of the dispute in 14% of disturbance calls, and in 29% of calls where the complainant complained of drunkenness on the part of the accused. Bard and Zacker also note that alcohol intoxication is less common in assaultive versus nonassaultive disputes—21% of assaultive disputes versus 32% of all calls recorded in this study.[199]

Bard and Zacker's results point to a tendency to assign excessive causal importance to the batterer's drinking. In my counseling clientele, abuser and abused often hold that battering occurs only when the abuser has been drinking. In most cases were this is asserted, close questioning uncovers assaults occurring when the abuser is sober. Nevertheless, some batterers do assault only when under the influence of alcohol. This still does not necessarily mean that the biochemical effects of alcohol cause assaults. As Gelles points out, the cause of assault can be attributed to alcohol in order to disavow responsibility for violent behavior, and drunkenness can be used as an excuse for a "time-out" from ordinary social norms.[200] Further, a spouse's drinking behavior can itself be a source of conjugal conflict at times escalating to violence.

CHILD ABUSE AND CONJUGAL ABUSE

First of all, conjugal abuse itself represents an indirect or emotional form of child abuse. Children usually witness the abuse of one parent by the other and are profoundly affected by the experience.[201] Hilberman and Munson state that neglect and emotional abuse are the norms in the parental treatment of children of violent couples.[202] Violent couples are often child-oblivious couples in contrast to the child-focused families so well known to family therapists.

Direct physical abuse of children is also a common concomitant of conjugal abuse. Straus, Gelles, and Steinmetz find that in the course of a year, 28% of the most conjugally violent couples who had children also abused the children; this is about double the overall annual national incidence of child abuse derived in the same study. Straus et al. find that 77% of the abusively violent couples who have children abuse their children at some time in the children's lives.[203] Steinmetz finds a significant correlation of .50 (p<.01) between marital aggression and parent-child aggression.[204]

Studies of battered women corroborate these results. Carlson found that 29% of woman batterers in her study were also alleged to have physically abused their children; Gayford reports that 54% of woman abusers were also child abusers, Roy reports 45%, Flynn reports 33%, and Dobash and Dobash report 23%.[205] The battered woman is also often a child abuser; 37% of women in Gayford's sample admitted to physically abusing their children.[206] The same proportion of battered women in Pfouts' study admitted to child abuse, but it should be recalled that most of Pfouts' sample were initially identified as cases of child abuse and/or neglect.[207] Hilberman and Munson report concomitant woman abuse and child abuse in 33% of their sample, while Prescott and Letko report a 43% rate in their sample.[208] Prescott and Letko note that in the majority of their child-and-woman abuse cases, the eldest child is singled out as the sole or primary child victim.[209] As previously mentioned, an association between woman abuse and sexual abuse of children has also been noted.[210]

To sum up, there are four possible patterns of conjugal abuse and child abuse. First, the spouse abuser may also be the sole child abuser. Second, the abused mate may be the only child abuser. Third, both parents may abuse the children. Finally, there may be no physical abuse of the children despite the presence of conjugal abuse. This last pattern appears to apply to a majority or near majority of couples experiencing conjugal violence. Naturally, these family patterns only apply to couples with children.

FAMILY HISTORIES OF VIOLENCE

Published studies record that between 23% and 68% of battered women are themselves offspring of violent relationships. Six studies find 23% to 40% of battered women witnessed violence between their parents,[211] while two studies find proportions of 63% and 68%.[212] The aggregate proportion of battered women who were born to conjugally violent parents is

33.8% out of 523 battered women surveyed in eight studies. Pagelow found 27.5% of her subjects considered themselves daughters of battered women.[213]

These prevalence figures for violence in the parents' marriage do not seem to diverge substantially from Straus et al.'s estimate that 28% of couples experience violence during their relationship. Still, Parker and Schumacher found a statistically significant difference ($p<.05$) between battered women and those assaulted no more than once, in which battered women were more likely to be offspring of violent couples. Parker and Schumacher also found that repeatedly assaulted women were significantly more likely ($p<.02$) to have witnessed violence between their parents than were women only assaulted once by their mates.[214] These findings, however, are based on a sample with the second highest incidence of violence between parents in the literature on violent relationships. Attempts to replicate this study's findings are necessary to see if this effect continues to hold true.

The proportion of woman batterers reported to have witnessed spouse abuse between their parents is consistently higher than that for battered women from the same samples. The proportion is reported as 50% in two studies, 53% in Pagelow, 51% in Gayford, and "over 50%" in Flynn.[215] These figures uniformly reflect the percentage of batterers known by their wives/partners to be children of assaultive couples, are not based upon direct reports from the batterers, and are consequently conservative.

The literature reports that between 10% and 33% of battered women studied were also abused as children.[216] Parker and Schumacher found no difference in the rate of childhood victimization of battered and nonbattered wives.[217] Two sources relate whether batterers were abused as children. Prescott and Letko found that at least 29% of the batterers studied were themselves physically abused as boys. This figure of 29% of the entire sample represents almost 46% of two dozen abusive husbands for whom the authors have reliable data since over a third of the subjects in the study did not know if their husbands/partners had been abused children.[218] Pagelow's sample reported that 48.1% of their husbands/partners experienced "extremely severe" parental physical punishment in childhood.[219]

Four references refer to combinations of domestic abuse in the histories of their samples. Dobash and Dobash find that 29% of battered women they studied and 59% of these women's abusers came from violent homes.[220] Roy finds that a third of battered women and 81% of woman beaters in her study had childhood histories of either witnessing conjugal abuse, experiencing child abuse, or both.[221] Ganley and Harris report 63% of their client woman batterers have such childhood histories.[222] Half of Hilberman and Munson's sample of abused women describe histories of violence between their parents, alcoholic fathers, and physical and/or sexual abuse as children.[223] Unfortunately, it is unclear from their report whether these authors mean that half of their sample had experienced at least one of these factors in their childhood or that half of the sample had experienced all of these phenomena.

Clearly, a violent family history by itself does not determine the occurrence of conjugal abuse. For example, the Dobashes report that 41% of batterers and 71% of victims in their study had nonviolent families of origin.[224] One-third of the women in Gelles' study who witnessed conjugal violence between their parents were not subsequently abused by their mates.[225] We need to know what influences the likelihood that the conjugal violence of one generation will be carried on to the next, as well as what factors act to prevent or to inhibit the intergenerational transmission of conjugal violence.

The intergenerational transmission of domestic or conjugal violence has been studied in two other works not yet mentioned in this regard. First, Carroll studied the relationship of physical punishment in childhood to marital happiness and to marital violence. He found that marital happiness is significantly lower ($p < .05$) among subjects who had received much physical punishment as children compared to those who had received low amounts of corporal punishment. He also found a tendency for encountering current marital violence to be associated with punishment by the same-sex parent. He states that this corroborates theoretical formulations by Aldous and Hill, and Hill et al., that the intergenerational transmission of violence most likely occurs in same-sex linkages.[226] Same-sex linkage also coincides with the findings reported earlier that woman abusers more often are offspring of violent couples than are battered women.

Straus et al.'s study is the other work yet to be mentioned. Straus, Gelles, and Steinmetz present very detailed data concerning how different biographical patterns of family violence affect rates of incidence for conjugal violence. Looking first at parental spouse abuse, Straus et al. found that witnessing parents attack each other was associated with a tripled rate of conjugal violence for both men and women. Thirty-five percent of male partners who had seen parental spouse assault engaged in some form of conjugal violence during the year studied, as opposed to 10.7% of husbands/partners never having witnessed violence between their parents. For women, the analogous figures are 26.7% versus 8.9%.[227]

People whose parents were never violent to each other experienced the lowest rates of abusive conjugal violence—about 2% for both woman abuse and husband abuse—half of the rate for the entire sample. Sons of the most conjugally violent parents perpetrated 900% more womanbeating in a year than sons of nonviolent parents (20% versus 2%). Daughters of spouse beaters committed over 500% more husband-beating than daughters of peaceable couples (13.3% versus 2%).[228]

The three coauthors next turn to the effect of having received corporal punishment from parents as a teenager upon rates of conjugal violence. Only about 6% of those not corporally punished as teenagers encountered any conjugal violence in the year, compared to 16% of the entire sample. The rate of abusive conjugal violence among the people who had been punished the most as teenagers was 8% for both genders, about double the overall sample rate, and quadruple the rate of about 2% for those not punished.[229]

To avoid confounds between physical punishment received and parental conjugal violence witnessed, the study team studied the subjects whose parents had nonviolent marriages. For this subgroup of offspring of nonviolent couples, the rate of woman abuse by male partners was double for those who were punished as teenaged boys compared to those who had not been punished. Women who were punished as teenagers also tended to be more violent partners than women who had not been punished, but this effect was less pronounced for women than for men.[230]

Finally, Straus et al. turn their attention to the effect of what they unfortunately call the "double whammy"—i.e., the childhood experience of both being an abused child and witnessing spouse abuse between the parents. They find that men with parents who were violent in both ways have an annual incidence rate for conjugal violence of over 25%, compared to a mean sample rate of 12% for men, and to a 6% rate for men whose parents were nonviolent in both respects. Women with "double whammy" childhood experiences have an incidence rate for annual conjugal violence over 20%, compared to the female sample mean of 12%, and the rate of 5% for daughters of doubly nonviolent parents. One-third of couples where at least one member of the couple had experienced both kinds of parental violence, themselves experienced conjugal violence in the target year. This is double the overall rate for annual conjugal violence of 16% obtained for the sample.[231]

Turning to the "double whammy" and abusive levels of conjugal violence, Straus et al. find that 10% of husbands who experienced both kinds of parental violence themselves committed severe woman abuse in the target year, compared to 3.8% for all husbands sampled. Women with the "double whammy" experience committed husband-beating at a rate of 13.2% annually, almost triple the overall rate of abusive conjugal violence committed by women. In couples where one or both members had experienced both kinds of parental violence, the annual rate of abusive conjugal violence was 15%, more than double the overall sample rate of 6%. Straus et al. state that people who have experienced the "double whammy" are five to nine times more violent in their conjugal relationships than people with nonviolent parents.[232]

These findings by Straus, Gelles, and Steinmetz certainly appear impressive and undoubtedly work in favor of the hypothesis that experiencing conjugal violence is associated with a violent family of origin. Nevertheless, significant causal associations have not yet been demonstrated between violence in the family of origin and subsequent conjugal abuse. This is partly because of differences in the methods of the studies conducted so far. Most studies discussed focused on woman abuse and child abuse in the family of origin, while Straus et al. look at conjugal violence by either parent and at parentally administered corporal punishment during the teen years. Further, the Straus et al. results do not necessarily reflect a causal relationship where violence in the family of origin leads to conjugal abuse in the individual's family of procreation. For example, these findings do not rule out hereditary transmission of aggression. As another alternative explanation, it could be that people who were punished as teenagers by their parents were more aggressive, antisocial types who were already prospective spouse assaulters, quite apart from the parents' behavior. Finally, it is unfortunate that Straus et al. sometimes cannot distinguish between rates of perpetrating conjugal violence and of being victimized by it. Their methods at times statistically combine rates of battering and being battered and relate those rates to the childhood experience of domestic violence by either present-day victims or batterers.

MISCELLANEOUS QUANTITATIVE FINDINGS

O'Brien found that violent divorcing couples were consistently lower than nonviolent divorcing couples in marital satisfaction derived from five selected behavior categories. He also found consistently more conflict over the same five areas among violent couples relative to nonviolent ones.[233]

Straus set out to test whether the cathartic expression of aggression tends to decrease violent behavior. He sampled 583 college students, obtaining 385 useable questionnaires referring only to intact families. His results tend to refute the catharsis hypothesis by showing positive correlations between verbal and physical marital aggression (R=.36) and between aggression against objects and aggression against mates (R=.74 for men, .76 for women). He found a negative correlation between conjugal violence and unaggressive verbal strategies of conflict resolution.[234] Later data from Straus, Gelles, and Steinmetz corroborate these findings. Rates of conjugal violence in the later study were found to increase as verbal aggression also increased. The quartile of couples highest in verbal aggression had a 56% annual rate of conjugal violence. For the top 5% in verbal aggression, the violence incidence rate was over 83%.[235]

In unrelated findings, Straus et al. found that conjugal violence was positively associated with higher scores on a checklist of 18 stress-inducing events, that violence was usually employed by the more powerful member of the couple, and that families where husbands and wives were equally powerful experienced less spouse abuse than couples where one member was clearly dominant. They also found that shared decision-making in couples with no dominant member decreased the rate of violence more than specialized decision-making in these couples.[236] These last findings are paralleled by Landis' finding that marital happiness tends to be higher in couples with a "50-50 distribution of dominance."[237]

Straus et al. and Gelles each studied the effect of the number of children on incidence of conjugal violence. Gelles found little relationship—a very slightly inverse one between number of children and the incidence rate of spouse abuse.[238] Straus et al. found increasing rates of woman abuse as the number of children rose from zero to five, followed by a drastic reduction; there was no woman abuse at all in families with at least six children. Husband abuse showed a less consistent, but overall positive, correlation than woman abuse for families with zero to five children.[239] These are very strange results; conjugal abuse is at its peak in families of seven and is entirely absent from families of eight or more members! One must assume that the advent of the sixth child by itself does not halt conjugal violence.

Star et al. administered a battery of psychological measures to their sample of 57 battered women. As a group, these women were solidly normal for most of the personality variables measured. Where they did diverge from the norms was as follows: they were more shy, reserved, and introverted, with a higher than average tendency towards social withdrawal. They were abnormally low in ego strength, while they were abnormally high in self-sufficiency, tension and frustration, impulsivity, and in persecutory feelings.[240] None of these findings necessarily reflect factors predisposing the women to becoming battered. All of Star et al.'s results may solely reflect the psychological effects of battering upon the victim.

Dobash and Dobash carried out an interesting and unique study of the social lives of battered women and their husbands. They found that husbands and wives went out together less and less as the marriage continued, while the men went out more and more with friends. As the marriage continued, the battered wives went out less and less with their friends. Dramatic changes are noted between social behavior during courtship and in the first year of marriage. These changes set the trends that continue into the later years of the relationship.[241]

Some writers have attempted to establish a relationship between suicide and woman abuse. Half of Gayford's sample of abused women made suicide attempts, and 16% said they really wanted to die.[242] Half of Star et al.'s group said they had considered suicide.[243] Regarding the batterer, Walker states that almost 10% of the men who had abused her subjects committed suicide after these women left them.[244] A similar percentage of my clientele in batterers' counseling have made unsuccessful suicide attempts. As mentioned earlier, murder-suicide is generally a domestic phenomenon.[245]

CLINICAL DESCRIPTIONS

Thus far the discussion has concentrated primarily upon quantitative data regarding conjugal violence. Next, recurrent themes in descriptive and clinical accounts of conjugal violence shall be reviewed. Due to the virtual nonexistence of accounts of couples experiencing husband-battering, the following discussion will be limited to relationships involving battered women and woman batterers. It will also be limited for the most part to an account of phenomena widely reported throughout the literature, avoiding idiosyncratic descriptions of battering relationships and their members, and emphasizing relationships involving chronic, repetitive battering.

Before proceeding, it is important to take note of two problems with personality profiles of battered women and woman batterers. First, as with any profile of a clinical or dysfunctional group, the tendency of those drawing the profile is to emphasize in their description the pathological or negative features of the group under study. Thus, the clinical descriptions of battered women and woman batterers that follow will accentuate the negative to a pronounced degree.

The second problem is that the clinical profiles to follow portray features that may be either causes or effects of battering. It is too often assumed that the battered woman's personality characteristics are causal or predisposing to her being battered. This grows out of the usual assumption of abnormal psychology that a profile of symptoms composing a given syndrome represents — at least in part — causal or predisposing factors. For example, a symptom such as a hand-washing compulsion is seen as either revealing underlying causative neurotic dynamics and/or as reflecting past experiences in which the symptom was learned. The symptoms — the individual's problems in living—thus give important clues about her/his history and personality. No such assumption should be made about battered women's condition of being battered.

No one has yet presented convincing evidence of factors which predispose women either to be battered or to abide in violent relationships. Given the epidemic extent of woman-battering, it is more than possible that random factors unrelated to individual psychology are the key determinants of which women become battered and which do not. In summation, it is important to remember that the personality profile of a survivor of battering may reflect the usual effects of violent abuse, and may have nothing whatsoever to do with causative or predisposing factors to becoming abused.[246] This point seems to be less true for perpetrators of battering since some predisposing factors—such as previous subjection or exposure to family violence—are strongly suggested by the available evidence. Still, with batterers as well, we should continue to question which of their characteristics point to causes of battering and which demonstrate effects of perpetrating abuse.

Characteristics Common to Both Batterers and Battered Women

Both battered women and woman batterers are described in the literature as having low self-esteem and negative self-images.[247] Consequent feelings of helplessness, powerlessness, fear, and inadequacy are common to both parties,[248] as are experiences of shame and self-contempt.[249] These feelings are usually more readily apparent in battered women, since negative feelings are strongly denied, repressed, or projected by woman abusers. Abusers in general only own up to feelings of this sort during the period of remorse which they often experience shortly after a battering incident or when their mates have fled them.

Both batterers and battered partners are noted for being extremely dependent in their relationships.[250] The violent male partners are probably even more dependent upon the battered women than vice versa.[251] The batterer's dependency upon his mate may not be superficially apparent until the woman has left or threatened separation, whereupon the abuser's dependency is vividly manifested.

The dependency between members of battering couples is often described as symbiotic or as a survival bond between the mates.[252] It seems that each member of the couple believes that he or she will perish without the other, that the survival of each can only occur if the conjugal relationship remains intact. This belief is related to their negative self-images, which cause the couple to doubt both their ability to live independently and to find other partners who will accept them. Of course, the survival bond attitude can have a sound basis in reality for a battered woman involved with a potentially homicidal abuser.

Another corollary of the mates' dependency is that battering relationships are not based on psychologically mature love, but rather upon need. In battering relationships, there is generally little of the intimacy and even less of the reciprocity necessary for genuine love. Especially among abusers, but to a lesser extent among victims also, the partner is not valued in her/himself as an independent individual, nor respected as one. Rather, the partner is valued for the gratifications and resources she or he provides. The members of the couple, however, usually mistake their intense bond with the partner for authentic love and may confuse sexual relations with genuine intimacy.[253]

Batterers and battered women both tend to deny or minimize the scope and severity of the violence in their relationships.[254] This protects the parties' fragile self-images by reducing both the brutality perceived in the batterer and the extent of victimization and humiliation felt by the battered woman. This denial of the violence by the couple also makes the conjugal relationship appear more viable and desirable to both.

Accompanying the denial of violence, there is rationalization by both mates concerning the source of violence. Violence is initially viewed by both parties as an isolated event triggered or even justified by behavior committed by the victim which in turn angered or provoked the abuser.[255] Over time, the battered woman may relinquish this view of the ongoing abuse, but the batterer is likely to hold tenaciously to this perspective.[256]

Members of violent couples are usually traditionalists in their views of family and sex roles.[257] Batterers adhere to rigidly traditional definitions of masculine sex roles and expect traditional femininity of their conjugal partners.[258] Batterers consequently have much difficulty with providing nurturant support to their mates and children, and they may avoid these functions entirely. They will usually refuse to perform domestic duties that they perceive as woman's work, even if the woman is disabled or is the only member of the couple who is employed outside the home. The women, on the other hand, generally expect their men to be dominant, the head of the household. As a rule, the women do not demand full and equal partnership in their marriages/relationships. They ordinarily resent filling in for their male partners if and when the man abdicates his traditional duties as leader of the family.

Impulsivity is often present in both mates.[259] In abusers, in addition to violent behavior, impulsivity generally takes the forms of low frustration tolerance, substance abuse, promiscuity, and/or spending sprees.[260] Either of the mates can act without taking stock of the possible consequences of his/her behavior. In the victim, this may be a learned response to abuse, arising out of despair. That is, since battered women are often in a position of "damned if they do and damned if they don't" perform a given behavior, it may no longer pay them to consider consequences before acting. To look into the future may be to face up to the likely prospect of further violence and may therefore be avoided. In woman abusers, impulsiveness could be a similar residual effect of childhood victimization. Thus, either mate may make choices which appear provocative or irresponsible to third-party observers, but which the individual does not experience as self-defeating or as counterproductive to the marriage/relationship.[261]

Jealousy and social isolation are also common to both mates.[262] The social isolation of the victim is usually more extensive than that of the abuser, however.[263] Conversely, while jealousy is frequent among victims as well as abusers, it is mentioned much more often as a salient trait of the batterer.[264]

Characteristics of Batterers

As mentioned, the literature reports that batterers generally suffer from poor self-esteem and negative self-images. The batterer usually carries the self-image of a loser or an underachiever, even though others may perceive him as a success.[265] He has often as a child experienced physical abuse and verbal denigration from one or both of his parents. Batterers also have high rates of exposure to parents or parental figures who were conjugally violent.[266]

Abusive husbands are generally possessive and jealous. They may be highly intrusive and keep their mates under surveillance.[267] Their jealousy is related to their self-contempt and dependency. They fear losing their female partners and simultaneously view this as a likely outcome of their own worthlessness.[268] If the woman does leave to avoid violence, the abuser often defends against his sense of worthlessness by attributing his mate's flight to her seduction by another man.

Extraordinary measures are often taken to prevent the woman's expected infidelity. Men at work may call home repeatedly to check up on their mates.[269] Lunch is often taken at home for similar reasons. The woman may be locked inside the home, denied a telephone to use, and forced to account under interrogation for her every move.[270] The batterer's jealousy may reach the level of an obsession or of delusional certainty of the mate's infidelity. There are several published accounts of situations where the abuser is not satisfied until his wife/partner confesses to nonexistent liaisons with other men. The woman may also be prohibited social life with women on the pretext of suspected or potential lesbianism.[271]

The procedures outlined above as expressions of jealousy also reflect the batterer's attempt to dominate and thoroughly control his mate, completely disallowing her autonomy.[272] These jealous activities also relate to the batterer's extreme dependency on the battered woman, and his consequent difficulty separating from her for even short periods. The measures taken to prevent the woman from having extramarital affairs simultaneously enforce isolation from social contacts upon her. The literature abounds with case histories that reveal further measures taken by batterers to isolate the woman socially, a process which Walker terms *social battering*.[273]

Social battering can take various forms. There are different ways of publicly humiliating the wife/partner such as verbal abuse, failing to show up at social events or else arriving intoxicated, flirtation in the mate's presence, bringing friends and acquaintances home at inconvenient or embarrassing junctures. Social battering also includes taking steps to alienate the battered woman's friends, or to alienate her from her friends, or to dictate her choice of friends. The batterer may pick fights while the couple is preparing for a social occasion, or he may make batterings a regular consequence of having been out to social engagements. The eventual and desired result of the abuser's social battering is that the victim will increasingly avoid attempts to go out and make social contacts. The woman's increased isolation in turn makes it more difficult for her to leave the batterer.[274]

A batterer also generally takes other steps to enhance his control over his mate and to promote the woman's dependency upon him. He may deprive her of economic necessities and keep complete control of the family finances.[275] This is often executed as a double bind in which the woman is not given adequate money or resources to perform the tasks she must perform if she is to escape battering. Thus, a husband may give his wife a pathetically small sum for the grocery budget, and then beat her for serving only inexpensive foods.[276] The woman's lack of money is a great obstacle to her if she wants to leave. The literature is full of examples of determined women who, over long periods of time, scraped together small amounts of cash in order to purchase transportation and depart the abusive situation.[277]

Batterers project the blame for their own violent behavior upon their wives/partners.[278] Thus, the batterer either denies or minimizes his violence, and he also describes it as the battered woman's fault anyway. Conjugal violence is portrayed by batterers as a necessary evil, a resort taken only because the woman "didn't do right." This attitude is a holdover from the traditional rule of thumb allowing husbands to chastise their wives for any reason whatsoever—even no reason at all. Complaining about unfair treatment, being unable to quiet the children at will, serving a meal ruined as it waited hours in the oven for the man's tardy arrival—all exemplify situations that batterers perceive as offenses by wives/partners that deserve punishment by a beating.

A close relative of projecting blame onto the battered woman is the batterer's set of unrealistic expectations of what she can and ought to do. For example, batterers seem actually to believe that their mates should be able to hush the children in a moment and to have dinner ready whenever the abuser arrives home, no matter how unexpected. The wife/partner may be viewed by the batterer as inadequate should he feel any dissatisfaction or unhappiness in his life, even if she is in no way a direct source of these feelings.

Jealousy, projection of the blame for violent behavior, and low self-esteem are all closely interrelated. Due to his fragile self-image, it is extremely difficult for the batterer to take responsibility for his violence and to acknowledge that his behavior is what has alienated his battered partner. Few ever admit that they realize they drove their mates away or frightened them off. Those of my counseling clients who have owned up to this realization uniformly referred to it as the aspect of their situation that was the most difficult for them emotionally. It is far less emotionally painful for the batterer to blame the battered woman for his own violent behavior and to blame her and her imaginary paramour if she flees the abusive situation.

Batterers are not brutal at all times, however. They present a dual personality, a Jekyll side with attractive traits as well as a Hyde aspect.[279] They can be kind, generous, and attentive to their mates and children. Child-like playfulness and zest are commonly noted in abusive men. Their female partners often perceive the men as exciting, vibrant, and passionate.[280] Batterers have adequate social skills much more often than not; they can be very charming and appealing.[280½]

The oscillation between benign and malevolent behavior makes the batterer highly unpredictable.[281] Battered women often do not feel able to predict or to anticipate beatings; for instance, this was true of 95% of Eisenberg and Micklow's subjects.[282] Victims may be beaten one day for overcooking an egg, but they receive no physical abuse at other times for seemingly more grievous offenses such as carelessly wrecking the car or assaulting the batterer.[283]

Another result of the batterer's dual personality is that he can present his good side, when necessary, in order to win the allegiance of intervenors. Thus, police answering domestic disturbance calls are often confronted with an angry and disheveled wife who then verbally abuses her apparently reasonable, calm, charming, and tolerant husband. The usual result in such a situation is that the police perceive the woman as a provocative bitch. Mental health workers may be seduced by the batterer in a similar manner and believe his allegations that his wife/partner provokes him into slapping her around a little, just to straighten her out.

Batterers do not limit their woman abuse exclusively to the physical mode. In fact, batterers always employ verbal and psychological abuse as well; often this includes verbal threats of renewed violence.[284] In this vein, Walker quotes a subject named Lorraine:

> There were two kinds of abuse, or maybe even three types. There was the verbal abuse of dirty name-calling and accusing. . .the complete tear-down of my ego or personality, and then there was the third kind, the physical, the actual hitting. . . .So there were really three kinds of abuse, and. . .they were all coupled together. . . .[285]

There is as yet no record of a battering relationship free from this linkage of verbal and psychological, in addition to physical, abuse.

A final important trait of batterers is one called "overkill" by Walker.[286] Overkill mostly refers to the relentless and excessive violence involved in woman abuse. Serum and Walker both note that, in contrast to Lorenz's findings concerning wolves, the batterer does not necessarily desist from his attack when the victim signals submission or surrender. Rather, beatings may continue even after the victim has lost consciousness or is dead.[287] Wolfgang found that spouse murders were the type most likely to involve superfluous violence—i.e., violence continuing after the killing was already accomplished.[288]

Batterers may also overkill with kindness. Walker cites cases where men have run up excessive debts in order to buy propitiatory gifts for their battered partners in remorse over having beaten them. One dramatic example was a woman hospitalized after a beating who received so many flower arrangements from her abusive husband that she ran out of space in her hospital room to display them.[289]

Characteristics of Battered Women

As mentioned already, battered women generally have low self-esteem.[290] They experience related feelings of worthlessness, humiliation, powerlessness, helplessness, self-blame, and shame.[291] Their shame is a major obstacle to seeking intervention, and it is all too often reinforced by an indifferent, critical, or even hostile social environment:

> The first feeling is the feeling of shame. That. . .kept me from telling anyone, from seeking any kind of help. . . .

When I finally decided to talk about my situation, I found that these feelings of shame were reinforced. Male friends invariably asked me what I had done to cause the beatings. . .I had a therapist who told me I was a masochist. My mother, when I finally told her, said that I was sick. A male doctor who treated the broken nose and concussion said that I should try and be a good wife. All these things just made me feel that, yes, this was my fault.[292]

The extreme social isolation of the battered woman exacerbates this shame-inducing effect. It is a momentous occasion when a battered woman summons her courage and reveals her plight to another person. Rebuffs of the type described in the above quotation reinforce the woman's shame and mitigate against her ever attempting to broach the subject of her abuse again. Some women simply despair of finding a sympathetic listener who will try to help. Others become convinced that their victimization is somehow their own fault.

Fear, paralyzing terror, and anxiety seem to be the most ubiquitous emotional experiences among battered women.[293] Victims of woman abuse are often immobilized by their fear of the batterer and his violence.[294] This fear can literally petrify the woman so that she is unable to resist an attack or retaliate:

The fear doesn't leave you. It's with you twenty-four hours a day.

I am fortunate; I am not enduring the agony any more, but the fear is still with me.

I was beaten so badly that my head was just one solid bruise. . .but I just stayed in my house. I didn't do anything, because I was so afraid.[295]

The battered woman's fear includes anticipation of further conjugal attacks and is magnified by the unpredictable nature of the assaults: "If he could justify being violent to the degree that he was, he could always become more violent. The threat was always there."[296] The woman's fear of the batterer often continues even if she leaves the abusive relationship.

In addition to fear of further conjugal assaults, the battered woman may have other fears. She may fear for the safety of her children or of her family of origin, in addition to her own safety. She may also fear her own anger and her potential for violent retaliation.[297]

The fear of retribution from the batterer for seeking help or for revealing the abusive situation is another major force obstructing the woman from seeking outside intervention. These fears are justified for the most part. Many of the most severe conjugal assaults and murders are in response to battered women's attempts to seek help or to leave.[298]

Another factor magnifying the battered woman's fear of her violent mate is that she often comes to believe in his omnipotence. This is partly a result of the intense dependency upon him that she experiences and that he often deliberately cultivates in her. It is partly a result of the fact that she knows he can do things that other people do not do—both positive and negative behaviors. It is also an effect of some batterers' extraordinary sensitivity to, and/or vigilance over, their women partners. Thus the woman may come to believe that leaving her man is impossible or futile because he can track her down wherever she goes and make her life even more miserable.[299]

Battered women tend to take responsibility for the batterer's violence, especially early on in the marriage/relationship. The woman at least initially believes that she can end her man's violence against her by altering her behavior in order to please him. This attitude gives her a sense of control over her fate and holds out for her the hope that nonviolence will eventually take ascendancy in the relationship. In accepting responsibility for the batterer's violence, the victimized mate is of course reacting in accordance with the expectations and attributions of those around her, often including her friends and relatives, as well as the batterer.[300]

Battered women generally feel guilty about being beaten. This guilt is related to her accepting the postulate that she is somehow responsible for the abuse. It can be easier psychologically for a battered woman to believe in the justness of her fate and to accept her beatings in return for the prospect of her eventual control over the violence.[301] To confront the arbitrary and unfair nature of the abuse is much more difficult emotionally and often leads to desperation.

In terms of psychiatric symptomatology, battered women resemble cases of agitated depression. As a result of prolonged stress, they often manifest psychosomatic symptoms such as backaches, headaches, and digestive problems. The battered woman may appear to have aged prematurely. Often there will be fatigue, restlessness, insomnia, or loss of appetite. Great amounts of anxiety, guilt, and depression or dysphoria are typical.[302] Too often their disorders are treated strictly as biochemically or intrapsychically based.[303] It is imperative for physicians, therapists, and other helpers to inquire about the possibility of battering when they see a woman who is married, cohabiting, "going steady," or similarly involved with a man, and who also appears to be suffering from agitated depression, anxiety neurosis, a psychosomatic illness, or similar problems.

Allusions to the positive characteristics of battered women are notable for their scarcity in the conjugal violence literature. When they appear at all in current publications, battered women's strengths are mostly implied between the lines of case historical reports. It is often implied in available case histories that battered women can be resourceful, persevering, brave, intelligent, and creative in their efforts to survive and to escape abuse. Still, when it comes to constructing overall psychological profiles of battered women, the tendency in the literature is very much to emphasize the negative attributes reported above: low self-esteem, helplessness, self-blame, shame, fearful paralysis, and dependency.

The tendency of clinical profiles to focus on battered women's negative attributes reflects the usual pathologizing bias of clinical psychological literature in general. It is intriguing to note, however, that woman batterers' redeeming qualities receive more direct mention in the battering literature than do battered women's positive characteristics. This occurs partly as a result of attempts to convey and to explain the continued attractiveness of many batterers to their abused partners. Nevertheless, this pattern in the literature also suggests a continued, subtle bias against identifying with battered women. It also reflects our cultural tendencies to value men more highly than women and to be more careful to temper criticism with praise when describing men rather than women.

Battered women's activists provide a strong contrast to the clinical descriptions of battered women, by explicitly emphasizing battered women's strengths. The following quotations are good examples.

> Women who come to shelters are already self-sufficient. Most have endured an incredible amount of physical and mental abuse, perhaps over a long period, while at the same time fulfilling their responsibilities of daily living.

> We acknowledge that battered women ride in the unstable, swift cart of an emotional roller coaster, but we must also realize they are capable individuals. . . .[304]

> . . .despite mythology to the contrary, battered women are actively engaged in changing their lives. . . .

> Most psychological theories misunderstand that battered women assess their reality continually and make choices based on what they find.

> "Battered women learn to be realistic, not helpless. . . .You learn not to ask for help because it's a waste of time."[305]

The last quote recalls Waites' analysis of enforced restriction of choice. In a situation of forcibly restricted choice, individuals are apt to make decisions which appear weak or counterproductive to observers unaware of the enforced restriction of the person's choices.[306] When enforced restriction of choice is taken into account, it often becomes clear that the restricted individual is startlingly successful at surmounting highly unfavorable conditions.

Changes Over Time in the Battering Relationship

Two works discuss the dynamics of the battering relationship as it persists over time. Walker offers what she calls the "cycle theory of violence."[307] Actually this is not really a theory, but rather a schema for conceptualizing about the violent conjugal relationship. She divides battering relationships into three phases, roughly equivalent to before, during, and after an acute battering incident. The three phases are cyclical in that the period after battering merges subtly with the period before the next violent episode.

Phase I of Walker's cycle is the tension-building stage. Minor battering incidents, involving verbal abuse, threats, and relatively mild physical force, occur during this time. The woman attempts to cope with these incidents in a variety of ways. Despite her attempts at adaptation, tension continues to mount between the mates to the point that it becomes unbearable. Walker describes the escalation of tension in Phase I, as it leads inevitably to another beating:

> As the batterer and the battered woman sense the escalating tension during this first phase, it becomes more difficult for their coping techniques to work. Each becomes more frantic. The man increases his possessive smothering and brutality. His attempts at psychological humiliation become more barbed, his verbal harangues longer and more hostile. Minor battering incidents become more frequent, and the resulting anger lasts for longer periods of time. . . .Exhausted from the constant stress, [the battered woman] usually withdraws more from the batterer, fearing she will inadvertently set off an explosion. He begins to move more oppressively toward her as he observes her withdrawal. He begins to look for expressions of her anger, sensing it even though she may still deny it or think she is successfully hiding it. Every move she makes is subject to misinterpretation. He hovers around her, barely giving her room to breathe on her own. . . .
>
> There is a point toward the end of the tension-building phase where the process ceases to respond to any controls. Once the point of inevitability is reached, the next phase, the acute battering incident, will take place.[308]

Phase II, then, is the actual beating. It is generally the shortest of the three phases, usually over within a day and almost never lasting over a week. In general, only the batterer can end Phase II, since both resistance or submission by the victim tend to be ineffectual at ending the assault. Exceptions to the above generalization would include successful physical retaliation by the battered woman and effective intervention by police or other third parties.

Phase III is "characterized by extremely loving, kind, and contrite behavior by the batterer."[309] The assailant realizes that he has gone too far and tries to make it up to the victim. The battered woman usually is enticed by the batterer's good behavior during this period into remaining with him. Despite this, it is immediately following Phase II or at the outset of Phase III that most battered women seek help, if at all. As Walker says:

> Since almost all of the rewards of being. . .coupled occur during phase three for the battered woman, this is the time when it is most difficult for her to make a decision to end the relationship. Unfortunately, it is also the time during which helpers usually see her. When she resists leaving. . .and pleads that she really loves him, she bases her reference to the current loving phase-three behavior rather than the more painful phase-one or phase-two behavior.[310]

Consequently, it is a corollary of Walker's work that the battered woman must be helped to recognize the three-phase cycle if she is to decide to leave the battering relationship.[311]

Dobash and Dobash describe the changes occurring routinely in the lives of battered women as the violence continues over time. Initially, the women shoulder most of the blame for what has happened. They seek to change their behavior in order to comply with the husband's wishes.

> It is only when these efforts fail to stop the violence that the woman ceases to view the beatings as a passing phase and, with great reluctance and horror, begins to view her husband as a violent man and their relationship as a violent one. It is at this point that she really begins to change and fear becomes an integral part of [her] daily life.[312]

Along with this change in the woman's attitude comes a reluctant loss of affection for the male partner, say Dobash and Dobash. "This loss of affection is often followed by a feeling of hate and an outraged sense of injustice."[313] The couple's sex life often deteriorates as a consequence.

Each successive battering leaves the woman with less hope, less self-esteem, and more fear. At this point, many women despair of improving the relationship and cease their efforts to do so. The batterer notices this and often believes an extramarital affair is the basis of the change in his partner's behavior. Meanwhile, the woman either turns inward and attempts to build a protective shell around her emotions that will allow her to cope, or she may consider her only means of escape to be suicide or murder. If this latter level of desperation is reached, the batterer may be surprised to find his mate retaliating for the first time against his assaults. She may also at this low point express indifference in response to his threats of violence or even murder. These latter behaviors arising out of the victim's desperation are often misinterpreted as signs of provocativeness.[314]

The Dobashes' discussion parallels Walker's three-phase cycle in many ways. Walker's cycle, however, gives the impression of a treadmill or stationary cycle where successive experiences of a given phase are identical. Dobash and Dobash give more of a sense of a progressive deterioration in the relationship while it endures. There is great consensus in the woman abuse literature—including Walker—that conjugal violence tends to increase in both its severity and frequency as the battering relationship continues over time.[315] Dobash and Dobash account particularly well for the effects of time upon the battering relationship.

_____ Chapter 4

THEORETICAL LITERATURE

There are numerous theories of family violence in general, of conjugal violence, of woman abuse in particular, or of male violence against
women. Gelles and Straus enumerate at least 15 distinct theories in their
theoretical review of violence in the family.[1] Their review overlooks theories of woman abuse as a phenomenon of misogynist violence, other feminist
theories of woman abuse, and of woman abuse and/or family violence as
involving coercive control situations. Taking into account theories not
mentioned by Gelles and Straus, there must be easily 20 distinct theories
of either family violence, woman abuse, or conjugal violence. This section
will not attempt to cover exhaustively all of the existing theoretical
perspectives. Instead, it shall survey important viewpoints derived from
five main types of theoretical models: psychoanalytic theory, learning theory,
a model of coercive control situations, sociological theories, and feminist
theories.

PSYCHOANALYTIC APPROACHES

Although belief in the masochism of battered spouses has widespread
public acceptance, there is no detailed exposition of the psychoanalytic
theory of female masochism as it relates to woman-battering. Rather, there

are only brief allusions to masochism, or interpretations of it, which clearly reflect the work of Freud and of Deutsch regarding masochism as a feminine trait.[2] To my knowledge, there is still no work of any length whatsoever that has been devoted to establishing this connection in a detailed, systematic way. The nearest approximations of such an effort follow:

A husband's behavior can serve to fill a wife's needs even though she protests it.[3]

The victim can always be assumed to have played a crucial role in the offense, and may have directly or indirectly brought about or precipitated their own victimization.[4]

If it is not safe to let oneself to be dominated, it is not possible to be fully feminine. . . .The nagging, aggressive woman is often unconsciously demanding that which she most fears. By irritating a man, making unreasonable demands and criticizing, she is really trying to evoke a dominant response. . . .Her aggression. . .is [both protecting] against male dominance and, at the same time, demanding it.[5]

[Regarding battered women,] there is a special aspect of. . .the masochistic person which merits examination. Masochism here does not imply enjoyment of suffering—the women, because of low self esteem, fail to view their role as underdog and therefore do not take the necessary steps to free themselves from this kind of relationship.[5½]

These statements all express untested assumptions. They may be accurate in some cases, but they have dangerous implications when overgeneralized. These authors neglect the batterer's role in the abuse, the transactional aspects of battering relationships, and the social pressures upon the victim to remain in a battering relationship. Whatever Storr believes, it is often even more unhealthy for a woman to stifle justified complaints than to "nag." Schultz's logic implies by extension that burnt toast, a normal disagreement, or an innocent visit from an insurance salesman can play "a crucial role" in justifying abuse or even murder. The passage from Shainess is vague, but it appears to assume fallaciously that all battered women can leave their relationships.

Masochism is in strict terms the direct enjoyment of painful stimuli. In the very strictest sense, masochism is the term for achieving sexual arousal and/or orgasm through experiences of physical pain. This definition can then be extended to include sexual arousal obtained by being humiliated, masochistic fantasies as opposed to actual behavior, and taking direct pleasure—at a milder level than orgasm or sexual arousal—in painful or humiliating experiences. These phenomena do indeed occur in human life.

Sado-masochism is the term incorporating the roles of both the subject and partner in masochistic sexuality. Sexual masochism and sado-masochism are basically synonymous. This sexual attitude should be clearly distinguished from sadism—i.e., sadistic sexuality practiced upon a partner who derives no pleasure from the pain or humiliation experienced. The difference between sadism and sado-masochism, in this view, is the presence or absence of direct, masochistic pleasure felt by the sadist's partner. Consent is omitted here because of the potential for the sadist of obtaining the partner's consent by physical coercion or intimidation. Many authors fail to differentiate sadism from sado-masochism and, thus, confuse unwilling victims with willing masochists.

From erotic and physically pleasurable experiences of pain, the definition of masochism can be extended further to include a purely psychological level of masochism. This level of masochism would include, for example, martyrish tendencies to take pleasure in self-sacrifice, self-castigating tendencies, a predilection for self-punishment in various forms, and suicidal thought or behavior. In particular, for orthodox psychoanalysis, this level of masochism includes such traditional feminine characteristics as passivity, submissiveness, self-sacrifice on behalf of one's family, and denigration of women relative to men. This type of masochism was thought by Freud and Helene Deutsch to be an experience innate to females.[6]

A further, and fallacious, extension of the definition of masochism is often made. In this fallacy, which was first described by Karen Horney, the actual experience of suffering is equated with a lust for suffering.[7] With respect to conjugal abuse, the question arises whether the abuse provides masochistic gratification to the battered partner, or whether those battered mates who choose to persist in the relationship do so in spite of the battering due to other advantages derived from maintaining the relationship. Furthermore, persisting in the relationship can often represent a hedonistic—that is, pleasure-maximizing—strategy which improves the battered woman's safety and chances of survival. Finally, the battered woman may remain with the batterer against her will. This occurs either because of the effectiveness of the batterer's direct measures to keep her with him, or as a result of the enormous social pressures impeding the battered woman's departure.

As mentioned, psychoanalytic theory views masochism as a fundamental attribute of the female personality. This position was first put forth by Freud and best articulated by Helene Deutsch. Rather than go into great detail about the Freudian theory of female personality, let us just note that according to Freud and Deutsch, masochism is a universal result of the libidinal economics of female development. This position is extremely controversial.

Modern developments such as changes in sex roles, in sexual mores, and new sexological findings have made the above theoretical stance even more suspect than when it was first advanced. Critics can now point to the importance of socialization in determining sex roles. They can also point to some erroneous assumptions of this theory in regard to female sexual physiology. Furthermore, contemporary society now expects women actively and hedonistically to enjoy sexual activities, rather than to submit to coitus in the passive and self-sacrificing fashion which Freud seems to have equated with female sexuality. Another problem of the theory of masochism as innate to the psychology of women is that it is hard to verify, either experimentally or clinically. Clinical examples of penis envy and feminine masochism could alternatively be interpreted as psychological reactions to the patriarchal oppression of women, rather than as innate responses to having female anatomy. Horney has noted that it makes sense to envy the penis when having one carries a multitude of social advantages.[8]

In regard to woman abuse, critics of the masochism approach point out that psychoanalytic views ignore the real constraints upon the battered woman that encourage her to remain in the battering relationship. Instead, psychoanalysis views the woman's motives solely as intrapsychic. Recognizing the limitations on the battered woman's options provides a more complete understanding of her situation, as well as alternative explanations for the persistence of some battered women in their violent relationships.[9]

Intrapsychic approaches erroneously assume that the battered woman can always leave her abusive mate. In fact, she cannot always leave, due to physical restrictions. Should she leave, this nearly always entails many disadvantages for her despite the potential halting of the abuse. It is vital to recall that leaving the batterer sets up only a *potential* for cessation of the violence since the batterer's violence can continue after the legal termination of the relationship.[10] In fact, leaving the batterer often increases the woman's risk of being murdered.[11] It is therefore worthwhile to look at the potential costs and benefits to the victim in leaving her partner. In this connection, Waites has noted that people often place higher priority on potential losses than on potential gains in weighing the merits of risky options.[12]

Critiquing the psychoanalytic theory of feminine masochism, Serum and Singer independently offer explanations of its popularity in application to battered women. According to each of them, this theory enables others to believe that the victim enjoys, or at least provokes, the abuse that she receives. This perspective in turn has soothing implications for those not involved in a battering relationship. It supports the assumption of justice in the world, while rejecting the possibility of random, undeserved, and unprovoked abuse.[13] It reinforces our sense of control over our fate.[14] The moral is that, "Since I'm not a masochist, I cannot become a battered mate. Thank God!" Unfortunately, this reassuring conclusion is inaccurate since conjugal abuse is often random, often unprecipitated by conjugal conflict,[15] and always undeserved.

Psychoanalytic perspectives on conjugal violence are uniform in their reliance upon concepts of provocation of the abuser by the battered partner. This in turn implies that violence in a conjugal relationship is a justifiable response to certain nonviolent but provocative behaviors by the partner who is attacked. As stated in the Introduction, I believe we must reject the view that initiating conjugal violence is ever justifiable or acceptable. Furthermore, even if it were granted that conjugal violence can be provoked, no psychoanalytic approach has explained the effectiveness of battered women's induction of violent responses in their mates. After all, even skilled hypnotists cannot cause subjects to commit assaults if the subjects wish to remain nonviolent.

This discussion has accorded psychoanalytic conceptions of battering more attention than they have really earned. Psychoanalytic theorists have paid little attention to conjugal violence. The few existing published applications of psychoanalytic theory to the subject of woman-battering have been peremptory and replete with logical problems in their basic assumptions. It is important to address the psychoanalytic approach, however, because it has exercised enormous influence upon public attitudes toward woman-battering and conjugal violence. Psychoanalytic influence is best seen in the continued prominence of the question, "Why does she stay?"[16] This question tends to presuppose either victim provocation in conjugal violence or unconscious masochism in the victim, if not both.

LEARNING THEORY

There are various types of learning theories, also often called *behaviorism*. The three preeminent forms of learning theory are classical conditioning, operant conditioning, and social-learning theory. The woman abuse literature has made much use of learning theories, especially Bandura's social-learning theory. Conjugal violence experts who apply learning theories extensively in their work include Ganley and Harris, Pagelow, Saunders, Serum, and Walker. In addition, most of the woman abuse literature implicitly or explicitly views battering as learned behavior, as do most counselors specializing in work with batterers to promote nonviolence.

As applied to conjugal violence, approaches based upon learning theories can help investigate factors reinforcing violent behavior that make violence by an individual mate more or less likely to occur. Learning theories can also investigate factors inducing battered mates to abide in a battering relationship. One disheartening aspect of battering is that the batterer receives much positive reinforcement from the battered woman in the form of compliance and submission.[17] The discharge of aggressive tensions through violence can also be a positive reinforcer for violent behavior. Learning theory thus points out the need for effective negative reinforcement of battering if it is to cease. Positive reinforcement of nonabusive behavior is also consequently important.[18]

The frustration-aggression hypothesis of Dollard and Miller has influenced much of the work on battering. This hypothesis predicts that aggressive responses will increase in frequency in response to frustration. When sociologists discuss stress and economic deprivation as contributors to conjugal violence, they reveal a debt to the frustration-aggression theory.[19] Research indicating a positive association between conjugal violence and frustrating factors such as unemployment, lower racial status, marital conflict, and lower income would corroborate the frustration-aggression theory.

A relevant finding from the research on operant conditioning is that intermittent, random, positive reinforcement produces the most persistent behavior patterns. Applied to battered mates, this may partly explain the persistent duration of their relationship with the abuser. The positive reinforcement of the victim for staying with her partner, which occurs during Phase III of Walker's schema, can accurately be called intermittent and random, or noncontingent. Thus, this viewpoint would predict that remaining in the relationship should become a behavior that is very difficult to extinguish.[20]

Bandura's work on learning aggressive responses through vicarious reinforcement or modeling is clearly relevant to battering.[21] These findings help explain the high prevalence among batterers of having witnessed as children conjugal or other family violence. Less well known, but equally valuable, is Bandura's description of social factors encouraging the learning of violent behavior—e.g., the influence of violence in the media and of military combat training.[22]

In general, learning theories have not specifically addressed conjugal violence, but have looked at aggression or violent behavior in general. One major exception to this is Walker's "theory of learned helplessness,"[23] which she uses to explain in part the battered woman's tendency to remain in the battering relationship. Walker's theory of learned helplessness is based upon studies conducted upon dogs:

> Seligman and researchers placed. . .dogs in cages and administered electrical shocks at random and at varied intervals. . .Dogs learned quickly that no matter what response they made they could not control the shock. The learning of the unpredictability and noncontingent nature of the aversive stimulus was of prime importance. At first the dogs attempted to escape. . . .When nothing they did stopped the shocks, the dogs ceased any further voluntary activity. When Overmier and Seligman attempted to change this procedure and teach the dogs that they could escape by crossing to the other side of the cage, the dogs still would not respond. . . .Even when the door was left open and the dogs were shown the way out, they remained passive, refused to leave and did not avoid the shock. It took repeated dragging of the dogs to the exit to teach them how to voluntarily respond again.[24]

Walker cites studies of other animals that have yielded similar results, as well as experiments with humans that have shown impaired later learning after exposure to inescapable aversive events.[25]

Walker believes that battered women are in a situation analogous to that of the dogs in the above studies by Seligman. Subjected to random and inescapable aversive events in the form of beatings,

> They learn that their voluntary responses really don't make that much difference in what happens to them. . . .It becomes extraordinarily difficult for such women . . .to believe their competent actions can change their life situation. Like Seligman's dogs, they need to be shown the way out repeatedly before change is possible.[26]

Thus, this theory explains not only the perseverance of battered women in their marriages/relationships, but the frequent necessity of several temporary separations before the relationship is eventually ended.[27]

The theory of learned helplessness emphasizes the victim's experiences within the conjugal relationship, thus deemphasizing the impact of her early life experiences. Walker does take earlier experiences into account; she believes that the socialization of women tends to inculcate in them a strategy of "giving their power away" and not taking competent, voluntary action on their own behalf. In connection with this, Walker says that 75% of her sample of battered women had a paternalistic, "Dresden doll" kind of upbringing.[28]

Serum criticizes Walker's theory of learned helplessness. Serum believes that active inhibition of assertive responses, rather than learned helplessness, better describes the individual process of responding to being battered. The advantage of her own outlook, says Serum, is that it explains the victim's experience of dread and anxiety even after she has left the batterer. Despite the absence of the batterer, the victim still persists in the pattern of active self-inhibition that she assimilated during her marriage/cohabitation.[29] Another feature of Serum's view is that it portrays the battered woman as an active survivor instead of as a passive, helpless victim. Serum is also more radical than Walker in her rejection of the importance of childhood experiences in predisposing a girl to become a battered woman, as shall be discussed later.

A disadvantage of Walker's theory of learned helplessness is that it neglects the social influences that encourage a victim to persevere in a violent relationship. Walker does integrate these influences into her overall description of the battered woman syndrome, however.[30] These social influences may reinforce the victim's experience of helplessness and despair since they certainly pose her additional obstacles to escaping the battering that she endures. As Walker herself notes, her theory of learned helplessness is only a partial explanation of the behavior of battered women.[31] Finally, her theory does not explain how some battered women manage to end their battering relationships after only a few assaultive incidents.

Pagelow takes social-learning theory on woman abuse an important step further. She reflects feminist concerns with institutional responses, women's resources, and sex role socialization, by hypothesizing that these factors combine to affect strongly each battered woman's decision whether or not to attempt to dissolve her violent relationship. Specifically, Pagelow hypothesizes that:

> The fewer the resources, the more negative the institutional response; and the more intense the traditional ideology of women who have been battered, the more likely they are to remain in relationships with the batterers and the less likely they are to perform acts that significantly alter the situation in a positive direction.[32]

By "traditional ideology" Pagelow means a "broad range of internalized beliefs in. . .the 'rightness' of the patriarchal-hierarchical order of the social structure."[33] For women, traditional ideology encompasses a high level of investment in a wife-and-mother role subordinate to the husband and an overall view of women as appropriately secondary to men in value and in power. Pagelow restricts her hypothesis to "secondary battering"—her term for second and subsequent battering incidents in a relationship after the initial violent incident or "primary battering". The hypothesis is formulated in the context of the social-learning theory of learning by vicarious reinforcement. Pagelow uses this theory to explain the learning and transmission of both traditional ideology and—especially in boys—violent domestic behavior.[34]

Pagelow does well in integrating social responses, values, and socialization into a social-learning framework for understanding woman abuse. Her hypothesis is elegant and relatively simple to test. However, her approach has several flaws.

Her emphasis on traditional ideology seems to imply that feminists and nontraditional women are immune from entrapment in battering relationships. This is not so. It is questionable whether feminists have even a diminished tendency relative to other women to be involved as victims in battering relationships. Pagelow also overlooks the batterer's contribution—by violence, threats, and other methods—to entrapping the battered woman and retaining her as a cohabitant mate. Also, she does not take into account changes in the battered woman's attitudes and life situation as the violent relationship continues. Finally, Pagelow's interest in "Why does she stay?," combined with the theoretical emphasis on the battered woman's ideology as contributing to the endurance of the battering relationship, at times appears to blame the victim for being abused. On the other hand, all of the above flaws in Pagelow's approach can be remedied while retaining her foundation of a truly social social-learning perspective on woman-battering.

COERCIVE CONTROL THEORY

The coercive control theory concentrates upon a specific sort of interaction, which Singer terms a "coercive control situation."[35] The analysis of woman abuse as a coercive control situation is advocated by Singer and by Serum[36] and is heavily indebted to research involving brainwashing and coercive control in social organizations such as concentration camps, Chinese thought reform or "brainwashing" prison programs, hostage situations, and coercively authoritarian religious cults.[37] This perspective is not clearly differentiated from a highly specialized social-learning approach. Also, both Singer and Serum consider their theories to be systemic in nature.[38] Steinmetz has also recognized similarities between brainwashing and the chronic battered woman syndrome.[39] Taking a similar view, Steven Morgan has coined the term *conjugal terrorism* for coercive control in woman abuse:

> Conjugal terrorism is a term describing the behavior of the violent husband, whose attitudes and behavior bear a remarkable resemblance to those of the political terrorist. Conjugal terrorism is the use or threatened use of

violence in order to break down the resistance of the victim to the will of the terrorist.[40]

Serum summarizes the view of woman abuse as a coercive control situation as follows: "The battered woman syndrome represents the breakdown of the personality in the face of severe external threat."[41] This severe external threat is provided by the coercive controller upon whom the victim's survival and/or well-being depends.[42] In woman abuse, the batterer functions as a coercive controller. Serum believes that anyone—no matter how strong their preexisting personality—breaks down under the influence of coercive control.[43]

Drawing upon Bettelheim's description of the psychological reactions of inmates of German concentration camps, Serum finds ten similar phenomena occurring in battered women and concentration camp prisoners.[44] These ten common features of concentration camp prisoners and battered women are:

> 1) guilt feelings, with an attendant sense of deserving the victimization; 2) significant loss of self-esteem; 3) detachment of emotion from incidents of severe violence, and extreme reactions to trivial incidents; 4) failure to observe the controller's rules because of the arbitrariness of punishment; 5) extreme emotional reactions; 6) difficulty planning for the future and delaying gratification; 7) fear of escaping the coercive control situation; 8) child-like dependency on the controllers, and identification with them; 9) imitation of controllers' aggressiveness, and adoption of their values; 10) maintenance of the hope that the controller is kind and just.[45]

Serum remarks that many of these same features—e.g., irrational guilt, low self-esteem, and fear of escape—are used by others to support the concepts of masochism or predisposing psychopathology in victims of conjugal abuse. By viewing these phenomena instead as the ordinary results of coercive control or brainwashing, there is a significant shift in the context of these phenomena.

Batterers employ many techniques documented in the literature on brainwashing. These include imprisonment or confinement; social isolation; beatings; torture; starvation or malnourishment; sleep deprivation; threats of murder or of torture; random and unpredictable leniency, coupled with equally unpredictable punishment; humiliation and revilement; complete prescription of the use of time and space; manacling or other forms of bondage; coerced false confessions; and other methods of directly inducing guilt such as denunciations of the victim to authorities or significant others. The effect of the victim's isolation and of the induction of fear in the victim is to increase the victim's suggestability to behave as dictated by the coercive controller. The victim's dependency upon the controller is enhanced by all of the techniques employed.[46]

Serum comments that studies of brainwashing do not seriously question the effectiveness of these techniques, nor do they seek to discover personalities strong enough to withstand brainwashing. No hypothetical attribution of masochism or weakness is made against prisoners who succumbed to brainwashing techniques. Rather, the brainwashing process is taken as sufficient explanation for its psychological impact.[47]

Why, then, are battered women subjected to almost identical conditions as brainwashed prisoners believed to be masochists and provocateurs, while the prisoners are not so accused? First, ignorance of the severity and sophistication of woman-battering obscures from many observers the similarities between the treatment of hostages, brainwashed prisoners, people interned in concentration camps, and battered women. Second, marriage or a conjugal relationship is assumed to be a relationship entered into voluntarily, while being imprisoned or held hostage are clearly involuntary situations. However, entering marriage or cohabitation can be a semivoluntary choice or even entirely involuntary, while leaving a legal marriage certainly is no matter of unobstructed free will.[48] This is even more true of conjugal relationships where one party is maintained in the relationship by physical coercion and/or physical restraints.[49]

Another major reason that battered women are accused of masochism and emotional immaturity and may be viewed as deserving their victimization—while the predominantly male victims of brainwashing are not—is that they are women. First, psychoanalytic precepts assume from the outset that women are masochistic. Other sexist attitudes also reinforce a negative evaluation of battered women. These include values that hold women responsible for the success of their marriages, perceptions of women as childish and immature, and the tradition of blaming women victims that is best demonstrated in connection with popular attitudes about rape.[50]

Part of the importance of the approach espoused by Serum and by Singer is that it raises the absolute antithesis to the ideas that battered women—or any battered mates, for that matter—are masochistic, provocative, or predisposed in some manner to be victimized. Unlike Walker's theory, the coercive control interpretation makes no acknowledgment whatsoever of the importance of predisposing factors existing in the battered woman before marriage/cohabitation. According to the literature on brainwashing, no predisposition to succumb to brainwashing is necessary or even relevant.[51] In disputing outlooks that invoke masochism, provocation, or predisposing factors, the coercive control model avoids conclusions that blame the victim or portray her as inviting abuse. This is an empirically testable position since research could conceivably demonstrate that there are important factors predisposing a woman to enter or to endure in a battering relationship.

The coercive control approach to conjugal violence does not encompass social and cultural influences upon violent couples and their individual members. Although Serum clearly accepts feminist and sociological analyses of social factors promoting woman abuse, this is not a primary interest of hers. Another problem of the coercive control model is that thus far it is vague about the minimum criteria that determine whether a situation indeed involves coercive control. Also, like most theories of battering, this one does not apply well to battering relationships that are terminated swiftly.

SOCIOLOGICAL THEORIES

The work of Simmel serves as a landmark precursor to sociological theories of conjugal and family violence. Simmel remarks that conjugal relationships are especially sensitive to even minor amounts of antagonism. His analysis begins the contemporary recognition that conflict is inevitable in the family and foreshadows our current knowledge that the family is an extremely violent institution:

> The more we have in common with another as whole persons. . .the more easily will our totality be involved in every single relation to him. Hence the wholly disproportionate violence to which normally well-controlled people can be moved within their relations to those closest to them.[52]

Current sociological theories of conjugal violence show their indebtedness to Simmel by emphasizing the inevitability of intrafamily conflict, rather than invoking models of family harmony and/or stable equilibrium.[53]

Goode's approach is referred to as the resource or ultimate resource theory of violence.[54] Goode states that force is one of the four major resources by which people can move others to serve their ends, the other three being economic resources, prestige, and likeability or attractiveness. Force functions as a deterrent to performing undesired acts and as an inducement to perform desired ones. In general, the more resources an individual or group has at its disposal, the less overt violence there will be. Violence still remains a potential resource even when not utilized since those with the most resources usually can also deploy more force than others with fewer resources.[55]

O'Brien invokes Goode's theory in order to explain the demonstrated increase in the incidence of conjugal abuse in couples where the woman has superior socioeconomic status, skills, or resources. He notes that violence is generally expected in a society when there is a threat by subordinates to the dominance of superordinates. The superordinates then attempt to enforce their dominance by violent means. Similarly, says O'Brien, when husbands fail to possess the superior skills or resources that are supposed to legitimize their classically superior status, one would expect them to use physical force as a last resort to maintain their traditional dominant position.[56] A corollary of O'Brien's argument is that either diminishing women's potential for achievement or obliterating the traditional expectation of husband superiority should decrease the prevalence of conjugal abuse. Of course, the latter alternative is much preferred over the former.

Leaving aside for now sociological feminist authors, the most important sociological theorist working on conjugal violence is undoubtedly Murray Straus, followed by his sometime collaborator Richard Gelles. Straus' theoretical approach to conjugal violence is not uniform throughout his works, however. He has presented at least three theories relating to conjugal violence: a sociological approach to family violence, a similar approach concentrating on woman abuse, and a general systems theory approach to family violence.[57] As a result of his shifting emphasis upon family violence in general or woman-battering in particular, Straus can sound like a feminist analyst when he is emphasizing woman abuse, or he can sound at odds with feminist theorists.

According to Straus, the foremost social factor influencing conjugal violence is the existence of cultural norms that permit conjugal violence, especially woman abuse. He loves to remark that "the marriage license is a hitting license."[58] The hitting license is both a widespread fact of life apparent in popular entertainment, old sayings, and social behavior, while at the same time it diametrically contradicts our stereotypical conceptions of marriage as tranquil, warm, secure, caring, and loving. Research shows that the hitting license is not limited to legal marriage, but also applies in practice to unmarried cohabitant heterosexual relationships.[59]

The hitting license aspect of marriage is part of the tradition of the rule of thumb. It is operating when battered partners are viewed as deserving of conjugal assaults. It is reflected in Stark and McEvoy's findings that 20% to 25% of Americans can readily approve in some circumstances of a mate slapping the other mate's face.[60] It is the probable reason for the results of studies showing that people do not intervene in assaults committed by a man upon a woman.[61] Like those who passively witnessed the Kitty Genovese rape-murder, onlookers do not intrude because they infer the interaction is a marital quarrel and, hence, none of their business. As mentioned in Chapter 1, the hitting license is also recognized by police and judicial procedures.

The tolerance of conjugal violence is related to our society's priority on the privacy of the home and of the nuclear family. Americans believe they should not intrude upon others' private affairs, and they expect their own privacy not to be violated by others. Family disputes are viewed as nobody else's business.[62] The Fourth Amendment to the Constitution is the legal representation of this attitude, and it has often been interpreted as an obstacle to police intervention in domestic assaults.[63]

Reinforcing the belief in the sanctity of the privacy of the home are our myths about the family. A major reason why people are not concerned about the lack of effective intervention to halt conjugal violence is that few realize its possible severity. For many people, conjugal violence conjures up images of one partner slapping the other partner at most a few times. It is shocking even for veteran shelter workers to hear of the many ways in which a home is literally converted into a torture chamber. This failure to realize the severity of conjugal violence—and the consequent shock when confronted with a true-life horror story—occurs because as a culture we think of conjugal and family relationships as anything but violent. Conjugal relationships and the family are supposed to be havens of love and warmth and tranquility. Violence is supposed to take place in the streets, not among intimates behind the closed doors of a dwelling.[64] Yet statistically women and children are in fact safer out on the streets than in the home.[65]

As Goode points out, the existence of domestic violence reflects the fact that force is a resource available in any social institution, and it is generally used for the purpose of maintaining the existing institutional structure.[66] Paralleling this, Straus believes that the more a society resorts to violence on the governmental level, the more violence is affirmed as a valid strategy for use by the members of that society. For Straus, war, police use of force, capital punishment, and corporal punishment in schools provide governmental models of the appropriate use of violence. Maintenance of world-wide armed forces and militaristic political ideologies also express the acceptance of violence by our most powerful and respected citizens.[67]

Straus notes that violence in the mass media both portrays the high level of violence and aggression in America, and also helps perpetuate that pattern.[68] A vicious circle is created, as exemplified by people who rush out to arm themselves after the news publicizes a rise in the crime rate. I would add here that one possible reason for research findings that violent couples tend as a group to be youthful may be the effect of television violence in inculcating violent behavior. Since older marrieds were less exposed to televised violence, continues this hypothesis, they are consequently less violent.

Ordinary American children witness thousands of violent acts—real and simulated—in the media as they grow up. This certainly does not help breed nonviolence, especially since nonviolent conflict resolution is very rarely portrayed in our media. Furthermore, film, television, and comics implicitly endorse conjugal violence by treating it in general as a humorous and/or trivial topic, rather than as a serious one. For example, Jackie Gleason gained fame in the character of a bus driver who routinely threatened his television wife. This sort of depiction of domestic violence as a comic subject still obtains; for example, on "Saturday Night Live" conjugal assaults are portrayed as humorous and trivial events.

The right to bear arms is a treasured American value that Straus believes has grievous consequences for conjugal relationships and the family. Not only does this right legitimize violent behavior, but a great many murders could be averted by stronger gun control or, in Straus' terms, "domestic disarmament."[69] Of course, disarming American families would deprive some battered partners—especially battered women—of a most effective deterrent against battering. Still, it seems that on the whole handgun registration and domestic disarmament would have beneficial effects on conjugal violence. Currently, the odds are that a gun bought "to protect the family" is instead more likely to be used against a family member.

Analyzing the structure of the family, Gelles and Straus together have developed a list of nine reasons why the family experiences such a high level of conflict and violence. First, there is the large amount of "time at risk" of family violence, arising because family members spend so much time together. Second, is the wide range of activities and interests included within the family, giving rise to more opportunity for conflict to occur. Third, many of these activities overlap or compete with each other.[70]

Fourth, the high level of emotional involvement in the family changes the intensity and meaning of frustrations experienced within the family. For example, it is much more hurtful to have a mate disapprove of one's appearance than a colleague or acquaintance. It is more painful to be refused conversation by a conjugal partner than it would be in other relationships.[71] The high level of emotional involvement in the family also makes it less desirable for family members to back down or to flee—the usual human and mammalian strategies for avoiding violence.[72]

Family conflict is also generated by the presumed right of family members to influence each other. There is a wide range of topics and behaviors that will provoke an argument in the family but would not lead to overt conflict in other relationships.[73] Alcohol abuse is a good example here; what we might well tolerate or merely sidestep in drunken strangers, we attempt to prohibit in children and mates. Furthermore, the right of family members to influence one another includes the perceived right to use physical force on family. This is especially, but not exclusively, true of the parent-child relationship, and it is also the rule for conjugal and sibling relationships.

Sixth, continue Gelles and Straus, conflict arises in families because at a minimum the family represents the differing outlooks of two genders or of two generations. In families with a heterosexual parent couple, the generation gap and the battle of the sexes are simultaneously present. Seventh, roles within the family are to a large extent assigned according to age and gender differences, rather than chosen upon the basis of interest and/or competence.

Eighth, the involuntary or semivoluntary basis of membership in the family gives rise to more negative feelings and resentment than are experienced in a voluntary group. It is much easier to quit the Elks or NOW than it is to quit a marriage or to end an unmarried cohabitant relationship. Finally, Gelles and Straus note that the privacy of the family insulates the family from potential sources of assistance or intervention.[74] This privacy does not apply solely to situations occurring behind closed doors. To reiterate, onlookers will very rarely intervene in a family fight—verbal or physical—going on before their eyes. Even in public, family members are relatively free to dispute and to fight physically, as if they were in the privacy of their own home.[75]

Straus points out that our societal unwillingness to acknowledge the family as a very conflict-laden group is itself a source of continued domestic violence. So long as we ignore the existence of family conflict or treat it as atypical, we will not be willing to instruct people in techniques for engaging in conflict effectively and nonviolently. Also, the victims of domestic abuse are inclined to believe their situations are unique because of the denial or minimization of the epidemic of family violence.[76] This promotes victims' ashamed reluctance to seek outside assistance.

The ubiquitous use of corporal punishment upon children has several implications for conjugal violence. First, childhood physical punishment sets a precedent for those who love an individual to be identical with those who beat her/him. Second, corporal punishment teaches that important matters legitimize the use of violence.[77] Third, it has been shown that physically punished children tend to be more aggressive, both as children and as adults.[78] Fourth, the legitimization of corporal punishment makes it harder to distinguish legitimate levels of family violence from abusive ones.[79] This carries over into the conjugal relationship where batterers often portray their violent behavior as the minimum necessary discipline. Last, parental punishment teaches that being hit is for the individual's own good.

Like feminist authors, Straus notes that the sexist structure of the family and of society promotes woman-battering. Social acknowledgment of the husband/male partner as head of the family sets an expectation that men will exercise dictatorial authority over their wives (or female partners) and families. One result of this is that men will resort to physical force when they cannot maintain by other means their authority as heads of their households. O'Brien's and Gelles' findings about the relationship of abuse to husband-wife discrepancies in employment and occupational status are relevant here.[80] The use of force against wives and female partners both protects male authority and is justified by the existence of male authority.[81]

The sexist economic system that discriminates against women seeking employment helps entrap battered women in their violent relationships. The jobs open to women are generally of lower status, involve more drudgery, and pay an average of 59% of male wages. Thus, battered women must often choose between poverty and enduring battering.[82] Many battered women with children are reluctant to deprive their children of material affluence by leaving the batterer.

The sexist division of labor in society assigns child-rearing responsibility to wives/women. This keeps them in a dependent and less powerful position if they bear children. There are only terribly inadequate child care services available to women who work—or who want to work—outside the home. Women who have worked as housewives rearing children are at a disadvantage in terms of seniority and occupational skills when they try to enter the paid-labor market. On the other hand, husbands basically need not fear that they will be responsible for *both* financial support of the children and child care should divorce occur.[83]

The myth that children need two parents present in order to develop to their full potential also helps to entrap battered women.[84] Many shelter residents find it a revelation relieving them of much guilt when shelter workers tell them that one nonviolent parent is better for the children than two parents in a violent relationship. The preeminence of the wife-and-mother role for women also works against battered women. Women get the sense that to succeed as women they must succeed in their conjugal relationships, and that they have an obligation to try their utmost to make these relationships work, thus preserving their families. Men are not taught to place a similarly heavy investment on the husband-and-father role.[85]

The socialization of women makes it easier for men to victimize women with battering. Women are not taught how to defend themselves physically to the same degree as men are. They are taught less achievement orientation, competitiveness, and assertiveness than men. Instead, they are encouraged to be passive, cooperative, self-denying, and to define themselves according to others' wishes and perceptions. This is also good preparation for enduring victimization without rebelling against it.

The negative image of women fostered in society views women as childlike, unreasonable, and overly emotional. As quasi children in a society that allows corporal punishment of children, women are more susceptible to physical punishment. This myth goes on to say that women are less reliable sources of information because of their feminine irrationality and emotionality.[86] Viewed as hyperemotional beings, women are perceived as likely to become upset easily over trivial matters such as a family spat, which they may then exaggerate to others. These latter myths work against women with amazing frequency as they seek assistance from intervenors such as police, judges, clergy, therapists, and physicians.

Straus lists Parsons' concept of compulsive masculinity with its "essential concomitant" of aggression toward women, as another effect of sexism that encourages woman abuse. The female mirror image of compulsive masculinity is a negative self-image derived from social devaluation of women and their attributes. According to Straus, women's negative self-image can in turn encourage their toleration of male aggression and violence.[87]

Straus describes a final influence of sexism in promoting woman-battering, which is the male orientation of the criminal justice system.[88] For some reason, he overlooks similar pro-male orientations in other systems of intervention such as religion, mental health services, medical services, and civil litigations. Viewing his work as a whole, it seems that Straus' intent is not to deny the male orientation of these other systems, but to emphasize the problem of masculine bias as it applies to the criminal justice system.

The sociological approach constitutes a partial theory of conjugal violence. The sociological perspective excludes individual psychological factors and also fails to account for purposive and dynamic aspects of violence between mates. A social-psychological approach is more complete than a strictly sociological view because social psychology incorporates psychological factors resulting from individual experiences and/or interpersonal interactions. Gelles provides a social-psychological model of child abuse, which is easily applied to conjugal violence as well.[89] Gelles combines the influence of socialization experiences and of individual psychodynamics with that of the social factors already mentioned. He relies naively upon the psychiatric psychopathological model of individual psychology, implicating "psychopathic states" as a contributor to abusive behavior.[90] Straus displays a similarly fallacious reliance upon psychopathological diagnosis when he considers the role of the batterer's individual psychology in woman-battering.[91] Since no psychodiagnostic category—or set of categories—has a lock upon spouse or child abuse, social-psychological theory is improved by including individual psychological factors without reference to diagnostic categories of psychopathology.

A more all-inclusive approach to conjugal violence is Straus' application of general systems theory. Straus lists several desirable features of general systems theory applications. First, general systems theory is equipped to include all major factors influencing battering either positively or negatively. Social, cultural, interpersonal, and intrapsychic variables can all be incorporated into this model, as well as the influence of sources of intervention.[92] Thus, this theory is especially helpful in assisting people studying conjugal violence to recognize and recall all major influences instead of concentrating upon some type of partial analysis.

The utilization of general systems theory implies a perspective upon relevant variables that transcends the correlational approach. The correlational approach only indicates a relationship between antecedents, consequences, and a given factor. In contrast to this, the systems theorist is both equipped and compelled by theory to specify the processes involved in the phenomenon to be studied. For example, rather than merely stating the effect that battering tends to recur, Straus has developed a cybernetic flow chart that indicates processes by which conjugal violence either escalates over time, or is maintained at a stable level, or is diminished over time.[93] Alternative courses of action are thus specified, as well as causal influences upon the choice of alternatives.

A key feature of this approach is its inclusion of feedback mechanisms which increase, decrease, and/or maintain the level of a given system product—for current purposes, conjugal violence. The use of feedback mechanisms recognizes that the family or couple is by nature a dynamic system, rather than in a state of stable equilibrium. This also implies the inclusion of the goals of the system or of the purposive nature of the system. The purposiveness of systems creates the potential for change in the structure of the system—morphogenic processes—in addition to the homeostatic processes that maintain the system structure.

The major drawback of the general systems approach is its complexity and its tendency toward abstraction. A universally applicable systems model must by nature abstract from the concrete details of individual situations. In some opinions, Straus' general systems perspective obscures more than it clarifies.[94] The potential inclusion of all major variables affecting a system product is very difficult to execute in practice, due to the multitude of factors involved and to their myriad interrelationships. Issues of comprehensibility and convenience encourage a continued partial focus, even in utilizing a general systems perspective. To illustrate this, Straus' flow chart consists of 15 steps—all of which are very condensed and can be elaborated in great detail—emphasizing the interpersonal and attribution processes covered by symbolic interactionism. Despite its condensation of material and its concentration upon a single partial theory, Straus' cybernetic diagram remains quite complicated.[95]

To review, Straus' relevant theoretical contributions take at least three forms. In one approach, he analyzes the structural and cultural factors in society and in the family that contribute to the existence of family violence.[96] His second perspective involves working this first analysis into an approach based on general systems theory.[97] A third perspective of his concentrates upon woman abuse or wife-beating, as he prefers to call it.[98] In some works, his analysis is quite feminist, although the farthest he will go in his analysis of sexism as a cause of woman abuse is to say that sexism is "perhaps the most fundamental" factor causing woman-battering.[99] At other times, he conflicts with feminist views as he interprets his research as indicating equal conjugal violence by males and females and in analyses where he emphasizes family violence.[100] Later in this chapter, I will discuss further the issue of studying battering as a subset of family violence or as woman abuse—a form of violence against women.

In the meantime, there are still two problems to be noted in Straus' theoretical works. One problem is the existence of cultural norms that oppose conjugal and woman abuse, by supporting nonviolence in the family and by defining the assaulting of females by males as unacceptable. This is not to deny the rule of thumb tradition, nor to discount the frequency in our society of woman abuse and of male violence against women in general. Rather, this poses the theoretical challenge of accounting for the interplay of contradictory cultural norms in order to explain the ascendance—in an individual, group, or culture—of one or the other set of norms.

A second problem in Straus' theories is his emphasis upon family conflict as the basis of family violence. Certainly family conflict often does act as the basis of family violence, and conflict is certainly positively correlated with the occurrence of violence. However, Straus tends to overlook the fact that batterers may commit conjugal violence in response to feelings—not necessarily of anger—generated entirely outside of the family or, at least, outside the conjugal relationship. Even where battering occurs in the context of conflict, the conflict is not necessarily conjugal— e.g., many a batterer has beaten his wife over a conflict with his boss. The conjugal conflict approach to conjugal violence also fails to explain why it is that men commit so much more conjugal violence than women since each partner presumably experiences an equal level of conjugal conflict.

FEMINIST THEORIES

There are a variety of feminist approaches to battering. Their unifying feature is their sociopolitical foundation for theoretical analysis, which views social phenomena as determined by the sexist, patriarchal structure of our society. This analysis sometimes includes the personal level as well. Feminist approaches differ as to whether patriarchy should be viewed as the exclusive—or merely the primary—determinant of social phenomena. This perspective can be applied to an extensive range of subjects—virtually any aspect of the social sciences and the humanities and to some topics in the physical sciences as well.

Feminism can be termed a sociological or social-psychological theory, depending upon the specific feminist viewpoint in question. There are some important features, however, that sharply distinguish feminist views from the sociological perspectives on conjugal violence already discussed in this work. The most important difference is the unanimous rejection by feminists of studying family violence or marital violence or spouse abuse, emphasizing instead woman abuse as the appropriate topic for study.[101] Some feminist authors treat woman-battering as an important subset of violence against woman;[102] others study woman-battering in relative isolation from other forms of violence against women.[103] But all feminist authors treat husband abuse as either nonexistent or trivial and therefore reject gender-neutral references to spouse abuse in favor of gender-specific terms such as woman abuse.

Feminist writers pointedly avoid categorizing woman-battering with other forms of intrafamily violence. Some go so far as to question the very existence of husband-battering;[104] others hold that battered men are comparatively rare and therefore of low priority for study and intervention.[105] Child abuse, parent abuse, and intersibling violence are infrequently discussed in feminist works on woman abuse, and then usually as concomitants or as residual effects of woman-battering.

The feminist definition of conjugal violence as predominantly woman abuse is eminently testable. While most authorities on battering agree that well over 90% of conjugal abuse is woman abuse, undoubtedly there will be further testing of this belief by attempts to ferret out battered husbands/male partners. Steinmetz is the chief proponent of the hypothesis that violence against male partners is as prevalent and as serious in our culture as is woman abuse.[106] Should Steinmetz's view be verified empirically, feminist approaches to conjugal violence as woman-battering would be discredited. The testability of this aspect of the feminist theory of woman abuse is a positive feature of the feminist perspective.

Viewing woman abuse as a type of male violence against women enables feminists to relate woman-battering to various topics overlooked by other theoretical views of conjugal violence. Feminist writers have connected woman abuse with such superficially diverse phenomena as rape, incest, pimping and prostitution, the foot-binding of women, the veiling and seclusion of women, mandatory clitoridectomy, infibulation, pornography, curfews and other behavioral restrictions upon women to define whether they are perceived as of chaste character, prosecution of witches, media encouragement of sadistic male sexuality, and economic restrictions upon women resulting in poverty for women without conjugal partners.[107]

Perhaps the clearest overlapping between woman-battering and other types of violent victimization of women involves rape. Women are frequently raped by their male conjugal partners. If one includes as rape nonforcible invocation of the male "conjugal privilege," then, under this definition, virtually all heterosexual conjugal relationships involve at least one incident of rape. Furthermore, rape can be an effective method for a man to obtain a wife/female partner.[108] Pagelow, for one, gives a chilling case history of a woman whose partner "married" her by raping and abducting her.[109]

Feminist theory enables us to see as more than coincidental the close similarities between public attitudes toward battered women and toward rape survivors. Both rape survivors and battered women are viewed by the public as provocative—or even deserving—of their victimization by men. Both groups are believed to enjoy this victimization, despite their protests otherwise. Both are told that they are responsible for whether or not their victimization occurs—e.g., rape victims dress seductively and/or are not careful enough, while battered women would no longer be battered if they performed better as wives/mates. Both are discouraged by shame and lack of public support from seeking help after their victimization. If they do seek help in spite of the negative social pressures, both rape survivors and battered women must prove themselves "worthy victims"[110]—e.g., strict sexual morality prior to the rape is demanded of the rape survivor, while battered women must prove themselves worthy by separating from their mates and by following through in assisting the prosecution of their mates. If they fail to prove themselves worthy victims, each group is again discounted as deserving or as enjoying the assaults upon them by men.

Conversely, little attention is paid to rapists and woman abusers in order to prevent or discourage their behavior. Women are taught various techniques which hopefully help them to avoid being raped, and women are socialized to be good wives and cater to their husbands. Men receive no consistent instruction not to rape and not to beat. Quite the opposite, masculine sexual competence is associated with aggressively pursuing, and even coercing, sexual contacts with women. Husbands are still encouraged in various ways to control their wives, using physical violence if necessary to achieve control. Feminism explains the denigration of women victimized by men and the simultaneous neglect or exoneration of male assailants as twin manifestations of our patriarchal culture, systematically maintaining male domination and oppression of women.[111]

Extensive reference to historical fact is another feature distinguishing feminism from other sociological approaches.[112] Feminist study of woman abuse has emphasized and described in detail the response tendencies of social institutions as key factors perpetuating woman-battering. Unlike other sociological views, feminists consistently view as a manifestation of sexism the failure of social mechanisms to halt or to discourage woman-battering.

Feminism is the most important theoretical approach to conjugal violence/woman abuse; a majority of writers in the field espouse feminist views, and every major author on the subject considers herself/himself a feminist. Foremost among these are Martin, Walker, Dobash and Dobash, Schechter, Barry, Pagelow, Davidson, Gelles, and Straus. Steinmetz— perhaps the author most condemned in feminist works—also considers herself a feminist.

Feminism not only permeates the existing literature on woman-battering and conjugal violence, but it spawned the investigation of this subject in the first place. Woman-battering was discovered in the 1970s to be a widespread and serious problem through the work of women's consciousness-raising groups inspired by the feminist political movement. The first battered women's shelters developed out of feminist organizations. These events marked the birth of modern inquiry into woman abuse in particular and conjugal violence in general.

Moreover, feminist work for the first time dictated that woman abuse would be studied in its own right. Previously, woman-battering and/or conjugal violence had been subsumed under various other topics—e.g., marital discord, murder, police work, alcoholism, neurology, probation work, violence in general—and thus made less visible. Feminism also established the values assumption that violence is not acceptable behavior in conjugal relationships. This contrasts dramatically with the assumptions of earlier works, such as those of Schultz and of Snell et al.[113] In establishing a new context for studying conjugal violence and dictating new values assumptions for that study, feminism has founded the dominant scientific paradigm for research in this field.[114]

One theme in feminist theory that is especially important to the present work has to do with the impact upon battered women of overall social economic discrimination against women. I will refer to this either as "feminist resource theory" or as the "feminist resource argument." Feminist resource theory states that societal economic discrimination against women encourages many battered women to persist in their violent relationships because of the material disadvantages they would encounter were they to leave the batterer and support themselves—and their children, if applicable—financially. Proponents of the feminist resource argument include Martin, Walker, Pagelow, Schechter, and Straus, among others.[115]

Feminist resource theory predicts that the more independent economic resources of their own battered women have, the more likely they are to leave their abuser. Conversely, feminist resource theory predicts that the fewer material resources the batterer provides, the more likely his wife/partner is to sever their conjugal relationship. Walker uses this last theoretical point to explain the proportional overrepresentation of welfare recipients among residents of women's shelters.[116]

As previously mentioned, feminist work on woman abuse can be divided into two major branches. One branch concentrates upon woman abuse with little or no mention of other forms of violence against women. The other promotes the view of woman abuse as a form of violence against women, closely related to other forms of violence by men against women. The following discussion will pay special attention to representatives of each of these two branches of feminist thought, respectively—Susan Schechter and Kathleen Barry.

Susan Schechter has articulated especially well a feminist theoretical analysis concentrating upon woman abuse. Schechter attempts to answer the question "Why are women abused by their husbands/male partners?" Schechter acknowledges that the perfect theory of woman abuse would include individual and interpersonal levels of analysis, but leaves these areas aside in favor of a feminist sociological analysis:

> Ideally, a theory of violence against women in the family will explain individual behavior adequately. However, here the priority is to understand why abuse is directed at women, not why each individual man abuses. . . . The task is to discover what social conditions produce this target [i.e., women] generation after generation.[117]

Schechter then cites the historical context of male domination within and outside the family. Within this context, battering is seen as having developed as a means of enforcing men's conjugal authority over their female mates. Male authority is also represented and upheld by our extrafamilial social institutions.

Schechter includes a socialist commentary that capitalism has left women especially vulnerable to battering as a result of the privatization of the family and the removal of women from the paid-labor market to unpaid homemaking. Our gender division of labor, says Schechter, not only assigns unpaid domestic duties to women but "adds a moral dimension to this assignment" by defining household responsibilities as women's moral obligation to fulfill. Sex role socialization for men to dominate actively and women to submit passively combines with institutional support for male authority over women and the economic dependency of women upon their male partners to promote the entrapment of battered women in battering relationships. Despite this, continues Schechter, battered women remain actively engaged in surviving and in changing their lives.[118] While some would argue with its socialist features, Schechter's work well represents current feminist thought concentrating on woman abuse.

Kathleen Barry offers a cohesive view of woman-battering as a subset of overall male violence against women. For Barry, woman abuse is but one type of female sexual slavery, which is defined as follows:

> Female sexual slavery is present in ALL situations where women or girls cannot change the immediate conditions of their existence; where regardless of how they got into those conditions they cannot get out; and where they are subject to sexual violence and exploitation.[119]

While the main topic of interest in Barry's work has been the enslavement of women on an international basis for use in the sexual industries of prostitution and pornography, her definition intentionally includes woman abuse, most incest situations, and many forms of sexual abuse of girls and young women. Woman abuse and incest do not merely repeat the characteristics of female sexual slavery in prostitution, says Barry. Rather, she notes two ways in which the institutions of family and prostitution depend upon one another. One is that intrafamily female sexual slavery promotes forced prostitution.

> . . .a significant proportion of street prostitutes come from wife-battering, child-abusing, incestuous homes. Many were the object of their father's incestuous assault and/or other abuse. Female sexual slavery is a family condition and a precondition to forced prostitution.[120]

The other link between family and forced prostitution is that marital or family relationships may themselves be instruments for the sexual enslavement of women. The institution of bride-price and the enticement of women by promise of marriage or conjugal relationship are important methods for procuring female sexual slaves.

> Where daughters are sold into marriage through practices of dowry or brideprice, we have both the preconditions and the practice of sexual slavery.[121]

> Women may be. . .fraudulently recruited by fronting agencies which offer. . .marriage contracts that don't exist. Or they may be procured through seduction by being offered friendship or love. Conning a young woman by feigning friendship or love is undoubtedly the easiest and most frequently employed tactic of slave procurers. . .and. . .the most effective.[122]

Marriage to a prostitute can also bring to a pimp such benefits as legal immunity and legal rights over his prostitute/wife's earnings as community property. A wife cannot be compelled to testify against her husband in criminal proceedings. Furthermore, many anti-procuring and anti-prostitution laws leave a loophole for pimps who are simultaneously husbands. "If the procurer married the girl to circumvent the law he cannot be prosecuted."[123]

Barry's contributions demonstrate the similarities between the techniques of woman-battering and the "seasoning" techniques employed by pimps and procurers. The discussion in Chapter 5 shall return to this point. Barry's concept of female sexual slavery provides an unusual and insightful frame of reference on woman abuse. Utilizing the category of female sexual slavery, woman abuse is isolated and demarcated from many other forms of family violence—e.g., intersibling violence, parent abuse, nonsexual forms of child abuse—while it is more closely related to the incestuous victimization of daughters and granddaughters and to other forms of sexual abuse. Female sexual slavery also includes phenomena that are typically extrafamilial, such as prostitution, pornography, and sex murders. Barry's approach thus contrasts with theoretical perspectives isolating and relating the various forms of intrafamily violence. Barry also discusses the function of female sexual slavery as sexual terrorism affecting all women, whether they are directly victimized sexually or not. Sexual terrorism creates a climate of fear that encourages women to restrict their choices while men are left unimpeded and, hence, relatively privileged.

There are many problems facing feminist views of woman abuse. These problems involve the theoretical challenge posed by other forms of family violence. Feminist authors thus far have been too vague about how to approach child abuse. The problem is whether to treat child abuse as a subject isolated from woman abuse, to attempt to combine some forms of child abuse with woman abuse, or to attempt a theoretical integration of all types of child abuse with woman abuse. Husband abuse poses a similar theoretical question to feminists: should it be subsumed as a special case under woman abuse, treated as an exceptional phenomenon that proves the rule, or should it be separated theoretically from woman-battering? Other parallel problems remain, involving the various other permutations of family violence—e.g., abuse of parents and elderly relatives, and violence between siblings.

EMPIRICAL AND THEORETICAL LITERATURE COMPARED

It is premature to describe most theoretical predictions about conjugal violence as either proven or refuted. Only a very few concepts of theoretical relevance have thus far been uncontroversially established. First, and foremost, it is now obvious that conjugal violence is a widespread and severe problem in contemporary society. In the face of crime statistics, 600 battered women's shelters, and the work of Straus et al., it would currently be absurd to state that "force is rare in modern marriage." Second, clinical observers agree that conjugal batterers can represent virtually any diagnostic category of psychopathology and, hence, that perpetrating battering is unrelated to psychiatric diagnosis.[124]

There is great consensus among published sources, both theoretical and empirical, that the overwhelming bulk of conjugal violence consists of woman abuse and that husband abuse is rare by comparison. However, this belief apparently is not unanimous at present.[125] Furthermore, those who deny absolutely the existence of violent conjugal abuse by women against their husbands/male partners have now been proven incorrect by scattered case reports. While relatively rare, battering of men by their female partners does occur.

There do not seem to be any more instances of indisputable empirical support for theoretical expectations about conjugal violence. Concepts of victim provocation have been universally rejected by the woman abuse literature. This rejection, however, has been substantiated by logical, conceptual arguments aimed at theoretical assumptions. Since it is a value-laden theoretical assumption, victim provocation is not readily susceptible to proof or disproof by empirical work.

As noted earlier, the existing empirical literature displays a trend for couples with lower socioeconomic status to report higher incidence rates of conjugal violence. While this trend may be due to greater candor among members of couples of lower status, it also tentatively supports both Goode's ultimate resource theory and the frustration-aggression hypothesis. It will be recalled that Goode's theory predicts an inverse relationship between the amount of resources available and the use of violence.[126] The frustration-aggression hypothesis predicts that greater levels of frustration will be associated with increased aggression. Also noted earlier, O'Brien has applied Goode's ultimate resource theory in order to explain the empirically derived increase in the incidence of conjugal violence among couples where the woman has superior educational and/or occupational status than her male partner.[127]

The empirical literature also supports the predictions of feminist resource theory; however, this support is quite tentative. It is derived from three studies that together show a trend for battered women possessing higher levels of resources to be more likely to seek outside intervention in order to halt the violence.[128] While no existing empirical results tend to disconfirm feminist resource theory, it is of course absurd to regard the literature just surveyed as having adequately confirmed this theory. Similarly, it would be absurdly premature to discuss at this point any further theoretical implications as having been tentatively supported or undercut by existing published research. This discussion will proceed by reviewing difficulties common to all of the existing theoretical literature.

UNIVERSAL PROBLEMS OF THE THEORETICAL LITERATURE

There are several problems common to all existing theoretical works on domestic violence. One is the failure to acknowledge and account for women who decide to break off violent relationships, and who manage successfully to do so early on, after only one or a few abusive incidents. Thus far the literature has been primarily concerned with battered women entrapped in violent relationships over relatively long periods of time. This concern is appropriate since longer enduring battering relationships tend to be both more physically lethal and more psychologically debilitating.

Despite this, there are good reasons to remember battered women who leave their violent mates relatively soon after abuse has begun in their relationships. For one, this helps balance the tendency to view battered women as hapless and helpless victims. Moreover, it points to even higher incidence and prevalence rates of violence against female conjugal partners than those already derived. Also, finding and studying women who rapidly broke off violent conjugal relationships could teach us more about how women are either entrapped in or able to free themselves from battering relationships. It is crucial to note that, in studying battered women who rapidly and successfully escaped their battering relationships, our intent must be to discover factors that enhance women's freedom, and not to find ways to blame the victims of prolonged battering.

A second problem has to do with conceptualizing the severity of abuse. Some observers might question the usefulness or advisability of attempting to define and to measure relative severities of abuse. In particular, such a pursuit could be misused in order to justify violent reactions to nonviolent, but emotionally abusive, behavior.

In my view, the utility of defining and measuring the relative severity of abuse is related to documenting the effectiveness of violence as a means of entrapping and controlling victims. It is too often overlooked how violence itself prevents escape from violence, as in the case of victims who are forcibly restrained or knocked unconscious. The coercive control model, on the other hand, provides a theoretical basis for predicting a statistical relationship between the magnitude of abuse suffered and the tendency to attempt to dissolve the marriage/relationship.

Coercive control theory leads me to predict that battered women will be more likely to attempt to divorce/break off at relatively low levels of abuse and less likely to try to dissolve their relationship at higher levels of abuse because coercive control takes stronger effect at these levels. Extremely severe levels of abuse might well be exceptions to the above principle since increased desperation for their survival would motivate many battered women to overcome coercive control attempts in order to try to escape. Developing a scale of the magnitude of conjugal abuse would be useful for testing the above hypotheses.

A related problem involves nonphysical forms of abuse, variously referred to as psychological, emotional, or verbal abuse. Many battered women describe the nonphysical forms of abuse as the most painful for them. The literature has reached a clear consensus that physical battering is always accompanied by verbal and psychological abuse from the batterer. Apart from this, however, no one has yet satisfactorily related the physical and nonphysical forms of battering to one another, either in terms of severity or of effectiveness in entrapping and controlling the victim.

The following theoretical difficulty, while not exactly universal, is very widespread. There is too great a tendency to conceive of conjugal violence as punishment or as negative reinforcement for unwanted behavior, while ignoring violence as a means in itself for gaining dominance. Perspectives based on learning theory or upon sociological theories are especially susceptible to this oversight. When a woman is beaten and physically prevented from visiting her friends, this incident does not necessarily function as punishment to dissuade her from visiting, but is primarily a method to prevent her physically from doing what she wishes. Victory achieved through physical combat should be distinguished from punishment or negative reinforcement.

As should be obvious by now, no theory copes well with the subject of battered male heterosexual partners. They are either dismissed from consideration or else overvalued by unnecessarily gender-neutral terminology. Even in the latter case, their existence is still not explained adequately. It seems that one could take battered husbands into account without negating the overwhelming relative predominance of battered women. By analogy, historians are able to discuss instances of unprovoked violence by native Americans without obviating the overall portrait of genocide by whites against native Americans.

Battering in homosexual relationships has not been adequately addressed as yet. Shelter and hotline workers are now well aware that violence occurs in both lesbian and gay male couples. It is impossible to tell at this time whether or not homosexual battering should be theoretically distinguished from heterosexual battering.

Like most of the existing published literature on all aspects of family violence, this work has avoided the issue of whether human violence in general—and domestic violence in particular—is inevitably a part of human experience. Similarly, works on woman abuse and family violence do not deal with the ultimate causes of human violence, whether it is innate or learned, and other related issues.

Reports on the Tasaday people seem to establish that family violence need not occur in human society. Still, further verification and more cross-cultural studies of this matter would be valuable. It would also be valuable for someone to investigate the literature on primate behavior—especially ethological field studies—to see whether and how violence occurs in quasi-familial primate relationships, and to relate this research to conjugal abuse in human behavior.

This concludes the discussion of universal theoretical problems regarding battering. Next will be a review and critique of two important theoretical controversies. The first concerns whether to take the perspective of family violence or of woman abuse; the other regards the hypothesis of intergenerational transmission of conjugal violence.

FAMILY VIOLENCE VS. WOMAN ABUSE

Feminist opponents of the family violence perspective rightly point out that the concept and terminology of family violence can obscure the fact that the great predominance of conjugal violence is directed against women. Feminists advocate asking why conjugal violence tends to victimize women so much more than it does men, rather than inquiring why the family is such a violent institution.[129] Also, the work of Barry on female sexual slavery and works on woman abuse as a coercive control situation pose formidable challenges to the family violence approach by demonstrating the tremendous relevance of certain dramatically nonfamilial situations to the study of woman abuse.

Barry's concept of female sexual slavery in particular suggests strongly that not all forms of family violence are similar enough to categorize together. Her view indicates that woman abuse and father-daughter incest are best not casually combined with violence among siblings, abuse of elderly men, socially legitimized corporal punishment of children, and other disparate forms of family violence—especially since woman abuse and incest bear more resemblance to forced prostitution and to other forms of extrafamilial female sexual slavery. Theorists taking the woman abuse approach are generally skeptical of the value of combining sibling violence, parent abuse, child abuse, and spouse abuse under the unified conceptual category of family violence. Combining these different forms of family violence may be analogous to adding together apples and oranges and grapes. While these are all indeed fruit, "2 apples + 3 oranges" is a more edifying phrase than "five pieces of fruit." Including various forms of family violence under one topic for study, if it is to be done at all, should facilitate or clarify study and intervention and must not increase inaccuracy, vagueness, or ambiguity.

There are two main arguments in favor of a family violence approach over the woman abuse perspective. One is that it is important to debunk the myth of the family as a haven from danger in favor of the cruel truth that the family is the most violent social institution, except for the military in wartime.[130] This argument notes that spreading the information that women face more danger in their own homes than from the more generally feared "violence in the streets" furthers the social and political needs of battered women.

The second major reason in support of a family violence perspective is that the various forms of family violence are interrelated. Along these lines, Gelles and Straus present their analysis of the shared causes of all forms of family violence in the institutional structure of the family.[131] Perhaps the most important factor making the family the training ground for violence is the traditional and continued legitimacy of corporal punishment of children and of wives.[132]

Different forms of family violence not only share common sociological contributing causes but are also statistically correlated within families. Families experiencing physical abuse of one type also experience increased rates of other types of family violence.[133]

Furthermore, different permutations of family violence are not only intercorrelated; one type of abuse may convert into another type or may directly cause another type. Thus, formerly battered children may later in life commit parent abuse against their once-abusive parent in order to avenge the child abuse that they endured earlier. Children often are battered when they try to protect their mothers from woman abuse. Parents—mostly mothers—may suffer conjugal violence when they try to stop their mate from child abuse. Battered women who have been beaten for their children's behavior—e.g., noisiness—sometimes commit child abuse in their desperation to control their children's behavior in hopes of avoiding further woman abuse.

Woman abuse theorists have not adequately accounted thus far for the connections between woman-battering and other forms of family violence. They have also not fully explained their decision not to examine types of family violence other than woman abuse. It should be noted here that some movement in this direction has already begun. In particular, some members of the National Coalition Against Domestic Violence have started to address, in relation to woman abuse, the issues of child abuse, incest, and the situation of the children of battered women.[134]

At this point, it seems that what is needed is an approach to family violence that carefully avoids obscuring the fact that men run a relatively minor risk of domestic victimization. The ideal view of family violence would also recognize forms of extrafamilial violence—such as sexual slavery—that are closely connected to intrafamily violence. A theory of violence against women and children would, as far as I can tell, best fulfill these requirements.

An approach emphasizing violence against women and children would of course recognize that most such violence occurs within the family and is committed by men. This approach could perhaps account for domestic violence against adult males as a special case or an exception that proves the more general rule. The traditional status of women and children as patriarchal property provides the factual starting point for this approach.

My advocacy of a theoretical perspective emphasizing violence against women and children is only the first step toward fully developing such a theory. The recommendation of this view is preliminary and tentative since presently unforeseen problems could prompt me to abandon this perspective. The violence against women and children perspective does carry with it a disadvantage relative to woman abuse theory; it might seem to promote a view which, like family violence theory, relegates woman-battering to the background. This is not at all my intent, but a pitfall to be studiously avoided. In fact, a theory of violence against women and children can, and should, perform the opposite function of bringing woman-battering into the foreground of issues concerning family violence and other violence against women and children. This approach can reveal that woman abuse is often the fundamental source of many other forms of violence that have previously been treated as unrelated to woman-battering.

THE INTERGENERATIONAL TRANSMISSION HYPOTHESIS

This discussion of the theoretical literature on conjugal violence has not so far dealt with the hypothesis that battering is passed on from one generation to the next—the intergenerational transmission hypothesis. This is because this hypothesis can be assigned to various theories; for example, psychoanalytic theories of transference or unconscious identification, the social-learning theory of learning by vicarious reinforcement, theories of other processes for assimilation of values permitting or encouraging battering, and genetic transmission of violent tendencies. This hypothesis can be variously interpreted to apply to the commission of conjugal violence, or to the tendency to become or to remain a battered partner, or to both the commission of and victimization by conjugal violence.

The concept of the intergenerational transmission of conjugal violence has been strongly criticized by some sources. Some feminist writers believe that the concept of intergenerational transmission of domestic violence distracts and detracts from the overriding priority of changing the sexist social system that is the major cause of woman-battering.[135] Also, many writers—including the current author—doubt that intergenerational transmission applies to the tendency to be battered by one's mate. Moreover, it is clear that some batterers experienced nonviolent childhoods, and that many people—especially women—from violent families of origin do not commit conjugal violence. Thus, the intergenerational transmission hypothesis will never account for all occurrences of conjugal violence, nor for all battering relationships.

I do not view the feminist analysis of woman abuse and the intergenerational transmission of the tendency to batter as mutually exclusive concepts. I believe that available research—including the current study—demonstrates a general tendency for the intergenerational transmission of the tendency to commit conjugal violence, but that this demonstrated tendency should not obscure the awareness of sexism as the fundamental source of woman abuse. Indeed, the sexist structure of society that perpetuates woman abuse is probably a necessary precondition to the intergenerational transmission of battering behavior. Given current information, it is justified to say that men who as children witnessed the most extreme sorts of abuse of power possible within a conjugal relationship under our social system are more likely as adults—but not inevitably guaranteed—to perpetrate such abuses in their own conjugal relationships. This does not mean, however, that interventions against conjugal violence must be limited to treating violent families and their descendants, while ignoring those aspects of the social structure which permit or encourage conjugal violence. Quite the contrary!

To draw upon an historical analogy, suppose that in the antebellum South there was a tendency for the most cruel slaveholders to rear descendants who in turn were very likely to become extremely cruel slaveholders. Proslavery forces might have interpreted this fact to their advantage in order to argue that the slave system could be maintained if extraordinarily cruel masters were counseled against their abusive behavior. Given our modern, abolitionist values regarding slavery, however, it is obvious that the major issue in halting cruelty against slaves was ending the institution of slavery that was itself a form of cruelty, and that permitted—if not encouraged—even more extreme abuses.

Similar attitudes should be applied to woman abuse. In order to halt woman abuse, it is vital to seek remedies for social factors that permit or encourage its existence. Sexism is the term for the set of social factors which together maintain greater male power and privilege in our society. Some of the main factors that compose sexism include lesser legal protection for wives and cohabitant girlfriends than for husbands/boyfriends—both in statutory law and in law enforcement practices; unequal pay scales that handicap women relative to men; unequal customs regarding family responsibilities that place upon women the burden of child care, of responsibility for conjugal satisfaction, and of stigma should divorce occur; highly differentiated gender stereotypes which discourage assertiveness and physical self-defense by women while promoting male ruthlessness and violence.[136] There are no policy or treatment implications of the intergenerational transmission hypothesis that should take equal priority with the urgent need to change the social conditions that constitute sexism.

Chapter **5**

COERCIVE CONTROL AND WOMAN ABUSE

This chapter will build upon the theme already expressed earlier that certain nonfamilial and nonmarital situations are extremely pertinent to woman abuse. In particular, there will be a detailed description of the impressive similarities between woman abuse and the Chinese Communist thought reform practices of the late 1940s and 1950s. This will be followed by a brief description of the resemblances of conjugal violence and thought reform to the seasoning practices employed by pimps and procurers in order to force women and girls into prostitution. Lastly, I will propose some implications of the fact that brutal institutions usually treated as the diametric opposite of conjugal and family life are so similar to violent conjugal relationships and violent families.

The endeavor that this chapter represents is intended to advance the study of woman abuse in particular—and family violence in general—under the coercive control model. The working definition of coercive control involves a controller who takes enormous power—usually through confinement or isolation—over a victim he seeks to control by demanding compliance and violently enforcing that demand. The captive victim is made very dependent upon the controller; in fact, usually the controller will have the power to dictate whether or not the victim survives. Along these lines, Singer describes coercive control situations as "high dependency, high control situations."[1] Examples of coercive control situations include concentration camps; hostage situations; the condition of political prisoners subjected to violence and abuse; forced labor camps; violently isolative religious cults such as the People's Temple; some types of child abuse, especially those involving severe threats against the life and/or sexual integrity of the child; thought reform prisons; female sexual slavery, including forced prostitution; and prolonged woman-battering.

It so happens that the two forms of coercive control situations to be compared here to woman abuse have the goal of inducing stable, long-term personality changes in the victim. These changes involve alterations in the victim's behavior, values, and attitudes. In thought reform, the goal was to reform the prisoner so that he came to support the Chinese Communist regime.[2] In seasoning women for prostitution, the goal is to persuade women whose preexisting values and attitudes are inconsistent with working as prostitutes to do so nevertheless.[3] The goal of inducing this sort of long-term personality change is not, however, a criterion for defining whether or not a situation involves coercive control. The compliance demanded by the coercive controller may be short term and relatively superficial, as in brief hostage situations.

An intended by-product of the following discussion will be a more concrete—and hence more horrifying—rendering of how deplorable the battered woman's condition can be. I had considered attempting an exhaustive catalogue of the techniques employed by woman batterers, the main purpose of which would have been to impress the reader with the fact that the home can readily be converted into a torture chamber. I came to realize that no written enumeration of battering techniques can truly exhaust the twisted, sadistic ingenuity of men who torture their female conjugal partners. Further, I am less competent than many others at recalling and/or inventing battering techniques.

The most important reason for my rejecting the undertaking of a catalogue of battering techniques was the possibility that such a work could be used as a source book on how to commit woman-battering. I therefore rejected the idea of creating such a dangerous and superfluous publication. Still, I hope that this chapter, as written, will manage to convey some of the abominable horror and misery of woman abuse.

The following discussion concentrates upon woman abuse and its parallels to thought reform and forced prostitution. Much of the discussion would apply equally well to husband abuse, but I see no reason to accord husband abuse equal billing with woman abuse through use of terms such as *conjugal abuse*. Some of the following discussion would also apply to child abuse, but I am not competent to draw richly detailed and reliable analogies between child abuse, thought reform, and seasoning. On the other hand, the focus on woman abuse reflects my own knowledge and experience. It also reflects my belief that woman abuse is the most critical form of family violence because of its higher lethality, its causative role in other types of family violence, and its political importance in a sexist society.

The following discussion concentrates upon individual and interpersonal levels of analysis, hardly even referring to higher-order sociological levels. Some of the analysis will also refer to the immediate environment created in the coercive control situation and is, thus, ecological, in a very constricted sense of the word. By overlooking society and its institutions, I do not mean to suggest that woman abuse—or coercive control, for that matter, is purely psychological. I firmly believe that society as a whole plays the crucial role in permitting the deployment of coercive control by batterers—i.e., woman abuse.

Another limitation of this chapter is that, like coercive control theory in general, it does not adequately account for battering relationships that the victims manage early on to escape successfully. Here I am concentrating upon more severe abusive relationships. The following discussion is offered in hopes of educating the reader and the public that the woman abuse our society tolerates resembles very closely other practices that are already generally deplored. Communicating this knowledge that woman abuse is akin to brainwashing and torture is, in turn, supposed to help shift our social perceptions and priorities, so society will no longer tolerate woman abuse but, instead, will seek to extirpate this evil completely.

THOUGHT REFORM AND WOMAN ABUSE

Probably the best-studied form of coercive control is "brainwashing." Brainwashing is the English mistranslation of "thought reform"—the Chinese term for techniques used shortly after the revolution in Communist China in order to induce behavioral and attitudinal changes in political prisoners. The principal procedures of thought reform used by the Chinese Communists were imprisonment, verbal humiliation, beatings, and other means of physical torture. These techniques were used to induce false confessions by captives, confessions to having committed exaggerated or patently unreal crimes.[4]

The battered woman's situation obviously resembles that of a prisoner subject to thought reform. Like brainwashed captives, battered women are subjected to verbal abuse, beatings, other forms of physical abuse, and to confinement or imprisonment. In fact, the restriction of the battered woman's free movement is probably the most important technique of woman-battering. Instead of using the fist as the primary symbol for battering, we should think of internment in the home—the woman is kept under lock and key, or the exit is blocked by a physically superior or armed captor. The first prerequisite for battering to occur is the presence of the victim. This is ensured by her forcible confinement.

Part and parcel of confinement is isolation. Walker in particular has given a fine description of the methods used by batterers to effect the social isolation of their battered mates. She terms these methods for alienating and cutting off the battered woman from the social network outside the conjugal relationship *social battering*.[5] Abduction of the battered woman by the batterer is often necessary in order either to ensnare her in the first place or to resume her confinement if she has escaped it for awhile. Thus, abduction is closely related to imprisonment and to the general restriction of free movement placed upon the battered woman. The woman abuse literature abounds with true stories of abduction and confinement of the battered woman by the batterer.[6] With political prisoners such as captives of brainwashing, abduction prior to imprisonment would be called "arrest" or "capture," but it amounts to the same thing.

The restriction of movement achieved through abduction and enforced confinement—with its consequent isolation of the victim from her/his supportive social network—is one key method for imposing coercive control common to both the situations of woman abuse and brainwashing. Another major technique of coercive control common to these two situations involves the induction of false or exaggerated confessions by the captive victim. In the thought reform prison, confession by the prisoner was regarded both as a symptom of increased compliance and as a stage in the establishment of extensive behavioral and attitudinal changes. Coerced false confessions gave thought reformers both justification for punishing their prisoners and a means of gauging the captive's progress in thought reform. The coerced false confession also destabilized the prisoner's beliefs and values through the effect of cognitive dissonance[6½] and, thus, helped to promote further change by the prisoner in the controller's desired direction.[7]

In woman-battering, the process of the batterer forcibly projecting responsibility for his violence onto the battered woman can be viewed as similar to brainwashing because it involves the induction of false or exaggerated confessions. This commonly takes two forms. In one, the batterer coerces a false confession from the battered woman in order to justify or to rationalize his assaulting her. Often this involves her confessing to nonexistent extramarital sexual contacts.

> Kellie recounted how she had been beaten and interrogated by her husband for at least four hours. He demanded she confess to having had sex with a mutual friend of theirs. She truthfully insisted that she had not had any extramarital sexual contacts, even though she was beaten almost continually for her refusal to confess. When her husband took out a sawed-off shotgun, loaded it, and demanded again that she own up to this imaginary sexual affair, she finally gave in and confessed in fear for her life. He continued to interrogate her at gunpoint, forcing her to fabricate details of her nonexistent tryst, especially specific sexual acts. Sixteen months after this interrogation ordeal, Kellie's husband would still cite her false confession to justify beating her.[8]

False confession need not involve extramarital sex; it can consist of owning up to any transgression that the batterer insists be confessed.

The second form of coerced confession in woman-battering is even more common than the first type. It consists of the battered woman agreeing that she was to blame for the batterer's violence or abuse. Any time that a battered woman attempts to mollify her abuser by apologizing and claiming her own fault for his abuse of her, this can be viewed as identical in kind to confessions elicited in brainwashing. These false confessions by woman abuse victims can be induced by the batterer through physical, emotional, or economic coercion, or through a mixture of the above. Like thought reform confessions, they are both a signal of obedience and a means for promoting increased compliance by the victim in both behavior and thought.

False or exaggerated confessions extracted by coercion from battered women also function in favor of the batterer on a social level, and not solely on the conjugal interpersonal level. Battered women can be coerced into taking blame in order to dissuade police officers from arresting the abuser. Especially if witnessed by a third person, false confessions can later be used against battered women in civil suits concerning divorce, custody and property settlements, child visitation rights, and damages. False confessions later recanted by the victim can be used to establish her unreliability as a witness in civil or criminal justice proceedings. Perhaps most important, confessions of this sort can be used to subvert the battered woman's reputation among her closest friends and family.

> One shelter resident described how her husband beat her in front of her parents for regularly visiting a male friend she had. Implicitly he was accusing her of infidelity, and either because of this or because of fear for

their own safety, her parents did not intervene to halt this assault. Seeing this, her husband escalated the beating and explicitly accused her of "whoring around" with this friend and with other men. Eventually she confessed to nonexistent affairs in order to attempt to stop the beating. From the time of this incident forward, she said, her parents held her to blame for subsequent assaults on her by her husband, because they believed him justified to beat her for being unfaithful.[9]

Similarly, therapists, physicians, ministers, social workers, and various other helpers can be turned against the battered woman by means of the technique of coerced false confession.

In order to illustrate further the resemblance of woman-battering to brainwashing and to elucidate better the techniques of battering, it will be instructive to compare in detail woman abuse situations with Schein et al.'s account of the procedures utilized in Communist Chinese thought reform prisons. The study by Schein et al. still enjoys a good reputation as an investigation of coercive control situations.[10]

Schein et al. borrow a self-concept theory from Lewin in order to analyze thought reform conditions. They divide the process of coercive persuasion (their preferred term for coercive control) into three parts: unfreezing, changing, and refreezing. Unfreezing involves changing the environment in order to disrupt the prisoner's equilibrium. The unfreezing process is intended to produce a psychological breakdown in the victim:

> If the unfreezing experiences had undermined or destroyed the prisoner's self-image and basic sense of identity, he found himself with a fundamental psychological problem to solve. . .the reestablishment of a viable self. In other words, the unfreezing process could precipitate. . .an identity crisis.[11]

Facing the complete breakdown of psychological equilibrium, the thought reform prisoner changes in order to construct a self-image that is defined by the coercive controller as acceptable. Refreezing is the process of the prisoner integrating and articulating changes in her/his values, attitudes, and beliefs.[12] While all three of these phases can be applied conceptually to woman-battering, the present discussion will now focus upon thought reform techniques for "unfreezing" the prisoner's psychological equilibrium and their resemblance to woman-battering.

Schein et al. enumerate five kinds of support that contribute to the prisoner's resistance to the process of thought reform. The five sources of the prisoner's resistance are: 1) desire to resist, or initial attitude of noncooperation; 2) physical strength and well-being; 3) social-emotional and cognitive support validating beliefs, attitudes, and values; 4) self-image;

and 5) basic personality integration, including intrapsychic defense mechanisms and basic superego values. A variety of unfreezing techniques are exerted by the controller against each type of support for the prisoner's resistance. Psychological collapse is supposed to result; the aim of unfreezing is "to reduce the prisoner psychologically to a nonentity."[13]

There are of course some important differences between brainwashing as practiced in China in the 1950s and woman abuse. One key difference is that, once they are married or cohabiting with the batterer, battered women generally will not have a strong inclination not to cooperate with their husband/partner. Most battered women early in their conjugal involvement feel committed to the conjugal relationship. For battered women, an initial, reflexive reaction to resist the batterer would best apply to the very early stages of acquaintance and courtship, if at all. This attitude would also apply to the phase—which many couples do not experience— where the cohabitant abuser is feared and hated by the victim. Thought reform prisoners, subjected to imprisonment and abuse by adversaries in a foreign land, would generally feel more motivated than battered mates to resist their coercive controllers. Of course, those battered women who are shanghaied or coerced into marriage/cohabitation would be in similar circumstances as thought reform prisoners with regard to their basic initial desire to resist the abuser.

Another crucial difference between battered women and thought reform victims derives from the batterer's simultaneous function not just as abuser, but—ostensibly, at least—also as the victim's most important source of love and acceptance. Verbal, physical, and sexual humiliations from a husband or lover take on an enormous impact that similar behavior by a foreign adversary would achieve with greater difficulty, if at all. The fact that the batterer often is simultaneously the most rewarding and most dangerous person in the battered woman's life poses tremendous psychological difficulties for the victim. This effect is duplicated in other coercive control situations by the controller's ability to reward and to punish, but it is probably milder in those situations where the controller is not in a love relationship with the captive. It will be useful at times to recall these differences as the discussion of the many similarities between woman-battering and thought reform proceeds.

For each of the five supports for resistance against thought reform, Schein et al. list imprisonment experiences that operate as unfreezing forces to undermine the prisoner's ability or motivation to resist. Acting against the prisoner's initial attitude of noncooperation, say Schein et al., are the following thought reform procedures: control of information, especially censorship of information unfavorable to the controller; exposure of the prisoner to others with favorable attitudes toward the controller; exemplary behavior of the captors; and convincingness of the interrogator's threats and protestations of leniency.[14]

It has been noted above that the fundamental desire to resist the batterer is probably not generally as strong in battered women as the desire of thought reform prisoners to resist their Communist Chinese captors. However, there are influences analogous to the above thought reform procedures that work against the battered woman when she does wish to defy or to resist the batterer. Foremost among these seems to be the battered woman's exposure to others with favorable opinions of her mate. Often when a battered woman attempts to reveal her plight as a victim of woman abuse, she meets responses of shock and disbelief predicated upon her violent mate's good reputation. Classic among these responses are, "But he's such a nice guy!" or "What did you do to get him so mad at you?" These responses can and do come from friends, family, and all types of professional intervenors—clergy, physicians, lawyers, police, and therapists. The effect is to invalidate the victim's own experience; to imply that she is either culpable, out of touch with reality, or a liar; and to dissuade her from further attempts to gain assistance by revealing her plight.

The above sequence is reinforced in its impact by the batterer's exemplary behavior. More often than not, he does appear to be "such a nice guy," perhaps even a veritable pillar of the community. Given our prevailing myth that nice men only become enraged or violent with good reason, and community response supporting the perception of the batterer as a nice guy, the logic of provocation and of being at fault becomes more enticing to the battered woman trying to make sense of her experience.

Like thought reform prisoners, battered women also are subjected to control of information pertaining to their coercive controller. Many battered women have pathetically little information about how their violent partner spends his time outside the home. Information about his employment or income production may be intentionally withheld from the battered mate. Friends and relatives may conspire—perhaps with good intentions—to keep family secrets that would reflect badly on the batterer—e.g., his extramarital affairs, bar brawls, or squandering of money may be concealed from the battered woman.

Meanwhile, the batterer—like a thought reform interrogator—insists to the victim that she is well treated by him or, at least, that she is treated well given her culpability or inadequacy as a mate. This stance undercuts the victim's experience of herself as abused and begs the question of what the controller considers maltreatment. In this connection, the batterer/controller threatens dire consequences if the battered woman refuses—

perhaps even if she hesitates—to comply with the controller's dictates.

Sapping the physical strength of the victim is, of course, one of the primary techniques of woman abuse. Schein et al. list the following thought reform methods for attacking the prisoner's physical well-being:

> inadequate diet; loss of sleep due to intermittent and continuous interrogation, or other pressures; disease related to other prison stresses, such as poor diet; lack of exercise; excessive cold in combination with inadequate clothing; physical pain induced by prolonged standing or squatting; physical pain and injury from wearing manacles and chains; physical pain due to proscription of defecation except at two designated 2-minute intervals daily; requirement prisoner not shift position, except with guard's permission; cuffing and beating.[15]

This represents only a partial list of techniques used to attack the physical strength of all coercive control victims, and it may not even exhaust the techniques used to this end by thought reform programs.[16]

It is obvious that "cuffing and beating" applies directly to the treatment of battered women. What has been less obvious so far to both researchers and to the general public is that physical battering is but one in an arsenal of coercive control techniques that are deployed against the victim, creating an overall context that is synergistically greater than the sum of its components. An important purpose of the present discussion is to demonstrate that the batterer's violence is accompanied by many other forms of influence that are very destructive to the battered woman's physical and psychological integrity.

Inadequate food, clothing, shelter, heating, and medical care are considered neglect when they occur in families. Many battered women and their families are subjected by the batterer to inadequate provision of the basic necessities of life. More often than not, this is not a matter of poverty. Quite often, the batterer will severely deprive his partner and/or children of necessities while he spends money on his selfish priorities such as alcohol or other drugs, gambling, sexual services, motorcycle accessories, custom car parts, travel, and sporting equipment. Perhaps the most common pattern is for the batterer's alcoholism to exhaust the couple's or family's finances, at times to the point of literally starving the battered woman and her children.

Subjecting the battered woman to exposure is a surprisingly common technique. I have heard numerous accounts, like those recorded by Eisenberg and Micklow, of batterers locking battered women out in bad weather while the women were inadequately clothed.[17] This type of exposure is not only physically debilitating but also emotionally humiliating if the woman is naked or in her underwear.

The battered woman may be prohibited by the batterer from either eating, drinking, urinating, or defecating, or from performing a mixture of these vital bodily functions. Consequently, many women arrive at the women's shelter malnourished, and some have been frankly starved. The women become more susceptible to disease as a result of the rigors of woman abuse. Medical care may be denied by the batterer; the classic example of this is the frequent refusal by batterers of medical treatment for the injuries their battered mates suffer during the conjugal assault.

Most battered women suffer loss of sleep. Anxiety-induced insomnia is common; the batterer also often takes steps to prevent his mate from sleeping. Sleep deprivation procedures include lengthy harangues and interrogations into the night; making loud noise with stereos, television, or machinery; threats of battering or murder if the woman falls asleep; and enforcement of the expectation that the battered woman be awake when her mate returns home. One of my clients in batterers' counseling said:

> I'd be out all night drinking and carrying on. I might not come home 'til dawn; I might not even come home for a couple of weeks. But when I'd return home—whenever that was—Sally had better be awake, with a meal waiting for me, or else I'd bounce her around the room. And she knew it. So when I'd be gone long periods of time on a binge, she would barely sleep—as little as possible, anyway—because she didn't want to get a beating.[18]

Inordinate demands regarding housework, child care, and work outside the home may be placed upon the victim by the batterer, which further increases the battered woman's physical exhaustion. Part of the batterer's refusal to assist with housework and child care may be a strategy of wearing out his mate by burdening her with numerous physically taxing obligations. Although working prisoners to exhaustion was apparently not part of thought reform procedures, hard labor is well known to have been utilized in prisons and concentration camps elsewhere.

Like thought reform prisoners, battered women subjected to extremes of confinement and/or physical restraint, such as binding, will suffer from a lack of movement and vigorous exercise. Use of manacles, handcuffs, and chains by batterers in order to restrain battered women physically does occur. Binding with rope is a more common technique. Victims may also be confined to very small spaces such as closets or trunks.

Forcing the prisoner to remain motionless in one position figures more prominently as a thought reform method than a woman abuse procedure. However, I have encountered battered women subjected to this technique.

Leannah's husband forced her to sit in a chair motionless for an entire night. At times she was tied to the chair, at other times untied but still not permitted to move. Throughout this time, her husband honed a large, sharp hunting knife, threatening to kill or to mutilate her if she so much as batted an eyelash. In the course of the night, he recounted many sadistic fantasies of how he would have liked to torture, maim, and/or kill her with the knife. Naturally, she was terrified. She finally got free because her husband fell asleep after at least twelve hours' vigil over her. She said of the incident, "You'd be amazed how fast you learn how to not blink an eyelash when your life depends on it."[19]

Schein et al. do not dwell much upon the techniques of torture used in thought reform. It is hard to say whether this is because Chinese thought reform de-emphasized methods of inflicting pain through ancient torture techniques, or because of Schein et al.'s perspective that physical torture was less of interest than the psychological debilitation induced by coercive persuasion.[20] In any case, methods that are more commonly thought of being applied to political prisoners or prisoners of war are used by batterers against battered women. Some torture techniques used against battered women are chillingly creative and sophisticated in their morbid, sadistic fashion. Apart from beatings, common methods of torture in woman abuse include cigarette burns; twisting limbs to, or past, the breaking point; submerging the victim to near drowning; choking and suffocating; bamboo or wood chips under the fingernails; mutilation with knives or sharp instruments; branding; introducing painful irritants to the eyes. All of these techniques are reminiscent of espionage fiction or of factual accounts of torture under political repression. To shelter workers, American homes at times seem to form a sort of "Gulag Archipelago" in which women and children are subjected to myriad atrocities.

Sexual means of debilitating prisoners' physical strength are also overlooked by Schein et al. Thought reform prisoners apparently were not subjected to sexual abuse.[21] Rape and sexual abuse are committed all too often against political prisoners as an intended component in a regimen of coercive control.[22] Battered women are frequently subjected to conjugal rape and/or other sexual abuses that amount to physically debilitating torture.

Conceiving a pregnancy can even be used by the abuser as a strategy to diminish the battered woman's physical strength. This technique appears to be unique to woman abuse.

After three pregnancies resulting in two live births, Laura had been warned by her physician not to have any more children. Her husband Karl, however, refused to allow her to be sterilized and insisted upon sex without contraception. A fourth pregnancy resulted. As the doctor had predicted, Laura nearly died giving birth to her third child. She was again advised to have surgery for sterilization. Her husband continued to prevent her from being sterilized. He locked her in their home and nailed the windows shut. When Karl persisted in demanding or forcing sex without contraception, Laura began to suspect that he was trying to murder her in this way. At this point, she began to plan her escape and managed within two months to flee to a women's shelter.[23]

Even in less extreme cases, as pregnancy progressively impedes the woman's speed and ease of movement, she becomes more vulnerable if assaulted, less able to defend herself, less able to flee successfully, and more dependent upon her abusive mate. (Of course, it is only some batterers who sire children with the primary purpose of enhancing coercive control over the battered woman.)

Schein et al. note the following thought reform procedures for undermining both the social-emotional and cognitive supports of prisoners' resistance: control of information, including censorship of mail; continuous repetition of one line, one type of informational input; no personal contact with outsiders; no close relationships permitted with anyone; introduction of testimonials by others lauding the thought reformers; continuous and unanimous condemnation of groups with which the prisoner identifies or of values to which the prisoner adheres; use of informers to create distrust among cellmates; and solitary confinement.[24] These procedures either isolate the prisoner from potential sources of social, emotional, and cognitive validation and reassurance or else they subject the prisoner to invalidation on the social, emotional, and/or cognitive level. All of these procedures are also used in woman abuse.

Isolation of the battered woman by the batterer, separating her from her friends or relatives by various means, results in the woman abuse victim being cut off from the external world, at times to the extent of solitary confinement. This makes it less likely that the victim can obtain either sympathetic assistance or supportive validation of her experience of subjection to coercive control. The batterer's techniques for isolating the battered woman have already been excellently described by Lenore Walker, especially in her chapter on "social battering," and hence need not be reiterated here.[25]

Schein et al.'s list of thought reform techniques places the batterer's verbal abuse of his victim in an unusual and conceptually productive context. Using Schein et al.'s study, it becomes obvious that the verbal abuse endured by battered women in part represents the continuous repetition of one line or type of information and includes the condemnation of groups with which the woman identifies and of values to which she adheres. Battered women may be verbally condemned in particular for being female; or for being members of their family, religion, race, culture, or political affiliation; or for their occupational or educational or class status. Ordinarily the batterer will insist upon his correctness and the laudability of groups or values with which he identifies, while the victim is harangued about her wrongness. Through subjection to this sort of treatment, battered women often come to question or to change their values, beliefs, and attitudes.

The creation of disunity and distrust among prisoners by use of informants has its analogies in woman abuse. In particular, the batterer may play the children's interests against those of the battered woman in order to foment divisiveness. For example, the batterer may assault or sexually molest the children in order to prove that their mother is an inadequate protector to be distrusted. Children can be enticed or coerced by the batterer to act as informants—even as false witnesses—against the battered woman. Similarly, the battered woman can be coerced into selling out her children's interests in favor of protecting herself. Friends and relatives are also manipulated by batterers to betray the battered woman in various ways. One typical example involves attempts by the batterer at the sexual seduction of the battered woman's best friend.

According to Schein et al., the following thought reform methods undermined the prisoner's self-image, sense of identity, or sense of integrity and inviolability:

> Humiliation, revilement, and brutalization; complete prescription of the use of time and space so that the prisoner would feel completely dependent on the authorities; identification of prisoner by number only; prohibition of any decision-making; unanimous perception of prisoner as a reactionary and criminal—denial of other roles; manacling and chaining prisoner to make him dependent upon others for basic bodily need management, or enforced self-derogation through lack of assistance with excretory functions; seducing or forcing the prisoner into making concessions which arouse guilt—e.g., false confessions; prevention of personal hygiene, demeaning punishments; insults and taunts; denial of any privacy— continuous scrutiny.[26]

Humiliation, revilement, and brutalization subvert the victim's self-image. Under continual verbal abuse in an extreme and unfamiliar situation, the victim eventually will find corroboration for the controller's insults and condemnation. As the prisoner/battered woman is reduced to an animalistic mode of living—or lower, in some cases—she will begin to feel less than human and may thus come to attribute to herself a sense of worthlessness or subhumanity.

Under verbal abuse, the prisoner/captive is described only in negative qualities that are often exaggerated or patently unreal. Thus, thought reform prisoners were treated and described solely in their role as "criminal reactionaries." They had no other mode of existence for their guards and captors save as criminals. Similarly, the batterer verbally abuses the battered woman as a "bitch," admitting no positive qualities to exist in her.

The dehumanization of battered women in some cases includes prolonged physical restraint obliging the woman eventually to soil herself with her own bodily wastes. All battered women face constricted decision-making powers and some experience a total prohibition on their independent decision-making. Similar to coercive controllers' identification of captives by number only, many batterers studiously avoid addressing—or referring to—their mates by name. Instead, she is referred to by her role— "the wife," "the old lady," "my woman"—and addressed without use of her name, sometimes without so much as the use of a pronoun. Avoiding use of the battered woman's name dehumanizes her in the batterer's perception as well as injuring her own self-image.

> For a long time, I wouldn't call Elizabeth by her name. She was "the wife"—my possession, like an object. I realized through counseling that I wouldn't call her Elizabeth—wouldn't even *think* of her by name—because to do that would be to recognize her as an independent human being.[27]

Many battered women experience extensive or complete prescription by the batterer of how to use their time and space. Certain rooms or areas of the house or apartment may be put off limits to her. Her time may be planned for her in such a way that any unforeseen interruption in the schedule will place the woman out of compliance with her schedule and, thus, subject to punitive measures.

> One woman came to the shelter shortly after being beaten for talking to a woman neighbor for a few minutes. Her boyfriend's objection was that he had left her a schedule to keep, and socializing wasn't part of it.

> Another woman discussed her intense anxiety each time she shopped for groceries. She was expected to return home by a certain time or else she would be beaten. Her husband said he assumed she was flirting or having an affair if she was late returning from the market. Thus, if the checkout lines were unusually lengthy, making her late, she faced a beating for supposed infidelity. She left her husband and fled to a friend's home after a grocery shopping trip in which long lines, a delay at the butcher window, and a flat tire made her over an hour late. She didn't want to face the physical danger at home, and so she decided not to return home.[28]

Jealousy is most often invoked as the pretext for batterers to deny their mates privacy. Some abusers keep their partners under constant, direct surveillance. Others hover around their partner as much as possible, and check up on her whereabouts by phone when they cannot keep watch. Sometimes a different reason is given to prohibit privacy. One shelter resident stated that her husband insisted that he accompany her everywhere, and she him, in the interests of "togetherness." In practice, this meant she could not urinate or defecate in private, nor even change her tampon in solitude.

A very important thought reform method involved either enticing or coercing the prisoner into concessionary actions that aroused guilt.[29] The guilt thus induced could be either emotional, intrapsychic guilt or could involve the appearance of culpability without the prisoner's actually feeling guilt. Sometimes both types of guilt could apply simultaneously. As an example of this last circumstance, a prisoner could give the appearance of culpability by confessing without feeling guilty and then feel guilt about the lie involved in the false confession.

The coercive extraction of false or exaggerated confessions from battered women has already been discussed earlier in this chapter. Coercing the battered woman into culpable activities is a related way to induce the appearance of guilt in battered women, and it will also effectively induce guilt feelings in some instances. Probably the most common illicit or culpable-seeming activities into which battered women are forced are: sex with one or more persons outside the conjugal relationship, illicit drug transactions, child abuse, or criminal activities such as larceny or passing bad checks. The batterer can then humiliate and/or blackmail the battered woman in various ways for her involvement in these activities, and he can also use these incidents to his legal advantage in divorce actions or related civil suits. This blackmail can be powerful enough to dissuade the woman from attempting either to flee or to sunder the relationship because she fears the potential impact of the batterer's denouncing her.

An analogous practice was used on Patricia Hearst by the SLA. She was raped by SLA members and forced to participate in a bank robbery. She was then forced to claim that she had joined the SLA of her free will, loved her fellow members, and had willingly participated in the bank robbery. This changed her status from a victim to be rescued by law enforcement officers into a hunted outlaw. This, in turn, decreased her motivation to be found by the police and increased her motivation to see the SLA evade arrest.[30] Similarly, battered women who have been coerced by their mates into illicit activities have less motive to receive third-party intervention, less reason to reveal their victimization, more motivation to comply with the batterer, and more reason to hope he will not face any negative repercussions for his abusive behavior.

There are other methods not yet mentioned for inducing guilt in the battered woman. She may be forced to neglect her children or relatives in favor of the batterer's demands. She may be made to feel guilty about not attempting to stop her violent mate from mistreating others, and the batterer may commit a host of cruelties with precisely this intention. Physical and/or sexual child abuse by the batterer appear to be common methods to induce guilt in the mother.

> He beat my little boy real bad. My son was bruised and bloody all over, and he looked just terrible for days. And my husband would point to him and say to me, "Don't you feel awful you didn't stop me?" or "You're some rotten mother not to try and protect your son." And it seemed to me after awhile that that was why he had beaten the child. Because the boy hadn't done anything wrong, nothing even to deserve a spanking, much less a beating.[31]

> I raped her daughters—my stepdaughters—right in front of her. I made her watch—every time I saw her look away, I threatened to shoot her and the girls. I had my .38 loaded and in my hand—that's how I made them all do what I said. I didn't do it for the sex. I didn't desire her daughters, really. I just wanted her to feel terrible that she had watched me do that to the girls without her trying to protect them. I wanted her miserable. I wanted her to doubt herself as a mother, to think she was a bad mother. So I gave her the biggest failure a mother could have.[32]

Of course, not all concomitant child abuse by woman batterers is intended primarily to abuse the battered woman emotionally and make her feel guilty. A surprising amount of batterers' child abuse, however, is committed for this purpose.

The following thought reform techniques were used to assault the prisoner's basic personality integration—his intrapsychic defense mechanisms, basic values, or superego functioning:

> Threats of death, of endless isolation and interrogation without release from prison, of torture and physical injury, of injury to family and loved ones—induction of anxiety and despair; rewards and indulgences used to tantalize and confuse; rejection of prisoner's values and morals, or depiction of prisoner's behavior as inconsistent with his professed values and morals—induction of guilt; continual criticism and rejection of prisoner;

continual projection of image that captors are operating according to higher moral and ethical principles than the prisoner.[33]

The rejection of the prisoner's values and morals, and the continual criticism and rejection of the captive are largely redundant with the continued verbal and physical revilement and brutalization of the prisoner already discussed. There is a slight difference here in that the rejection and derogation carry a moral authority with them, reflecting the higher moral plane on which the coercive controller supposedly exists relative to the captive. In woman-battering, the traditional moral obligation of wives/female partners to obey their husbands/male partners is often invoked by the batterer for similar effect.

Schein et al. consider the use of random, noncontingent reinforcement by unpredictable rewards and punishments to be relatively unimportant as a thought reform technique.[34] Lifton, however, views this process as crucial to the effectiveness of thought reform.[35] Serum, Singer, and Walker all consider the ambiguity induced by random, noncontingent rewards to be a very important influence contributing to the breakdown of the battered woman.[36] Walker views this battering tactic as the means of inducing learned helplessness in the battered woman. Thus, the use of rewards and indulgences to tantalize and confuse is central to Walker's theory of learned helplessness.[37]

Faced with unpredictable consequences for their actions, battered women can become oblivious or indifferent to the possible repercussions of their behavior. This in turn can contribute to their appearing "provocative" or blameworthy to outside observers.[38] For example, a woman can become quite apathetic about her household chores when she faces an equal likelihood of being beaten for doing the chores or for neglecting them. Police called in to intervene in a subsequent assault committed on her by the batterer may then perceive her as a slovenly housekeeper and may sympathize with the batterer over her apparent sloppiness.

The various types of threats associated with thought reform, and with other types of coercive control, figure very prominently in woman abuse. The threat of physical injury and torture of the battered woman is omnipresent in any relationship where battering has occurred on repeated occasions, as well as in most relationships where violence has happened once or rarely. Threats against the safety of the battered woman's children, relatives, friends, and/or pets are nearly as ubiquitous in battering relationships as direct threats against the woman herself. Under such threats, many battered women heroically refuse to flee or heroically resume cohabiting with the abuser rather than place others—such as their children or parents or siblings—in jeopardy.[39]

The frequency of weapons threats by batterers is reminiscent of the mock executions staged by Iranian terrorists upon their captive American diplomats. In some violent households, these mock executions or death threats become almost routine, although the victims rarely—if ever—become accustomed to them. Straus et al.'s survey findings imply that at least 190,000 American men each year threaten their wives/female partners with a knife or gun, and that they do so an average of four or five times apiece. The same figures indicate that each year at least 144,000 male partners shoot, stab, or shoot at their female mates an average of over five times apiece.[40]

Verbal and behavioral death threats by the batterer can be reinforced and given enhanced impact by his actually murdering. Some battered women know their mates have already committed murder in the past; ·many are involved with combat veterans who have killed as part of warfare. Some batterers get away with child murder, or they make credible attempts on the life of the battered woman or of one of her children. Pets are killed quite often by batterers in order to appear capable of killing; consequently, their death threats against people seem more plausible.

Schein et al. believe that the induction of guilt in the prisoner plays a special role in unfreezing the prisoner and making him willing to comply. They describe nine bases by which thought reform prisoners could be considered guilty by the captors.[41] All nine types of guilt attributions are also made by batterers against their victimized mates. In both situations, these types of guilt are invoked by the captor in order to justify his maltreatment of the victim.

It should be noted that these reasons for assessing culpability involve sham or pseudo guilt, and that I judge neither thought reform prisoners nor battered women truly guilty. Rather, this discussion deals with the ways in which patently false attributions of guilt are substantiated by coercive controllers against their captive victims. Furthermore, guilt "established" on these grounds is often effectively induced in the prisoner subjected to coercive control. In woman abuse, this contributes to the battered woman taking the blame for her abuser's cruelty to her.

The first type of pseudo guilt is guilt by association, in which "the prisoner is guilty if he has associated with any others who are themselves guilty."[42] Good examples of this in woman abuse would be the woman being held culpable for associating with individuals the batterer dislikes, or with people of whom he disapproves—e.g., single women, divorcees, lesbians, gay men, people of "wrong" races or religions. Second is guilt by intention, in which the prisoner is guilty for exhibiting motives which could lead to actions deemed harmful to the controlling captor.[43] In woman-battering, culpable intention would include any display of a wish to leave. Having knowledge of a battered women's shelter or hotline would be punishable on such grounds. If the woman talks with any extrafamilial person, the batterer can interpret this as her showing guilty intent to leave the conjugal relationship.

Guilt for incorrect attitudes negative to the controller or for doubting any decision by the controller comes third. In other words, the captive is expected to accept the controller with unquestioning obedience.[44] This is part of the ancient marriage vow, which in practice extends to unmarried cohabitants, and it is enforced violently upon battered women. Fourth is guilt for thinking differently from the captor.[45] This type of guilt proscribes battered women from expression of their personal perspective.

Guilt for having knowledge which could in any conceivable way be used against the controller is the fifth type of sham culpability listed by Schein et al.[46] This type of guilt is especially germane to woman abuse. Virtually all battered women can be deemed guilty by the abuser on this count. The woman's experience of having been battered by her mate is in itself dangerous knowledge that could harm the batterer's social reputation. Quite likely, the battered woman will have other kinds of knowledge potentially dangerous to the batterer if revealed. This could concern his child abuse, criminal activities, substance abuse, sexual proclivities, business schemes, or family secrets, among other things.

Sixth is guilt for taking action harmful to the controller's interests, which is assessed without regard for whether the victim intended harm to the controller or not.[47] When a batterer assaults his mate for her delaying dinner by getting stuck in a traffic jam and returning home late, he can be said to be operating on this type of pseudoculpability. Any brief separation in which the woman flees the batterer can also be considered blameworthy by the batterer on the same grounds of being contrary to his self-interest.

On the other hand, the prisoner/battered woman can be judged miscreant for failure to take action supportive of the coercive controller's preferences.[48] This helps explain why battered women may sometimes be hostile—or even assaultive—towards police intervening in a conjugal assault. Her failure to support her mate against the police in this situation would be considered a serious, physically punishable offense by the batterer. The batterer therefore would likely escalate the conjugal assault once the police were out of his way. Additionally, failure by the battered woman to do every conceivable deed to please her mate would in the batterer's eyes amount to guilt by omission, which he could then punish at will.

The eighth form of sham guilt involves culpability over having one or more characteristic personal faults.[49] The batterer commonly invokes the battered woman's real or drummed-up personal faults—such as nagging, laziness, drug abuse, or mental illness—to justify his maltreatment of her. The last type of pseudoguilt is guilt for having dangerous social origins. In thought reform, this related mostly to the bourgeois, capitalist origins of thought reform prisoners.[50] In woman abuse, the batterer can charge this type of culpability in relation to the woman's race, class, ethnicity, religion, or family background. Furthermore, the abuser can consider his mate to have dangerous social origins, punishable by battering, simply because she is a woman.

It is time to summarize the resemblances between thought reform or brainwashing and woman abuse illustrated in the preceding discussion. In both situations a male captor or set of captors subjects the prisoner to enforced confinement involving a regimen of physical brutality and violence, imposed physical hardship, dehumanization, and verbal and emotional abuse. The threat of the victim's death is usually presented by the captor in word and/or deed. Escape is either literally impossible, or very nearly so, or else escape is the most dangerous of all the prisoner's alternatives. Throughout both the thought reform and woman abuse ordeals, the captor portrays himself as utterly laudable, worthy, and inviolable, while demonstrating to the victim that she or he is entirely guilty, worthless, and eminently violable.

As described above, there is shocking similarity between the specific procedures and techniques of thought reform and woman abuse. Along with physical and emotional abuse, confinement and coerced false or exaggerated confessions figure prominently in both contexts. The technique of inducing guilt feelings in the victim or, at least, of extracting from the victim protestations of her/his culpability involves nearly identical methods and attribution processes in both thought reform and woman-battering.

The intended results of both thought reform and woman abuse are also similar. Thought reform is intended to produce a psychological breakdown so that the prisoner becomes malleable. It is said to induce a personality change in the prisoner, brainwashing him into compliance with his captors.[51] In woman abuse, the process involves a male captor (the batterer) breaking a woman's spirit and bending her to his will. That the purpose and result of woman abuse may not be consciously premeditated, while thought reform was a carefully conceived procedure, is irrelevant to the aim and usefulness of the present discussion. What is important here is the chilling overall similarity of woman-battering to brainwashing.

If better known, the similarity between battering and brainwashing could have significant political consequences. Many people support a policy of preserving families and/or conjugal relationships intact. These individuals might change their priorities and their policy preferences if they learned that sometimes "preserving the family" amounts to aiding and abetting the brainwashing process of coercive control.

COERCIVE CONTROL AND PIMPING

Kathleen Barry shows in *Female Sexual Slavery* that forced female prostitution involves coercive control practices very similar to thought reform. This is especially easy to see in light of the preceding discussion. The process used to coerce women into prostitution is called "seasoning," and is analogous to the unfreezing process of thought reform. Says Barry of the seasoning process:

> Seasoning is meant to break its victim's will, reduce her ego, and separate her from her previous life. All procuring strategies include some form of seasoning. . . . Seasoning inculcates dependence and indebtedness in the victim. . . .
>
> In breaking down their victims, some procurers rely only on the dependency that results from taking their acquisition so far away from home that [she] can't get back without money for transportation. . . . Harsher methods may involve beating, rape, sodomy, drugging, and starvation before turning a female out on the streets or over to a brother.[52]

The parallels between the above methods of seasoning and those of thought reform are obvious enough to bear no further comment. Like thought reform, the purpose of seasoning is to inculcate in the victim behavioral and attitudinal changes desired by the controller. Barry quotes a pimp on this subject:

> You create a different environment. It's a brainwashing process. . . . When you turn a chick out, you take away every set of values and morality she had previously and create a different environment. . . .
>
> Turning out a square broad means literally changing her mind[53]

The outcome of successful seasoning is "perfect obedience in the newly procured woman."[54] As a result of this process, the pimp gains complete authority over the prostitute.

The pimp-prostitute relationship bears great resemblance to woman abuse. In fact, since pimps often establish cohabiting or even marital relationships with their prostitutes, pimping can be thought of as a special variety of woman abuse. Accounts of woman abuse include examples of husbands either pimping battered wives or forcing them to have unpaid sex with certain individuals.[55] Linda Lovelace's autobiographical work recounts how her former husband used violence to turn her out as a prostitute once they were married, eventually resulting in his forcing her to work as a pornographic film star.[56] Thus woman-battering can lead to pimping, and pimping always entails woman abuse.

Both prostitution and a violent conjugal relationship may be entered into by the female victim as a matter of either free choice, restricted choice among limited alternatives,[57] or no choice due to forcible coercion. Says Barry,

> Seasoning does not always precede prostitution. It is as effective in forcing some women to remain in prostitution as it is in putting others into it. Some women who willingly try out prostitution do not realize until later that they cannot get out. When they try to leave their pimp, the physical brutality and torture have the same effect as [they] would have had. . .earlier.[58]

Similarly, most battered women enter willingly into marriage or cohabitation with the batterer and do not experience abuse at his hands until after marriage/cohabitation.

According to Barry, the most common strategy used by pimps in order to obtain women to function as prostitutes is a technique similar to courtship. Barry calls this strategy "befriending or love and romance."[59]

> A procurer's goal is to find naive, needy teenage girls or young women, con them into dependency, season them to fear and submission, and turn them out into prostitution.[60]

> When a pimp hits on a female who is resistant, "prudish," or scared, he will not introduce prostitution immediately. He'll just be a nice guy who buys her a meal and offers her a place to stay. Finally he professes his love to her. When a sexual relationship between them is established and he is sure she loves him, he employs the "if you love me, you'll do anything for me" line. To prove her love she must have sex for money with [a stranger]. . . . If she resists or refuses, he will likely pout, . . .and insist that she does not truly love him. To restore his affections, she finally agrees. . . ., believing that one time won't hurt. He has her hooked. . . . After she turns one trick, he starts pimping her, giving her nightly quotas, taking the money she earns, and making her believe that she is truly a slut and that only he out of the goodness of his heart will have anything to do with such a despicable creature.[61]

Compare the above to the behavior of a batterer in counseling with the author:

> We'd been married a couple of years, and I was really bored with our sex life. I wanted to swing [i.e., to exchange sexual partners with another couple] and I told Liza that. When she wouldn't do it, I beat her up a few times—once real bad—and generally kept on her until she finally agreed. All along I felt she'd do this for me if she really loved me. Then, once we started swinging with different couples, I'd beat her up if she'd enjoyed sex with the other guy too much. I felt she had turned into a slut. But I kept pressuring her to do more and more degrading things in front of me with other guys. And she'd hesitate, and I'd say "If you really love me," and she'd agree, and then later I'd near kill her if she had enjoyed it or seemed to enjoy it.[62]

As shown by Barry, when a man courts a woman successfully, it will sometimes lead not to marriage but to forced prostitution. Conversely, woman-battering can closely resemble pimping when the batterer forces his female partner to have sex with others. Finally, as discussed previously, marriage can itself be a procuring or pimping method. Marriage to a prostitute gives the pimp certain legal advantages relative to an unmarried pimp-prostitute relationship. The prostitute/wife cannot be compelled to testify against a pimp who is her legal husband. The law recognizes the right of a pimp legally married to a prostitute to part of her earnings and other property as their communal property. He has a greater ability to get authorities to track down a fleeing wife as a missing person, than he would have if he asked authorities to help him recapture a fleeing prostitute who is not his legal wife.

The similarity between thought reform and seasoning demonstrates that forced prostitution is indeed a coercive control situation. That is, in this situation a powerful controller demands compliance of an individual dependent upon him, enforces that compliance with violence on some occasions, and either prevents the victim from escaping alive or makes this possibility very unlikely. It is also obvious that forced prostitution is so similar to woman-battering that it can be considered a type of woman abuse. Despite this, pimp-prostitute relationships are not generally conceptualized as relationships of a conjugal or familial nature. Thus, forced prostitution provides another close parallel to woman abuse that is nevertheless usually considered neither a conjugal nor a familial phenomenon.

It is frightening to think of conjugal or familial life as closely resembling either thought reform or forced prostitution. It is even more chilling when other coercive control situations are demonstrated to be all too pertinent to woman abuse. I am not the first to draw these analogies. Singer has shown the relevance of hostage situations and of coercive religious cults to the study of woman-battering.[63] Steinmetz has recognized the similarity between brainwashing and woman abuse.[64] Most influential upon my current approach to coercive control has been Camella Serum, whose work has related Bruno Bettelheim's descriptions of the treatment of concentration camp inmates to phenomena in woman abuse and has compared brainwashing to woman-battering.[65]

From these studies, it has become compellingly—though terrifyingly—obvious that some conjugal relationships or families resemble a prison or concentration camp or torture chamber more than they exemplify the usual, positive connotations of the words "couple" or "family." The following news article illustrates how a familial home can be converted quite literally into a prison.

> "Children freed from father's jail." Melbourne, Australia (AP)—Police stormed a fortress-like home here. . .to free the last of eight children jailed up to ten years by their father. . . .
>
> The four children still inside, aged 2 to 12, were freed. . .about 7 a.m. as their father. . .slept.
>
> The children were found healthy though unnaturally pale and one of them screamed as she was brought outside because she had not seen normal light for many months. . . .
>
> [The father], whose wife also lived in the house, was charged with four counts of unlawful imprisonment and one of assault.
>
> Police learned of the children's captivity. . .from. . .neighbors of the family who were told of the bizarre situation by [the] 16-year-old daughter.
>
> She broke out of the intensely-guarded house. . .after her father slapped her for eating food other than at the one prescribed daily meal allowed under his rigid rules. . . .
>
> Soon afterwards, three of the older children fled. . . .
>
> The house was boarded-up with blacked out windows; rigged with alarms and sirens; surrounded by floodlights and had a 15-foot-high galvanized iron fence. . .that set off the alarm system when touched.[66]

One wonders how the teenaged daughter managed to escape in the first place; conjecture along these lines summons up images from tales of escape by prisoners of war. Perhaps she tunneled out of the family compound.

WHEN IS A FAMILY NOT A FAMILY?

The ordinary connotations of "family" include love, gentleness, warmth, intimacy, and safe haven.[67] While "family" may carry for some people overtones of conflict, inhibition, distance, and betrayal, these latter connotations of family are much more unusual than the positive ones at the top of this paragraph. Most certainly, few people—if any—mentally associate "family" with imprisonment or torture. Even persons with excellent reasons to equate family with danger, terror, and abuse do not seem to do so.

> I asked Johnny why he only associated with members of his family. The question truly perplexed me because I perceived his family as dangerous, if not downright lethal. To explain my bewilderment, I recited to him a long series of betrayals, violations, and assaults committed by his family. Some of the more lurid examples included: Johnny's father routinely firing guns in the house and regularly assaulting Johnny's mother with a knife; severe beatings of the children by each parent; Johnny's uncle raping Johnny's mother in full view of most of her children; his uncle's later attempted rape of Johnny's wife; death threats—often punctuated with gunfire—from all but one of his brothers and male cousins. Despite all of this, and more, Johnny visited almost all of his nearby relatives on a regular basis, and had no friendships—or even strong acquaintanceships— outside of his family. He explained this to me:

> "These people are my family, my blood. Nobody's going to love me or treat me better than them. I figure if they pull all these stunts on me, I can't afford to trust strangers. Outsiders'll just raise even worse hell."[68]

It is extremely difficult to maintain simultaneous awareness of the family as the nurturant haven it should be and as the tormenting prison that it all too often is. Such awareness is important to halting domestic abuse, however. If blinded by the positive connotations of family to its potential for torture and coercive control, helpers and policy makers will be, at best, ineffective in halting family violence, and they more likely will unintentionally help perpetuate abuse.

Marital and family therapists know better than to undertake systems-oriented therapy interactions with a captor and his hostage(s). Yet, through ignorance of coercive control in domestic situations, many marriage counselors and family therapists attempt family systems therapy with violent couples or families who in essence constitute captor-hostage relationships. I would hope that intervenors and policy makers concerned with preserving and strengthening families do not intend to promote battering or domestic coercive control, but that they also do so unintentionally, through ignorance.

In order to overcome the problems and potential disservices caused by a definition of family that includes coercive control situations, I would like to suggest redefining our concept of family. The only acceptable alternative to such a redefinition is to increase public cognizance that a family can literally be a torture chamber and, at this point in history, often is. Continued widespread ignorance of domestic torture and captivity is, of course, unacceptable.

I recommend dividing the concept of family as currently defined[69] into two subsets—families and familoids. The basic body integrity or inviolability of all members would be a new, additional criterion for a group related by ancestry, marriage, and/or adoption to be classified as a family. Relatively unrestricted movement of all members—appropriate to their age and mental capabilities—is here considered to be a vital aspect of bodily integrity.

Familoid is a word I have created by combining *family* and the suffix *-oid*. A familoid is very similar to a family; it is a group that would otherwise be termed a family except that at least one member is subjected to coercive control at the hands of another member. In a familoid, at least one member poses a serious threat to the life and/or sexual integrity and/or free movement of at least one other member. The most common types of familoids involve severe woman abuse and/or severe child abuse.

I have invented the term *familoid* for the following purposes. The concept of familoid is intended to communicate the principle that there are certain extreme domestic situations—familoids—in which family therapy should not be conducted with the entire group. The issue of preserving or strengthening the family cannot apply to familoids since a familoid is, by definition, not a family. Somewhat less important, the novelty of the term familoid is also meant to lend added impact to the concept that some groups related by ancestry, conjugal relationship, and/or adoption resemble prisons or coercive control situations more than they resemble a family. Familoid, then, should introduce an important clarifying distinction for use by intervenors and policy makers, between ordinary families and extraordinarily dangerous "nonfamily" families.

The new word is not very important. What is important is for helpers to realize that not every family should be preserved and/or offered family therapy together. What is important is for the public to recognize that extremely violent domestic groups no longer merit the label "family" —with its positive connotations—and that consequently battered women's shelters do not "break up families," but rather assist the survivors of families that have already been destroyed from within.

It may be that it is unnecessary to coin a new label—"familoid" or whatever—to convey the above messages effectively. At present, however, the argument that battered women's programs cannot break up families that have already ceased to function as families often functions to no avail, falling instead on deaf ears. I would hope that the device of using familoid—a new term that captures the concept of a dangerous pseudo-family—will help overcome some of these difficulties.

PART II

THE CURRENT STUDY

Chapter 6

METHOD

SETTING

The settings from which the subjects for the study were obtained are the main service of the Domestic Violence Project—SAFE (Shelter Available For Emergency) House—and its affiliated program of counseling for violent mates. I will often refer to these settings simply as the shelter and the counseling service or batterers' counseling service. The Domestic Violence Project (DVP) is a nonprofit corporation that evolved from a feminist task force on woman abuse that began in 1975, sponsored by the National Organization for Women. Incorporated in 1976 as the NOW Domestic Violence Project, DVP began with two functions: 1) providing shelter to battered women in the homes of volunteers; and 2) seeking an independent facility as a source of temporary refuge for battered women. The shelter facility—SAFE House—was opened on March 1, 1978, and consists of a house in a secret location in the Ann Arbor area.

In May 1979, DVP started providing counseling to violent mates. The rationale for this was to break the cycle of conjugal violence by helping batterers halt their violent behavior. This counseling was provided at a public office at first located in Ann Arbor, and then moved to Ypsilanti in July 1981.

SAFE House is Washtenaw County's main shelter for battered women. It provides temporary shelter for battered women and their children. Residents may stay at SAFE House for up to 30 days (a time limit that is extended in case of need) in order to recuperate from assaults, to avoid sustaining further assaults or threatened initial assaults, and to plan for their futures. Most often their future plans involve the decision whether to continue their marriage/relationship or to seek to terminate it. Peer counseling is provided at the shelter to the women residing there in order to assist them in their choices by informing them of their legal rights, available community resources, and options. As a matter of policy, SAFE House workers do not suggest to the women what they should do next in their lives. Residents are neither encouraged nor discouraged from making a given decision. SAFE House endorses the right of women to determine their own destinies—to terminate or to resume a relationship, to take or to relinquish possession of their property, to maintain or to relinquish custody of their children—as they desire for themselves. Residents are free to end their stay in the shelter at any time.

SAFE House is one of the oldest battered women's shelters in the United States. As such, it is in many ways a prototypical battered women's shelter. Other, newer shelters have adopted SAFE House as a model or have used training materials based upon the work of SAFE House. This may be an important consideration in relation to the potential for generalizing the results of this study to apply to battered women taking shelter elsewhere.

The shelter has a peak capacity of about 25 persons—a few more if the resident population includes infants who sleep in cribs. The average stay in shelter is nearly two weeks. Over two-thirds of the women—nearly all of the women with offspring not yet fully grown—bring their children with them to the shelter. While the main purpose of SAFE House is to provide temporary shelter for women battered by their male partners/husbands, the shelter is occasionally used by women who are in different predicaments. These include battered daughters, battered mothers or mothers-in-law, women battered by their female lover, and survivors of rape and/or incest. The shelter does not provide residence to adult males.

The shelter serves as a referral and advocacy service for residents. Residents are referred to any social, legal, law enforcement, medical, mental health, vocational, educational, or other services that they may need or desire. Shelter workers—women's advocates, to use their official job title—do their utmost to ensure the quality of shelter life and, also, of outside services to shelter residents. They advocate for shelter residents if and when they receive less-than-optimal services from another agency. There is a program of child care, including preventive education about violence and sexual abuse. During the school year, children residing in the shelter attend classes in the local school system at their appropriate grade level.

To gain entry into SAFE House, a woman must be an adult or emancipated minor who either has been assaulted by one of the following—her husband, her cohabitant partner, a noncohabitant partner, a former husband/lover—or is in imminent danger of an assault by her intimate or formerly intimate partner. As previously noted, some occasional exceptions to these criteria are made for women victimized by other forms of familial and/or sexual violence. The prospective shelter resident must be assessed by shelter workers as psychologically capable of functioning adequately in the communal environment of the shelter. Therefore, women with acute psychiatric problems or chronic, severe psychiatric disabilities are often refused entry to SAFE House and referred elsewhere. Similarly, a prospective resident must be judged free from chemical dependency upon alcohol, narcotics, or unprescribed drugs in order to be admitted. She must be relatively free of acute medical problems or else she will likely be referred to a hospital. She must be willing to abide by the rules of the shelter, which stipulate curfew hours; maintenance of the secrecy of the shelter location; no use of alcohol or other recreational drugs during her stay; and nonviolence, including refraining from corporal punishment of children in the shelter. On occasion, a prospective shelter resident will decide against entering the shelter because she objects to one or more of the rules. If the shelter is full to capacity, a woman calling for shelter will either be wait-listed for entry or will be referred to other nearby shelters, as she prefers. Finally, a prospective resident with good alternative sources of safe emergency shelter is sometimes advised not to come to the shelter, but, instead, to utilize one of her alternatives for shelter and to stay in touch by phone. This occurs most often when the shelter is near its capacity in order to conserve shelter space for battered women in more urgent need.

The DVP batterers' counseling services primarily provide individual, group, and crisis hotline counseling to people who have assaulted their partners or who fear they may imminently become violent with their conjugal partners. In all cases, the purpose of counseling is to enable counseling clients to halt or to prevent conjugal abuse. Couples and family counseling is also occasionally offered at DVP. In most couples, one member is the batterer and the other the battered partner; these can be termed "unilaterally violent couples." In couples and family counseling cases, the batterer is treated as the index client. In a very few client couples, both partners are deemed equally violent—that is, of equal physical danger to one another and of equal likelihood to initiate a conjugal assault—and both partners are treated as index clients. This latter type of couple will be called a "reciprocally violent couple."

Counseling sessions are generally offered once per week at the public office of the DVP. The counselor is also available any time that he is home to take crisis phone calls from clients. Clients are directed and encouraged to use the crisis hotline as an alternative to violent behavior. While both the batterers' counseling service and SAFE House are affiliated as branches of the DVP, DVP batterers' counseling clients are not necessarily the partners of SAFE House residents; only about 40% of batterers' counseling clients are SAFE House residents' partners. Therefore, the battered partners of the counseling sample are to be distinguished from SAFE House residents, and the assailant partners of SAFE House residents are likewise to be distinguished from batterers' counseling clients.

The vast majority of counseling clients are men who batter their wives/partners. Only a very few of these abusive men come from reciprocally violent couples; the bulk of the couples are unilaterally violent. Even rarer than reciprocally violent couples among batterers' counseling clients are women who unilaterally assault their husbands/partners. The counseling service has, on occasion, served gay and lesbian batterers. It has also occasionally served clients who were otherwise involved in domestic violence: battered men, battered women, child abusers, parent abusers, adult survivors of child abuse, sibling abusers.

In order to obtain batterers' counseling at DVP, a client needs only to agree to work with the counselor on halting his violent behavior. As of this writing, clients are expected to pay for counseling services if they are financially able to do so. The counseling clients to be discussed in this study were offered free counseling services, however. Over 90% of batterers' counseling clients are voluntary, while the rest initiate counseling as a condition of a probation sentence. However, of the voluntary clients in abusers' counseling, nearly all initiate counseling either after their partner has left them (for temporary shelter or for permanent residence elsewhere) or because their partner has threatened to leave unless they undertake counseling to end their violence. Only a tiny minority of counseling clients speak of ending their violence as their priority irrespective of whether their marriage/relationship continues. Consequently, it appears that the primary motivation for clients initiating batterers' counseling is their wish to resume, or to maintain, their threatened marriage or primary affectional relationship. It will be useful to recall the preceding as discussion now turns to the method of the study.

METHOD

The present study involves two subject samples, one composed of SAFE House residents and one of DVP batterers' counseling clients. The SAFE House sample consists of 300 consecutive residents who took refuge at the shelter between September 1978 and October 1980, and who were battered by their male conjugal partners. Women taking shelter from other sorts of violence were not included in the study sample. Also, a few women were sheltered at SAFE House on multiple occasions during the period studied. In these cases, only data regarding the woman's first shelter stay were included for use in this study.

The counseling sample consists of 119 men who received batterers' counseling at DVP during my tenure there as a paid batterers' counselor (May 14, 1979 through December 31, 1981). All 119 of the men were assessed as unilaterally violent woman abusers. Those few counseling clients who came from reciprocally violent couples were excluded from this study, as were counseling clients who were violent female partners, battered men, or involved in other ways in family violence.

Most of the data used here come from two sources: 1) SAFE House intake forms for the shelter sample, and 2) batterers' counseling files, especially intake information, for the counseling sample. Reports by the partners of counseling clients about the pattern of abuse they endured were collected when possible, either from SAFE House intake forms or from direct interviews that I conducted. Also, in December 1981, 21 shelter workers and ex-shelter workers were distributed a questionnaire about their judgments as to whether or not the former shelter residents studied had resumed cohabitation with their abusive partner within one year of departure from SAFE House. The only other data source used was public divorce records available at the Washtenaw County Clerk's office.

Data was gathered from the shelter sample concerning 43 variables. Four of these were scored on two coding scales apiece, resulting in a total of 47 possible raw variable scores collected for each shelter resident. A list of these 47 variables, with their associated definitions and coding scales, appears in Appendix A. Some further variable scores were derived from the raw data scores. For example, the age difference between each pair of partners was computed based on the ages given for each shelter resident and her abusive partner.

Forty-one of the 43 shelter sample variables studied were derived from information on the SAFE House intake form. A sample shelter intake form appears in Appendix B. The shelter intake forms have good face validity. They are designed to record relevant information in a way that promotes clear and easy administration. Shelter workers are trained to administer intake questionnaires in order to ensure consistency in the administration of the forms and in the definitions used in gathering information. While the intake form is designed primarily as a tool for case management, many questions on the form were included for the secondary purpose of research about battered women and their families. The shelter intake forms remained nearly unchanged throughout the period of the study, with only one major exception, as follows.

The question about the number of conjugal assaults sustained by a shelter resident was typically gathered through an open-ended question, "How many times have you been assaulted by partner?" For the first 49 of the 300 cases studied, however, the form provided for the number of assaults to be recorded as a positive number from 1 through 7, or else as "Innumerable" for women assaulted eight or more times. The "Innumerable" response was not scored for purposes of this study, but was treated as a missing response.

Responses such as "innumerable," "countless," "lost count," "too many to say for sure," were also quite common among the 251 cases where the number of assaults was gathered by open-ended questioning. All responses of this kind were left unscored. This situation clearly poses some problems in the interpretation of statistical analyses involving the number of assaults. In an effort to handle this difficulty, a variable was included which categorized the number of assaults into three divisions: 1) 0-3 assaults; 2) 4-7 assaults; and 3) 8 or more assaults. On this latter variable, responses like "countless" and "innumerable" were scored in the third category, "8 or more assaults." This still does not resolve all of the problems in analyzing data concerning the number of assaults as shall be seen later when the results of this study are described.

For most shelter sample variables, I could assume good interscorer reliability for the information recorded. Variables of this type would refer to objective facts that were not very charged emotionally such as the woman's age, how many children she had, her place of residence, her partner's age, and his occupation. Inspection of the records of 16 shelter residents who were readministered intake questionnaires as they returned for multiple shelter stays confirmed the above assumption; there was enormous consistency for each of these respondents between information gathered in intakes administered independently on each entry into shelter.

There were certain variables derived for the shelter sample which seemed more susceptible to a possible lack of interscorer reliability. These variables seemed more likely to be affected by the set of the intake worker because they included information that was more qualitative and more emotionally charged than other variables. Therefore, one-way, fixed effects analyses of variance were conducted to investigate whether there was a significant interscorer difference among the 40 intake workers on any of the following variables:

> number of times assaulted; annualized rate of the recent frequency of assaults; severity of worst assault; severity of last assault; whether resident's mother was a battered woman; whether the shelter resident was physically abused as a child by her parents; whether the woman alleged child abuse by her partner; whether the resident reported substance abuse by her partner; whether the resident sustained assaults while she was pregnant; and whether the shelter resident ever employed forcible self-defense against conjugal assaults.

The analyses of variance conducted revealed that there were no significant interscorer differences in recording any of the above variables. Nearly significant interscorer differences ($.05 < p < .20$) were found concerning the severity of assaults. Closer inspection showed that these results derived primarily from interviews conducted by a particular worker. This worker functioned as a backup intake worker who was specifically assigned less urgent intake cases when other workers were occupied with emergencies. Consequently, it would seem that the less severe scores she recorded did not result from inconsistency in the administration of intake questionnaires but, instead, resulted from the process of assigning workers to intake duties. In conclusion I feel confident that there was good interscorer reliability for all of the shelter sample variables studied.

Rather than describe at this time the definitions and scoring criteria used in determining scores on each variable, most of these descriptions will be deferred until the discussion of the study results in Chapters 7 through 10. This will make it easier for the reader to recall the relevance of scoring procedures to the statistical results derived. In the meantime, the reader can refer to the appropriate appendix for a list of the criteria used in scoring and defining the data collected from the two samples. Discussion will be limited for now to the procedures used for determining the outcome of shelter residents' relationships with their violent partners.

Each of the 21 shelter workers was sent an outcomes questionnaire regarding all of the women who had been in SAFE House concurrently with the worker's employment there. For each former resident, the worker was asked to indicate to the best of her knowledge whether or not the woman had resumed cohabiting with her abusive partner within one year of her exit from SAFE House or whether this information was unknown to the worker. Nineteen of the 21 workers returned the completed questionnaire, a response rate of 90.5%.

In order to determine whether residents resumed or terminated cohabitation with the batterer after they left SAFE House, the following standards were used. Cohabitation was rated as having terminated under the following circumstances: if two or more shelter workers unanimously agreed that the given woman had not resumed cohabiting with her abuser; if at least two-thirds of a group of at least four shelter workers agreed that the woman had not resumed cohabiting with her original partner; if a less-than-two-thirds majority of workers were corroborated by objective proof that cohabiting had not resumed; or if there was clear documentation that cohabiting had not resumed, regardless of shelter worker judgments on this issue. The same criteria were applied in reverse for rating cohabitation as having resumed after the woman left SAFE House: unanimous agreement by at least two shelter workers that cohabiting had resumed; or two-thirds agreement among at least four workers; or a simple majority of workers corroborated by objective proof; or irrefutable objective documentation that cohabiting had resumed.

In some cases, it became clear that a woman had resumed cohabiting with her abusive partner, but had later separated from him for at least one year prior to the administration of the outcomes questionnaire. For these cases a third outcomes category was added, "cohabitation currently terminated after initial recohabitation." In other cases, it was clear that cohabitation had ended for at least one year prior to the outcomes investigation, but it was unknown whether there had been any intervening period of resumed cohabiting between the woman's exit from the shelter and the outcome investigation; this type of outcome formed a fourth category. If none of the above criteria applied, or if the woman came from a noncohabitant relationship, then the outcome of the relationship could not be assigned to any of the above four categories and the outcome was therefore considered unknown. To recapitulate, the four scoreable categories of the shelter outcomes variable were: 1) cohabitation terminated with no resumption; 2) cohabitation resumed; 3) cohabitation resumed at first, but has since terminated for at least a year; and 4) cohabitation terminated, but not known if there was a period of resumed cohabitation after the woman left the shelter.

From the original four category outcome variable just described were derived two additional outcomes variables. Both additional variables were divided into two simple categories and are therefore dichotomous variables. The first variable simply recorded whether or not there was any resumption of cohabiting after each resident left the shelter. The other dichotomous outcome variable reflected whether or not cohabitation was terminated by the time of the study's outcomes investigation. Criteria for considering an outcome to be unknown were identical for all outcomes variables.

Using the above method, outcomes could be rated for 187 shelter residents' conjugal relationships, leaving the outcome unknown in 113 cases. In 85.9% of their individual judgments on outcomes, the shelter worker's rating was the same as the final outcome rating for the given resident's relationship. This represents high reliability for the outcomes ratings.

The counseling sample data includes 37 variables, four of which were scored on two coding scales apiece, resulting in a total of 41 possible raw variable scores gathered from each counseling client. A list of these 41 variables, with their associated definitions and coding scales, appears in Appendix C. Some further variable scores were derived from the original 41 variables scored, similar to the method described for the shelter sample.

All but a dozen of the counseling sample variables studied were obtained from the DVP batterers' counseling files, especially the intake form. The other dozen variables were gathered from the battered women partners of the counseling clients. These latter data were obtained for 89 partners of the 119 clients, either from SAFE House intake forms or from direct interviews. In all, 48 of the counseling clients (40.3%) were partners of SAFE House residents. Of these 48, only 25 had partners who were included in the shelter sample, while the other 23 had partners who were not included in the shelter sample because they arrived at SAFE House after the October 1980 close of the study period for the shelter sample. Of the 71 counseling clients not involved with SAFE House residents, I was able to interview 41 of their partners (57.7%).

The intake form and intake procedures were consistent throughout the period studied. A sample DVP batterers' counseling intake form appears in Appendix D. I saw all 119 counseling clients in my role as batterers' counselor, and all data come from case records pertaining to the clients. In order to test whether I changed my data collection methods over time and, thus, affected the reliability of the data gathered, the sample was divided in half, into the first 60 and the following 59 cases. One-way, fixed effects analyses of variance were conducted comparing the data gathered from the two halves of the sample for each variable. These analyses of variance revealed no significant effects attributable to my procedures as counselor and researcher.

Four significant results were derived, however, from the analyses of variance for the 41 variables. The earlier clients had as a group attended significantly more counseling sessions and had recorded longer periods of nonviolence than the later clients. These results obviously occurred because the first 60 clients had a substantially longer period of time in which to attend sessions and to accrue a record of nonviolent behavior. The two other significant results of these analyses are: 1) the first 60 clients as a group reported significantly shorter (p<.02) average intervals between intake and the first conjugal assault in their relationship; and 2) the partners of the earlier clients on the average reported almost significantly (p=.051) more severe last assaults prior to intake than did partners of the later clients. It is clear to me that these results have nothing to do with my methods of gathering data and, thus, do not demonstrate any lack of reliability in the data collection procedures for the counseling sample.

It remains uncertain whether the above significant outcomes of the analyses of variance of the interval since the first conjugal assault and of the woman's report of the severity of the last assault are due to random factors or to change in the clientele over time. The only change of which I am aware is that later clients were as a group less likely to have experienced their partner's departure for shelter. One would expect two significant results (p<.05) in a battery of 41 statistical analyses in any case, and so it may very well be that these latter two significant results are indeed due to random chance. In any event, they appear to pose no problems for the interpretation of the study results.

LIMITATIONS OF THE PRESENT STUDY

The two major data-gathering instruments in this study are the intake forms from SAFE House and the DVP batterers' counseling service. Both of these forms were designed primarily as tools for case management and only secondarily as research tools. Both forms are psychologically unsophisticated; neither form collects data pertaining to intrapsychic factors, personality variables, nor subjective experiences. Both forms rely instead upon social and familial data of a relatively objective nature. Some desirable sociological data pertaining to the subjects are also unavailable. The chief example of this is the educational level of shelter residents and of batterers' counseling clients, which was not asked because it was considered unnecessary and somewhat demeaning to clients to be questioned about their education by workers who were generally—and often obviously— college educated.

The shelter form in particular can be a rather crude research device. Often it poses questions without giving the kind of clear definitions that would be preferred for research purposes. The specific implications of this problem will be discussed in detail whenever appropriate in the account of the results of this study. For now, I will take one example to illustrate this problem of vagueness. The shelter sample data regarding the women's childhood exposure to conjugally violent parents are derived from answers to the question, "Was your mother a battered woman?" Often residents asked the intake worker for the intended definition of a battered woman, but, far more often, they merely replied "Yes" or "No," using their own subjective definitions. Thus, no uniform definition of a battered woman or woman abuse was applied to the data for this variable, and the nature of the predominant functional definition in the sample is unknown. This problem of unstated definitional criteria applies to much of the data from the shelter sample and for some of the counseling sample data as well. I will be careful to reveal this problem and its implications whenever it is relevant to the discussion of the study results.

It is important to remember that the data obtained and the research results derived in this study will reliably apply only to battered women accepted as SAFE House residents and to woman batterers in counseling at DVP. That is, the data does not represent battered women in general nor woman abusers in general, but only those who sought and received the services of DVP. The results are likely to be generalizable to battered women and violent male partners receiving services at similar programs around the country, but this generalizability is not guaranteed and is, of course, difficult to substantiate. In making inferences about the data, one must bear in mind that members of violent couples who get help at domestic violence programs probably differ in some ways from battered women and woman abusers in general. The works of Gelles and of Carlson, mentioned earlier, are the only empirical studies of which I am aware that indicate some possible differences between battered women who receive outside assistance and those who do not.[1]

Obviously, the criteria for acceptance into SAFE House, described earlier, affect the research results and their relevance to other residents of women's shelters. The rules and procedures for accepting shelter residents influence the characteristics of the shelter sample, and in a way that may differ from procedures at other battered women's shelters. Fortunately for the goal of applying this research elsewhere, many shelters for battered women employ similar admission practices. This is due in part to the role that SAFE House has played as a prototypical shelter and, in part, to commonalities in the shelter experience across the nation.

Both the shelter and counseling sample characteristics are affected by the surrounding community from which the clients come. The counseling sample is undoubtedly influenced by the predominant motives of the batterers in initiating counseling—to maintain or to regain their ongoing relationship with their abused partner or to fulfill a probation sentence.

Batterers who enter counseling at DVP clearly form a small minority of all the woman abusers in the surrounding community: 119 clients were seen in two-and-a-half years, while it can be conservatively estimated that over 2000 men batter their wife/female partner each year in Washtenaw County alone. Only about one-eighth of all partners of SAFE House residents ever receive batterers' counseling from DVP. Batterers who are willing or eager to let go of their mates are certainly not adequately represented among the counseling sample members, about 90% of whom came to counseling in order to retain or to retrieve their partner.

A further limitation of this study involves the problem of conceptualizing and measuring the severity of conjugal abuse. The current study uses only objective behavioral measures of physical abuse, thus neglecting verbal and emotional forms of abuse, and treating sexual abuse as if it were psychologically identical in its impact to other forms of physical abuse. While a substantial proportion of battered women—perhaps a majority— report that verbal, emotional, and/or sexual abuse caused them the most misery, studies of conjugal abuse have not thus far attempted to address the issue of nonphysical abuse in their efforts to conceptualize levels of severity of conjugal abuse. The notion of different degrees of severity of abuse is important for some aspects of the study of conjugal abuse—e.g., for documenting the hypothesized escalation of abuse as the marriage/ relationship continues. In any case, this study fails to improve upon the existing literature by also measuring the severity of conjugal abuse based upon behavioral measures of physical violence.

The data from both the shelter sample and the counseling sample utilize two scales as indexes of the severity of woman abuse—the CRT and Gelles scales already described in Chapter 2 and also listed in Appendix B.[2] These scales have many deficiencies as measures of the severity of violence. They are certainly not interval scales, and are not reliable as ordinal reflections of the injury or life threat created by a particular assault. Consider this example, using the Gelles scale. A slap can be fatal—e.g., an open-handed karate blow, while pushing someone down can be much less physically damaging. When scoring on the Gelles scale, however, pushing someone down is always scored "6" while a slap is always scored "4." The use of these scales in the current study is further complicated by the fact that they were not designed for collecting data from clinical records, but for use in face-to-face survey research interviews. Despite all of these problems, short of developing a new scale for measuring the severity of conjugal abuse, these scales are the best measure available for use in the current study.

Since most of the data for both samples were obtained from counseling interactions—especially intake interviews—there was inevitably some altering of interview procedures to meet the needs of various clients. This occurred despite the overall consistent guidelines for intake interviews because the interviews were first and foremost service-oriented and functioned only secondarily as research interviews. In particular, when shelter residents or batterers' counseling clients were emotionally or physically overtaxed by interviews, the interviews were greatly abbreviated. Interviews would be cut short, for example, if a shelter resident was exhausted, or if a counseling client was late and another client was awaiting his appointment, or if clients at either setting were very upset or agitated. The above procedures resulted in a great deal of missing data. Large sample sizes were chosen for this study because of this issue, and also because many unknown outcomes ratings were expected regarding the shelter sample.

ADVANTAGES OF THE STUDY

There are also advantages, however, in deriving data from clinical interactions. Help-oriented interviews promote greater self-disclosure than survey research that has no obvious direct benefit to the respondents. Furthermore, the batterers' counseling interactions promoted higher and more reliable reporting rates for various stigmatized behaviors in the following way: these interactions offered me much material that I could judge for myself, rather than relying solely upon client self-assessments. Thus, many counseling clients initially claimed that they had nonviolent family backgrounds, but they later recounted incidents that were clearly physically abusive. Clients in these cases had either suppressed reporting these incidents to me, or had repressed memories of these incidents from themselves, or else quite often they did not themselves judge the incidents to be abusively violent. My consequent knowledge of these events resulted in much more reliable information concerning violence in the families of origin of the counseling clients than could be obtained through survey research.

The principal advantage of the current study is that it undertakes statistical analyses of many factors that have important theoretical, empirical, and clinical implications. As was discussed in the literature review chapter, tests of the statistical significance of empirical findings have been far too scarce in the literature on conjugal abuse. Another advantage is that this study could be undertaken with relative ease and rapidity. This advantage offsets to some extent the disadvantage of not having more sophisticated research instruments. Unfortunately, it would require two years or more to design better research instruments and administer them to comparably large samples of battered women in shelter and woman abusers in batterers' counseling.

THE HYPOTHESES TO BE TESTED

The hypotheses tested in the present study were in large part determined by the nature and availability of the relevant data. I did not generate a protocol of theories or hypotheses to test, and then design my data-gathering techniques accordingly. Rather, the available data in DVP files were examined to see which hypotheses could be tested. This admittedly represents a cart-before-the-horse strategy, but this is excusable because of the infancy of research in conjugal violence. Due to this approach, my expectations regarding the results of hypothesis-testing were of secondary importance to the opportunity to conduct statistical analyses of the available data.

There was one exception to the above strategy for designing the present study. Despite the lack of already available shelter outcomes data, I decided to gather information as to whether or not each shelter resident broke up with her abuser. This information was collected in order to investigate what factors would facilitate—or impede—a battered woman's ability to leave the batterer. This issue was chosen for study because I had a unique opportunity to gather reliable shelter outcomes data by surveying my co-workers at DVP and because of the popularity of the question of why battered women stay with their violent mates.

The statistical analysis in this study can be divided into five different categories, according to the type of hypotheses tested. These categories are: 1) hypotheses as to whether the sample populations differ significantly from the overall population with respect to a given variable; 2) hypotheses about the congruence—or lack thereof—between victims' and perpetrators' reports about the woman abuse they have endured/committed; 3) hypotheses about predictors of whether or not the battered woman's abusive relationship will terminate or continue; 4) hypotheses about predictors of the magnitude of woman abuse, across battering relationships; and 5) hypotheses concerning predictors of the outcome of batterers' counseling. Tests of the first category of hypotheses involved comparing the sample data to available census statistics on the overall population of heterosexual couples. The statistical procedures involved most often were Pearson X^2 statistics to compare overall distributions or else t statistics to compare the sample means with estimated population means.

The congruence between the reports by batterers' counseling clients and by their abused partners of the violence they have perpetrated/endured was tested by paired t tests of the differences between each batterer and his victimized partner in their reports regarding several variables measuring conjugal violence. Differences between shelter residents who terminated and those who resumed cohabiting with their abusers mostly were tested by either t tests of the difference between the means of the two groups on a given variable or by Pearson X^2 analysis of the distributions of the two groups over a given variable. Probit analysis of the relationship between shelter outcomes data and each measure of the magnitude of abuse was also undertaken to see if significant linear or curvilinear statistical relationships could be derived between these sets of variables.

Hypotheses regarding factors affecting the level of violence were tested by correlating violence variables with other variables. Some t tests were also used to compare mean levels of violence between two comparison groups—e.g., alcoholic and nonalcoholic batterers. When t tests could not be used due to unequal variances in the two comparison groups, Mann-Whitney U tests were applied instead. Relationships between batterers' counseling outcomes and other counseling sample variables were discovered by computing the correlations between each outcomes variable and the other counseling sample variables. For all five categories of hypotheses in the study, the null hypothesis in virtually every statistical test was that no difference (or no correlation) would be derived.

The literature review in Part I foreshadows much of the hypothesis-testing conducted in the present study. Also, reports of the published precedents for each specific statistical analysis in this study will accompany the descriptions of quantitative results in Chapters 7 through 10. Therefore, the hypotheses to be tested will for now be briefly enumerated without citations of their published foundations.

I expected both the batterers and the battered women studied not to deviate statistically from the overall population of couples on the following variables: age; age at marriage/cohabitation; race; and number of children. It was expected that shelter residents would not differ from Michigan women in general in their rate of employment outside the home. Batterers were expected to match the overall population of Michigan men in their level of educational achievement.

Based upon previous research, the study samples were expected to deviate from the overall population of couples regarding several characteristics. Age differences between partners were expected to be more extreme on average. The rate of premarital pregnancy resulting in live birth was expected to be higher. Overrepresentation of unmarried cohabitants relative to legal marrieds was expected; welfare recipients were expected to be disproportionately common among shelter residents. Batterers were hypothesized to have unusually high rates of unemployment, alcoholism or problem drinking, military service, childhood exposure to conjugal violence, and childhood exposure to child abuse. Based purely upon the clinical impressions of myself and other shelter workers, a relatively high prevalence of interracial couples was predicted for the two samples, as well as a high rate among shelter residents of previous subjection to child abuse.

Based on the woman abuse literature, the one existing empirical study, and my own clinical experience as a batterers' counselor, it was expected that the counseling clients in the sample would report less violence than their battered mates would report. Therefore, it was expected that, relative to his wife/partner, each member of the counseling sample would report committing fewer assaults, a lower estimated frequency rate of his assaults, less time elapsed since the first assault in the relationship, and less severe and less dangerous behavior by him as he perpetrated both the last and worst conjugal assaults.

Shelter residents who resumed cohabiting with their violent mates were expected to resemble battered women terminating cohabitation on the following variables: age, race, previous experience in counseling or psychotherapy, tendency to retaliate in physical self-defense, and involvement with an alcoholic batterer. Also, no linear or mean differences were predicted between these groups for the time elapsed since the first conjugal assault; the length of the relationship; the number, frequency, or behavioral severity of conjugal assaults experienced. These latter variables were also examined by probit analysis for expected curvilinear relationships consistent with coercive control theory. It was hoped that the abuser's involvement in the affiliated batterers' counseling program would not affect the likelihood of termination or resumption of cohabitation. However, I feared that the abuser's involvement in batterers' counseling would increase the likelihood of recohabitation since shelter residents with mates in counseling would have higher hopes for the abuser to reform.

Unmarried cohabitants were predicted to be more likely to break up than legal marrieds because they did not face the legal obstacle of divorce proceedings. Concomitant child abuse by the batterer was expected to be associated with a higher probability that the conjugal relationship would dissolve, as was the batterer having a record of violent extrafamilial crime. Shelter residents with prescriptions for psychoactive medications were expected to be more likely to remain in violent relationships than shelter residents not taking tranquilizers. Battered women resuming cohabitation with batterers were expected to have higher rates of childhood exposure to conjugal violence and to child abuse than battered women terminating cohabitation.

The number and the length of previous, conflict-related conjugal separations were expected to differentiate strongly between shelter residents terminating cohabitation and resuming cohabitation. Higher numbers of previous separations and longer separations were predicted to be associated with conjugal breakup. Similarly, shelter residents terminating cohabitation were expected on the average to have experienced previous separations more recently than recohabiting shelter residents. As an indicator of motivation to leave the relationship and take shelter, women ending their relationships were expected on the average to have traveled greater distances to the shelter.

The impact of economic resources upon the outcomes of shelter residents' relationships was reflected in several variables. I predicted that the more economic resources a battered woman had, the more likely it would be for cohabitation to end. Conversely, it was expected that the more monetary resources that the violent mate provided, the less likely cohabitation would be to end. Consequently, the following factors were expected to be associated with higher rates of conjugal breakup: paid employment for the battered woman; her receiving welfare payments; her having older, more independent children, or fewer children. Relationships where the battered woman provided more financial support than the batterer were expected to be particularly likely to terminate. Conversely, among shelter residents' mates, paid employment, higher levels of education, and higher occupational status were expected to be associated with cohabitation being more likely to resume.

In examining factors associated with higher levels of conjugal violence, I was especially interested in seeing if longer-lasting relationships tended to have higher levels of violence, if previous estrangement was associated with more serious conjugal violence, and if physical self-defense by the battered woman had a statistical tendency to be met with an escalation in the batterer's violence. I hoped to establish that there were no racial differences in the severity of violence. The correlations with the measures of the severity of violence were derived for every variable to see if any unforeseen statistical relationships would also crop up.

In similar fashion, all batterers' counseling sample variables were correlated with batterers' counseling outcomes to see what statistical relationships—if any—might be derived between counseling outcome and other factors. I expected higher levels of concordance between batterers' and victims' reports to be associated with better counseling outcomes. Greater numbers of assaults, more frequent and/or more severe assaults, violence during pregnancy, and the batterer having a violent family of origin were all expected to be associated with poorer outcomes in batterers' counseling.

CHARACTERISTICS OF THE SHELTER SAMPLE

The 300 shelter residents in the sample range in age from 16 to 55, with a median age of 26 and average age of 27.7 years at the time of the intake interview. Only 6.6% of the women were age 40 or over at intake, and only 9% were teenagers; 26.7% were in their 30s, while 57.6% were in their 20s, by far the most heavily represented decade. The racial mix of the women was 79.3% white, 16.7% black, and Asian and Hispanic, 2% each.

The women were accompanied to the shelter by an average of 1.84 children apiece. This does not reflect the total number of children that they had borne and/or reared since it excludes those left at home, adopted out, deceased, with relatives or previous husbands/partners of the residents, in boarding school, or living independently. Forty of the women (13.3%) brought no children with them; most of these 40 women were childless. Thirty percent brought one child to SAFE House, an additional 30% brought two, almost 16% brought three children, and under 11% brought four or more children to the shelter. No woman was accompanied by seven or more children, partly because of the shelter's limited capacity and partly due to other logistical difficulties. The children ranged in age from newborn to 22 years old. The average age of the youngest child of each mother in the shelter was 3.3 years; the average age of the eldest child in shelter with each mother was 7.2 years. Of the 260 women with children for whom data are available, 32.4% had given birth to at least one premaritally conceived child, and an additional 11.6% were raising one or more children without ever having been legally married to the fathers of their children.

Over 94% of the women had been residing in Michigan prior to taking shelter, with 5.7% coming to SAFE House from outside the state. Washtenaw County residents accounted for over half of the sample (51.4%), and were distributed within the county as follows: 30.4% of the entire sample were from Ypsilanti or Ypsilanti Township, 10% were from Ann Arbor, and 11% were from the out-county area. The six counties bordering Washtenaw County contributed almost 35% of the sample: 18.4% from Wayne County, 6% from Oakland, 5% from Monroe, 3% from Livingston, and the remainder from Jackson and Lenawee Counties. Genesee County was the only other county represented by a portion of the sample as large as 3%.

The violent mates of the shelter residents ranged in age from 17 to 65, with a mean age of 30.9 years and a median age of 28.8. The racial distribution of shelter residents' abusive partners was 71% white, 25% black, 3% Hispanic, 1% Asian, and less than 1% native American. Among 225 assailant partners for whom there is information, their mean and median educational levels were just over 11 years. Almost 53% of the men had either completed high school or passed a high school equivalency exam. Over 20% had studied at the college level, and over 6% had bachelor's or graduate degrees.

Turning to economic variables, 22% of the women in the shelter sample had full-time paid employment on intake, while 4% had paid part-time jobs, and two (0.7%) were laid off and receiving unemployment benefits. This leaves 73.3% of the women who apparently were full-time homemakers. A little over 30% of the women were receiving general assistance or ADC welfare benefits on intake. Nearly 37% of the women brought a car with them—usually their own, occasionally one borrowed from relatives or friends.

The shelter residents' mates had a full-time employment rate of 72.6%, including 5.1% self-employed. About 3.5% were not in the job market because they were either retired, disabled, or full-time students. The remainder of the assailants (26.4% of the 295 men for whom there is employment information) were not employed. These men would not necessarily be termed unemployed according to the Labor Department definition of able, available, and actively seeking work, however.

Looking at the relative income-earning status of the shelter residents and their respective mates, nearly 20% of the women were the sole income earner in their family (including women receiving welfare), while in nearly 35% of the couples, each member of the pair had an independent income source—i.e., "two-paycheck households." In almost 11% of the couples, there was no apparent income source whatsoever. The male partner was the sole income producer for nearly 35% of the couples represented in the shelter sample.

Almost 77% of the women were legally married to the batterer and cohabiting with him prior to shelter entry; one of these couples had divorced and remarried one another. Another 4.7% of the women were still legally married to their abusers, but they were legally or informally separated prior to taking shelter. Unmarried cohabitants composed 14% of the sample; 11.7% were still cohabiting just prior to intake, 1% were cohabiting with their divorced ex-husband, and 1.3% had separated prior to intake from their unmarried, formerly cohabitant partner. Noncohabitant relationships that had never been cohabitant composed 3.4% of the sample. Two women

(0.7%) were fleeing divorced ex-husbands with whom they were not cohabiting.

The length of the relationship/marriage between shelter residents and their partners ranged from less than one month long to 30 years and nine months, with a mean duration of six years and a median duration of four years, five months. The shelter residents had separated from their partners an average of 3.1 times apiece prior to taking shelter. Twenty-seven percent of the women had never left their male partners for a conflict-related conjugal separation of at least a day. Twenty-six percent had experienced a single previous separation, 17% had been separated twice, and 30% had separated from their partners three or more times. Over two-thirds of the women who had previously separated from their husbands had experienced at least one conjugal separation within one year of their entry into SAFE House. The mean length of their most recent previous separation was three months; its median length was about 27 days. Twenty-nine women had been separated from their partners for at least six months (16.3% of women with available information on this topic), and 11 had been separated at least one year (6.2%).

On the average, an interval of about four-and-three-quarters years had elapsed from the first assault in the relationship until the shelter intake. The median for this interval was three years. Six percent of the women were taking shelter within two months of the first conjugal assault that they had endured.

When asked how many assaultive incidents they had sustained at the abuser's hands, 91 women (33%) gave unscoreable responses such as "countless" or "innumerable." Considering only the 186 scoreable responses, the shelter residents had endured an average of 59 assaults each, with a median of 7.4 assaults each. These figures are conservative estimates for the sample as a whole since the excluded unscoreable responses reflect high numbers of assaults. Prior to intake, each woman had on the average been experiencing over five assaults every four weeks for an annualized frequency rate of over 65 conjugal assaults per year. Over 20% stated that they were being assaulted twice or more per week.

Sixty-two percent of the women who had ever been pregnant during their abusive relationships had been assaulted during a pregnancy; 4% knew that they were pregnant during the shelter stay. Fifty-four percent had forcibly retaliated in self-defense against the batterer on at least one occasion; 37% said that they did so sometimes, often, or usually. Seventy-eight percent of the sample arrived at SAFE House within one week of the last assault they had experienced. Half arrived within one day of the most recent violent incident.

About 90% of the sample had endured conjugal violence at least as severe as a punch. Two-thirds had experienced at least one assault where they were extensively beaten up, or worse. One in six had been threatened with a knife or gun by their partners, and one in 30 had been attacked with a knife or gun by her mate.

Taken together, the 300 women reported on intake a total of 28 fractures that they had sustained from assaults by their violent partners. The most commonly reported fractures reported were of the nose or jaw. The women also reported a total of 22 serious injuries not involving bone fractures. These included chronic back injuries, torn ligaments, dislocations, ruptured eardrums, broken teeth, lacerations, stab wounds, and bullet wounds. Twenty-five women—one in 12 of those sampled—reported forcible marital rape (or conjugal rape) or other forms of forced sex, and three reported knowing of incestuous assaults upon the children by the batterer.

Since all of the figures just discussed refer solely to injuries reported and recorded on intake at the shelter, and since the topic of previous injuries was not a major focus of the intake interview, all of these reports must be regarded as very conservative reflections of the injuries and sexual abuse sustained by the women in the shelter sample. The frequency of references on intake to marital rape and other forced sex is especially remarkable. Since sexual abuse is a very sensitive matter, it is most typical for sexually abused shelter residents to reveal the sexual abuse they have endured only after they have been in the shelter for a time and have developed trust in one or more of the women's advocates working there.

Despite the major injuries just discussed, only 24% of the battered women had ever received medical treatment for injuries sustained during a conjugal assault. Very often the women desired medical treatment, but they were prevented by their partners from obtaining it. Although a minority of the women had received medical treatment for the assaults, 69% of the women had experienced at least one conjugal assault that resulted in police intervention. Over 17% had received multiple visits from police related to incidents of woman abuse.

Over half (52%) of the women had received prior mental health services of some kind—counseling, psychotherapy, or marital therapy—not including the crisis counseling that resulted in their taking shelter. Eighteen percent of the sample brought psychoactive prescription medications with them to SAFE House. Minor tranquilizers were most common among these, accounting for over 44% of psychoactive prescriptions brought in, followed by prescription painkillers (32%). After the DVP batterers' counseling services had opened, 12% of the sample subjects' partners obtained at least one counseling session there. Overall, 8.3% of the shelter sample's violent mates were seen in the DVP counseling services.

The sample considered 68% of their partners to be either active or former problem drinkers. Nearly one-fourth of the batterers were alleged to abuse prescription drugs, of which amphetamines, minor tranquilizers, and barbiturates had the highest rates of abuse. One-third of the assailant partners were alleged by shelter residents to abuse nonprescription, "street" drugs. Marijuana was the overwhelming favorite in this latter category, figuring in nearly 92% of the street drug abuse specified. This last result probably is related to the decriminalized status of marijuana possession in Ypsilanti and Ann Arbor. One-third of the shelter sample's assailant partners were known by their mates to have been charged with violent crimes against persons outside their current conjugal relationship. Nearly one in six (15.7%) of the abusers had been convicted of at least one crime of extrafamilial violence.

Outcomes of the shelter residents' relationships were rated in 187 cases (62.3% of the sample). Of these 187 cases, 63.7% were known to have resumed cohabiting within one year of exit from SAFE House with the abuser who had originally driven them to take shelter at SAFE House. Of this latter group, however, about one in nine (7% of all known outcomes in the sample) were known to have experienced the long-term termination of cohabitation after one period of resumed cohabitation. For fifty-seven women (30.5% of known outcomes), cohabitation never resumed with the abuser from whom they had fled to the shelter. In 11 cases (5.9% of known outcomes), cohabitation had terminated by the time of the outcomes investigation, but it was unknown whether or not there had ever been an intervening period of recohabitation.

It was not entirely a matter of each shelter resident's preference whether cohabitation with the batterer resumed or ended after she left the shelter. Many of the relationship outcomes are directly attributable to the actions of the male partners. Frequently a man would forcibly intrude into his partner's new home and establish cohabitation with her in this way, regardless of her preference. In a few other cases, men refused to recohabit with shelter residents who were willing to do so. This is why the foregoing discussion of outcomes has been worded in terms of "cohabitation terminating or resuming," rather than referring to women terminating or resuming cohabitation.

CHARACTERISTICS OF THE COUNSELING SAMPLE

The 119 batterers' counseling clients who compose the counseling sample range in age from 19 to 55 years old, with an average age of 30.1

years and a median age of 28.5. Fifty-four percent were in their 20s, one third were in their 30s, 10% in the 40s, two clients were teenaged (1.7%), and two clients were between 50 and 55 years old. Over 77% were white, 21% black, and there was also one Asian client and one Hispanic client (0.8% each).

Nearly one third of the men had neither sired children nor had ever cohabited regularly with children. The rest had either fathered children, lived with children, or both. Of the men who had sired children, nearly half had either impregnated their legal wives premaritally (41.3%) or were raising their children without being legally married (8%). Overall, the rate of premarital pregnancy was 35.6% for the legally married men in the sample.

The area in which the counseling clients resided was bounded by Detroit on the east and Jackson on the west, by Flint to the north and the Ohio border to the south. Washtenaw County residents composed 71.8% of the group: 32.7% of the sample were from Ypsilanti, 23.6% from Ann Arbor, and 15.5% from the out-county area. Wayne County was represented by 14.5% of the sample. Livingston, Jackson, and Monroe Counties were the place of residence for four clients apiece (3.6% each). Two clients (1.8%) came from Hillsdale County, and one (0.9%) from Genesee County.

At the time of the counseling intake, 71.2% of the counseling sample were employed full time, including 8.5% who were self-employed. Twenty-two percent were unemployed on intake, 3.4% were disabled or retired, and 3.4% were full-time students. An additional 8.5% of the sample were employed when they initiated counseling, but they experienced at least one period of unemployment while they were still involved in counseling. The unemployment rate for the sample—excluding men who were disabled, retired, or students—therefore ranged between 23.6% and 32.7%.

Nearly three-fourths of the clients (72%) still were legally married to their partner: 59% said they were still cohabiting with their legal wife; 13% considered themselves separated. An additional client (0.8%) was divorced from his most recent partner. Eleven percent of the clients were from continuing unmarried cohabitant relationships; another 8% had cohabited unmarried, but they already considered the relationship separated or dissolved at the time of intake. The final 8% of the clients were involved in noncohabitant relationships. The length of involvement in the relationship averaged four-and-three-quarters years, and ranged from three months to over 31 years. About half of the clients (49.2%) came from relationships no longer than two-and-a-half years in duration.

The average interval between counseling intake and the date of the client's first reported conjugal assault in the then current relationship was three years, according to the clients' reports, and ranged from two weeks to almost 18 years. The clients' wives/partners reported an average interval of 4.7 years between the first conjugal assault and the counseling intake interview. Median time elapsed since the first assault was two years for the clients' reports, 3.1 years according to their partners.

Clients reported an average of 16.3 assaultive incidents that they had initiated during their marriages/relationships. The number of conjugal assaults reported by clients ranged from zero to "thousands" (scored and treated as 998 for the statistical purposes of this study). Nine percent of the clients insisted they had never assaulted their partners; I disbelieve all of these reports. Twenty percent said they had committed only one conjugal assault; only one of the 18 men in this group was corroborated by his woman partner as having committed a sole attack upon her. Over half of the men reported three or fewer assaults. The clients' 54 partners who reported scoreable quantities of the assaults that they had sustained reported an average of 37 assaultive incidents in their relationships, with a range from one to 998 violent incidents. The median for the women's reports was 5.8 assaults. Twenty-two percent of the women reported three or fewer assaults. Whereas just 4% of the men reported committing 20 or more conjugal assaults, 24% of the women reported enduring at least 20 conjugal assaults, and this latter percentage does not include several women who reported "countless" assaults. For 41 clients and their partners who each gave scoreable independent reports of the number of assaultive incidents, each batterers' counseling client reported an average of 45.4% as many assaults as did his mate. To say the same thing another way, each female partner of the 41 counseling clients reported an average of 120% more assaults than her partner had reported.

The annual frequency rate of assaultive incidents reported by the counseling clients ranged from 0 to 329 assaults per year—i.e., nine assaults every ten days, with an average estimated frequency rate of 11 assaults annually. The median frequency of conjugal attacks estimated by the men was once or twice per year—1.42, to be precise. For the 66 partners of counseling clients who gave estimates of the annual frequency rate of conjugal assaults, the derived average frequency rate was 40.6 assaults per year, while the range of responses was zero to 365 assaults annually. The median of the female partners' estimates was 8.5 attacks each year. Over 21% of these women stated that they were physically abused on at least a weekly basis, while only 3.7% of the men in counseling estimated that they perpetrated assaults weekly or more often than weekly.

Of 53 counseling clients who were involved with their partner during at least one pregnancy, 34% disclosed perpetrating an assault upon their pregnant mate. Of their 50 partners for whom information is available, 56% stated that they were assaulted while pregnant. Thirty percent of the counseling clients with children disclosed perpetrating physical child abuse, and another 12% disclosed perpetrating borderline child abuse. Forty-four percent of the wives/partners with children alleged child abuse by their partner, while 56% did not consider their mate to be child-abusive.

Over one-third of the counseling clients discussed assaultive incidents that they and/or the researcher classified as beatings. Four men (3.5%) stated they had assaulted their partners with a knife or gun on at least one occasion. Two-thirds of the men disclosed using violence against their mates at least as severe as punching. Nearly one out of five (18.5%) of the clients' female partners reported enduring at least one incident of conjugal assault involving a knife or gun. About half of the women reported beatings (48%). Together, about two-thirds (66.3%) of the partners of counseling clients reported violence at least as severe as beatings, and exactly seven out of every eight of the women reported sustaining conjugal violence at least as severe as punching.

The counseling clients had inflicted a variety of physical injuries upon their mates. Seven were known to have knocked their mates unconscious, and at least two more had strangled their partners to unconsciousness. At least two woman had required stitches to close cuts inflicted during assaults. One woman had contracted pleurisy after being beaten in the back. Another had experienced a very severe kidney bruise due to battering. Fractures were rife; as a group, the mates of the counseling clients had sustained at least 17 bone fractures, as well as numerous broken teeth. Seven of these fractures were facial—five of the nose and two of the jaw. There were also two known skull fractures, one of which resulted in nearly fatal epileptic seizures as an after effect. Six fractures involving the trunk were reported—four cases of broken ribs, one of broken vertebrae, and one of a broken collarbone. Two reported fractures involved an arm or a hand. Two wives of counseling clients were known to have sustained loss of vision from head injuries inflicted by their partners. The above undoubtedly is not an exhaustive list of the serious physical injuries inflicted by counseling clients upon their mates. It reflects only those injuries revealed to the counselor by the clients or by their battered partners.

Turning to the counseling clients' childhood exposure to family violence, over 71% of the sample were known to be reared in child-abusive families or environments; 69.3% revealed being childhood victims of physical and/or sexual abuse, while another 2% witnessed—without being directly victimized—the physical and/or sexual abuse of a sibling by their parent(s). Of those who specified their childhood abuser, 42% were abused solely by their father, 19% solely by their mother, and 17% by both natural parents. The other 22% were abused by other relatives, including step-parents, or by parent surrogates—e.g., workers in an orphanage. Two of every seven clients stated that they were not battered as children, but it is almost certain that some of these men would be considered to be formerly battered children if more were known about their histories.

Two-thirds of the clients reported knowing of conjugal abuse occurring between their parents or step-parents, or parent and his/her unmarried cohabitant partner while the client was a child. The great majority of these cases involved a father or father surrogate assaulting the mother or stepmother, but there were a few cases recorded of conjugal abuse committed by the mother or stepmother of a client against the father or stepfather. Looking at childhood exposure to some form of family violence, 79.8% of the counseling clients were undoubtedly exposed to either child abuse, conjugal abuse, or both, while there is no known childhood exposure to family violence for only 20.2%. This last percentage is a maximum estimate of the proportion of counseling clients who came from nonviolent family backgrounds; the actual proportion could well be lower.

In addition to exposure to family violence, it is known that 8.2% of the counseling sample were veterans of military combat. This represents over one-quarter of the military veterans in the clientele. In all, 29.1% of the sample were veterans of the military.

Fifty-six percent of the counseling clients considered themselves not to be problem drinkers, and another 5.5% considered themselves borderline cases with respect to problem drinking. About 21% presented themselves as successfully reformed alcoholics, and 17.3% had an ongoing, self-described problem with alcohol consumption. As counselor, I considered only 21% of my clientele to be unambiguously free from difficulties with alcohol, and I termed 4.6% to have borderline cases of problem drinking. I considered 10% of my clients to be successfully reformed alcoholics, and I assessed over 64% as having at intake an active alcohol problem. Just over half of the wives/partners interviewed considered their mates to be active problem drinkers, and another 2.6% termed their mates ex-alcohol abusers, leaving 47% of the women who considered their partner not to be a problem drinker.

Turning to other substance abuse, 39% of the clients disclosed that they abused drugs other than alcohol. Marijuana was by far the most prominently mentioned of these other drugs. To my knowledge, less than 2% of the clients were addicted to narcotics during their involvement in counseling. A similar proportion abused a tranquilizer (Valium) during the period they were in counseling. An additional 4% of the clients disclosed suicide attempts utilizing overdoses of various drugs, including aspirin and caffeine tablets. Twenty-seven percent of the counseling clients' mates stated that the men abused drugs other than alcohol. Marijuana again figured prominently in these reports, followed by a reported 5% rate of abuse by the batterers of amphetamines and/or barbiturates.

Turning to counseling outcomes, I as counselor was subjectively somewhat satisfied with the level of domestic nonviolence achieved by 26% of the clients, and fully satisfied with the progress of 10% of the clientele. The sample members attended an average of 9.7 counseling sessions apiece. No clients made satisfactory progress toward nonviolence in 7 or fewer sessions, yet about two-thirds of the clients did not attend the necessary 8 or more counseling appointments. In fact, 58% attended four sessions or fewer, not including another 18 men not in the sample, who made appointments to begin batterers' counseling and never arrived. The median of the number of sessions attended by each client was 2.96, the mode was 2 (24% of the sample). Attending four sessions seemed to be a turning point for clients; of the 42% of the sample who remained in counseling past the fourth session, 80% attended at least eight sessions and 63% attended a dozen or more. Thirty-two percent of the clients were known to have remained domestically nonviolent for a period of at least four months after initiating counseling, and 18% experienced documented nonviolent periods of at least six months' duration after beginning counseling. The average documentable period of nonviolence by counseling clients after having attended counseling was 3.15 months, with 68% of the clients failing to reach this average.

Chapter 7

COMPARISONS OF THE SAMPLES TO THE GENERAL POPULATION

As noted before, the statistical analysis in this study can be divided into five different categories, according to the type of hypotheses tested. These categories are: 1) hypotheses as to whether the sample populations differ significantly from the overall population with respect to a given variable; 2) hypotheses about the congruence—or lack thereof—between victims' and perpetrators' reports about the woman abuse they have endured/committed; 3) hypotheses about predictors of whether or not cohabitation between the battered woman and the batterer will terminate or continue; 4) hypotheses about predictors of the magnitude of woman abuse across battering relationships; and 5) hypotheses concerning predictors of the outcome of batterers' counseling. Without much further ado, I will describe in Chapters 7 through 10 the results of the statistical analyses conducted. Chapter 11 ends this work with a summary and discussion of the statistical results of this study.

AGE CHARACTERISTICS

Five previous studies of battered women have derived average ages for the battered women ranging from 26.8 to 37 years,[1] for an aggregate average age of 31.1 years. Previous studies of woman batterers derived mean ages ranging from 32 to 35 years.[2] The current study falls close to the age spectrum established in the existing literature, with mean ages of 27.7 years for the shelter residents, 30.9 for the assailant partners of the shelter sample, and 30.1 for the batterers' counseling sample.

No previous study has compared the age distribution or mean age of the sample studied to that of the general population of couples. Straus et al. found by far the highest rates of conjugal abuse among couples composed of men and women aged 30 or less.[3] In order to determine whether the present study populations deviated from the general population of couples with respect to age, a Pearson X^2 analysis was conducted, comparing the sample age distribution to U.S. census figures.[4] Comparison for age was limited to legal marrieds—separated or cohabiting—because of limitations in the census data. The Pearson X^2 results are shown in Table 2.

Table 2   Comparison of Age Distributions: Married Sample Members Compared to Overall U.S. Married Population

Sample Name	Age (in years)											X^2	$p<$
	14-17	18-19	20-24	25-29	30-34	35-39	40-44	45-54	55-64	65-74	75+		
Shelter Residents													
—Observed	3	21	68	67	51	15	7	9	2	0	0		
—Expected	1	3	23	31	31	27	22	45	36	19	5	355.22	.001
Shelter Residents' Violent Partners													
—Observed	1	3	56	64	54	24	24	7	7	1	0		
—Expected	1	1	14	27	29	26	22	45	41	25	10	295.91	.001
Batterers' Counseling Clients													
—Observed	0	0	17	27	17	11	8	3	1	0	0		
—Expected	0	0	5	9	10	9	8	16	14	9	4	105.78	.001

The table shows that the age distributions for all of the samples of legal marrieds deviate very significantly from the national age distribution for legal marrieds. This is due in large part to the scarcity of sample subjects 40 years or older. Further statistical analysis shows that the sample age distributions still deviate significantly from the national age distribution among legal marrieds, even if comparison is limited to ages 44 and below, as seen in Table 3. The 20s age decade is much more heavily represented in the study sample than one would expect based on U.S. census data.

Table 3 Comparison of Age Distributions (Through Age 44 Only): Married Sample Members Compared to Overall U.S. Married Population

	Age (in years)							X^2	p<
Sample	14-17	18-19	20-24	25-29	30-34	35-39	40-44		
Shelter Residents									
—Observed	3	21	68	67	51	15	7		
—Expected	1	5	38	53	52	45	38	127.90	.001
Shelter Residents' Batterer Partners									
—Observed	1	3	56	64	54	24	24		
—Expected		2	27	51	55	49	42	55.45	.001
Batterers' Counseling Clients									
—Observed	0	0	17	27	17	11	8		
—Expected	0	1	10	18	19	17	15	15.99	.01

These findings do not of themselves substantiate the inference that conjugal violence is most prevalent among couples in their 20s and 30s. Since these are help-seeking samples, many other factors related to help-seeking probably contribute to these results. Younger adults may be more aware of services for battered women and woman abusers. They are possibly more willing to avail themselves of these services due to contemporary values that place less stigma upon separations, divorce, and help-seeking. A sense of resignation to a violent relationship may also play a role in the scarcity of middle-aged and elderly people in the shelter and counseling samples. Also, alternative sources of shelter are available to senior citizens, and they may divert elderly battered women from the shelter clientele. The results may also reflect shelter service delivery, which may be conducting publicity and outreach that is more effective with younger women than with middle-aged and elderly women. It is still important to recall that the work of Straus et al. has indicated that couples under 30 years of age may be most prone to conjugal violence.[5]

Next, consider the age difference between partners in violent relationships. In Gelles' sample, conjugal violence was most likely to occur in couples where the male partner was older than the female partner, but frequent violence—occurring monthly or more—was most common among couples where the woman was older than the man.[6] The present study compared the age difference between shelter residents and their male partners to national census figures.[7]

The analysis showed that the overall distribution of age differences did not deviate significantly from national figures ($X^2=6.334$, df=6, p<.25). There was, however, a nearly significant overrepresentation in the shelter sample of couples where the man was younger than the woman ($X^2=3.359$, df=1, p<.10). This latter result mildly replicates Gelles' finding that younger-male/older-female couples were at greatest risk of frequent conjugal abuse.

The median age at marriage of legal marrieds in the shelter sample was compared to national figures on median age at first marriage, again using Pearson X^2 methods. The relevant national median ages at first marriage are 23 years old for husbands and 21 years for wives.[8] The shelter sample medians are 21.6 years for the violent husbands and 19.1 years for the battered wives. The X^2 results show that significant proportions of both the wives and husbands in the shelter sample fall below the national median age at first marriage for their gender. For the wives, the relevant statistic was $X^2=6.418$, df=1, p<.025, while for the husbands it was $X^2=7.175$, df=1, p<.01. These results are all the more impressive when one recalls that the sample medians do not exclusively reflect ages at first marriage but also include some spouses' ages at the beginning of their second or subsequent marriages. The results again reflect the relative youth of the legal marrieds in the shelter sample, but they also reflect a tendency for battered wives in the sample, and for their violent husbands, to marry at earlier ages than American legal marrieds in general.

RACIAL CHARACTERISTICS

The race of battered women and batterers is routinely reported in the research on battering. To date, these reports have never included any assessment of the significance or triviality of the racial composition of the samples studied. This is deplorable research practice since it leaves results very vulnerable to racist interpretations that blacks and/or other minorities are more heavily implicated in conjugal violence than are whites.

The current sample is a good example of the above since both samples include higher proportions of blacks than the 13% of the Michigan population that blacks comprise. However, in comparing the racial distributions of the shelter residents and counseling clients to the racial distributions that one would expect based on clients' place of residence, the obtained racial distributions of shelter residents and counseling clients are not different than would be predicted by random chance.[9] For the racial composition of shelter residents, $X^2=5.311$, df=4, p».25; for the counseling clients, $X^2=3.561$, df=4, p=.50 (approximately). Thus, we can be confident that these two samples are racially distributed according to random chance.

Assailant partners of shelter residents are more likely to be black than one would predict based on random chance, ($X^2=20.472$, df=4, p<.001). This is attributable to a relatively large proportion of shelter residents (7.8%) coming from couples consisting of a white woman and black man. National census figures for 1980 record only a 0.34% proportion of legally married black-white interracial couples,[10] compared to 4.9% in the shelter sample. The obtained sample proportion diverges radically from the national figures (p<.001), but this statistical effect still pertains to only a small part of the shelter sample.

NUMBER OF CHILDREN

The shelter sample average of 2.12 children under 18 years of age per each woman cohabiting with children matches the Michigan mean for 1976 of 2.06 children living in each family with children.[11] However, the sample distribution of the number of children in each family differs radically from the overall state distribution, as Table 4 shows.

Table 4   Number of Children Residing With Each Shelter Resident: Observed and Expected Distributions

	Number of Children				
	None	One	Two	Three	Four or More
Observed	40	91	90	47	32
Expected	131	58	57	30	24

$X^2=113.39$, df=4, p<.001

This is directly attributable to the relative scarcity in the shelter sample of women not living with children. If consideration of the distribution of the number of children is restricted to women cohabiting with children, the obtained sample distribution is extremely close to the expected distribution ($X^2=0.578$, df=3, p».90). The relative absence in the sample of women not living with children is in large part an effect of the rarity in the sample of middle-aged women and of the absence of elderly women—the two groups who are most likely to have adult children no longer residing with them. These results may also reflect a tendency found by Straus et al. for the rate of woman abuse to rise as household size increased.[12]

Table 4 shows that women rearing three or more children are more common in the sample than one would expect by random chance.

PREMARITAL PREGNANCY RATES

Gelles has alluded briefly to premarital pregnancy and to pregnancy occurring early on in a marriage as factors associated with woman abuse. Star found that 17% of her sample of battered women were pregnant before marriage or cohabitation with their abusive partners. In Gayford's sample, the rate of pregnancy prior to marriage or cohabitation was 67%.[13]

The present researcher hypothesized that marrying to legitimize a child would be associated with greater resentment by one or both mates at being married to each other, which in turn would be associated with greater conflict in the marriage. Marital conflict has been shown to be positively associated with the occurrence of conjugal violence.[14] Therefore, it was expected that a greater prevalence of premarital pregnancies brought to term would be found in the study samples than in the population at large.

For the purposes of this study, a premaritally conceived child was defined as any child born either before, or less than 7 months after, the parents' legal marriage. Offspring of relationships prior to the parents' marriage were not counted. Children conceived and reared by parents not legally married to one another were classified as nonmaritally conceived. It could not be determined with any regularity whether nonmarital conceptions precipitated cohabitation by the parents, or if they occurred after their cohabitation had already begun. Cases were treated as unknown where the parentage of the children and/or the chronology of births and marriage were ambiguous.

Applying the existing data on the prevalence of children conceived out of wedlock to the racial compositions of the samples, one would expect 30.1% of the shelter sample and 30.8% of the counseling sample to have children conceived either premaritally or nonmaritally.[15] The obtained rates were 42.9% of the shelter sample and 33.6% of the counseling sample. Both obtained rates exceed the expected rates, the shelter sample by a very significant degree (t=4.41, df=251, p<.001, one-tailed). The counseling sample rate exceeds its expected rate to a statistically insignificant extent (t=0.642, df=109, p>.25, one-tailed). Limiting analysis solely to married members of the shelter sample, one still finds a significantly higher rate of premarital conception of children than would be predicted by random chance (t=3.14, df=216, p<.001, one-tailed).

EMPLOYMENT RATES

Studies of the employment rates of woman abusers have uniformly reported high rates of unemployment among the samples of batterers.[16] To my knowledge, no one has investigated the employment status or employment rates of battered women. The feminist resource theory, however, implies that those women who are not employed outside the home are likely to be more entrapped as battered women since greater financial resources make it easier to leave a violent husband/male partner.

For the current study, expected rates of nonemployment were computed, based on unemployment figures, data on labor force participation rates, the racial composition and the place of residence of the sample subjects.[17] These expected rates were then compared to the derived sample rates of nonemployment. The term *nonemployment*, as used here, is to be distinguished from the usual labor statistics definition of unemployment. The sample data simply reflects whether shelter residents, counseling clients, and assailant partners of shelter residents held paid jobs or not. There is not sufficient data available to determine if subjects were participating in the work force under the conventional definition used in labor statistics to determine unemployment rates.

Given the work force participation rates for women, the prevailing unemployment rates over the study period for the areas of residence of the shelter residents, and the racial composition of the sample, one would expect 56% of the shelter sample not to be employed outside the home—i.e., to be either unemployed or to be homemakers.[18] The derived sample rate of 71.7% nonemployment diverges very significantly from the expected rate, ($X^2 = 27.57$, df$=1$, p$<$.001). The shelter sample members were much less likely to be employed outside the home than Michigan women in general.

Given the work force participation rates for men, the prevailing unemployment rates over the study period for the areas of residence of the shelter sample, and the racial distribution of the assailant partners of the shelter sample, one would expect 26.9% of the partners of shelter residents not to hold jobs. That is, 26.9% of the batterers should be either unemployed, in the ordinary labor statistics sense, or not participating in the work force.[19] In fact, 28.8% of the assailant partners of shelter residents were recorded as not holding jobs. This result does not differ significantly from the expected rate, ($X^2 = 0.638$, df$=1$, p$>$.25). It should be noted, however, that this finding pertains only to nonemployment and does not pertain to unemployment rates. Given the available data, one cannot rule out the possibility that the shelter partners suffer a higher unemployment rate, in the conventional definition, than the general male population.

Similar findings pertain to the counseling sample as well as to the shelter partners. An expected nonemployment rate of 27.2% was computed for the counseling sample.[20] The derived rate of 28.1% was very close to the expected rate ($X^2=0.044$, df=1, p».75). Further study using the conventions of labor statistics would be desirable in order to determine whether or not batterers suffer from higher unemployment rates than American men in general.

WELFARE RECIPIENT STATUS

Walker argues that battered women receiving welfare are more likely to take shelter than those not receiving welfare since welfare recipients face little or no financial loss in leaving their violent mates.[21] Based on this argument, it was hypothesized that welfare recipients would compose a significantly higher proportion of the shelter sample than of the general population of women in Michigan. This hypothesis was borne out by the study data.

The best estimate of the proportion of Michigan women receiving welfare payments between 1978 and 1980 is 10%.[22] The obtained sample proportion of 30.3% welfare recipients differs very significantly from the expected proportion ($X^2=137.81$, df=1, p<.001). Even if the expected proportion of welfare recipients is doubled to 20%, the obtained proportion still exceeds very significantly the expected proportion ($X^2=20.02$, df=1, p<.001).

MARITAL STATUS

Studies by Yllo and Straus, by Carlson, by Gayford, and by Star et al. indicate that violent couples are more likely than American couples in general to be unmarried cohabitants.[23] The current study replicates this result. Based upon national census figures for 1980, one would expect no more than 3.2% of the couples studied to be unmarried cohabitants.[24] Among legally married and/or cohabiting couples represented in the shelter sample, 12.5% are from unmarried cohabitant relationships. This differs dramatically from the census-derived expectation ($X^2=77.61$, df=1, p<.001). Similarly, 13% of the counseling sample in legally married or cohabitant relationships come from unmarried cohabitant relationships. This result likewise dramatically exceeds the census-derived expectation ($X^2=34.375$, df=1, p<.001). These results are partly attributable to census underestimates of the number of couples cohabiting without being legally married. Despite this, the actual proportion of unmarried cohabitants in the general population would need to exceed 9%—almost triple the census proportion—before the derived shelter sample proportion of "living-togethers" differed insignificantly from the proportion in the general population. The actual national proportion of "living-togethers" would need to exceed 7.5% in order to trivialize in similar fashion the obtained proportion among the counseling sample.

CHILDHOOD EXPOSURE TO CONJUGALLY VIOLENT PARENTS

Published studies record findings that between 23% and 68% of battered women sampled witnessed as children violence between their parents.[25] Of these studies, six found prevalences of battering in the families of origin of battered women that do not appear to diverge much from Straus et al.'s conservative estimate that 28% of cohabiting heterosexual couples experience conjugal violence during their relationship.[26] One important study, however, found that battered wives using the Baltimore Legal Services Corporation for divorce cases were significantly more likely to report violence between their parents than were nonbattered wives who were divorce clients of the same agency.[27]

In the present study, data on shelter residents' childhood exposure to conjugal violence between their parents is based on responses to the intake question, "Was your mother a battered woman?" The intended meaning of this question, as operationalized by interviewers, is, "Did your mother (or primary cohabitant mother figure) ever to your knowledge endure any violence whatsoever from your father (or father figure)?" Difficulties with the wording of the question are clear; it is susceptible to simple Yes-No answers. Such simple answers will probably lower the reported incidence of woman abuse because some respondents will state that their mothers were not battered even though they were mildly or infrequently assaulted. When shelter residents inquired about the interviewer's definition of "battered woman," they were informed that any violence was to be counted for a "Yes" response. Many respondents, however, answered "Yes" or "No" without requesting clarification. The wording of the question also omits violence against fathers or father figures in shelter residents' families of origin. While two residents mentioned that their fathers were battered husbands, it is possible that some women did not volunteer relevant information of this type.

The intended definition of the question, as used in the current study, is quite close to Straus et al.'s Violence Index, measuring any conjugal violence at the level of pushing or worse. These authors found that 28% of intact, cohabiting American couples reported at least one incident of conjugal violence occurring during the course of their relationships.[28] Straus suggests doubling this figure to arrive at a more accurate estimate of the true prevalence of conjugal violence in America.[29] Straus et al. also report that 12.6% of couples had experienced conjugal violence at least as serious as punching on at least one occasion.[30] Among the shelter residents, 31.4% of 242 respondents reported violence between their parents. This result does not differ significantly from Straus et al.'s prevalence estimate of 28% (t=1.178, p›.10, one-tailed).

For the counseling clients, the presence or absence of conjugal battering in their families of origin was determined through clinical interviews. Any report of violence between parents resulted in a client being categorized for purposes of this study as having been exposed to conjugal abuse between his parents. Undoubtedly some clients withheld relevant information from the counselor or failed to identify conjugal abuse between their parents by the same definition as the researcher would. Thus, the reported rate of exposure of the counseling clients to conjugal violence between their parents is a conservative or minimum estimate of their actual rate of exposure to conjugally abusive parents. Just under two-thirds (66.3%) of counseling clients interviewed on this topic reported violence between their parents. This figure obviously differs very significantly from Straus et al.'s prevalence rate of 28% (t=8.4, df=97, p‹.001, one-tailed); it even differs significantly from Straus' suggested prevalence estimate of 56% (t›2, df=97, p‹.025, one-tailed).[31] Unless the actual prevalence rate of conjugal violence in the United States exceeds 58.1%, the counseling sample has a significantly higher rate of exposure to conjugally violent parents (at the p‹.05 level) than the general American public.

It is also nearly certain that a higher proportion of counseling clients than of shelter residents were exposed to conjugally violent parents (t=6.13, df=338, p‹.001). Part of the reason that exposure to conjugally violent parents was found among a higher proportion of counseling clients than shelter residents is the greater amount of interview time and closer questioning used in determining counseling clients' family background of battering, relative to interviewing shelter residents about their family history of conjugal violence. Still, these procedural differences do not seem to account for the major portion of the difference between counseling clients and shelter residents in childhood exposure to conjugally violent parents. Unless the actual rate of conjugal battering among parents of the shelter sample were at least 57%—instead of the reported 31.4%—the differences between the shelter and counseling samples remain statistically significant at the p‹.05 level. It is very unlikely that there was so much underreporting on this topic in the shelter sample.

CHILDHOOD SUBJECTION TO CHILD ABUSE

Unfortunately, there is no existing research estimating the probability that an adult American was formerly abused as a child by her/his parents or parent figures. Consequently, there are no national estimators with which to compare the sample prevalences of past subjection to physical child abuse. Among the shelter sample, nearly 30% of the women considered themselves to have been physically or sexually abused by a parent while they were children. This prevalence of child abuse among shelter residents closely resembles the 26% prevalence of formerly battered daughters among Parker and Schumacher's sample of legal clients who were both battered and nonbattered women (t=0.59, df=339, insignificant difference).[32] Straus et al. found an annual incidence rate of physical child abuse of 14% among couples rearing children, which could easily accrue to a 30% rate of physical child abuse over individuals' entire childhoods.[33] Therefore, it tentatively appears that battered women residing at SAFE House are not any more likely than American women in general to have been battered children during their youth.

The men in the counseling sample report a much higher rate of childhood subjection to physical abuse by their parents. Among the counseling sample members, 61.4% report being physically abused during childhood by at least one of their parents. An additional 8% of the counseling sample reported ambiguous incidents that were classified as borderline child abuse, and yet another 2% reported witnessing their parents physically or sexually abusing at least one of the respondent's siblings.

To my knowledge, there is no existing research on the prevalence of child abuse in the childhood of adult American men. It is clear that the 61.4% prevalence of physical abuse in the childhoods of the counseling sample is a significantly higher prevalence than the 30% prevalence in the shelter sample (t=5.83, df=390, p<.001). The higher rate among counseling clients is again partly attributable to the longer interview time and closer questioning involved in gathering the counseling sample data, compared to the shelter sample data. On the other hand, unless the actual rate of subjection to child abuse among shelter residents were 52% or higher, the child abuse subjection rate among the counseling clients would remain significantly greater than that of the shelter residents. It is unlikely that shelter residents underreported their histories of child abuse to the degree necessary to create inconsequential differences between the child abuse subjection rates of the shelter and counseling samples.

EDUCATIONAL LEVEL OF ASSAILANT PARTNERS

Gelles found that rates of woman abuse were highest among men with some high school education short of graduating, and that woman abuse rates decreased steadily at higher levels of education. Parker and Schumacher found a statistically significant tendency for conjugally non-violent men to be more likely than batterers to have graduated high school. Straus et al. found contradictory results; in their study, male high school graduates had the highest rate of perpetrating woman abuse, while men with either less than eight years' education or some college education short of a bachelor's degree had the lowest rates of woman abuse.[34] Available Michigan census figures enable a comparison between the overall 1970 distribution of the educational level of men over 25 years old and the obtained distribution of educational experience among male partners over 25 years old of the shelter sample.[35]

While the overall obtained distribution differs significantly from the expected distribution ($X^2=18.835$, df=9, p<.05), closer inspection reveals that this is due mostly to differences between the observed and expected distributions at the very lowest and highest levels of education. Men who have completed less than five years of school and men who have attended graduate or professional programs past the bachelor's degree level are both far more rare in the sample than should be expected. If one compensates for this by combining the categories for the lowest and highest educational levels, using one category for 0-4 years' education and one category for 13 or more years' education, one finds that the obtained sample distribution is not significantly different from the expected sample distribution ($X^2=8.946$, df=6, p>.10).

Overall, the husbands and partners of SAFE House residents seem to be more educated than Michigan men in general—based on 1970 census figures. One would expect 51.2% of the sample to have graduated high school or received high school equivalency degrees, while in fact 55.7% have. It is clear that Parker and Schumacher's finding of a lower proportion of high school graduates among violent husbands in their sample does not hold true for this sample.[36] Similar to the findings of Straus et al., men with eight years' or less education are underrepresented in the sample relative to the overall population. Unlike Straus et al.'s findings, men with some college education but no bachelor's degree comprise a higher proportion of the sample than of the male population of the state.[37] This may be due to the high concentration of colleges and universities in the area served by SAFE House. The fact that only census figures from 1970 were available for computing the expected distribution of educational experience also contributes to the finding that the sample of shelter partners are, on the whole, more educated than the overall male population in Michigan since the general level of education has increased over time. The rarity of men with graduate and/or professional training among partners of shelter residents probably reflects more upon issues of service utilization and service delivery than upon the relative frequency of woman abuse among highly educated men.

ALCOHOL ABUSE AMONG BATTERERS

Batterers are notorious as problem drinkers. Both the general public and the published literature portray woman abusers as having a pronounced tendency toward alcoholism. Published studies report rates of alcohol abuse ranging from 44% to 85% among the batterers studied.[38] These rates are quite impressive, but none of them have been compared to the estimated rate of alcohol abuse in a given community.

When shelter residents were asked to give their subjective opinions as to whether their partner abused alcohol, 63.7% of those responding replied that they considered their mates active alcohol abusers and another 4.3% considered their mates to be past or reformed alcohol abusers. In the counseling sample, only 17.3% of the men considered themselves on intake to have an active problem with their alcohol consumption, while another 26.4% considered themselves to be either reformed or borderline problem drinkers. As counselor, I considered 64.2% of my clients to suffer from unambiguous cases of problem drinking or alcohol addiction, while I considered another 14.7% to be either reformed or borderline problem drinkers. Of the 77 wives/partners of counseling clients asked if they considered their mate to be a problem drinker, 50.6% responded in the affirmative.

The highest available estimate of the rate of problem drinking among males in Washtenaw County is 27.3%, and this is an inflated estimate. Besides being intentionally exaggerated, this rate includes by definition not only the proportion of men physically and/or psychologically addicted to alcohol but also those whose consumption of alcohol has been linked to any problem behavior such as violence, work dysfunctions, drunk driving, and other alcohol-related behaviors leading to arrest, injury, and/or treatment for alcohol abuse.[39] Under this definition, the actual rate of problem drinking among men in Washtenaw County is probably lower than 27.3%. Even compared to this intentionally high estimate of the rate of male problem drinking in Washtenaw County, the obtained sample rates of woman abusers with a history of alcohol abuse are all significantly higher (see Table 5).

Table 5 Batterers' Reported Rates of Problem Alcohol Use, Compared to the Expected Rate of 27.3%

Source of Reported Rate	N=	Rate (%)	t=	p< (one-tailed)
Assailant Partners of Shelter Residents				
—As reported by woman partner	278	68.0	15.23	.001
Batterers' Counseling Clients				
—Self-reports	110	38.2	2.56	.01
—Self-reports, active alcohol problems only	110	17.3	−2.35	NS
—Wife/partner's report	77	53.2	5.10	.001
—Counselor's report	109	74.3	11.01	.001
—Counselor's report, active alcohol problems only	109	64.2	8.65	.001

Only the rate of active alcohol abuse admitted by the counseling clients fails to exceed significantly the maximum estimated prevalence in the local male community of alcohol abuse. This admitted rate is an obvious under-statement by the clients. If one includes the proportion of self-described borderline and ex-problem drinkers in the counseling sample, the obtained rate again exceeds the expected rate by a statistically significant margin.

MILITARY EXPERIENCE AMONG BATTERERS

Straus states that there is a higher rate of perpetration of woman abuse among men employed in weapons-carrying occupations such as the military, law enforcement officials, and security guards.[40] Based upon this, one might expect woman abusers to be more likely to be military veterans than nonviolent husbands/male partners. The proportion of the counseling sample who were military veterans is 29.1%. This is very close to the overall state rate of 27% military experience among men (t=0.494, df=109, p>.25).[41]

Chapter 8

CONCORDANCE BETWEEN VICTIMS' AND ASSAILANTS' REPORTS

Probably the foremost characteristic of the woman abuser discussed in the existing literature is his tendency to minimize and/or to deny his violent behavior.[1] Most of the literature describing this phenomenon is composed of clinical impressions derived from therapeutic contacts with batterers and battered women. No published source suggests that battered women as a group tend to overreport or exaggerate the violence done to them. Rather, battered women are viewed as likely to underreport or to tone down their accounts of their assailant partners' violence.[2]

Only one work has addressed with systematic research the issue of whether batterers underreport their violence. Bulcroft and Straus have shown that men are much less reliable reporters of their conjugally violent behavior than women are of their own conjugal violence against their husbands/male partners. In the Bulcroft and Straus study, husbands sampled admitted to perpetrating only 52.7% as much violence as their children claimed to have witnessed them commit, while wives in the sample confessed to committing 164% of the conjugal violence that their children reported the women to have perpetrated. That is, husbands reported committing over 47% less, while wives reported committing 64% more, conjugal violence than their children reported witnessing them perpetrate.[3]

Based on the woman abuse literature, the one existing empirical study, and my own clinical experience as a batterers' counselor, it was expected that the counseling clients would report less violence than their battered mates would report. Therefore, it was expected that, relative to his wife/partner, each member of the counseling sample would report committing fewer assaults, a lower estimated frequency rate of his assaults, less time elapsed since the first assault in the relationship, and less severe and less dangerous behavior by him as he perpetrated both the last and worst conjugal assaults. These expectations were tested by paired one-tailed t tests of the difference between the female partner's report and that of the counseling client who was involved with her.

Table 6 displays the results of the paired t tests conducted on the partners' reports. Table 6 clearly demonstrates that the woman abusers in counseling reported perpetrating very significantly lower quantities of violence in their relationships and very significantly less severe violence, relative to their partners' accounts of violence in the relationship. Overall, each abuser reported an average of 45.4% as many assaults as his mate did, at an estimated frequency that averaged 40% of the frequency estimated by his abused partner, over a period of time that averaged 66% of

Table 6   Paired t Tests of the Difference Between Reports from Each Batterers' Counseling Client and His Wife/Partner

Variable	N=	Mean of Counseling Clients' Reports	Mean of Reports by Clients' Female Partners	t (Paired t Test)	p‹ (One-tailed)
Reported Number of Assaults	41	3.95	12.15	3.072	.002
Annual Frequency of Assaults	44	3.93	26.86	2.187	.0175
Elapsed Time Since First Assault (Months)	40	30.5	48.12	3.615	.0005
Severity of Last Assault					
—CRT Scale	69	5.84	6.97	3.816	.0002
—Gelles Scale	69	4.52	5.35	2.983	.0025
Severity of Worst Assault					
—CRT Scale	78	7.01	8.36	6.109	.0001
—Gelles Scale	78	5.37	6.38	5.430	.0001

the period which his partner stated had elapsed since the initial assault in their relationship. These figures, and the statistical analysis summarized in Table 6, clearly document the expected underreporting of abuse by the batterers.

The disparity represented here between the batterers' and battered women's reports, highly significant and divergent as it is, is much less than would be expected from the overall population of members of battering relationships due to the following methodological effects. The disparity between reports of the number of assaults was diminished by the exclusion once again of women who gave unscoreable responses such as "countless" assaults. Thus, these accounts could not be compared to each of their partners' reports, which in general were dramatically lower.

The method used for recording the men's and women's reports of the number and estimated frequency of assaults intentionally diminished the divergence between mates' reports. In order to prevent my manipulating the data in order to promote the research hypotheses, the data were processed in a way that acted against supporting the hypotheses. Men's responses were rounded up while women's responses were rounded down. For example, the response "7 or 8" would be scored 7 for a woman and 8 for a man; "5 to 10" would similarly be scored 7 for a woman and 8 for a man. The one exception to this procedure occurred in cases where both members of a couple gave identical responses; in these cases, the responses were scored alike so differing reports would not be created out of accounts that were in agreement. Thus, if a batterer said there were "7 or 8" assaults and his partner also said "7 or 8", their responses would both be scored the same—either 7 or 8, chosen arbitrarily.

Care was taken throughout the scoring procedures to avoid the temptation, stemming from the research hypotheses, of inflating the women's reports or of deflating the men's reports. Instead, I took steps to interpret the battered women's reports conservatively while interpreting the batterers' counseling clients' reports liberally. For example, one woman reported that she had been assaulted "at least two dozen times—oh easily! easily that! probably more." Her response was scored as 24 assaults. A batterer allowed that he had attacked his wife "maybe 15 times, but I really think more like eight to ten times"; this was scored as 15 assaults. These methods of course constricted the divergence between the batterers' and battered women's accounts of the violence in their relationships.

The self-selected nature of the counseling sample also affects the disparities between partners' reports in a conservatizing manner. The counseling sample, after all, represents a group of woman batterers who are, on the whole, more willing to admit that they have a problem of woman abuse than are batterers in general. Quite a few men called me as counselor to inquire about the whereabouts of partners in refuge, but they declined offers of a counseling appointment on the grounds that they had never committed any violence against their partners. These men of course do not appear in the sample. Some of the counseling clients had discussed their conjugal violence with their mates prior to their early counseling sessions; this would tend to increase the agreement between the man's and woman's perceptions and accounts of the violence.

Factors in the context of the counseling interaction also increased the tendency for counseling clients to disclose their abusive behavior more fully than they would elsewhere, which in turn increased somewhat the concordance between their disclosures and their partners' reports. Since they were being interviewed at a highly specific conjugal abuse clinic, counseling clients had less incentive to be secretive about their violent behavior than they might otherwise be. Since they were always informed that their counseling was strictly confidential, clients were aware that none of their statements about their behavior could be used against them in any prosecution or litigation. This situation contrasts sharply with questioning from police, judges, and other legal officials, where the information disclosed could be used in criminal prosecution or sentencing, or in civil matters such as decisions regarding child custody or child visitation rights. In these legal situations, batterers have heightened motivation to deny or to minimize their abusive behavior.

Indeed, the counseling interaction that is the source of the data used here is probably the only context in each counseling client's life where he had an incentive to admit to being violent. This occurred because clients who steadfastly denied a problem of woman abuse were soon refused further counseling. Several clients grudgingly admitted to assaulting their partners upon being threatened with denial of further counseling; in these cases, the clients' eventual admissions of committing violent abuse are used for the research data. (Clients owned up to violent behavior under threat of termination of counseling in order to fulfill the implicit or explicit demands from their partners that they pursue batterers' counseling in order to halt their violence.) Even with this incentive to confess to conjugal violence in a safe context, 7% of the sample (9% of those giving scoreable responses) insisted that they had never assaulted their mates. Twenty percent acknowledged a sole assaultive incident, and another 11% reported committing only two assaults. This compares to none of the 56 reporting partners of the counseling sample stating there had been no assaults, and under 11% reporting one to two violent incidents in their relationships.

Given the various factors just described that enhance the concordance between the separate reports by each member of a couple, the lack of
concordance in the statistical results is all the more staggering. Recall that
for only one variable—the frequency rate of violence—was the likelihood
greater than one in a hundred that the observed differences between partners'
reports were due to random chance and not to systematic, nonrandom
processes. For that variable, the probability of random effects was still less
than one in fifty-seven. It could hardly be more clearly demonstrated that
the counseling clients reported committing much less conjugal violence of
a much less severe nature than their wives/partners reported enduring.

The reader might still conceive that the disparity between the batterers'
and battered women's reports may be due as much or more to the victims'
exaggerating the abuse they endured, rather than to the perpetrators deny-
ing or minimizing the abuse they committed. Recall, however, that all
published sources suggest that, in general, battered women underreport
the violent abuse that they have endured.[4] Furthermore, based upon my
own clinical experience, I am convinced of the correctness of these published
observations. The differences observed in this study between partners' reports
do not reflect any noticeable tendency by battered wives to exaggerate or
overreport the violence and abuse that they have experienced. My experience has been that battered women are indeed far more likely to underreport
the abuse they endure than overreport it.

Like anyone subjected to trauma, battered women are likely to use
coping mechanisms of repression, denial, and/or rationalization. Thus,
many battered women tend to repress experiences of being abused or to
minimize or rationalize the abusive violence they have endured. Anyone
who has sympathetically interviewed battered women over time during
their stay in shelter has seen them recall more incidents of abuse than
they initially remembered due to the opportunity to reflect upon their
relationships. This last phenomenon also can occur as a result of a woman
redefining her concept of abuse to include milder, or more subtle, forms
of abuse than she had initially perceived as abusive. In contexts other than
shelters, battered women may underreport the violence that they have
endured in order to avoid being viewed as deviant, ill, or blameworthy, or
in order to enhance their credibility to the listener.

Certainly some battered woman somewhere has at some time in history exaggerated the abuse done her, but it seems clear that a tendency to
exaggerate abuse does not apply as a general principle to battered women.
Instances of exaggerated reports by battered women of the abuse they
have sustained are exceptional. In my counseling experience, those rare
women who have exaggerated their accounts of abuse by their male part-

ners have been atypical of battered women in other ways as well. They have been unilateral husband abusers or reciprocally violent wives/partners seeking to justify their violence either through rationalizations about self-defense or by projecting their own violent behavior onto their mates. (These identical psychological defenses are of course even more commonly employed by men who batter their female partners.) It should be noted again that reciprocally violent couples do not figure at all in this section of the results of the study, nor do women who batter male partners because all of the statistics presently under discussion refer to, and were derived from, the counseling sample.

A few additional factors were analyzed for concordance between partners. For 33 couples, separate reports were available from each partner as to whether conjugal assaults had occurred during any of the woman's pregnancies. In six couples (18%), the man denied committing any violence during the woman's pregnancy, while the woman reported him battering her during at least one pregnancy. In one couple (3%), the man admitted battering his mate while she was pregnant, and she reported no battering during her pregnancies. Fifteen couples (46%) agreed that there had not been assaults during pregnancy, and 11 couples (33%) agreed that the man had assaulted the woman while she was pregnant. Analysis of these independent responses by a one-tailed binomial test of symmetry reveals a nearly significant trend for batterers to underreport abuse during the mate's pregnancy ($p < .063$).

For 46 couples with children, there were separate reports as to whether each partner considered the woman batterer to be a child abuser also. Twenty-four of the couples (52%) agreed that the batterer was not a child abuser. Two batterers reported committing child abuse although their mates did not describe them as child abusers (4%). Thirteen couples (28%) agreed that the violent mate was also a child abuser. Seven batterers (15%) who were described by their partners as child abusers denied committing child abuse. Again a one-tailed binomial test of symmetry reveals that this finding also represents a nearly significant discordance between partners' reports ($p < .09$).

The concordance between partners concerning the batterer's substance habits was also investigated, to see if there was any difference in the level of conjugal agreement regarding his substance abuse, compared to that regarding his violent behavior. Since comparable judgments by the counselor on the clients' alcohol abuse were also available, these were also investigated for agreement with the counseling clients and the female partners of the counseling sample members.

There was significant disagreement between the counseling clients and their mates regarding the batterers' alcohol abuse. Among 70 couples giving independent judgments regarding the man's alcohol abuse, 16 (23%) were composed of women alleging alcohol abuse by male partners who denied being problem drinkers when interviewed themselves. In seven couples (10%), the man admitted a past history of alcohol abuse while his wife/partner did not mention any alcohol abuse by him. The rest of the 70 couples (67%) agreed about the man's status as an alcohol abuser. Despite this, the men still show a significant tendency to report being alcohol abusers less often than their mates allege them to be alcohol abusers (one-tailed test of binomial symmetry, $p<.05$).

Client agreement with the batterers' counselor was even lower regarding whether or not the client was a problem drinker. In 28 cases, client and counselor agreed that there was no history of problem drinking; in 40 cases, they agreed that there was. This left 38 cases (35.8%) where the counselor considered the client to be a problem drinker, while the client denied abusing alcohol. A one-tailed binomial test of symmetry revealed a very significant difference between the counselor's and the client's tendencies to describe the client as a past or active alcohol abuser ($p<.0001$).

For 64 cases where judgments regarding her mate's alcohol abuse are available from the female partner of the batterers' counseling client, there is nearly as little concordance between the counselor and the women as there was between the clients and the counselor. The counselor and the client's partner agreed in 18 cases that the client was not a problem drinker and in 35 cases that he was, for an overall rate of agreement of 74.6%. This left two cases (3%) where the client's mate termed him an alcohol abuser and the counselor did not, and 16 cases (22.5%) where the counselor alleged alcohol abuse by the client while the client's partner did not. The tendency by the counselor to allege more alcohol abuse by the clients than do the clients' mates is very significant ($p<.001$).

Turning to abuse of substances other than alcohol, counseling clients and their wives/partners are in much greater agreement on this issue than they are about alcohol abuse, child abuse, or any aspects of the conjugal violence they have committed/endured. Their overall rate of agreement was 87%. In six cases out of 70, men confessed to substance abuse that their partners did not report (8.7%), and in 3 cases women reported substance abuse that their mate denied. Analysis by a one-tailed binomial test of symmetry revealed no tendency at all for batterers to report engaging in less substance abuse, not including alcohol abuse, than their partners alleged. This is due in part to a common view in Washtenaw County that defines the use of recreational drugs—especially marijuana—as nondeviant behavior and, hence, not a subject to hide.

To sum up this section, the data show very low levels of client-partner concordance in their independent reports of the quantity, frequency, and behavioral severity of conjugal assaults; the elapsed time since the first assault in the conjugal relationship; whether the client assaulted his partner while she was pregnant; whether the batterer was also a child abuser; and whether the batterer was also an alcoholic or problem drinker. These low levels of concordance can be interpreted as reflecting shame or defensiveness on the part of counseling clients regarding these matters. The high concordance between the counseling clients and their mates regarding abuse by the men of substances other than alcohol seems to reflect the clients' reduced shame and defensiveness on this last topic.

FACTORS RELATING TO THE TERMINATION OR RESUMPTION OF COHABITATION BETWEEN THE BATTERED WOMAN AND BATTERER

The coding criteria for determining shelter sample outcomes—cohabitation resumed or terminated—have already been described in Chapter 6. The present section shall discuss the relationship of the outcomes categories to other variables. Before proceeding with this, however, it is important to note some possible confounds in the outcomes definitions. First, the criterion for considering cohabitation terminated—one year without resuming cohabitation—fails to exclude a few relationships where cohabitation will resume after separations of a year or longer. This fact is demonstrated in the shelter sample. Of those shelter residents who had experienced a conjugal separation prior to the shelter stay studied, 4.5% had resumed cohabitation with their abusers after separations of at least one year's duration.

Second, appealing to omniscience about the outcomes of the shelter residents' relationships, it is certain that some women categorized in this study as having resumed cohabitation, actually had their relationships eventually terminate after one period of resumed cohabitation. There are also probably some cases of cohabitation here considered terminated, where in fact the couple have resumed cohabiting. Despite these problems with the accuracy of the scoring of outcomes, I believe that the following analyses of statistical relationships between the outcomes and other factors remain valuable and statistically representative of the actual experiences of the shelter sample members.

It is also important to recall once again that the outcome of each shelter resident's relationship does not depend solely upon her will. Instead, the outcome also reflects the preference and behavior of each woman's violent partner in an interaction with each woman's will and behavior. Still, in the following statistical analyses, most of the time the underlying issue of interest will be which factors encourage battered women to decide to attempt to end their violent relationships or else which factors discourage them from this decision.

For purposes of semantic convenience, I will use the following terminology in discussing outcomes categories. If a woman never resumed cohabiting with her assailant partner after she left the shelter, the outcome will be referred to as "terminated immediately." If a woman stopped cohabiting after an initial period of resumed cohabitation, the outcome will be referred to as "terminated eventually." The outcomes for 11 women known to have terminated cohabitation by the time of the study, but for whom it is not known whether they initially resumed cohabiting or not, will also be referred to as "terminated eventually."

WHETHER PARTNER SOUGHT BATTERERS' COUNSELING

Hope that the abusive partner will reform and cease his violent behavior is a major motive for those battered women who decide to return to their husbands/partners.[1] Therefore, it might be expected that relationships in which the assailant received batterers' counseling would be more likely to resume than those where the assailant did not seek counseling. Conversely, however, the assailant's involvement in counseling could represent one last test of his capability of reforming, which in many cases he will fail. This latter effect could explain a positive association between assailants' involvement in counseling and the termination of cohabitation.

Pearson X^2 analysis reveals that there was a nearly significant tendency ($p < .08$) for cohabitation to be more likely to resume if the abusive partner entered counseling at DVP. While 65% of batterers not entering counseling resumed cohabitation, 83% of those in counseling at DVP experienced the resumption of cohabitation with their wives/partners. Of the relationships where cohabitation resumed and the assailant began counseling, 25% later experienced the termination of cohabitation. This compares to a rate of eventual termination of 8.1% for those relationships where cohabitation initially resumed and the batterer never received counseling at DVP. Consequently, the interaction between the outcome of the relationships and the counseling status of the batterer was statistically significant (p<.05). The tendency for cohabitation to terminate eventually was smaller for those couples where the batterer sought counseling at DVP (37.5%) than for those where the batterer did not receive batterers' counseling (44.2%), but this result is statistically insignificant (p>.50).

AGE

No age-related variables in the study were significantly associated with any of the three outcomes variables. That is, the age of the battered woman, her violent partner's age, and the age difference category for the couple— woman younger, equal ages, man younger—all yielded insignificant statistical results when tested for possible associations with the outcomes variables.

RACE

No racial factors were found to be significantly associated with the outcomes of the shelter sample's relationships. The race of the woman did not affect the likelihood of cohabitation resuming or terminating; neither did the race of the assailant. The racial composition of the couple— intraracial or interracial—likewise had no statistical bearing on outcome.

NUMBER OF CHILDREN AND AGE OF CHILDREN

It was expected that women with fewer children would be more likely to terminate cohabitation, and that more children would pose greater obstacles to the woman leaving the relationship. The more children a woman has, the greater her maternal obligations are in terms of the amount of effort required to care for the children and the financial needs of the family. The data did not reveal the expected effect, however. Women who terminated cohabitation—whether immediately upon leaving the shelter or eventually—had no fewer children than women whose cohabitation resumed. In fact, women who terminated cohabitation had just slightly more children on the average than those whose cohabitation resumed (2.03 children vs. 1.84, respectively). This difference was not all statistically significant.

Work by Gelles has already suggested that battered women who seek intervention to halt the abuse they are suffering tend to have older children than those battered women who do not seek outside intervention.[2] Other writers have also alluded to this effect.[3] Therefore, it was expected that mothers of older children would be more likely to break up with their violent mates. This expectation was not supported by the data. For mothers whose cohabitation terminated, both their youngest and oldest children were not significantly older than the youngest or oldest children of mothers who recohabited with their abusive partners.

ECONOMIC FACTORS

The reader will recall that feminist resource theory predicts that battered women will be more likely to terminate relationships with men who provide fewer material resources, and that the more economic resources of her own a battered woman has, the more likely she is to terminate her violent relationship. Based on feminist resource theory, one would expect a higher rate of cohabitation terminating among women employed outside the home, relative to those without work outside the home. The data reveal statistically insignificant trends in the expected direction. Among full-time homemakers, 31.5% terminated cohabitation without ever recohabiting after their shelter stay, compared to 33.3% of women employed part time outside the home and 35.1% of women with paid full-time employment. Half of the women employed outside the home (full or part time) eventually terminated cohabitation, compared to 41% of the women without employment outside the home. These differences remain statistically nonsignificant trends.

It was expected that welfare recipients would be more likely to end cohabitation than women not receiving welfare since welfare also represents an income source independent of the batterer. There was a nearly significant trend for welfare recipients to be more likely than nonrecipients to experience the immediate termination of cohabitation ($X^2=2.596$, df$=1$, p$<.11$). The strength of this tendency did not persist in relation to the eventual termination of cohabitation, although welfare recipients were insignificantly more likely to end cohabitation eventually (50% of the welfare recipients vs. 40.7% of nonwelfare recipients, p$=.25$).

Feminist resource theory would also predict that battered women would be more likely to end relationships with batterers who are not employed, compared to relationships involving batterers with gainful employment. This prediction is clearly supported by the data on immediate terminations. For 50 assailants without gainful employment—men whose job status was given as "not employed," "disabled," "retired," or "student"—the rate of immediate termination was 48%, compared to a 26.6% rate of immediate breakup for couples involving assailant partners who were listed as full-time workers or self-employed ($X^2=7.4$, df$=1$, p$<.01$). Similarly, a one-way analysis of variance showed significant differences in the rate of immediate breakup across the five categories of assailant job status—not employed, self-employed, full-time employed, disabled/retired, student; p<.03. Self-employed men experienced by far the lowest rate of cohabitation terminated immediately, 9.1%.

The above significant relationships between the assailants' employment status and the rate of immediate termination of cohabitation do not hold true for the relationship between assailant employment status and an outcome of eventual termination. This association is in part diluted by fluctuations in assailant job status over time, which are not available in the present data. While couples involving self-employed men remain the least susceptible to eventual breakups, their rate of dissolution rises to over 27%. Couples where the men are without jobs experience a 50% rate of eventual termination, compared to almost 41% for couples with men who are employed full time by an employer other than themselves.

The outcomes variables show no significant relationship with the occupational status of the assailant partner. Whether the batterer's occupational status is scored on Hollingshead and Redlich's seven point scale,[4] or on a simplistic scale of "white collar/blue collar/other," no statistically significant relationship with shelter outcomes can be derived.

As expected, the strongest relationships between the outcome of the shelter residents' relationships and the economic factors studied are derived from investigating the relative economic position of the battered woman and her violent mate. Looking at the employment status of each shelter resident and of her mate, and at the woman's welfare recipient status, it was obvious that in 33 couples the battered woman was producing more income than her mate. Among these 33 couples, the rate of immediate termination of cohabitation was 54.5%, compared to a rate of 27.7% among couples where the batterer was an equal or greater income producer than the battered woman. That is, couples where the battered woman was unambiguously the main producer of income were twice as likely to break up immediately, as were couples where the batterer was producing an income nearly equal, equal, or greater than that produced by the battered woman. Statistically, this difference in rates of immediate termination is very significant ($X^2=8.78$, df=1, p<.005).

The same statistical relationship applies at a nearly significant level to the eventual termination of cohabitation ($X^2=3.8$, df=1, p<.053). Couples where the battered woman was the main income producer were about one-and-a-half times more likely to break up eventually than were couples where the batterer was an equivalent or greater income producer than the shelter resident. The rates of eventual termination of cohabitation were

57.6% among couples where the shelter resident was the main income earner, compared to 39.1% among the rest of the shelter residents' relationships.

PSYCHOACTIVE MEDICATIONS AND PREVIOUS COUNSELING

It was feared that battered women who receive either psychotherapy, counseling, and/or psychoactive medications would be encouraged by such treatments to adapt or acquiesce to their abusive relationships, rather than attempt to terminate the relationships. Regarding this issue, the outcomes of shelter residents who had previously received counseling and/or psychotherapy for problems associated with conjugal abuse were compared to the outcomes for those who had not. Outcomes for shelter residents were also compared according to whether or not they received psychoactive medications.

By psychoactive medications are meant minor tranquilizers, antidepressants, prescription sleeping pills, prescribed stimulants, and prescribed pain medications. The heroin substitute Methadone, the anti-alcoholism drug Antabuse, antiseizure medications, alcohol, and psychoactive "street" drugs are excluded from this analysis. Major tranquilizers or "antipsychotic medications" are also excluded here. All three shelter residents who were taking this last type of medication, and for whom there are outcome data available, resumed cohabiting with their abusers; this occurred mainly because these women's psychotic or borderline psychotic conditions made it all but impossible for them, the shelter staff, and the other shelter residents to coexist and work effectively together, as would be necessary in order for them to avoid recohabiting with their abusive mates.

Statistical analysis showed little effect of previous mental health services upon the outcomes of shelter residents' relationships. Whether or not the shelter resident had previously received counseling and/or psychotherapy was associated with a difference in the rate of immediate termination of only 2%, and only 3% in the rate of eventual termination. Further, previous counseling did not decrease the rate of termination of cohabitation, but it was instead associated with slight, statistically insignificant increments in those rates.

Shelter residents taking prescribed psychoactive medications, other than major tranquilizers, were more likely to resume cohabiting with their abusers than were battered women not taking this sort of medication, to a substantial but not statistically significant degree. Overall, 79% of the women in the shelter who had psychoactive prescriptions resumed cohabiting with their abusers, compared to 64.5% of shelter residents without psychoactive prescriptions ($X^2=1.96$, df=1, p‹.20). Shelter residents with psychoactive prescriptions were also less likely to have cohabitation terminate eventually than were those women without such prescriptions (34.6% vs. 44.5%), but this latter difference is statistically trivial (p›.33).

MARITAL STATUS

It was expected that cohabiting couples where the partners were not legally married to one another would be more likely to break up than legally married couples since "living-togethers" face fewer legal obstacles to dissolving their relationships than do legal marrieds. The data do not support this expectation at all, however, and instead indicate no effect of marital status upon outcome. "Living-togethers" represented in the shelter sample were slightly more likely to experience immediate termination of cohabitation than were legal marrieds in the sample, but the legal marrieds had a barely higher rate of eventual termination than the "living-together" couples. Both of the above differences were statistically trivial.

LENGTH OF RELATIONSHIP

There are two contradictory hypotheses regarding the possible association between the length of the battering relationship and the likelihood that the relationship will end. On the one hand, one could expect women to be more likely to leave long relationships because of the time that it takes for battered women to recognize that the violence by their partners is unlikely ever to halt.[5] On the other hand, one could expect women to be more likely to leave relatively new relationships, while they are less likely to be resigned or habituated to a violent relationship and have invested less of their lifetime in their current conjugal relationship. As a group, women with relatively new marriages/relationships may be younger, may have fewer children, and may be more recently involved in the paid work force; all of these factors tend to make it easier for a woman to attempt to dissolve her conjugal relationship.

The data show no important difference between the mean lengths of the marriage/relationship for shelter residents who terminated cohabitation and those who resumed cohabitation with their partners (p›.50). As seen from Table 7, the data do show that shelter residents with relationships less than one year old are less than half as likely to experience the immediate termination of cohabitation as are shelter residents from lengthier relationships (14% vs. 31%). The data also indicate that the peak likelihood of immediate termination occurs among relationships between five and seven years old (41%). The rate of immediate termination rises steadily as the relationship gets longer, up until five to seven years' duration, and then the likelihoods decrease again.

Table 7   Percentage of Women Terminating Cohabitation, By Length of Marriage/ Cohabitation

Type of Termination	0-1 Year	1.1-2 Years	2.1-3 Years	3.1-4 Years	4.1-5 Years	5.1-7 Years	7.1-9 Years	9.1-12 Years	Over 12 Years
Immediate	14.3	32.0	35.7	35.3	36.8	40.9	28.6	28.6	29.4
Eventual	36.4	42.3	50.0	38.9	40.0	56.5	37.5	35.7	35.3

Judging from this, it would appear that the shelter residents were more reluctant to leave more recently formed relationships and more likely to give those relationships another try. This is corroborated by a large increase in the tendency for newer relationships to terminate eventually—within two years of the shelter stay studied. While the trend over the age of the relationship in the rate of termination is suggestive, it should be noted that the differences among termination rates for the various durations of the relationships are not statistically significant.

TIME ELAPSED SINCE THE INITIAL CONJUGAL ASSAULT

This variable is similar to the overall length of the relationship, but it reflects the fact that conjugal assaults may either predate cohabitation/ marriage in a given relationship or may not begin until a couple has cohabited for some period of time. On the average, women who terminated cohabitation had endured a shorter interval of time since the initial battering incident than had women who resumed cohabiting with their violent mates. These differences were not statistically significant, however (55 months for women who resumed cohabiting, 48 months for those who did not, $t=0.773$, p>.44).

Women who entered the shelter within one year of the first assault in their relationship had above-average rates of both immediate and eventual termination of cohabitation (38% and 52% respectively, vs. overall rates of 33% immediately and 43% eventually terminating). Women who had survived in the same battering relationship for over a decade had the lowest rates of both immediate and eventual termination (23.5% and 29.5%) among any of the categories of elapsed time since the initial battering. As shown in Table 8, peak rates of termination—both immediate and eventual—were recorded for shelter residents who had endured from four to five years of battering.

Table 8 Percentage of Women Terminating Cohabitation, By Elapsed Time Since First Conjugal Assault

Type of Termination	0-1 Year	1.1-2 Years	2.1-3 Years	3.1-4 Years	4.1-5 Years	5.1-7 Years	7.1-11.9 Years	12 or More Years
Immediate	37.9	35.7	25.0	38.9	40.0	23.5	33.3	23.1
Eventual	51.6	43.3	33.3	47.6	53.3	52.4	36.7	23.1

NUMBER OF PREVIOUS SEPARATIONS

Both Walker, and Hilberman and Munson suggest that a battered woman will tend to leave her abusive partner four or five times for temporary separations before the relationship is dissolved.[6] These authors also imply that, on the average, women who continue cohabiting with their violent partners have not previously experienced as many as four to five temporary separations from the violent mate. Separations as used here means the halting of cohabitation by the partners for at least one day in the context of conflict in the relationship. This does not refer to other contexts of separation such as business travel by one of the partners.

The present data clearly support the published hypotheses. The average number of previous separations among women who resumed cohabiting with the batterer was 2.42, compared to 5.07 among shelter residents who never resumed cohabiting after they left the shelter. This difference is statistically significant ($t=1.85$, $df=163$, $p<.05$, one-tailed). Women who had experienced one or no separations previous to entering SAFE House were only about half as likely as those who had experienced two or more prior separations to terminate their cohabitation immediately (23% vs. 44.6%).

OTHER FACTORS REGARDING PREVIOUS SEPARATIONS

One would expect battered women who terminate cohabitation to have experienced separations previous to their entering the shelter that were more recent than the separations experienced by shelter residents who later resumed cohabitation with the batterer. This is because less time between shelter entry and the previous conjugal separation would be associated with more frequent and severe violence and/or with a greater inclination in the woman to extricate herself from cohabiting with the batterer. The length of the last separation serves as an obvious indication of the avoidance of recohabitation already demonstrated by a given battered woman earlier in her relationship. Longer separations can also serve as rehearsals in preparation for permanently ending the violent relationship. It is therefore obvious that longer previous separations should be associated with later lengthy separations.

The data support the above expectations. Women who terminated cohabitation immediately had on the average experienced significantly more recent separations previous to taking shelter than women who later recohabited with their partners (10.6 months vs. 20.2 months since the last separation, t=2.1, df=97, p<.02, one-tailed). This effect also applied significantly to the difference between women who terminated eventually and those women who resumed cohabitation (20.9 months average among recohabiting women vs. 11.2 among eventual terminators, t=2.35, df=104, p<.011, one-tailed).

Turning to the duration of the last conjugal separation prior to each woman's entry into SAFE House, women who immediately terminated cohabitation averaged significantly longer prior separations than women who resumed cohabitation with their mates (124 days vs. 63 days, t=1.95, df=97, p<.03, one-tailed). This significant effect also extends to the difference in the average length of separation between shelter residents eventually terminating cohabitation and those resuming cohabitation (114 days' duration vs. 63 days, t=1.74, df=103, p<.05).

MAGNITUDE OF ABUSE: NUMBER, FREQUENCY, AND SEVERITY OF CONJUGAL ASSAULTS

There are 15 variables in this study that reflect different—though often interrelated—measures of the magnitude of physical abuse sustained by the shelter residents. These include seven first-order variables: 1) the total number of assaults committed upon the victim; 2) the estimated annual frequency of the occurrence of those assaults; the severity of assaultive behavior during the last violent incident before shelter entry, measured on 3) the CRT scale, or 4) the Gelles scale; 5 and 6) the severity of assaultive behavior during the worst assault, measured on the same two scales; and 7) the extrapolated number of conjugal assaults, based on the regression of the reported number of assaults upon the elapsed time since the first assault in the relationship. By multiplying together pairs of the above seven variables, an additional eight severity variables were derived: 1) frequency of assault multiplied by the reported total number of assaults; 2) frequency multiplied by the extrapolated total of assaults; the behavioral severity of the worst assault, as measured independently on the CRT and Gelles scales, multiplied by: 3 and 4) the frequency of assault; 5 and 6) the reported number of assaults; and, 7 and 8) the extrapolated number of assaults.

The extrapolated number of assaults was derived in an effort to provide a quantitative estimate of the number of violent incidents endured by the many women in the sample who reported "countless" or "innumerable" assaults by their mate. The estimated annual frequency of violent episodes is based upon the recent rate of occurrence of assaults, estimated by the shelter resident on intake. It is generally not the same number as the number of assaults divided by the time since the first conjugal assault. Rather, it tends to be a higher number, reflecting an escalation of violence by the batterer over the period just prior to the battered woman's entry into shelter.

The variables derived by multiplying together the number, frequency, and severity of assaults were computed in an attempt to replicate previous work by Gelles. Gelles found a nonsignificant statistical trend for a combined rating of the frequency and severity of violence reported by battered women to be a good predictor of whether the battered wives that he studied eventually divorced. This same combined rating of frequency and severity of violence was also the best predictor in Gelles' study for whether or not battered women sought intervention against the conjugal violence they were sustaining.[7] Unfortunately, Gelles does not state precisely the mathematics he used in computing his combined rating for the level of violence. Therefore, the current study employs a variety of measures in an attempt to replicate or contradict Gelles' findings.

Different theories predict different relationships between the outcome of the violent relationship and the magnitude of violence endured by the battered woman and perpetrated by the batterer. A commonsense, hedonistic hypothesis is that the more severe the violence, the greater the likelihood that the battered woman will attempt to break up the marriage/relationship. A simplistic approach emphasizing masochistic features of the battered woman would predict the opposite—a negative association between likelihood of breakup and severity of violence. Coercive control theory would predict a curvilinear relationship between these factors; it would expect relationships involving low and high levels of conjugal violence to be the most persistent relationships, while it would predict those violent relationships involving moderate and extremely high levels of violence to be the most likely to end. These expectations would not necessarily be inconsistent with statistical findings of a linear association—positive or negative—between the magnitude of violence and the likelihood of dissolution of the relationship, however.

Investigation of the violence magnitude variables by means of t tests comparing shelter residents terminating cohabitation to shelter residents resuming cohabitation revealed no significant differences between the mean of the two groups for any of the 15 variables measuring the magnitude of abuse. The finding nearest significance among these analyses was that women eventually terminating their relationships had reported on intake a higher average frequency rate of abusive incidents than those who continued cohabitation (annualized rates of 73.6 assaults per year vs. 45.9; $t=1.708$, $df=150$, p<.09, two-tailed). There were no average differences on the magnitude variables between women immediately terminating cohabitation and the rest of the shelter sample that even approached statistical significance.

On all variables derived from or measuring directly the annualized recent rate of occurrence of the assaults sustained by shelter residents, the nonsignificant trend was for women terminating cohabitation, immediately or eventually, to report having endured more frequent abusive incidents during the period shortly before they took shelter, compared to shelter residents who recohabited with their abusers. On most variables measuring or derived from the number of assaults sustained by shelter residents, the trend was for women who terminated cohabitation to have endured fewer assaults on the average than women who resumed cohabitation; the exceptions to this trend were the two variables derived by multiplying the frequency rate of violent incidents by the total number of assaults or by the extrapolated number of assaults. Thus, it seems that shelter residents terminating cohabitation experienced more rapidly escalating violence from their mates, and they took shelter before they had endured as many assaults overall as women who recohabited with the batterer.

Of the CRT and Gelles scales, the Gelles scale measure of the behavior during the worst assault mentioned by the shelter resident differentiated most strongly—but not significantly—between the groups terminating and continuing cohabitation. Of all 15 variables measuring the magnitude of abuse, the Gelles scale displayed the greatest difference between immediate terminators and women who resumed cohabitation ($t=1.296$, $df=141$, p<.20, two-tailed), with terminators having endured more severe assaults on the average. The variable derived by multiplying the Gelles scale score for the worst assault times the frequency rate of assaults was the second strongest differentiator (after frequency of violence) between women eventually terminating cohabitation and those resuming cohabitation ($t=1.647$, $df=125$, p<.11, two-tailed). This recalls Gelles' finding of a nonsignificant trend in which the combined frequency and severity of conjugal violence was the best predictor of eventual divorce among couples represented in his sample.[8] Setting the preceding remarks aside, it is important to recall that the main result of these t tests on the 15 magnitude of abuse variables is to demonstrate no significant linear differences—positive or negative—between shelter residents terminating and resuming cohabitation.

This lack of derived positive or negative linear relationships does not mean, however, that the likelihood in the shelter sample of termination of cohabitation is relatively stable across all levels of the magnitude of the violence. Rather, it is clear that curvilinear statistical relationships between the intensity of abuse and the outcome of the marriage/relationship apply better to the sample data than do linear relationships. Probit analysis of the abuse magnitude variables and the immediate or eventual outcomes of the relationships without exception revealed that, for each magnitude variable, higher-order exponents of the variable were stronger predictors of outcome than the linear—that is, first-order, level of the variable. Cubic (third-power) and quartic (fourth-power) levels of the frequency rate of violent incidents were relatively strong predictors of the eventual outcomes of shelter residents' relationships (probit analysis, p<.11 for each). So were cubic and quartic levels of the two variables that multiplied the frequency rate by the reported or extrapolated number of assaults (p<.17).

To assist the reader in visualizing what these curvilinear relationships imply, a quartic curve relating the sample data on the magnitude of violence to the shelter outcomes would be a curve shaped somewhat like a "W." A curve of this sort shows the greatest likelihoods of termination to occur at very low, moderate, and very high levels of violence, while lowest likelihoods of termination occur at low and high levels of violence. Cubic curves are shaped roughly like an "S" lying on its side; it is harder to generalize what cubic curves represent in the data from this sample. The cubic curves can also be conceptualized as the quartic "W" shape minus either its first descending line or its last ascending line.

PHYSICAL RETALIATION IN SELF-DEFENSE BY THE WOMEN

Pfouts found in her sample a subgroup of battered women who routinely retaliated against their mates' assaults, and whose marriages/relationships were simultaneously the most enduring among Pfouts' sample.[9] Walker's analysis of learned helplessness seems to lead to the opposite expectation—that battered women who defend themselves by fighting back physically would tend to experience themselves as less helpless and, therefore, are more likely to leave their abusive partners than women who do not react in physical retaliation.[10] Whether the battered women retaliated in physical self-defense never, rarely, often, or usually had very little statistical effect on the immediate or eventual outcomes of their relationships. The observed, nonsignificant trends mildly corroborate both Pfouts' finding and the learned helplessness hypothesis. As would be predicted from a learned helplessness approach, women who never used physical means of self-defense had the most durable relationships; 74% resumed cohabiting and only 36% eventually terminated cohabitation with the violent mate. Reminiscent of Pfouts' results, women who usually responded in forcible self-defense also tended to endure in their relationships; 70% resumed cohabiting, while 43% eventually terminated cohabitation. Forty percent of women who used physical self-defense either often or rarely immediately terminated cohabiting, and half of these women eventually terminated.

CONJUGAL ABUSE OF SHELTER RESIDENTS' MOTHERS

Various theoretical arguments can be made in order to support the hypothesis that daughters of battered women will be more likely to remain in violent relationships than daughters of women who were not battered. Some theoretical processes that support the above expectation are: learning by vicarious reinforcement, or modeling; unconscious identification and/or transference; acceptance of conjugal violence as normal or tolerable or inevitable; assimilation of values that dictate preserving marriage at great cost, or at all costs; and membership in an undifferentiated family of origin, among others. Gelles, however, found a statistically insignificant tendency for battered women who had observed conjugal violence between their parents to be more likely to divorce their husbands than battered wives who were daughters of conjugally nonviolent couples.[11]

The present study mildly supports Gelles' empirical findings. In the shelter sample, a little more than two out of every seven women considered themselves to be daughters of battered women. These shelter residents who were daughters of battered women were slightly more likely than the other shelter residents to terminate cohabitation immediately (38.6% vs. 31.8%, p».40), and they were also more likely to experience the eventual termination of cohabitation (52% vs. 40.4%). This latter statistical effect approaches significance enough to be termed a substantial trend ($X^2=1.88$, df$=1$, p‹.18).

CHILD ABUSE SUSTAINED BY SHELTER RESIDENTS

I had expected that shelter residents who had been subjected to physical and/or sexual child abuse earlier in their lives would be less likely to end their violent marriages/relationships. My basis for this expectation was the belief that battered women who had also been battered children would be more likely to perceive domestic violence as normal and/or inevitable, less likely to view domestic nonviolence as a realistic potential alternative, and, consequently, less likely to leave their mates in an attempt to achieve domestic nonviolence in their lives. This expectation was not at all supported by the data, however. The data show literally no statistical association between outcomes of the relationships and the women's experiences as abused or nonabused children.

CONCOMITANT CHILD ABUSE BY THE BATTERER

To some battered women, child abuse by their mate is more unacceptable than his woman abuse.[12] Many shelter residents note child abuse by their mate as a precipitant of their decision to enter shelter. As a consequence of this, I expected a higher rate of termination of cohabitation among battered women who reported child abuse by their mates than among those involved with batterers whom they did not consider child abusers. This hypothesis was contradicted by the data, which showed insignificantly higher tendencies ($p>.50$) for cohabitation to continue between battered women and child-abusive batterers.

DISTANCE TRAVELED BY BATTERED WOMEN TO SHELTER

I also expected the distance from the woman's original residence to the shelter to be positively associated with the rate of termination of cohabitation. This is because the distance a woman traveled in order to get to SAFE House reflected either her determination to leave her mate, the necessity of her leaving for her or her children's survival, or both. In order to measure distance, five categories of distance were developed based on the woman's residence: 1) Ypsilanti or Ann Arbor; 2) Washtenaw County, but outside of Ypsilanti and Ann Arbor—the out-county area; 3) counties in Michigan bordering Washtenaw Co.; 4) more distant areas of Michigan; and 5) outside Michigan. The rates of immediate termination among women in these five residence categories showed nearly significant differences ($X^2=8.746$, df=4, $p<.07$) and in pretty much the expected manner. Women from out-of-state were most likely to terminate immediately (45.5%). They were followed by Michigan women from outside Washtenaw County (41.4%); whether or not they were from a county bordering Washtenaw did not affect the termination rate. Women from Washtenaw County had the lowest rate of immediate termination (24.2%), and there was an unexpected dramatic difference between the rates for out-county residents compared to Ypsilanti-Ann Arbor residents (12% vs. 28.6%, respectively). The near significance of the above statistical analysis does not depend on the uniquely low termination rate among Washtenaw out-county residents, however. If shelter residents are grouped into three residency categories—Washtenaw County, all other Michigan, and states other than Michigan—the observed differences in the termination rates become statistically significant ($X^2=6.37$, df=2, p<.05) and follow the expected pattern.

ASSAILANT'S LEVEL OF EDUCATION

Since higher education is associated with greater material resources, feminist resource theory would predict that the marriages/relationships of more educated batterers will be more likely to endure than those involving less educated batters. Overall, the data support this expectation. It shows a significant difference between the average educational levels of shelter partners who resume cohabitation and those who terminate cohabitation immediately (11.4 vs. 10.6 years, respectively; t=1.861, df=142, p<.04, one-tailed).

Dividing the abusive partners of shelter residents into five educational categories—elementary, some high school, high school graduate or equivalent, some college, college graduate—one finds a steadily declining rate of termination through the first four categories, although there is an unexpected upswing in terminations among relationships involving the most educated batterers (see Table 9).

Table 9   Termination Rates of Shelter Residents' Relationships, By Educational Experience of the Batterer

	Elementary	Some High School	High School Graduate	Some College	College Graduate
Immediate Termination	45.5%	38.6%	30.0%	14.3%	42.9%
Eventual Termination	50.0	46.7	40.4	34.8	42.9

This pattern is not statistically significant ($X^2=5.98$, df=4, p<.21), however. A similar trend persists concerning the rate of eventual termination of cohabitation (see Table 9), but this relationship is even more insignificant statistically ($X^2=1.47$, df=4. p>.80).

ASSAILANT'S ALCOHOL ABUSE

Whether or not the woman considered her partner to be an active or past alcohol abuser had no impact upon the rate of termination of cohabitation. Relationships involving alcoholic batterers were a bit more likely to end (immediate termination: 34.7% vs.30.3%; eventual termination: 43.9% vs. 40.6%), but these differences were well within the range of random differences (p›.50).

BATTERER'S CRIMINAL RECORD OF VIOLENT OFFENSES

Overall, 33.8% of shelter residents stated that their mate had been formally charged and/or convicted of a violent crime, not including the assaults upon the shelter residents. It was hypothesized that when the batterer had been charged with violent offenses other than conjugal assaults, it could affect the outcome of the relationship in two contradictory ways. This situation could intimidate women into being more likely to remain in the relationship. On the other hand, it could hasten the woman's coming to perceive her partner as a violent individual, which in turn would encourage her to dissolve the relationship.[13] While the first hypothesis of an intimidation effect is rejected by the results, the latter hypothesis of an attribution effect is supported here.

The abusive mates are divided into three categories: 1) no known charge for violent offenses; 2) charged once with a violent offense; and 3) convicted of a violent offense and/or charged with more than one violent offense. Assaults upon the shelter resident are not included as violent offenses for the purpose of the above categorization. The three violent offense categories show nearly significant differences in their outcome rates. For immediate terminations, shelter partners with no known charges of extraconjugal violence and those with only one known charge of such violence experience lower rates of termination than batterers in the most violent category—convicted or multiply charged (30% vs. 27% vs. 52%, respectively, $X^2 = 5.02$, df=2, p‹.10). This relationship is even stronger for rates of eventual termination (never charged—41%, one charge—33%, convicted and/or multiple charges—63%; $X^2 = 5.61$, df=2, p‹.10).

Chapter 10

ADDITIONAL RESULTS

FACTORS RELATING TO THE LEVEL OF VIOLENCE

This section shall deal with six measures of the degree of violence suffered by the battered women of the shelter sample and with whether certain factors are statistically related to the magnitude of the abuse that took place. The six variables of interest are: 1) the reported number of assaults; 2) the annualized frequency rate of conjugal assaults prior to shelter entry; 3) the preceding two variables multiplied together; 4) the extrapolated number of assaults; 5 and 6) the severity of the worst assault, as measured separately by the Gelles and CRT scales. As Table 10 shows, these six measures for the most part have statistically significant, high intercorrelations.

Aside from other measures of the intensity of violence, the variables most strongly correlated with the reported number of conjugal assaults were: 1) the elapsed time since the first conjugal assault, $r=.503$, $p<.0001$; 2) the length of the marriage/relationship, $r=.266$, $p<.0005$; 3) the age of the battered woman, $r=.213$, $p<.0005$; 4) the length of the last separation (if any) prior to shelter entry, $r=.258$, $p<.01$; 5) whether the woman was assaulted while pregnant, $r=.221$, $p<.01$; 6) the age of the youngest child (if any), $r=.200$, $p<.015$; 7) the age of the batterer, $r=.166$, $p<.025$; 8) the woman's previous experience in counseling/psychotherapy, r=.149, p<.05. The variables most strongly correlated with the extrapolated number of

Table 10   Correlations Between Variables Measuring The Magnitude of Conjugal Violence

Variable	Reported Number of Assaults	Annual Frequency Rate of Assaults	Number of Assaults Multiplied by their Frequency	Extrapolated Number of Assaults	Worst Assault, CRT Scale
Annual Frequency Rate of Assaults	.388[5]				
Frequency Multiplied By Number of Assaults	.799[5]	.562[5]			
Extrapolated Number of Assaults	1.000[5]	.263[5]	.799[5]		
Worst Incident −CRT Scale	.162[2]	.176[2]	.091	.114[1]	
−Gelles Scale	.240[3]	.167[2]	.156[1]	.166[2]	.553[5]

[1]p<.10
[2]p<.05
[3]p<.01
[4]p<.001
[5]p<.0001

assaults form a similar list: 1) time elapsed since the first conjugal assault, r=.682, p<.0001; 2) length of the relationship, r=.503, p<.0001; 3) age of the battered woman, r=.380, p<.0001; 4) the age of the youngest child, r=.376, p<.0001; 5) the age of the batterer, r=.333, p<.0001; 6) the age of the oldest child, r=.320, p<.0001; 7) whether the woman was assaulted during a pregnancy, r=.194, p<.005; 8) the length of the last separation, r=.205, p<.01; 9) whether the male partner also abused the child(ren), r=.135, p<.03; and 10) whether the shelter resident's mother was a battered woman, r=−.124; p<.055.

Factors reflecting age and time play a more prominent role among the correlates with the extrapolated number of conjugal assaults because the extrapolated number of assaults is derived from a time-dependent variable—the elapsed time since the first assault. The length of the relationship and age of each partner are useful predictors of the number of conjugal assaults mainly because they are strongly related to the time elapsed since the first assault in the relationship. The length of the most recent separation prior to shelter entry is not so much a predictor as an effect of the recurrent violence. Still, these statistical relationships can be of use in the process of clinically assessing a battered woman's predicament when available information for some reason is not complete or detailed. Violence during pregnancy exemplifies the sort of partial information that an intervenor may have that predicts relatively well the magnitude of conjugal abuse that is occurring.

Apart from other measures of the degree of violence, the annualized frequency rate of violence is significantly correlated only with the length of the most recent separation (r=.166, p<.05) and with the approximate distance between the battered woman's residence and the shelter (r=.127, p<.05). However, the frequency rate is also a relatively good predictor of the eventual outcome of the termination of cohabitation (r=.138, p<.09, fifth highest correlation with eventual outcome in the data set). It has the strongest correlation with outcome of any variable that measures the magnitude of conjugal violence.

The variable derived by multiplying together the reported number of assaults and the frequency rate of violent episodes is most strongly correlated with similar variables as the number of assaults: 1) elapsed time since the first assault, r=.375, p<.0001; 2) length of most recent separation, r=.369, p<.0005; 3) length of the marriage/relationship, r=.250, p<.0015; 4) the age of the battered woman, r=.211, p<.01; 5) use of street drugs by the woman abuser, r=.184, p=.02; 6) woman's previous experience in counseling/psychotherapy, r=.149, p<.06; 7) age of the batterer, r=.141, p<.07; and 8) violence during pregnancy, r=.152, p<.08.

The severity of the worst assault mentioned in the shelter records, as measured on Straus et al.'s CRT scale, was significantly correlated with the following (excluding other measures of the magnitude of conjugal violence): 1) whether the battered woman ever received medical treatment for a conjugal assault, r=.260, p=.0001; 2) alcohol abuse by the violent mate, r=.245, p=.0001; 3) approximate distance of the woman's home from the shelter, r=.167, p<.01; 4) whether the battered woman was abused as a child, r=.126, p<.05; and 5) whether the police were ever called during a conjugal assault, r=.111, p<.09. The Gelles scale score for the worst assault shows somewhat distinct statistical relationships from the CRT scale. The Gelles scale scores were most strongly correlated with the following variables: 1) whether the assailant partner had been charged with violent crimes against persons other than the shelter resident, r=.218, p<.001; 2) the approximate distance between the woman's residence and the shelter, r=.162, p<.02; 3) whether the woman ever received medical treatment for a conjugal assault, r=.146, p<.03; 4) the shelter resident's previous experience in counseling/psychotherapy, r=.144, p<.03; and 5) the number of children residing with the woman at SAFE House, r=.112, p<.09.

The difference between the two lists of strong correlations with the CRT and Gelles scales suggests that the CRT is in general a more sensitive measure of the injury caused by a conjugal assault. The Gelles scale quite likely has less correlation than the CRT with the batterer's alcohol abuse because—unlike the CRT—the Gelles scale as used here does not reflect those incidents involving weapons threats that do not result in stabbing or shooting. In this sample, such incidents were often alcohol related. On the other hand, the Gelles score for the worst conjugal assault outstrips the analogous CRT score as a correlate or predictor of both the immediate and eventual termination of cohabitation in shelter residents' conjugal relationships.

It is important to recall that all of the preceding correlational relationships apply to the study data and are not necessarily generalizable to other populations of battered women seeking help. These correlations are quite likely not generalizable to battered women who do not seek intervention from shelters, hotlines, counselors, and other services. This may explain why the present data for the most part do not replicate Straus et al.'s finding of a fairly strong, positive correlation between the number of children in a family and the level of conjugal violence.[1] With the exception of the nearly significant correlation between the number of children and the Gelles score for the worst conjugal assault, this statistical relationship did not prevail in the current study. Straus et al.'s finding of course pertained to a sample composed of a large majority of couples who were identified as conjugally nonviolent, while the present study pertains to self-identified battered women and their mates.

Conjugal Estrangement and Weapons Violence

There was an important relationship between the severity of violent incidents, as measured on the CRT, and the degree of physical proximity or estrangement in the relationship. Women who termed their relationship status as separated—whether from legal marriage or from living together, divorced, terminated, and/or noncohabitant had suffered more serious worst assaults, to a statistically significant degree, compared to women who considered themselves as married or actively living together ($X^2=18.06$, df=8, p<.025). In particular, women from these more estranged relationships were significantly more likely to have suffered threats and/or actual assaults involving knives and guns ($X^2=4.54$, df=1, p<.05). Overall, 40% of the women from the estranged relationships had been threatened and/or assaulted with a gun or knife compared to under 16% of the women from active or less estranged relationships. These weapons threats surely were part of the women's motive for leaving their relationships, but the weapons incidents should also be viewed as indicative of the batterer's escalating response to the battered women's attempts to get him out of her life. This finding recalls Boudouris' research, which found that 40% to 50% of its sample of couples involved in conjugal murder were not cohabiting at the time of the murder.[2]

Defensive Physical Retaliation by the Battered Woman

Existing studies of battered women report that physical retaliation in self-defense by the woman is usually met with intensified violence from the batterer. Carlson reports that 77% of the battered women who did fight back reported that their mates escalated the violence in response. At least one-sixth of Pagelow's sample or at least 25% of those who did fight back had the same experience. Pfouts noted that, in the most violent couples in her sample, all of the women generally fought back.[3] Therefore, in the current study, it was expected that physical retaliation by the shelter residents would be associated with more severe violence by the batterer. This hypothesis was not supported by the data, nor was the converse hypothesis that retaliatory self-defense would be associated with a diminished magnitude of violence by the batterer.

The data do show, however, that women who rarely physically retaliated suffered significantly more severe worst assaults on the average than the rest of the shelter sample—those who never retaliated, often retaliated, and usually retaliated. The group who retaliated rarely comprises one-sixth of the sample. It is largely composed of those women who abandoned the strategy of physical retaliation against assaults because they perceived this strategy as only aggravating their predicament. The data thus corroborate statistically these women's perceptions. The data also suggest that battered women tend to arrive at the best possible self-defense strategy for their situation. The woman's reactions, after all, cannot be expected to halt her mate from battering her.

Race of Assailant

As expected, there were no significant differences between the degree of violence suffered by shelter residents abused by white assailants and those abused by black assailants. In the counseling sample, reports from black and from white clients concerning the number of assaults they had perpetrated were distributed in a significantly different fashion (Mann-Whitney $U=432$, $N=88$, $p<.04$), with whites reporting having committed more assaults than blacks. The distributions of the reports of each racial group on the frequency of violent incidents were different to a nearly significant degree (U=393, N=80, p<.055), again with whites reporting more frequent violence than blacks. These results do not appear to be a function of more defensive denial by blacks nor of more candid self-disclosure by whites since the female partners of the whites in the counseling sample reported a higher median number of assaults (median test, p<.16) and a distribution skewed toward more frequent assaults than did the mates of blacks in the counseling sample (U=261, N=65, p<.125).

Alcohol Abuse by the Batterer

In the shelter sample, mates of former and active alcohol abusers reported significantly more severe average worst assaults than those not involved with alcohol abusers (t=3.89, df=233, p<.0001). Turning to the extrapolated number of conjugal assaults committed, alcoholic batterers were reported to have committed a significantly higher median number of assaults (median test, p<.05). There was also a nearly significant difference between alcoholic and nonalcoholic partners of shelter residents in the distributions of the extrapolated number of assaults (U=7209, N=275, p<.085). Alcoholics were extrapolated to have committed a mean of 96 assaults, compared to a mean of 72.4 conjugal assaults for the batterers who were not problem drinkers. Compared to nonalcoholic assailants, alcoholic batterers were significantly more likely to have used a gun or knife to threaten shelter residents or actually to shoot or stab them: in the shelter sample, 22% of alcoholic batterers were involved in a weapons incident, compared to under 8% of nonalcoholic woman abusers in the sample.

Similar effects occurred in the counseling sample. The group of counseling clients whom the counselor considered to be borderline, former, or active problem drinkers reported a distribution of CRT scores for the worst assault that was skewed to higher severity than that of the rest of the sample, to a degree approaching statistical significance (U=678, N=104, p<.105; median test, p<.075). The mates of batterers who were not problem drinkers in the counseling sample reported less severe average worst assaults than did the partners of alcohol-abusing counseling clients (t=1.86, df=74, p<.07, two-tailed; U=389, N=76, p<.085). Alcohol abusers in the counseling sample were significantly more likely than other counseling clients to have their mates report violence—or threats of violence—involving weapons (22% vs. 11%). Problem drinkers were more likely to have beaten up their wives/partners or worse (CRT score>9, 74% vs. 50%; X^2=3.715, df=1, p<.06), than counseling clients without a drinking problem.

Abuse of Other Substances by the Batterer

Other forms of substance abuse—that is, excluding alcohol abuse—by the batterer were also correlated with reports of more severe violence. In the shelter sample, women battered by substance-abusing assailants generated distributions of reports that were significantly higher in the combined frequency and number of assaults that they endured (U=2384, N=159, p<.04) and showed trends for having sustained more severe worst assaults as measured on both the CRT scale (median test, p<.10) and the Gelles scale (U=5291.5, N=229, p<.10).

Similar effects were more pronounced in the counseling sample. Substance abusers as a group reported significantly more severe worst assaults than non-substance-abusing batterers (still excluding alcohol abuse) on both severity scales (for the CRT, U=861.5, N=105, p<.005; for the Gelles scale, U=1013.5, N=105, p<.04). The partners of counseling clients corroborate this difference between substance-abusive and non-substance-abusive batterers on the CRT scale in reports of the most severe assaultive behavior in the relationship (U=3674.5, N=73, p<.005), though not on the Gelles scale scores of assaultive behavior. While shelter residents reported approximately equal tendencies to use weapons in conjugal assaults by both substance-abusing and non-substance-abusing batterers (16.5% vs. 18.4%, respectively), partners of counseling clients reported significantly different tendencies by the men to employ weapons in conjugal assaults (37% of substance-abusing counseling clients vs. 10.9% of other counseling sample members; X^2=7.13, df=1, p<.01).

Violence in the Batterers' Families of Origin

A possible corollary of the hypothesis of intergenerational transmission of family violence is that batterers from violent families of origin will commit more conjugal assaults and/or more severe conjugal violence than batterers reared in nonviolent family settings. No published research thus far has addressed the issue of whether batterers from violent families of origin tend to be more violent than batterers reared in nonviolent families. Instead, existing research has investigated the correlation between individuals' childhood exposure to spouse and/or child abuse exclusively in terms of the subjects' subsequent commission or noncommission of family violence.[4]

The present study investigated whether the counseling sample showed any tendency to commit more severe, more frequent, or greater numbers of conjugal assaults, according to whether or not the batterer was reared in a violent family. Counseling clients who were raised by conjugally violent parents showed a nearly significant tendency to report having committed more severe worst assaults upon their mates (for the CRT scale: t=1.54, df=93, p<.07, one-tailed; U=787, N=95, p<.075; median test, p<.035; slightly less improbably findings on the Gelles scale). Batterers reared by conjugal abusers also displayed a mild tendency to report having committed more conjugal assaults (U=575, N=77, p<.20).

Available reports from partners of counseling clients corroborated only the last of the above findings, however. Women involved with counseling clients from conjugally violent families of origin reported enduring more conjugal assaults than women involved with men not exposed as boys to conjugal abuse (U=123.5, N=42, p<.04; median test, p<.10). On the CRT and Gelles scales for the severity of assaultive behavior, the counseling clients' mates reported slightly higher average scores for men reared by conjugally nonviolent parents, contradicting the trend shown in the reports by the counseling clients. The strongest of these contradictory trends among the female partners was that their reports concerning batterers who were sons of violent couples showed a lower median severity of conjugal assaults than reports concerning counseling clients reared by conjugally nonviolent couples, to a nearly significant degree (median test, p<.08).

Similar effects were derived concerning counseling clients' subjection to physical child abuse. Counseling clients who were abused as children confessed to committing significantly more severe assaults than those who were not battered as boys (for the CRT scale: t=2.11, df=94, p<.02, one-tailed; for the Gelles scale: t=2.19, df=94, p<.02, one-tailed). Reports from the batterers' partners failed to corroborate this effect. The women reported equal average severities of assaultive behavior by men formerly abused as children and by men who were not battered children. Counseling clients who were battered children also reported committing significantly more conjugal assaults on the average than those who were not battered children (27.3 vs. 4.2 average assaults; U=506, N=79, p<.035). This finding was corroborated by the batterers' wives/partners (58.6 vs. 7 conjugal assaults on average; U=120.5, N=43, p<.125).

Identical effects resulted when clients subjected as children to both spouse and child abuse were compared to the rest of the counseling sample—i.e., counseling clients exposed to either spouse or child abuse, or to neither. Batterers' counseling clients exposed to both conjugal abuse and child abuse in their families of origin, on average, reported committing significantly more severe assaultive behavior than the rest of the counseling sample (for the CRT: t=2.45, df=89, p<.01, one-tailed; for the Gelles scale, t=2.33, df=89, p<.015, one-tailed). Again, however, the reports from the batterers' wives/partners failed to corroborate this effect and, instead, displayed barely higher average severities of conjugal assaults by the men not exposed to both conjugal violence and child abuse. Reports from counseling clients and their partners agree in reporting a significantly greater average number of assaults committed by men formerly subjected to both child and spouse abuse, compared to the rest of the counseling clients. On the men's reports, the "double-exposed" group confessed an average 35.5 conjugal assaults, compared to an average of 4.3 assaults for the rest of the counseling sample (t=1.15, df=71, p<.13, one-tailed; U=463, N=73, p<.025). The women partners reported an average of 77.6 assaults by "double-exposed" mates, compared to 12. 2 assaults on the average by men not exposed to both child and spouse abuse (t=1.31, df=39, p<.10, one-tailed; U=123, N=41, p<.025).

We can draw the following conclusions from the above results. The batterers' counseling clients who were reared by conjugally violent couples had committed a significantly higher average number of conjugal assaults than clients reared by conjugally nonviolent parents. Counseling clients who were formerly battered children had committed a significantly higher average number of conjugal assaults than those who were not formerly battered children. Counseling clients exposed in their families of upbringing to both child abuse and conjugal violence committed significantly more conjugal assaults on average than those not "double-exposed" to family violence. Counseling clients exposed as children to child abuse, conjugal abuse, or both in their family of upbringing showed strong tendencies to confess to more severe assaultive behavior against their mates than counseling clients not exposed to child abuse, conjugal abuse, or both, respectively. Judging from their mates' reports, however, whether or not counseling clients were reared in violent families had no statistical effect on the actual average severity of the worst conjugal assault in the relationship. No differences were found based on the assailants' previous exposure—or lack thereof—to family violence in the frequency of incidents of conjugal violence.

PREDICTORS OF BATTERERS' COUNSELING OUTCOMES

Before discussing counseling outcomes, a few words are in order about the approach to batterers' counseling which I used in my role as counselor. The batterers' counseling rendered was directive. By the end of the first counseling session—and sometimes during the phone call seting up the first appointment—I had stated to each and every client that conjugal violence was unacceptable and unjustifiable behavior. Aside from a few of the earliest counseling cases, I also explicitly stated to all that child abuse and all other forms of family violence were similarly unacceptable behaviors.

I would call this a directive client-centered approach. Unconditional positive regard was clearly restricted to the client as a person and was defined as not extending to all of his behavior. Given my rejection of the clients' violent behavior, the clients' low self-esteem, and the high probability that clients had experienced a good deal of rejection and abuse in their relationships with others, I needed to make great compensatory efforts to communicate to the clients my perception of them as fundamentally acceptable, worthy human beings.

The counseling approach could thus be termed supportive in two ways. First, it was supportive of the clients' self-esteem. Second, it was supportive in the usual sense of a supportive psychotherapy concentrating on building and strengthening ego skills. Once battering had been defined as the problem, the major focus of batterers' counseling in the early sessions was to assist clients in devising strategies for successfully avoiding further violent behavior. This would include using crisis telephone supports, leaving the partner for short periods of time in order to ensure prevention of assaultiveness, negotiating instead of dictating, and communicating about anger and other feelings without resort to verbal or physical abuse. Issues of emotional awareness were discussed mainly as a way to help clients discover cues and warning signs associated with times when they were most likely to attack their loved ones so that batterers could effectively avoid turning violent.

Batterers' counseling was a problem-oriented approach, focusing on violence and the avoidance of further violence. Woman abuse was not construed as a symptom of more fundamental psychological problems. Hence, counseling interactions tended to concentrate directly upon woman-battering. When other aspects of clients' lives were discussed, it was in the context of investigating their relevance to the priority problem of battering. If I discovered that a topic was not relevant to the woman abuse problem, I did my best to steer the interaction back to issues pertinent to battering. Only if battering behavior seemed to be effectively halted or in long abeyance, did I take time to pursue topics with the client that were not of direct relevance to the conjugal violence.

I conceptually de-emphasized uncovering traumatic aspects of the clients' early histories. In practice, however, counseling interactions often harked back to violence in clients' families of origin that had provided them a violent model of conjugal and/or family behavior. The point of these discussions was not to abreact early trauma, but to note how clients' violent reactions and values justifying violence had been learned by them so that they could learn different response strategies for the present and future.

While the problem requiring counseling intervention was defined behaviorally and short-term strategies for avoiding violence were concrete and behavioral, the counseling did not take a behaviorist approach. Issues of reward and punishment were not given great importance. Relaxation techniques were rarely used due to usually unfavorable client responses when these methods were attempted. The approach was pragmatically problem oriented, but it relied upon a humanistic model of mostly conversational interaction.

The major emphasis was upon alternatives to violence and upon learning interior or exterior signals that indicated when it was especially important for the client to remember to execute those alternatives. I developed this overall emphasis in response to my perceptions of the clientele as a whole. Batterers tended to discuss violence as inevitable: "What else could I do?" I would respond to expressions of the unavoidable nature of violence with lengthy lists of acceptably nonviolent alternatives. Some of the alternatives mentioned were intentionally peculiar, absurd, or humorous in order to offer a sense of a very broad repertoire of potential behavioral alternatives.

Batterers also tended to discuss their violent behavior as sudden, unforeshadowed, and out of their control. My responses emphasized that the violence was attended by early warning signs. "Violence is not like a bolt of lightning from a clear blue sky. There are storm clouds that gather beforehand that you can learn to notice so that you're not caught unaware by your own behavior." As counselor I repeated over and over, in many and various ways, that clients were in control of their behavior and responsible for it.

Firm but gentle confrontation of the clients' rationalization or denial of their violence was another common type of counseling intervention. Confrontation was especially important if a client refused to admit that he had committed conjugal violence or denied that violence was a problem in his marriage/relationship. I generally attempted to balance confrontation with support in hope of maintaining or establishing rapport with the client and of avoiding rejection of the client as an individual. Discussion can now proceed to the statistical results regarding the outcomes of the batterers' counseling approach just described.

There were three estimators of the outcome of batterers' counseling for each counseling client: 1) the longest domestically nonviolent interval in the client's life after initiating counseling that is known to me; 2) the number of batterers' counseling sessions attended; and 3) my subjective rating of the counseling outcome on a five-point scale. The first two counseling outcome measures are fairly self-explanatory, except that one needs to be aware that the nonviolent interval measure is affected by the fact that follow up by the counselor after termination of counseling was not extremely thorough. I did follow up reliably upon most counseling clients who attended six or more sessions, but follow up was much less systematic for clients with briefer involvement in batterers' counseling. Follow-up data used to derive the nonviolence interval are also based in part upon chance encounters between ex-clients and myself, and upon other uncontrolled factors such as which ex-clients chose to call or to write me after leaving counseling. The nonviolence interval also reflects information from shelter files about which partners of counseling clients called for further assistance against battering after the counseling client had initiated counseling, and when such calls were received at the shelter.

My subjective rating of outcome does not reflect an attempt at developing an objective rating system for counseling outcomes. The higher the score given on the five-point scale, the more change toward domestic nonviolence I attributed to the client. I was very conservative in giving out high scores. The highest score—five—was reserved for clients whom I felt showed strong potential for permanent domestic nonviolence; there were only five clients in this category. Seven clients who had recently initiated counseling at the time of the study were not given outcome rating scores at all because it would have been premature to do so.

Note that the preceding two paragraphs have employed the term *domestic nonviolence* instead of *conjugal nonviolence*. This refers to an issue that arose in the counseling of a few clients who misjudged my expectations and transferred their assaultive behavior to their children while remaining conjugally nonviolent. The counseling outcomes do not reflect known incidents of child abuse as occurring during "nonviolent" intervals. Thus, all of the outcomes measures more accurately reflect the clients' known progress in halting all forms of intrafamily assaults, not just conjugal assaults.

The three outcomes measures all intercorrelate very strongly. The correlation between the longest known interval of domestic nonviolence and the number of counseling sessions attended was .732. The correlation between the subjective five-point rating and the number of sessions attended was .583. For the subjective rating and the longest nonviolent interval, the correlation was .713. All three of the above correlations are significant at the $p<.0001$ level. The strength of these intercorrelations is all the more impressive in light of the subjectivity of the counselor's outcome rating.

Table 11 displays the strongest predictors of the two objective counseling outcomes variables. As can be seen from Table 11, the lists of predictors for the number of sessions attended and for the longest known nonviolent period are very similar.

Table 11 shows that the strongest predictor of the objective outcomes is the concordance between the Gelles scale scores of the counseling client's and his wife/partner's independent accounts of the worst assault in their relationship. The clients' accounts of their most severe violent behavior are similarly strong predictors of the objective outcomes measures. The positive correlation means that, in general, when a counseling client reported perpetrating more severe conjugal violence, it was associated with attendance at more counseling sessions and with longer intervals of domestic nonviolence. This effect, taken together with the predictive importance of the concordance between clients' and their mates' reports, seems to indicate that more candid reports from the batterers' counseling clients were associated with better objective outcomes.

The significant positive correlations between counseling outcomes and severity scores also indicate that those clients who perceive their violent behavior as more severe tend to be more motivated, both to remain in counseling and to maintain nonviolent behavior. A similar interpretation holds for the positive correlation between objective counseling outcomes and the admission of having committed battering upon a pregnant woman, and for the positive statistical relationship between outcomes and clients reporting conjugal violence between their parents. The reports of childhood exposure to conjugally violent parents do not just reflect candor by the clients. Familiarity with conjugal abuse and its negative effects and the wish to behave differently than a violent parent did serve as additional motives for the counseling client to change.

I have no easy interpretation for the strong negative relationship between the partner's terming the counseling client a problem drinker and the objective counseling outcomes. Naturally, it reflects poorer outcomes among counseling clients considered problem drinkers by their wives/partners. The reasons behind this effect are open to speculation.

The strongest predictors of the counselor's subjective outcome score are somewhat distinct from the predictors of the objective counseling outcomes. The strongest predictor is whether or not the counseling client's partner was in SAFE House prior to his beginning counseling. Those clients who initiated counseling without their partner having entered SAFE House had significantly higher average subjective outcome scores than husbands/partners of SAFE House residents ($p<.01$; $r=.285$). This effect undoubtedly is due in large part to the motivation among many partners of SAFE House residents merely to retrieve their wives/lovers rather than

Table 11   Correlations of Selected Variables With Objective Measures of Batterers' Counseling Outcomes

Variable	Counseling Sessions Attended $(r=)$	Rank	Longest Nonviolent Interval $(r=)$	Rank
Male-Female Concordance, Gelles Scale Score for Worst Assault	.292[3]	1	.246[2]	2
Gelles Score for Worst Assault, Batterer's Report	.241[2]	2	.183[1]	5
Alcohol Abuse by Batterer, Alleged by Woman Partner	−.275[2]	3	−.254[2]	1
Assault During Pregnancy Reported by Batterer	.302[2]	4	.210	8
Worst Assault Reported by Batterer, CRT Scale	.203[2]	5	.196[2]	3
Conjugal Abuse Between Batterer's Parents	.195[1]	6	.200[1]	4

[1] $p < .10$
[2] $p < .05$
[3] $p < .01$

halt their violent behavior. It also may reflect greater motivation to change among men who seek batterers' counseling in response to milder leverage than their mates' leaving and taking shelter.

The other three strong predictors of the subjective score for counseling outcomes were again related to the severity of the reported conjugal violence. These were: 1) the client's report of his most violent behavior in the relationship, as scored on the CRT scale ($r = .21$, $p < .05$); 2) his mate's account of the worst violence she suffered at his hands, as scored on the CRT ($r = .22$, $p < .06$); and 3) the counseling client's and his partner's concordance in their independent reports of the most severe violence, as scored on the Gelles scale ($r = .22$, $p < .06$). Once again, reports of more severe conjugal violence were associated with better counseling outcomes.

It is important to note that I expected only one of these strong predictive relationships—the positive association between outcome and male-female concordance in independent reports of the most serious conjugal assault. It is also important to note that male-female concordances for the number of assaults committed and for the frequency of violent episodes did not prove to be important counseling outcomes predictors, nor did the concordance for the severity of conjugal violence as measured on the CRT scale. Of the concordance statistics gathered, only male-female concordances on the Gelles scale scores for the worst assaultive behavior proved to be a strong predictor of counseling outcome.

It appears that the difference between the CRT and Gelles scales in the predictive strength of concordance scores may have to do with the Gelles scale not capturing data relating to weapons threats while the CRT does. Apparently, for the initial counseling sessions, a batterer's reluctance to disclose weapons threats when he has, in fact, perpetrated such threats is not more predictive of poorer counseling outcome than if the client does, early on, reveal such an incident to the counselor. Therefore, since the CRT scale provides a way to score weapons threats while the Gelles does not, the male-female concordance on the CRT scale is weakened as a predictor of counseling outcomes, while the male-female concordance on the Gelles scale is not affected in this way.

I expected more severe violent behavior by the counseling client, a history of exposure to conjugally abusive parents, and reports by clients of battering their pregnant mates to be negatively correlated with good counseling outcomes, if at all strongly correlated with counseling outcomes. The positive correlation between counseling outcomes and these latter factors was entirely unexpected. Of course, all of these predictive relationships only hold with certainty for the counseling sample in this study. They are quite likely generalizable to similar populations—i.e., batterers voluntarily seeking counseling for assistance in halting their violence against their wives/partners. There is no reason to believe that these findings would generalize to the entire general population of batterers. Thus, I still believe that more severe violent behavior and a violent family background would be predictors of poor counseling prognosis among the general population of woman batterers. For those exceptional woman abusers who do voluntarily seek counseling, however, it appears that reporting these factors is associated with better prognosis.

Chapter 11

SUMMARY AND DISCUSSION OF RESULTS

In many important aspects, the study samples match the adult population of Washtenaw County and southeastern Michigan. The racial makeup of both the shelter sample and the counseling sample is identical to the racial composition of the overall population in the catchment area of the two services. Except for underrepresentation of the extreme high and low ends of the continuum, the distribution of the educational level of the assailant partners of shelter residents is no different than one would expect from a random sample of Michigan men. The batterers' counseling clients are no more likely than Michigan men in general to be military veterans. For each shelter resident cohabiting with children, the mean number of children living with her is 2.1, the overall state average. The SAFE House residents studied appear not to differ from adult American women in general in the rate with which they were as children exposed to either conjugal or child abuse in their family of upbringing.

The joblessness rates among male partners of shelter residents, and among the counseling clients, are very closely matched to the prevalence of joblessness that one would expect among men in southeastern Michigan during the study period. Due to the youth of the shelter partners and counseling clients, however, the obtained joblessness rates include fewer retired or disabled nonparticipants in the work force than would be expected of Michigan men overall. Therefore, the apparent conformity between the expected and observed joblessness rates for batterers does not rule out the possibility that the batterers experienced an unemployment rate—in the conventional labor statistics sense—that was significantly higher than the average one for the area during the study period.

The study samples do differ statistically in some major respects from the general population of married/cohabiting adults. Compared to the general U.S. population, the women in the shelter sample were more likely to have experienced a premaritally conceived birth, to be a member of an unmarried cohabiting couple instead of a legal marriage, and to be involved in an interracial conjugal relationship. Compared to Michigan women in general, the shelter residents were more likely not to be employed outside the home and to be welfare recipients.

All of the samples studied—shelter residents, their assailant partners, and counseling clients—differed significantly from the general U.S. married/cohabitant population in their age distributions. This was due to very little representation of persons aged 40 years and over among the samples, and the overrepresentation of people in their twenties among those younger than age 40. The significantly lower median age at marriage of legally married shelter residents relative to the general population of married women and the underrepresentation in the shelter sample of women not living with children are results related to the unusual age distribution of the shelter sample. It is impossible to say whether these age-related results primarily reflect patterns of service delivery and utilization, a higher risk of conjugal violence among younger couples, or an interaction of these two factors.

Both the counseling clients and the shelter residents' violent partners display very high rates of problem drinking. The counseling clients also show dramatically high levels of exposure to conjugally violent parents and of early subjection to physical child abuse. About 80% of the batterers' counseling clients were sons of conjugal batterers, or were formerly battered children, or were both. Not all of the remaining 20% of counseling clients should be assumed to come from nonviolent family backgrounds since some of the clients probably successfully withheld or suppressed information regarding their early exposure to family violence. Also, a few clients orphaned early in life were counted as from nonviolent families because they did not know of any violence in their families of origin. Still, for these few cases, the reports on the family of origin are particularly unreliable and may slightly diminish the derived rates of violence in the counseling clients' families of origin.

The study results comparing counseling clients' accounts of their conjugal violence with independent reports from the wife or woman partner involved could scarcely show a more dramatic divergence between partners' reports. As predicted by the previous literature, the violent men report committing far less conjugal violence, more infrequently, and of a less dangerous nature than do their victims, the battered women. Considering that the counseling sample probably represents a more candid group than woman batterers in general, and that the mathematical procedures in this study were designed intentionally to increase male-female agreement, these dramatic male-female differences become truly staggering.

Regarding the severity of conjugal violence, the findings statistically document the statements in the existing literature that, as time goes on, conjugal violence tends to escalate in its severity and in the frequency of its occurrence. A strong link between weapons violence by batterers and estrangement in the marriage or conjugal relationship has been demonstrated. The results also show that batterers who abuse alcohol and/or other drugs have a tendency as a group to commit more physically dangerous assaults than batterers who are substance-temperate.

It tentatively appears that the study data could represent a first step toward establishing a curvilinear relationship between the battered woman's tendency to break away permanently from her violent mate and the degree of abuse that he inflicts upon her. At the least, the study unambiguously suggests the advisability of further research on the hypothesis of a curvilinear statistical relationship between the permanent rupture of battering relationships and the magnitude of the conjugal abuse involved.

As suggested in the existing literature, previous behavior regarding conjugal separations was a strong predictor of the termination or resumption of cohabitation with the abuser after the shelter stay. Shelter residents who immediately stopped cohabiting with the batterer had on the average experienced just over five previous conjugal separations, significantly more than the average number of previous separations among women who recohabited. This figure is also very close to that predicted by Walker, and by Hilberman and Munson, for battered women sundering their marriages/relationships.[1] Women terminating cohabitation had also experienced conjugal separations prior to the shelter stay that were significantly more recent, and significantly longer on the average, than those experienced by women resuming cohabitation. The likelihood of termination of cohabitation reached its peak at five to seven years' duration of the relationship.

The study results clearly demonstrate the importance of economic considerations in the shelter residents' decisions whether or not to attempt to terminate their conjugal relationships. In general, the data show that the greater the woman's economic resources were, relative to her mate's income, the greater the likelihood was of cohabitation terminating—presumably at the woman's instigation. Couples where the battered woman was unambiguously the main income producer were twice as likely to experience immediate breakups as the rest of the shelter sample. In fact, a majority (54.5%) of the couples primarily supported by the battered woman's income broke up immediately.

Of the couples in the shelter sample where the batterer was not employed, almost half (48%) broke up immediately, a significantly higher termination rate than the rate among couples where the batterer had a job. Among the relationships terminating immediately, the assailants had a significantly lower mean educational level than the batterers from relationships where cohabitation resumed after the woman left SAFE House. Since more education is positively correlated with earning more income, the above result concerning the assailants' education can also be interpreted as reflecting the relative income production of the two groups of assailant partners. The results also show a trend for shelter residents who receive an independent income by virtue of being welfare recipients to be more likely to break off cohabitation, and a slight tendency for battered women having a job outside the home to be more likely to terminate cohabitation.

All of the following variables lacked any significant association with shelter outcomes: age of the battered woman or of her assailant partner; race of the shelter resident or of her assailant partner; racial composition of the couple—intraracial or interracial; the number of children living with the woman; the age of those children (if any); the occupational status of the assailant (on either of the two scales used to measure this variable); whether or not the couple was legally married, or had ever been legally married; whether the woman in shelter had been a battered daughter earlier in her life; whether or not the woman considered her mate a child abuser; whether or not the woman alleged alcohol abuse or other substance abuse by her mate. Whether or not the shelter resident had been reared by a conjugally violent couple also showed no significant impact on the outcomes data. However, this last factor did exhibit a trend in an unexpected direction—namely, that women with childhood exposure to conjugal violence in their families were more likely to terminate cohabitation with their violent partners.

DISCUSSION

Probably the most impressive findings in this study concern the dramatic disagreements between counseling clients and their abused partners in their descriptions of the conjugal violence that has occurred in their relationships. The available data cannot prove whether it is the men's reports or the women's reports that are the more accurate. However, the existing literature suggests that, in general, battered women give conservative reports of the violence that they have endured. Furthermore, no published source suggests that battered women have any general tendency to exaggerate or to fabricate their accounts of conjugal violence. My clinical experience—including certain logical impossibilities offered by counseling clients—has led me to an unshakable conviction that batterers do in general tend to minimize and/or deny their violent behavior. The findings regarding batterers' counseling outcomes seem to support the widespread impression among batterers' counselors that good counseling outcomes are associated with the client's recognition that his woman abuse is a serious problem.

Battered women and batterers can encounter a variety of people called on to intervene in some manner related to conjugal violence. These intervenors include police officers and sheriff's deputies, judges, prosecutors, lawyers, Friend of the Court officials, probation officers, physicians, nurses, social workers, psychotherapists, psychological counselors, marriage counselors, clergy, and shelter workers. Many of these intervenors face difficulties in assessment and deciding upon an intervention strategy that are complicated by the divergence in the conjugal partners' accounts of the problem. Often it is important—or at least would be desirable—to know which partner's report is the more accurate. A typical example is the police team in which one officer hears a husband describe a minor spat, while the wife in a separate room describes to the other officer a dangerous felonious assault or even an attempted murder. Based on these reports, the police must decide whether to make an arrest, inform the woman of the availability of emergency shelter for her, or leave the couple alone to "work things out." It is clear that the police decision in this situation has extensive implications for each member of the couple involved and upon the continuation or cessation of the conjugal violence.

The existing literature on battering documents an overwhelming tendency for intervenors to disbelieve the battered woman and to believe the batterer.[2] As a consequence of this issue, one of Pizzey's favorite adjectives for woman batterers is "plausible."[3] The batterer's plausibility is due to many factors, including myths and customs that portray women as less reliable reporters than men; the predominant tendency by usually male intervenors to identify with the man involved; the batterer's social skills and charm; myths and prejudices supporting violence against wives/girlfriends/women; the myth that violent men are obviously different, and not regular or nice guys.

The present study demonstrates, however, that in general intervenors should give more credence to the battered woman's report than to the batterer's when their two reports differ. In order to be more fair, more accurate, and more helpful, we need to treat batterers as implausible informants. This is not to say that all battered women are angels who never lie. There are instances where intervenors must decide in which partner's report to place more trust. In such cases, it seems clear that intervenors will make fewer mistakes and better protect human safety by favoring the battered woman's account.

To the extent that this study and future research show couples involved in woman-battering to be otherwise ordinary Americans, the feminist analysis of woman abuse is supported. The feminist view of battering rejects the view that battered women or woman batterers are deviant according to some psychological or sociological criteria. Instead, this analysis emphasizes the tragic normality of battering under sexist patriarchal traditions. This study is only a first attempt to explore the issue of the deviance or nondeviance of members of woman-battering relationships. This investigation has unfortunately failed to address many important factors, especially variables related to social status.

In revealing that SAFE House residents apparently do not differ from adult American women in general in the prevalence of violence in their families of upbringing, this study similarly supports feminist theory. These findings tend to contradict analyses that view battered women as women susceptible to entering violent relationships due to processes such as transference, unconscious identification, modeling, vicarious reinforcement, or the assimilation of family values regarding conjugal or family violence. Those shelter residents who were as children exposed to family violence also do not show any overall statistical tendency—as evidenced in terminating or continuing cohabitation—toward increased resignation to, or acceptance of, the abuse that they endure. In fact, the women in this study who were daughters of conjugally abusive couples were more likely to experience the termination of their marriages/relationships than women reared by conjugally nonviolent couples. These findings also contradict hypotheses based upon concepts of transference, unconscious identification, modeling, or assimilation of family values condoning conjugal violence, which would predict that women from violent childhood homes would show a heightened tendency to resume cohabitation with their abusive mates relative to shelter residents with nonviolent childhood histories.

That shelter residents are not more likely than American women in general to have had domestically violent childhoods has some important implications for therapeutic intervention with battered women. Many clinicians believe that, in therapy with battered women, the woman's tendency to choose a mate similar to her violent father should always be a major focus.[4] The present study contradicts this belief by demonstrating that there is no general tendency for the sample of shelter residents to be daughters of woman abusers. These results do not rule out the possibility—indeed, the inevitability—that childhood exposure to spouse and/or child abuse will be an important issue in counseling some battered women. Still, the data indicate that a childhood history of family violence is no greater an issue in mental health intervention with battered women than it would be with anyone. Furthermore, the presence or absence of a childhood history of family violence apparently does not statistically affect the battered woman's decision regarding terminating or resuming cohabitation with her violent partner.

These findings also suggest that preventive interventions aimed at helping children avoid future violent conjugal relationships are no more indicated for daughters of battered women than for girls in general. In fact, the somewhat greater tendency to recohabit with violent partners shown by the women who were not exposed to conjugally violent parents suggests that preventive intervention may be more important for daughters of conjugally nonviolent couples. On the other hand, the very high rate of family violence in the counseling clients' families of origin supports the concept of the intergenerational transmission of battering behavior. These results leave open the question whether this intergenerational transmission is due to unconscious identification, modeling or vicarious reinforcement, assimilation of values permitting or encouraging conjugal violence, genetic inheritance of violent tendencies, or an interaction of some or all of the preceding factors. It is my conclusion that the hypothesis of the intergenerational transmission of violence holds true for the commission of conjugal violence, but that there is no tendency for the role of battered mate to be transmitted intergenerationally. I view the sexist structure of our society as an absolutely crucial support for the intergenerational transmission of the perpetration of woman-battering.

It is important to note that none of the statistical deviancies found in this study can account in total for the cause(s) of woman abuse. For example, while 80% of batterers' counseling clients were exposed while boys to family violence, certainly some were not—perhaps as many as 20%. One must be careful to note that some deviations that are statistically significant are not at all important as causal generalities. For example, black-white interracial relationships are overrepresented to a very improbable degree in the shelter sample, but they still only comprise a small proportion of that sample.

The relationship between conjugal estrangement and the most severe forms of violence—weapons incidents—demonstrates the great physical risk that a battered woman incurs in her attempt to end a relationship with a batterer. Boudouris has already pointed out that 40% to 50% of conjugal murders occur while the couple is no longer cohabiting, and the National Crime Survey found that about one-fourth of wife assaults reported were perpetrated by the divorced ex-husbands of the victims.[5] Both Gayford and Roy have established that fear of continued violence by the batterer is a leading reason why battered women resume cohabitation with their abusive mates.[6] This information has crucial importance for intervenors working to assist battered women; one must continually bear in mind the danger involved in any attempt the battered woman may make to end her abusive relationship. This information also speaks eloquently to the absolutely essential need—in the absence of effective legal protection—for battered women to have resources providing safe emergency refuge, primarily battered women's shelters or volunteer home networks designed for battered women.

Similarly, adequate safety precautions must be taken in assisting battered women, either once they leave the woman's shelter or if they do not use shelter services in the first place. These precautions of course are subject to the given woman's preference. Some women who break off their conjugal relationships will want to hide from their former mates, and some will not. Intervenors must take steps to ensure that the woman's decisions regarding safety precautions are informed by a realistic assessment of the risk of further violence by her violent former mate. Unfortunately, one cannot rely upon the goodwill and reasonableness of the batterer to leave his ex-partner alone; I am aware of batterers who returned to kill their ex-wives after divorces and separations of several years' duration.

I would like to reiterate my values concerning the outcomes of shelter residents' relationships. I do not take the view that all battered women must terminate—or must attempt to terminate—their marriages/relationships with their abusers. Rather, my perspective is that battered women have the right to make an informed choice whether to attempt either to continue or to terminate their violent relationships, and whether to recohabit with or to separate from their violent mates. This informed choice should include supplying the battered woman with the information that batterers are extremely unlikely to halt their violence—even with counseling—and that the batterer's violence will in general tend to escalate in frequency and severity as the relationship continues.

I also recognize that decisions regarding ending or continuing the relationship may not be the top priority issues for a given battered woman, and that living without conjugal violence may likewise not be a high or top priority for a given battered woman. On the other hand, given that conjugal violence does tend to worsen as the relationship persists, given the difficulty and obstacles women face in breaking off a marriage/conjugal relationship, and the courage required to attempt to break up, I always consider the dissolution of a violent relationship to be a good and desirable outcome. It is of course especially desirable that there be no continued violence by the batterer, but this is not a matter the battered woman can control at all.

The continuation of a relationship as a battering relationship is *always* a bad outcome, but there are exceptional instances where the recohabitation of a battered woman with her formerly abusive mate does not involve further conjugal abuse. Furthermore, some battered women want to give their mate another chance to prove he can reform his behavior before sundering the relationship. Intervenors working with women who feel this way should raise the option of not giving the batterer any more chances as a valid alternative, but they should affirm whatever decision the woman makes. The only exception to this general rule would be situations where it seems virtually certain that a woman will be murdered or severely injured if she recohabits with her mate. Also, there will be situations where a woman's decision to recohabit will pose grave physical and/or sexual danger to one or more of her cohabiting children; in such cases, child protective services must immediately be informed and mobilized on behalf of the welfare of the endangered child or children.

Shelter residents whose partners entered batterers' counseling were more likely to resume cohabiting with their mate, but they were about equally likely as other shelter residents to terminate cohabitation eventually. This result seems to reflect an initial increase in the women's hope for, or belief in, their partners' potential to halt their conjugal violence when the batterers attend counseling. Some batterers' counselors refuse to inform their client's partner that the batterer is in counseling in order to offset this last effect. My own practice has been to speak to battered women— individually or in groups—in order to educate the women as to what results they can realistically expect if their partners get batterers' counseling and, also, to train shelter workers so that they can pass on the same information to the battered women whom they serve.

The findings of this study suggest that, of battered women who experience repeated conjugal separations and recohabitations, many—if not most—are experiencing a process in which they become progressively more likely to end their conjugal relationships. For many—perhaps for all— battered women who use conjugal separation as a coping strategy, the process of leaving their abusers and then returning to them is not an endless treadmill. Rather, it is a progressive process in which women exert increasing leverage upon their violent mates to change, while the women simultaneously become more familiar and more competent with living separately from their mates. Successive separations may also afford the battered woman opportunities to build up her resources—financial, educational, and occupational—in order to effect eventually a successful termination of her violent relationship. Apparently few battered women are willing to relinquish immediately their hopes and dreams of conjugal happiness in their current relationship, as indicated by the peak likelihood of divorce or breakup occurring after five to seven years' duration of the relationship—or after four to five years have elapsed since the initial conjugal assault in the relationship. This fact should not surprise us, however, nor should it be morally repellent as if people are ethically obliged to terminate their conjugal relationship should their mate assault them.

To reiterate, the study findings indicate that the process of separating and recohabiting by battered women is not an endless back-and-forth shuttle in static equilibrium, but rather a progressive process toward change in the violent relationship, including the termination of that relationship. The view supported by the data is very much at odds with a common public attitude that there is little point in sheltering battered women since they just go back home anyway. The perspective that battered women are obliged to terminate their conjugal relationships is based upon the destructive notion of the worthy victim discussed by Eisenberg and Micklow.[7] This latter viewpoint is usually associated with the belief that battered women do not, in general, live up to this supposed obligation to end their violent conjugal relationships. These suppositions are often invoked in order to support an analysis of battered women as masochists. The current study demonstrates, however, that battered women in fact do experience permanent breakups from their abusers with some regularity; over 30% terminated cohabitation beginning directly with the shelter stay studied, and over 43% within two years of that shelter stay. Thus, battered women do tend to leave their abusers on a permanent basis, they tend to go through several temporary conjugal separations before making a permanent conjugal break, and they are not obliged in the first place to prove themselves worthy victims by breaking off their violent conjugal relationships.

The demonstrated tendency for battered women with greater economic resources to be more likely to terminate their battering relationships is very important. In light of these results, women having equal access to the paid work force and receiving equal pay for comparable work as men can be seen as not only a fundamental matter of gender justice but also as a source of leverage to stop woman-battering. Job training, career counseling, and job placement programs designed wholly or largely for women—e.g., displaced homemaker programs and educational programs for nontraditional students—should function similarly to reduce the prevalence and perpetuation of battering relationships.

INDICATIONS FOR FUTURE RESEARCH

Due to the newness of research into battering, probably every topic studied in this work deserves further investigation. Many topics not treated adequately here—e.g., socioeconomic and intrapsychic factors—also require further research efforts. The type of research that is most urgently needed has not yet been mentioned at all in this work, but this omission will now be corrected.

For the near future, the most important research into conjugal violence will attempt to distinguish what types of interventions by various social agencies will be most effective in halting or preventing conjugal assaults. A first breakthrough study of this kind was just released during the writing of this work. The study in question compared three police intervention strategies and their effectiveness in deterring further conjugal assaults.[8] It is precisely this sort of research—only not limited solely to police interventions but also including judicial, medical, social service and mental health interventions—that is most critically needed for the present.

APPENDICES

APPENDIX A

Table of Variables
Collected from the Shelter Sample

N=300 (approx.), unless otherwise noted

Variable Number and Name	Coding Criteria	Descriptive Statistics	Remarks
1. Case number	Self-explanatory	N/A	Confidential for researcher use only
2. Intake worker	One i.d. number per intake worker	N/A	
3. Age of shelter resident	In years, at last birthday before entry	Mean =27.7 Range: 16-55 Median=26	
4. Place of residence	17 categories, mostly by county in Michigan. Also, Ann Arbor, Ypsilanti and out-of-state each given separate category.	30% Ypsilanti; 10% Ann Arbor; 11% Washtenaw Out-county; 18% Wayne County; 6% out-of-state	
5. Race	white, black, Asian, Hispanic, native American	79% white, 17% black 4% other	Comparable to area population at large
6. Number of children	Not total number, but children living with woman at/around time of shelter entry	Mean=1.84 Range: 0-6	
7. Age of youngest child	In years, at last birthday for children counted in variable 6 (V6) above	Mean=3.3 Range: 0-21	N=254
8. Age of eldest child	See V7 above. If there is only one child, he or she is counted on both V7 and V8	Mean=6.2 Range: 0-23	N=251

Variable Number and Name	Coding Criteria	Descriptive Statistics	Remarks
9. Employment status	1=Not employed outside home; 2=Part time and/or receiving unemployment compensation 3=Full time	73% not employed; 22% full-time employed	To be distinguished from Labor Dept. definitions
10. Welfare benefit status	Status on entry into shelter. 1=Not receiving welfare; 2=Receiving welfare	30% welfare recipients on entry	Significantly greater proportion of welfare recipients than general MI. women's population
11. Automobile in woman's possession at shelter?	1=No, 2=Yes	37% brought automobile	
12. Prescription drugs in woman's possession	1=None; 2=Yes, non-specific; Other categories for: minor tranquilizers, major tranqs., antidepressants, sleeping aids, sleeping aids + painkiller/minor tranq., sleeping aid + other, painkiller, methadone	Only 18% brought any sort of prescription medication	Partly attributable to shelter restrictions on drugs and alcohol
13. Previous involvement in counseling and/or psychotherapy?	Does not include crisis counseling leading directly to shelter stay, nor irrelevant types of counseling (e.g., academic counseling much earlier in life). 1=No, 2=Yes	52% have been in some type of counseling/ psychotherapy	
14. Marital status	Relative to current abusive partner. 1=Married, 2=Living together, 3=Separated from marriage, 4=Sep'd from living together, 5=Divorced, 6=Noncohabitant active relationship, 7=Non-cohabitant broken-off relationship, 8=Divorced and remarried same husband, 9=Divorced but still cohabitant	77% married; 12% living together; 3% noncohabitant; 5% separated from marriage	Living-togethers significantly over-represented compared to USA census figures

Variable Number and Name	Coding Criteria	Descriptive Statistics	Remarks
15. Length of relationship	In months. Since marriage for marrieds; since initiation of cohabitation for cohabitants; since beginning of relationship for noncohabitants	Mean=72.5 (6 years) Range: 1-369 (30.75 years)	
16. Number of previous separations	Minimum 24 hours apart from husband/partner. Not legal separations necessarily, but in context of conflict.	Mean=0.9 Range: 0-75 Median=0.9	
17. Time elapsed since last separation	In months, up to 99. Not scored if no previous separations have occurred	Mean=14.7 Range: 1-99 Median= 6.1	N=179
18. Length of last separation	In days, up to a maximum of 999.	Mean=90 Range: 1-999	N=178
19. Elapsed time since first assault	In months.	Mean=56.6 Range: 1-348 Median=38.3	
20. Total number of conjugal assaults endured	To a maximum of 999.	Mean=59 Range: 1-999	N=186. Many unscoreable responses, such as "countless," "innumerable," etc.
21. Frequency of assaults	Annual rate based on woman's estimate. Daily= 365, monthly=12, etc.	Mean=65.3 Range: 1-365 Median=11.5	N=242
22. Self-defense by woman (i.e., physical retaliation)	1=Never; 2=Not generally, rarely; 3=Yes, sometimes; 4=Yes, generally or often	46% Never; 37% Sometimes, often, or usually	N=239
23. Exposure to battering as a child	1=No exposure; 2=Father (figure) beat mother (figure); 3=Mother (figure) beat father (figure)	30.6% are daughters of wifebatterers/ battered wives. 0.8% exposed to husband-battering.	N=242. Similar to Straus et al.'s national prevalence findings.

Variable Number and Name	Coding Criteria	Descriptive Statistics	Remarks
24. Abused as a child?	1=No; 2=Yes, non-specific. Separate categories for abuse by father, by mother, by both parents	29.9% abused as children by one or more parent(s)/ parent figure(s)	
25. Ever beaten during pregnancy?	By current partner. 1=No 2=Yes	62% beaten during pregnancy	N=255
26. Does batterer also abuse your/his child(ren)?	1=No, 2=Yes	44% alleged to be child abusers	N=269
27. Elapsed time since last beating	In days	Range: 1-547 Median=1.1	
28. Severity of last assault	Using Straus' CRT scale, ranging from 1 to 11. 1=No violence; 2=Threat; 3=Violence against objects only; 4=Threw something; 5=Pushed/grabbed/shoved; 6=Slapped; 7=Kicked/bit/punched; 8=Hit/tried to hit with an object; 9=Beat up; 10=Threatened with knife or gun; 11=Used knife or gun		N=252
29. Severity of last assault	Using scale devised by Gelles, ranging from 1 to 10. 1=No violence; 2=Pushed/shoved; 3=Threw object; 4=Slapped or bit; 5=Punched or kicked; 6=Pushed down; 7=Hit with hard object; 8=Choked; 9=Stabbed; 10=Shot.		N=250

Variable Number and Name	Coding Criteria	Descriptive Statistics	Remarks
30. Severity of worst assault	On CRT scale; see V28 above.	87% punched or worse 66% "beaten up" or worse	N=239
31. Severity of worst assault	On Gelles scale, see V29 above.		N=239
32. Number of assaults, by category	1=0-3 assaults ever; 2=4-7 assaults; 3=8 or more conjugal assaults		N=274 an initial attempt to deal with problems in scoring the number of assaults.
33. Was medical treatment received for injuries sustained?	1=Never; 2=Yes, but not for the last assault; 3=Yes, for last assault; 4=Multiple times, including for last assault; 5=Multiple times, not including last assault.	24.3% have received medical treatment at least once for injuries sustained during a conjugal assault.	
34. Were the police called?	Scored same as V33 above.	69% have received police intervention at least once.	
35. Age of assailant partner	Self-explanatory.	Mean=30.9 Range: 17-65 Median=25.8	
36. Race of assailant	Scored same as V5 above.	71% white, 25% black	
37. Educational level of assailant partner	Last grade completed. Bachelor's degree=16, Master's degree=18	Mean=11.2 Range 2-18 Median=11.1	N=225
38. Husband/ partner's employment status	1=Unemployed; 2=Part-time employed; 3=Self-employed; 4=Full time; 5=Disabled or retired; 6=Student	26.4% described as unemployed	

Variable Number and Name	Coding Criteria	Descriptive Statistics	Remarks
39. Husband/ partner's occupational status	Seven-point scale adopted directly from Hollingshead and Redlich. 1=Executives and proprietors of large concerns, major professionals; 2=Managers & proprietors of medium-sized concerns, lesser professionals; 3=Administrative personnel of large concerns, owners of small independent businesses, and semiprofessionals; 4=Owners of little businesses, clerical and sales workers, technicians; 5=Skilled workers; 6=Semiskilled workers; 7=Unskilled workers.		
40. Husband/ partner's occupational status, Scale II	1=Disabled/Retired/ Student 2=Blue collar 3=White collar		An admittedly awful scale devised for purposes of comparison to existing research literature
41. Has partner ever been charged with a violent crime by anyone other than respondent?	1=No, not to respondent's knowledge; 2=Yes; 3=Yes, and convicted; 4=Multiple charges; 5=Multiple convictions	34% have been charged with a crime of violence by someone other than their wife/ partner	
42. Does partner abuse alcohol?	1=No; 2=Yes, in past 3=Yes, currently	68% alleged to be alcohol abusers	N=278
43. Does partner abuse prescription drugs?	1=No; 2=Yes, non-specific; 3-9=Additional categories for various drugs	24% abuse prescription drugs. Minor tranquilizers and amphetamines most popular.	

Variable Number and Name	Coding Criteria	Descriptive Statistics	Remarks
44. Does partner abuse non-prescription drugs?	Scored same as above variable (V43).	34% rate of abuse of street drugs— marijuana foremost with 18.5% rate reported	
45. Outcome	1=Resumed cohabiting with assailant within one year, and remained with him; 2=Terminated cohabitation after initial recohabitation; 3=Terminated cohabitation without recohabitation; 4=Cohabitation terminated by 3/82, recohabitation issues unclear. Scoring based on information from shelter workers, from Washtenaw Co. divorce records, and from shelter records.	56.7% recohabit with abuser; 7% terminate relationship after initial recohabitation; 30.5% terminate relationship without recohabiting after their shelter stay; 5.9% fall in Category 4	N=187, Outcome unknown for 113 cases
46. Did partner get counseling at DVP's affiliated batterer's program?	1=No, 2=Yes	8.3% received counseling at DVP	
47. Premarital pregnancy	1=No premarital pregnancy 2=Premaritally pregnant 3=Nonmarital pregnancy/ birth	56% not pregnant before marriage; 32.4% premaritally pregnant; 11.6% pregnant nonmaritally (i.e., rearing children unmarried)	N=259, Does not include pregnancies and births sired by previous husbands/ partners

APPENDIX B
The Shelter Intake Form

SAFE HOUSE

INTAKE FORM

SAFE HOUSE CASE # _____

Arrival Date: _____

Time of Intake: _____

Location of Intake: _____

Intake Worker: _____

INTAKE SUMMARY:

1. NAME OF CLIENT: _____
                               (first)   (last)   (maiden)

2. PREVIOUS PHONE #: _____ 3. AGE: _____
                                                          (date of birth)

4. PREVIOUS ADDRESS: _____
                           (street)   (city)   (state)   (zip)

5. SOCIAL SECURITY #: _____ 6. RACE _____

7. REFERRED BY: _____
                       (agency)   (worker)   (phone)

8. # OF CHILDREN: _____

9. NAMES OF CHILDREN RESIDING AT SAFE HOUSE:
    (first)   (last)   (birthdate)   (age)   (grade)

  1. _____
  2. _____
  3. _____
  4. _____
  5. _____

10. WHO SHOULD WE CONTACT IN CASE OF EMERGENCY? _____
                                                               (name)

_____
  (relationship)   (address)   (zip)   (phone)

11. ROOM ASSIGNED: _____

- -

EXIT SUMMARY

1. Date of Discharge: _____ Exit Worker: _____

2. I _____ of my own accord am departing SAFE

   HOUSE with my children _____

   and my personal belongings.

                                Signed: _____

                               Witness: _____

3. New Address: _____

4. New Phone: _____ 5. Follow-up Worker: _____

Reminder: If client is returning to visit or to stay, she must call first.

SAFE HOUSE   SAFE HOUSE CASE # _____
INTAKE FORM

12. CLIENT RESOURCES: (be specific with names, phone numbers amounts, etc.)
    1. EMPLOYED: _____ WHERE: _____
    2. WELFARE: _____CASEWORKER: _____
    3. PRIVATE FUNDS: _____
    4. AUTOMOBILE: _____
    5. ITEMS BROUGHT TO SHELTER: _____
       _____

13. WHAT DOES CLIENT NEED?
    ___ MEDICAL ATTENTION   ___ CHILDREN'S SCHOOLING
    ___ D.S.S.   ___ LEGAL INFO &/OR REFERRAL
    ___ CLOTHING   ___ HOUSING
    ___ OTHER _____
14. IS CLIENT/CHILDREN ALLERGIC TO ANY MEDICINES? _____
    _____

15. IS CLIENT/CHILDREN CURRENTLY TAKING
    ANY PRESCRIPTION DRUGS? _____
    _____

16. DOES CLIENT HAVE ANY PRESCRIPTION DRUGS WITH HER? IF YES,
    PLEASE LIST AND GIVE NAME OF ATTENDING PHYSICIAN _____
    _____

17. NAME OF CLIENT'S DOCTOR: _____ ADDRESS & PHONE _____
    _____ NAME, ADDRESS, & PHONE # OF
    CHILDREN'S DOCTOR _____
18. HAS CLIENT OR ANY OF HER CHILDREN BEEN EXPOSED TO ANY
    CONTAGIOUS DISEASES IN THE LAST THREE MONTHS? _____
18a. HAVE CHILDREN HAD THEIR SHOTS? _____
19. ANY SPECIAL DIET REQUIREMENTS? _____
20. HAS CLIENT EVER RECEIVED COUNSELLING? _____ WHERE? _____
21. ANY RELIGIOUS NEEDS? _____
- -
RELEASE OF LIABILITY:
I agree to sign the attached RELEASE OF LIABILITY and to abide by the rules and
regulations of SAFE HOUSE. I understand that my temporary residence can be
terminated at any time if I violate house rules.
SIGNED: _____ WITNESS _____
DATE: _____
I give my permission for a SAFE HOUSE worker to transport my child(ren) to receive
medical care in case of emergency. I also give my permission for my child(ren) to be
given any medical treatment needed in the event of any emergency in which I cannot
be reached.
SIGNED: _____ WITNESS: _____
DATE: _____

SAFE HOUSE   SAFE HOUSE CASE # _____
INTAKE FORM
<u>ASSAILANT INFORMATION</u>

1. NAME _____

2. ADDRESS _____

3. PHONE # _____ 4. AGE/DATE OF BIRTH _____

5. SOCIAL SECURITY # _____ 6. RACE _____

7. LAST GRADE COMPLETED: _____

8. EMPLOYED? _____ WHERE? _____

9. OCCUPATION _____

10. DESCRIPTION OF ASSAILANT: _____
                             (height)   (weight)   (coloring)   (other)

11. AUTOMOBILE OF ASSAILANT: _____
                            (color)   (year)   (make)

12. DO YOU THINK YOUR PARTNER WILL TRY TO FIND YOU? _____

13. HAS YOUR PARTNER EVER BEEN CHARGED WITH ASSAULT BY
    ANYONE OTHER THAN YOURSELF? _____

    A. STATE _____ YEAR _____ CHARGE _____

    B. CONVICTIONS _____

15. DOES ASSAILANT ABUSE ALCOHOL? _____

16. DOES ASSAILANT ABUSE PRESCRIPTION DRUGS? _____

17. DOES ASSAILANT ABUSE NON-PRESCRIPTION DRUGS? _____
- -
- -

PHOTO RELEASE
    I agree to have my photograph taken at SAFE HOUSE for the purpose of recording
my physical abuse and the most recent physical assault. This photo will be on file and
available for any court action for evidence.

SIGNED: _____ DATE: _____

WITNESS: _____
- -

Photograph taken by: _____ Date: _____
                         (signature)
Witness: _____

SAFE HOUSE   SAFE HOUSE CASE # _____
INTAKE FORM

<u>ASSAULT INFORMATION</u>
1. WHAT IS YOUR MARITAL STATUS?
   ____ MARRIED   DATE _____
   ____ SEPARATED   DATE _____
   ____ DIVORCED   DATE _____
   ____ LIVING TOGETHER   DATE _____
2. ANY PREVIOUS SEPARATIONS? _____
   A. HOW MANY? _____
   B. WHEN WAS THE MOST RECENT? _____
   C. HOW LONG DID IT LAST? _____
3. WHEN WAS THE FIRST TIME YOUR PARTNER ASSAULTED YOU? ____
4. HOW MANY YEARS HAVE YOU BEEN ASSAULTED? _____
5. HOW MANY TIMES HAVE YOU BEEN ASSAULTED BY PARTNER? ____
6. HOW OFTEN DO THE ASSAULTS OCCUR
   (WEEKLY, MONTHLY, ETC.) _____
   A. HOW DOES THE ASSAULT USUALLY BEGIN?
      (IS HE DRUNK, VERBAL ARGUMENT, ETC.) _____
      _____
      _____
      _____

   B. DO YOU DEFEND YOURSELF? _____
   C. OTHER INFO ABOUT "TYPICAL" ASSAULT _____
      _____
      _____
   D. WAS YOUR MOTHER A BATTERED WOMAN? _____
7. WERE YOU ASSAULTED BY YOUR PARENTS? _____
8. DID YOUR PARTNER EVER ASSAULT YOU
   WHILE YOU WERE PREGNANT? _____
9. HAS THE ASSAILANT EVER PHYSICALLY ASSAULTED
   ANY OF YOUR CHILDREN? _____

SAFE HOUSE   SAFE HOUSE CASE # _____

INTAKE FORM

10. DATE OF THE MOST RECENT ASSAULT: _____

10a. DESCRIBE MOST RECENT ASSAULT _____

_____

_____

_____

11. WAS MEDICAL TREATMENT RECEIVED? _____

    A. HOSPITAL NAME AND ADDRESS _____

    B. PHYSICAN'S NAME & PHONE NUMBER _____

12. WERE THE POLICE CALLED? _____

    A. WHICH DEPARTMENT _____

    B. OFFICERS' NAMES _____

    C. TIME AND PLACE _____

    D. WERE THERE ANY EYE-WITNESSES? _____

    E. DO YOU WISH TO PROSECUTE? _____

13. IF NO TO QUESTION 12, HAVE YOU EVER CALLED THE POLICE? _____

14. MAY WE PHOTOGRAPH YOUR INJURIES FOR COURT PURPOSES? ____

15. DO YOU HAVE A RESTRAINING ORDER? _____

16. DO YOU HAVE A CUSTODY ORDER? _____

APPENDIX C

Table of Variables
Collected from the Batterers' Counseling Sample

N=119 (approximately), unless otherwise noted

Variable Number and Name	Coding Criteria	Descriptive Statistics	Remarks
1. Case number	One i.d. number per case	N=119	Confidential for researcher use only
2. Age of client	Self-explanatory	Mean=30.1 Range: 19-55 Median=28.5	
3. Race	See V5 in Appendix A— same coding scheme	77% white; 21% black; 1% each, Asian and Hispanic	Random distribu- tion reflecting catchment population
4. Employment status	1=Unemployed at time of intake interview; 2=Part-time employed; 3=Self-employed; 4=Full-time employed; 5=Disabled/ retired; 6=Student; 7=Experienced unemploy-ment during counseling, but employed at time of intake	22% unemployed at intake; 8.5% more experience unem-ployment during period in counseling	
5. Marital status	In relation to battered partner. 1=Married; 2=Living to-gether; 3= Separated from marriage; 4=Separated from living together; 5=Divorced; 6=Nonco-habitant, active relationship; 7=Noncohabitant, termi-nated relationship	59% married; 11% living together 22% separated from marriage or living together; 8% noncohabitant	
6. Length of marriage/ relationship	In months. See V15 in Appendix A for coding scheme	Mean=56.8 Range: 3-379 Median=32	

Variable Number and Name	Coding Criteria	Descriptive Statistics	Remarks
7. Client self-report of alcohol abuse	1=None; 2=Borderline; 3=Yes, in past; 4=Yes, current alcohol abuse	21% self-describe as past alcohol abuser; 17% disclose current alcohol abuse	
8. Other substance abuse by client?	1=None; 2=Yes, non-specific; 3-56= Various categories for specific drugs/drug combinations	38.2% rate of substance abuse; marijuana foremost at 33.6%	
9. Veteran's status	1=Not military veteran; 2=Veteran	29.1% are veterans	Does not diverge from statewide proportion of male population
10. Combat experience	Scored for veterans only. 1=No combat experience; 2=Combat experience	28.1% were in direct combat	N=32
11. Children?	1=None; 2=Has sired children and/or cohabits with children (his or step-children)	67.5% have children	
12. Abused as a child?	1=Not physically abused as child; 2=Physically abused, nonspecific abuser; 3=Abused by father (figure); 4=Abused by mother (figure); 5=Abused by both parents/ parent figures; 6=Abused by other relative or authority figure; 7=Border-line abuse; 8=Witnessed abuse of one or more sibling(s), but not himself physically abused	61.4% directly abused; 8% subjected to borderline physical abuse; 2% witnessed physical abuse of a sibling	N=101
13. Exposed to battering as a child?	1=No; 2=Yes, at least one incident of violence beween parents/parent figures	66.3% exposed to conjugal abuse in family of origin	N=98
14. Is client also a child abuser?	1=No child abuse committed; 2=Borderline physical child abuse; 3=Clear physical child abuse	30% disclose committing unambiguous physical child abuse; 11% more disclose borderline abuse	N=70. Scored for men with children or step-children only

Variable Number and Name	Coding Criteria	Descriptive Statistics	Remarks
15. Elapsed time since first assault in relationship/ marriage	In months, client's report.	Mean=36.1 Range: 0-212 Median=24.3	N=74
16. Frequency of assaults	Annual rate, from client's report. Daily=365, etc.	Mean=11 Range: 0-329 Median=1.4	N=82
17. Violence during wife/partner's pregnancy?	1=No; 2=Yes. Scored only if wife/partner has been pregnant during relationship	34% reveal violence during mate's pregnancy	N=53
18. Severity of worst assault	From client's report, on CRT scale. See V28 in Appendix A for coding scheme	38% disclose beating or worse	
19. Severity of worst assault	From client's report, on Gelles scale. See V29 in Appendix A for coding scheme	76% disclose punching or worse	
20. Severity of last assault	Same as V18. CRT scale.		
21. Severity of last assault	Same as V19. Gelles scale.		
22. Elapsed time since last assault	In days, from client's report.	Range: 2-275 Median=13.5	N=85
23. Number of conjugal assaults	Total in this relationship, from client's report. Maximum possible score=998	Mean=17.3 Range: 0-998 Median=2.8 8% deny that assaults have occurred	N=90
24. Outcome	Counselor's subjective evaluation as of 3/82. 1=No progress at all; 2=Slight improvement; 3=Fair improvement; 4=Good improvement; 5=Excellent progress		
25. Longest known interval of domestic nonviolence	After initiating counseling, that is. In months.	Mean=2.2 Range: 0–16 22% known to exceed 3 months of nonviolence	

Variable Number and Name	Coding Criteria	Descriptive Statistics	Remarks
26. Number of counseling sessions attended	Maximum possible score=99	Mean=10 Range: 1-99 Median=3 29.9% attend 10 or more sessions	
27. Premarital pregnancy	1=No premarital pregnancy; 2=N/A, no pregnancies in relationship; 3=Yes, wife premaritally pregnant; 4=Nonmarital pregnancy and child rearing	28.2% rate of premarital pregnancy; 5.5% nonmarital pregnancy rate	
28. Elapsed time since first assault in marriage/ relationship	In months, from partner's report	Mean=56.3 Range: 0-300 Median=38	N=64
29. Number of assaults	Reported by partner, to a maximum of 998	Mean=37 Range: 1-998 Median=5.8	N=54. Statistically very divergent from the men's reports
30. Frequency of assaults, partner's report	See V16 above—same coding scheme	Mean=41.6 Range: 0-365 Median=8.7	N=66. Statistically very divergent from men
31. Partner's report of violence during pregnancy	See V17 above—same coding scheme	56% report violence during pregnancy	N=50
32. Does partner allege child abuse by batterer?	Scored for clients with children only. 1=No; 2=Yes	44% allege physical child abuse by their mate	N=57
33. Elapsed time since last assault	From woman's report, in days.	Range: 2-300 Median=12.8	N=57
34. Severity of last assault, woman's report	CRT scale. See V28 in Appendix A for coding scheme.		N=73

Variable Number and Name	Coding Criteria	Descriptive Statistics	Remarks
35. Severity of last assault, woman's report	Gelles scale. See V29 in Appendix A for coding scheme.		N=73
36. Severity of worst assault, woman's report	CRT scale. See V34 above, V28 in Appendix A for coding scheme.		N=80
37. Severity of worst assault, woman's report	Gelles scale. See V35 above, V29 in Appendix A for coding scheme.		N=80
38. Alcohol abuse by client	From woman's report. 1=None; 2=Past alcohol abuse only; 3=Current alcohol abuse	50.6% allege current alcohol abuse	N=77
39. Substance abuse by client	From woman's report. See V8 above for coding scheme.	73% say no substance abuse by their partners. 25% allege marijuana abuse.	N=77
40. Source of information obtained from female partner of client	1=Shelter records; 2=Directly interviewed by researcher		N=89
41. Counselor's assessment of client's alcoholism	See V6 above—same coding scheme.	64% assessed as current problem drinkers; 10% ruled ex-problem drinkers; 21% viewed as unambiguously non-alcoholic	N=109

APPENDIX D:
The Batterers' Counseling Intake Form

Assailant Intake Information

Case # _____

Date of intake: _____

Intake worker: _____

NAME _____

ADDRESS _____

PHONE #: _____

REFERRED BY: _____

AGE/DATE OF BIRTH: _____

OCCUPATION: _____

PLACE OF EMPLOYMENT: _____

_____ HOW LONG? _____

PREVIOUS COUNSELING, PSYCHIATRIC TREATMENT, ETC.: _____

_____

_____

MARITAL STATUS, AND RELEVANT DATES: _____

_____

_____

SUBSTANCE FACTORS: _____

_____

_____

LEGAL ISSUES: _____

_____

VETERAN'S STATUS: _____

COMBAT DUTY: _____

WEAPONS IN CURRENT POSSESSION: _____

_____

CLIENT'S CONCERNS: _____

_____

_____

ASSAILANT INTAKE INFORMATION, page 2

FAMILY CONSTELLATION (GENOGARM):

CHILDHOOD ABUSE HISTORY

ABUSED AS CHILD? _____

_____

WITNESSED SPOUSE ABUSE? _____

WITNESSED CHILD ABUSE? _____

HISTORY OF MARITAL VIOLENCE (INCLUDING FREQUENCY

AND SEVERITY): _____

_____

_____

_____

ADDITIONAL NOTES, WORKER'S ASSESSMENT, AND PLAN(S): _____

_____

_____

_____

_____

_____

_____

Using page 4 of the shelter intake form (see Appendix B above), the counselor would ask the following questions, not necessarily in the following order:

1. When did you first assault your wife/partner?
2. How many times have you assaulted your wife/partner, in total?
3. About how often do you assault her (daily, weekly, monthly, etc.)?
4. Give a description of a typical assault.
5. Describe the worst assault you have committed against your wife/partner.
6. Did you ever assault your partner while she was pregnant?
7. When was the last time you assaulted your wife/partner?
8. Describe the most recent assault.

NOTES

INTRODUCTION

1. Conservative estimate based upon statistics for spouse murders appearing in *FBI Uniform Crime Reports*, 1974-1983. The figure does not even include murders where the victim-perpetrator relationship is given as "boyfriend-girlfriend".

2. Ann Ganley (Public lecture on men who batter. Delivered at the Forum on Working With Men Who Batter, Milwaukee, Wisconsin, August 8, 1982.)

CHAPTER 1

1. R. Emerson Dobash and Russell Dobash, *Violence Against Wives* (New York: The Free Press, 1979); Suzanne Steinmetz, "The battered husband syndrome," *Victimology* 2, Nos. 3-4:499-509.

2. Dobash and Dobash, *Violence Against Wives*; Maria Roy, "A current survey of 150 cases," in *Battered Women*, edited by Maria Roy (New York: Van Nostrand Reinhold, 1977), 25-44.

3. Dobash and Dobash, *Violence Against Wives*.

4. Dobash and Dobash, *Violence Against Wives*.

5. Dobash and Dobash, *Violence Against Wives*.

6. R. Emerson Dobash and Russell Dobash, "Wives: the 'appropriate' victims of marital violence," *Victimology* 2, Nos. 3-4:426-442.

7. Dobash and Dobash, "Wives: the 'appropriate' victims of marital violence."

8. Terry Davidson, *Conjugal Crime* (New York: Hawthorne Books, 1978); Roy, "A current survey of 150 cases."

9. Davidson, *Conjugal Crime*, 103.

10. Del Martin, *Battered Wives* (San Francisco: Glide Publications, 1976).

11. Martin, *Battered Wives*.

12. John Stuart Mill, *The Subjection of Women* (New York: D. Appleton and Co., 1870).

13. Davidson, *Conjugal Crime*, 104.

14. Dobash and Dobash, *Violence Against Wives*.

15. Martin, *Battered Wives*.

16. Dobash and Dobash, *Violence Against Wives*, 31.

17. Susan Brownmiller, *Against Our Will: Men, Women, and Rape* (New York: Simon and Schuster, 1975).

18. Dobash and Dobash, *Violence Against Wives*.

19. Mill, *The Subjection of Women*, 57.

20. Mill, *The Subjection of Women*, 64-65.

21. Mill, *The Subjection of Women*, 63.

22. Dobash and Dobash, *Violence Against Wives*.

23. Martin, *Battered Wives*.

24. Sue Eisenberg and Patricia Micklow, "The assaulted wife: 'Catch-22' revisited" (Unpublished paper in the library of the Domestic Violence Project; revised and edited version published in *Women's Rights Law Reporter*, Spring/Summer 1977); Martin, *Battered Wives*.

25. Quoted in Dobash and Dobash, *Violence Against Wives*, 63; also quoted in Eisenberg and Micklow, "The assaulted wife: 'Catch-22' revisited."

26. Roy, "A current survey of 150 cases."

27. Dobash and Dobash, *Violence Against Wives*.

28. Davidson, *Conjugal Crime*.

29. Rita Henley Jensen, "Battered Women and the Law," *Victimology* 2, Nos. 3-4:587-589.

30. Martin, *Battered Wives*, 37.

31. Ibid.

32. Eisenberg and Micklow, "The assaulted wife: 'Catch-22' revisited"; Martin, *Battered Wives*; Lisa G. Lerman and Franci Livingston, "State legislation on domestic violence," *Response* 6, No. 5 (September/October 1983).

33. Eisenberg and Micklow, "The assaulted wife: 'Catch-22' revisited."

34. Eisenberg and Micklow, "The assaulted wife: 'Catch-22' revisited"; Maria Roy, "A current survey of 150 cases"; Lenore Walker, *The Battered Woman* (New York: Harper Colophon, Harper and Row, 1979).

35. Murray Straus, "A sociological perspective on the prevention and treatment of wife-beating," in *Battered Women*, ed. Maria Roy, 194-239.

36. Martha H. Field and Henry F. Field, "Marital violence and the criminal process: neither justice nor peace," *Social Service Review* 47:221-239.

37. Eisenberg and Micklow, "The assaulted wife: 'Catch-22' revisited"; Martin, *Battered Wives*.

38. Eisenberg and Micklow, "The assaulted wife: 'Catch-22' revisited."

39. Field and Field, "Marital violence and the criminal process: neither justice nor peace."

40. Camella S. Serum, "The effects of violent victimization in the family" (Paper presented to the Michigan Coalition Against Domestic Violence, December 3, 1979. Notes in author's possession.)

41. Martin, *Battered Wives*; Roger Langley and Richard Levy, *Wife-beating: The Silent Crisis* (New York: Dutton, 1977).

42. *NOW Times.*

43. Eisenberg and Micklow, "The assaulted wife: 'Catch-22' revisited"; Martin, *Battered Wives*; Michigan Women's Commission, *Wife Assault in Michigan* (Lansing, MI: Michigan Women's Commission, 1977).

44. Martin, *Battered Wives*; Walker, *The Battered Woman.*

45. Davidson, *Conjugal Crime*; Dobash and Dobash, *Violence Against Wives.*

CHAPTER 2

1. Ernest R. Mowrer and Harriet R. Mowrer, *Domestic Discord* (Chicago: University of Chicago Press, 1928).

2. Leroy G. Schultz, "The wife assaulter: one type observed and treated in a probation agency," *Journal of Social Therapy* 6:103-111.

3. Mirra Komarovsky, *Blue Collar Marriage* (New York: Random House, 1962).

4. John Snell, Richard Rosenwald, and Ames Robey, "The wife-beater's wife," *Archives of General Psychiatry* 11 (August 1964):107-112.

5. Ronald R. Mowat, *Morbid Jealousy and Murder* (London: Tavistock, 1966).

6. R. Reynolds and E. Siegle, "A study of casework with sado-masochistic marriage partners," *Social Casework* 40:545-551.

7. Mary Lystad, "Violence at home: A review of the literature," *American Journal of Orthopsychiatry* 45, No. 3:328-345; Stuart Palmer, *A Study of Murder* (New York: Crowell, 1960).

8. Komarovsky, *Blue Collar Marriage*; Mowrer and Mowrer, *Domestic Discord.*

9. John O'Brien, "Violence in divorce-prone families," *Journal of Marriage and the Family* 33:692-698, reprinted in *Violence in the Family*, ed. Suzanne Steinmetz and Murray Straus (New York: Harper and Row, 1974).

10. Steinmetz and Straus, eds., *Violence in the Family.*

11. Martin, *Battered Wives.*

12. Davidson, *Conjugal Crime*; Martin, *Battered Wives*; O'Brien, "Violence in divorce-prone families"; Steinmetz and Straus, eds., *Violence in the Family.*

13. Maccoby and Jacklin, cited in *Battered Wives*, Martin:16.

14. Lenore Walker, *The Battered Woman.*

15. Murray A. Straus, "Wife-beating: how common and why?" *Victimology* 2, Nos. 3-4:443-459.

16. J.C. Carroll, "The intergenerational transmission of family violence: the long-term effects of aggressive behavior," *Aggressive Behavior* 3:289-299; Richard J. Gelles, *The Violent Home* (Beverly Hills, CA: Sage Publications, 1972); Parker and Schumacher, "The battered wife syndrome and violence in the nuclear family of origin: a controlled pilot study," *American Journal of Public Health* 67 (1977):760-761.

17. Parker and Schumacher, "The battered wife syndrome and violence in the nuclear family of origin."

18. Gelles, *The Violent Home.*

19. Richard A. Bulcroft and Murray Straus, "Validity of husband, wife, and child reports on conjugal violence and power" (Unpublished paper in author's possession. Copies available from Family Violence Research Project, Department of Sociology, University of New Hampshire, Durham, NH); Steinmetz, "The battered husband syndrome"; Suzanne Steinmetz, "The use of force for resolving family conflict: the training ground for abuse," *Family Coordinator* 26, No. 1:19-26; Murray A. Straus, "Cultural and social organizational influence on violence between family members," in *Configurations: Biological and Cultural Factors in Sexuality and Family Life*, ed. Raymond Price and Dorothy Barrier (Lexington, MA: Lexington Books, D. C. Heath, 1974); Murray A. Straus, "Leveling, civility and violence in the family," *Journal of Marriage and the Family* 36:13-30.

20. Murray A. Straus, Richard J. Gelles, and Suzanne Steinmetz, *Behind Closed Doors: Violence in the American Family* (Garden City, NY: Anchor/Doubleday, 1980); David Owens and Murray A. Straus, "Social structure of violence in childhood and approval of violence as an adult," *Aggressive Behavior* 1, No. 3:193-211; Suzanne Steinmetz, "Wife-beating, husband-beating: a comparison of the use of physical violence between spouses to resolve marital fights," in *Battered Women*, ed. Maria Roy, 63-72; Deirdre A. Gaquin, "Spouse abuse: data from the National Crime Survey," *Victimology* 2, Nos. 3-4:632-643.

21. Gelles, *The Violent Home.*

22. Gelles, *The Violent Home.*

23. Snell et al., "The wife-beater's wife."

24. Langley and Levy, *Wife-Beating: The Silent Crisis.*

25. Steinmetz, "The battered husband syndrome."

25½. Natalie Shainess, "Psychological aspects of wife-battering,"in *Battered Women*, ed. Maria Roy.

26. Snell et al., "The wife-beater's wife."

27. Walker, *The Battered Women.*

27½. Shainess, "Psychological aspects of wife-battering."

28. Camella S. Serum, "Battered women and batterers" (Lecture presented at the Hoyt Conference Center, Eastern Michigan University, Ypsilanti, MI, May 9, 1979.)

29. Dobash and Dobash, *Violence Against Wives*; Martin, *Battered Wives*; Jane Roberts Chapman and Margaret Gates, eds., *The Victimization of Women* (Beverly Hills, CA: Sage Publications).

30. Serum, "Battered women and batterers"; Walker, *The Battered Woman.*

31. Murray A. Straus, "A general systems theory approach to the development of a theory of violence between family members," *Social Science Information* 12 (1973): 105-125; Richard J. Gelles, "No place to go: the social dynamics of marital violence", in *Battered Women*, ed. Maria Roy, 46-63; Eisenberg and Micklow, "The assaulted wife: 'Catch-22' revisited."

32. Martin, *Battered Wives*; Lenore Walker, "Battered women and learned helplessness," *Victimology* 2, Nos. 3-4:525-534; Parker and Schumacher, "The battered wife syndrome and violence in the nuclear family of origin"; Jane Pfouts, "Violent families: coping responses of abused wives," *Child Welfare* 57, No. 2:101-111; Serum,

"Battered women and batterers"; among others.

33. Pfouts, "Violent families: coping responses of abused wives," 110.

34. Walker, *The Battered Woman*, 15-16.

35. Dobash and Dobash, *Violence Against Wives*.

36. Martin, *Battered Wives*.

37. Steinmetz, "The battered husband syndrome."

38. Straus, "A general systems theory approach to the development of a theory of violence between family members."

39. Lystad, "Violence at home: a review of the literature."

40. Langley and Levy, *Wife-Beating: The Silent Crisis*.

41. Steinmetz and Straus, eds., *Violence in the Family*, 6.

42. Murray Straus, "A sociological perspective on the prevention and treatment of wife-beating," in *Battered Women*, ed. Maria Roy.

43. *Victimology* 2, Nos. 3-4.

44. Bonnie Carlson, "Battered women and their assailants," *Social Work* 22: 455-460.

45. John J. Gayford, "Wife battering: a preliminary survey of 100 cases," *British Medical Journal* 1 (1975):194-197.

46. Dobash and Dobash, *Violence Against Wives*.

47. Roy, "A current survey of 150 cases."

48. Dobash and Dobash, *Violence Against Wives*.

49. Barbara Star, Carol G. Clark, Karen M. Goetz, and Linda O'Malia, "Psychosocial aspects of wife battering," *Social Casework* (1979):479-487.

50. Mildred Daley Pagelow, *Woman-battering: Victims and Their Experiences* (Beverly Hills, CA: Sage Publications, 1981).

51. Pagelow, *Woman-battering: Victims and Their Experiences*, 245.

52. Suzanne Prescott and Carolyn Letko, "Battered women: a social psychological perspective," in *Battered Women*, ed. Maria Roy, 72-96.

53. Margaret Ball, "Issues of violence in family casework," *Social Casework* 58, No. 1:3-12.

54. J.P. Flynn, "Recent findings related to wife abuse," *Social Casework* 58, No. 1:13ff.

55. Janet Geller, "Reaching the battering husband," *Social Work with Groups* 1, No. 1 (Spring 1978); Janet Geller, "A treatment model for the abused spouse," *Victimology* 2, Nos. 3-4:627-632.

56. Mowrer and Mowrer, *Domestic Discord*.

57. Elaine C. Hilberman and Kit Munson, "Sixty battered women," *Victimology* 2, Nos. 3-4:460-471.

58. Pfouts, "Violent families: coping responses of abused wives."

59. Bruce J. Rounsaville, "Battered wives: barriers to identification and treatment," *American Journal of Orthopsychiatry* 48, No. 3:487-494.

60. Snell et al., "The wife-beater's wife."

61. Snell et al., "The wife-beater's wife."

62. Walker, *The Battered Woman*.

63. Serum, "Battered women and batterers"; Serum, "The effects of violent victimization in the family"; Dan Saunders, "Marital violence: dimensions of the problem and modes of intervention," *Journal of Marriage and Family Counseling* 3, No.

1:43-55; Anne Ganley and Lance Harris, "Domestic violence: issues in designing and implementing programs for batterers" (Paper presented to the American Psychological Association, August 29, 1978); Margaret T. Singer, "The nature of coercive control" (Paper presented to the Michigan Coalition Against Domestic Violence, December 3, 1979).

64. J. C. Carroll, "The intergenerational transmission of family violence."

65. Gelles, *The Violent Home.*

66. Richard J. Gelles, "Abused wives: why do they stay?" *Journal of Marriage and the Family* 38, No. 4:659-666; Gelles, "No place to go"; Richard J. Gelles, "Power, sex, and violence: the case of marital rape," *Family Coordinator* 26, No. 4:339-347; Richard J. Gelles, "Violence and pregnancy," *Family Coordinator* 24, No. 1:81-86.

67. George Levinger, "Sources of marital dissatisfaction among applicants for divorce," *American Journal of Orthopsychiatry* 26:803-807, also reprinted in *Violence in the Family*, ed. Suzanne Steinmetz and Murray Straus.

68. Marjory D. Fields, "Wife-beating: facts and figures," *Victimology* 2, Nos. 3-4:634-647.

69. O'Brien, "Violence in divorce-prone families."

70. Eisenberg and Micklow, "The assaulted wife: 'Catch-22' revisited."

71. Field and Field, "Marital violence and the criminal process: neither justice nor peace."

72. Parker and Schumacher, "The battered wife syndrome and violence in the nuclear family of origin."

73. Morton Bard, "The study and modification of intrafamilial violence," in *Violence in the Family*, ed. Suzanne Steinmetz and Murray Straus; Morton Bard and Joseph Zacker, "The prevention of family violence: dilemmas of community intervention," *Journal of Marriage and the Family* 33 (November 1971):677-682; Morton Bard and Joseph Zacker, "Assaultiveness and alcohol use in family disputes," *Criminology* 12, No. 3 (November 1974):283-292.

74. Gelles, *The Violent Home*; J. Boudouris, "Homicide and the family," *Journal of Marriage and the Family* 33, No. 11 (November 1971): 667-676; Dobash and Dobash, *Violence Against Wives*; Darrel Stephens, "Domestic assault: the police response," in *Battered Women*, ed. Maria Roy, 164-172; David Ward, Maurice Jackson and Renee Ward, "Crimes of violence by women," in *Crimes of Violence*, ed. Donald Mulvihill and Melvin Tumin (Washington, DC: U.S. Government Printing Office, 1969), 843-909.

75. Komarovsky, *Blue Collar Marriage.*

76. Steinmetz, "The use of force for resolving family conflict: the training ground for abuse."

77. Straus, "Cultural and social organizational influence on violence between family members"; Straus, "Leveling, civility and violence in the family."

78. Straus, "Cultural and social organizational influence on violence between family members."

79. Bulcroft and Straus, "Validity of husband, wife, and child reports of conjugal violence and power."

80. Gaquin, "Spouse abuse: data from the National Crime Survey."

81. Owens and Straus, "Social structure of violence in childhood and approval of violence as an adult."

82. Steinmetz, "Wife-beating, husband-beating."

83. Straus, Gelles, and Steinmetz, *Behind Closed Doors*.

84. Straus, "Wife-beating: how common and why?"

85. Steinmetz, "The battered husband syndrome."

86. Richard J. Gelles, "The myth of battered husbands," *Ms.* (November 1979).

87. Kersti Yllo and Murray A. Straus, "Interpersonal violence among married and cohabiting couples," (Unpublished paper in author's possession; available from Family Violence Research Project, Department of Sociology, University of New Hampshire, Durham, NH.)

88. Straus et al., *Behind Closed Doors*; Straus, "Wife-beating: how common and why?"

89. Straus, "Wife-beating: how common and why?"

90. Ibid.

91. Ibid.

92. Bulcroft and Straus, "Validity of husband, wife, and child reports of conjugal violence and power."

93. Straus, "Wife-beating: how common and why?"

94. Steinmetz, "The battered husband syndrome."

95. Gelles, *The Violent Home*; O'Brien, "Violence in divorce-prone families."

96. Gayford, "Wife battering: a preliminary survey of 100 cases"; Gelles, *The Violent Home*; Martin, *Battered Wives*; Walker, *The Battered Woman*.

97. Serum, "Battered women and batterers."

98. Margaret Elbow, "Theoretical considerations of violent marriages," *Social Casework* 58, No. 9:515-526.

99. Serum, "Battered women and batterers."

100. Dobash and Dobash, *Violence Against Wives*.

101. Gelles, "Abused wives: why do they stay?"

102. Carlson, "Battered women and their assailants"; Gelles, *The Violent Home*; Gelles, "Abused wives: why do they stay?"

103. Levinger, "Sources of marital dissatisfaction among applicants for divorce."

104. Ibid.

105. Straus, "Wife-beating: how common and why?"

106. Eisenberg and Micklow, "The assaulted wife: 'Catch-22' revisited"; Gayford, "Wife battering: a preliminary survey of 100 cases"; Beverly Nichols, "The abused wife problem," *Social Casework* 57, No. 1:27-32.

107. Walker, *The Battered Woman*.

CHAPTER 3

1. Boudouris, "Homicide and the family"; Gelles, *The Violent Home*; Gelles and Straus, "Determinants of violence in the family."

2. Gelles, *The Violent Home*; Gaquin, "Spouse abuse: data from the National Crime Survey."

3. Dobash and Dobash, "Wives: the 'appropriate' victims of marital violence."

4. Dobash and Dobash, *Violence Against Wives*.

5. Steinmetz, "Wife-beating, husband-beating."

6. Gaquin, "Spouse abuse: data from the National Crime Survey."

7. Fields, "Wife-beating: facts and figures"; Gelles, *The Violent Home*; Martin,

Battered Wives; Palmer, *A Study of Murder*; Steinmetz, "The use of force for resolving family conflict: the training ground for abuse."

8. Mowat, *Morbid Jealousy and Murder*.

9. Dobash and Dobash, "Wives: the 'appropriate' victims of marital violence."

10. Mowat, *Morbid Jealousy and Murder*.

11. Dobash and Dobash, "Wives: the 'appropriate' victims of marital violence."

12. Fields, "Wife-beating: facts and figures"; Mowat, *Morbid Jealousy and Murder*.

13. Dobash and Dobash, "Wives: the 'appropriate' victims of marital violence"; Steinmetz, "The battered husband syndrome."

14. Dobash and Dobash, "Wives: the 'appropriate' victims of marital violence"; Martin, *Battered Wives*.

15. Ward et al., "Crimes of violence by women."

16. Laura Meyers, "Battered wives, dead husbands," *Student Lawyer* 6, No. 7:46-51.

17. Stuart Palmer, *The Violent Society* (New Haven, CT: College & University Press, 1972).

18. Boudouris, "Homicide and the family."

19. Gelles, "Power, sex, and violence: the case of marital rape."

20. Fields, "Wife-beating: facts and figures"; Martin, *Battered Wives*.

20½. Bard, "The study and modification of intrafamilial violence."

21. Levinger, "Sources of marital dissatisfaction among applicants for divorce."

22. Fields, "Wife-beating: facts and figures."

23. O'Brien, "Violence in divorce-prone families."

24. Parker and Schumacher, "The battered wife syndrome and violence in the nuclear family of origin."

25. Ball, "Issues of violence in family casework."

26. Saunders, "Marital violence: dimensions of the problem and modes of intervention."

27. Mowrer and Mowrer, *Domestic Discord*.

28. Rounsaville, "Battered wives: barriers to identification and treatment."

29. Hilberman and Munson, "Sixty Battered Women."

30. Dobash and Dobash, *Violence Against Wives*; Gayford, "Wife battering: a preliminary survey of 100 cases"; Star et al., "Psychosocial aspects of wife battering."

31. Gelles, *The Violent Home*.

32. Komarovsky, *Blue Collar Marriage*.

33. Steinmetz, "Wife-beating, husband-beating."

34. Straus, "Leveling, civility and violence in the family."

35. Steinmetz, "The use of force for resolving family conflict: the training ground for abuse."

36. Bulcroft and Straus, "Validity of husband, wife, and child reports of conjugal violence and power."

37. Straus, "Wife-beating: how common and why?"

38. Straus, "Wife-beating: how common and why?"; Straus, Gelles, and Steinmetz, *Behind Closed Doors*.

39. Straus, "Leveling, civility and violence in the family."

40. Steinmetz, "The use of force for resolving family conflict: the training ground for abuse."

41. Straus, "Wife-beating: how common and why?"

42. Ibid.

43. Suzanne Steinmetz, *The Cycle of Violence: Assertive, Aggressive, and Abusive Family Interaction*, 2nd edition (New York: Praeger, 1977).

44. Straus, Gelles, and Steinmetz, *Behind Closed Doors*.

45. Steinmetz, "The battered husband syndrome"; Steinmetz, "The use of force for resolving family conflict: the training ground for abuse."

46. Gaquin, "Spouse abuse: data from the National Crime Survey"; Levinger, "Sources of marital dissatisfaction among applicants for divorce."

47. Martin, *Battered Wives*.

48. O'Brien, "Violence in divorce-prone families."

49. Dobash and Dobash, *Violence Against Wives*.

50. Straus, Gelles, and Steinmetz, *Behind Closed Doors*.

51. Steinmetz, "The battered husband syndrome."

52. Steinmetz, *The Cycle of Violence*, 18 (Frontmatter).

53. Bulcroft and Straus, "Validity of husband, wife, and child reports of conjugal violence and power."

54. Author's process notes. All names are pseudonyms.

55. Gelles, *The Violent Home*.

56. Stark and McEvoy, cited in "Cultural and social organizational influence on violence between family members," Straus.

57. Straus, "Wife-beating: how common and why?"; Steinmetz, "The battered husband syndrome."

58. Martin, *Battered Wives*.

59. Eisenberg and Micklow, "The assaulted wife: 'Catch-22' revisited"; Gayford, "Wife battering: a preliminary survey of 100 cases"; Pagelow, *Woman-battering: Victims and Their Experiences*; Parker and Schumacher, "The battered wife syndrome and violence in the nuclear family of origin"; Snell et al., "The wife-beater's wife."

60. Star et al., "Psychosocial aspects of wife battering"; Walker, *The Battered Woman*.

61. Eisenberg and Micklow, "The assaulted wife: 'Catch-22' revisited"; Gayford, "Wife battering: a preliminary survey of 100 cases"; Star et al., "Psychosocial aspects of wife battering."

62. Eisenberg and Micklow, "The assaulted wife: 'Catch-22' revisited"; Gayford, "Wife battering: a preliminary survey of 100 cases"; Star et al., "Psychosocial aspects of wife battering"; Pagelow, *Woman-battering: Victims and Their Experiences*.

63. Straus, Gelles, and Steinmetz, *Behind Closed Doors*; Gaquin, "Spouse abuse: data from the National Crime Survey."

64. Gelles, *The Violent Home*; O'Brien, "Violence in divorce-prone families."

65. Dobash and Dobash, *Violence Against Wives*; Martin, *Battered Wives*; Walker, *The Battered Woman*.

66. Gelles, *The Violent Home*.

67. Gaquin, "Spouse abuse: data from the National Crime Survey."

68. O'Brien, "Violence in divorce-prone families"; Serum, "Battered women and batterers"; Serum, "Violent victimization."

69. Yllo and Straus, "Interpersonal violence among married and cohabiting couples."

70. Carlson, "Battered women and their assailants"; Gayford, "Wife battering: a preliminary survey of 100 cases"; Star et al., "Psychosocial aspects of wife battering."

71. Yllo and Straus, "Interpersonal violence among married and cohabiting couples."

72. Straus, Gelles, and Steinmetz, *Behind Closed Doors*.

73. Ibid.

74. Gelles, *The Violent Home*; Straus, Gelles, and Steinmetz, *Behind Closed Doors*.

75. Straus, Gelles, and Steinmetz, *Behind Closed Doors*.

76. Flynn, "Recent findings related to wife abuse"; Owens and Straus, "Social structure of violence in childhood and approval of violence as an adult."

77. Komarovsky, *Blue Collar Marriage*; Straus, Gelles, and Steinmetz, *Behind Closed Doors*.

78. Eisenberg and Micklow, "The assaulted wife: 'Catch-22' revisited"; Walker, *The Battered Woman*; Geller, "Reaching the battering husband".

79. Walker, *The Battered Woman*; Davidson, *Conjugal Crime*.

80. Steinmetz and Straus, eds., *Violence in the Family*; Robert Whitehurst, "Violently jealous husbands," in *Sexual Issues in Marriage*, ed. Leonard Gross (New York: Spectrum Publications, Inc., 1975), 75-85; William Goode, "Force and violence in the family," *Journal of Marriage and the Family* 33 (November 1971):624-636; William Goode, "Violence between intimates," in *Crimes of Violence*, ed. Donald Mulvihill and Melvin Tumin. (Washington, DC: U.S. Government Printing Office, 1969).

81. Levinger, "Sources of marital dissatisfaction among applicants for divorce."

82. Bulcroft and Straus, "Validity of husband, wife, and child reports of conjugal violence and power."

83. Goode, "Force and violence"; Whitehurst, "Violently jealous husbands."

84. Straus, Gelles, and Steinmetz, *Behind Closed Doors*; Gaquin, "Spouse abuse: data from the National Crime Survey."

85. Gelles, *The Violent Home*.

86. O'Brien, "Violence in divorce-prone families."

87. Straus, "Cultural and social organizational influence on violence between family members."

88. Straus, Gelles, and Steinmetz, *Behind Closed Doors*.

89. Gelles, *The Violent Home*.

90. O'Brien, "Violence in divorce-prone families."

91. Gelles, *The Violent Home*.

92. Straus, Gelles, and Steinmetz, *Behind Closed Doors*.

93. Eisenberg and Micklow, "The assaulted wife: 'Catch-22' revisited"; Gayford, "Wife battering: a preliminary survey of 100 cases"; Hilberman and Munson, "Sixty battered women"; Prescott and Letko, "Battered women: a social psychological perspective"; Star et al., "Psychosocial aspects of wife battering."

94. Geller, "Reaching the battering husband."

95. Gelles, *The Violent Home*.

96. Straus, Gelles, and Steinmetz, *Behind Closed Doors*.

97. Parker and Schumacher, "The battered wife syndrome and violence in the nuclear family of origin."

98. O'Brien, "Violence in divorce-prone families."

99. Cited in *Battered Wives*, Martin.

100. O'Brien, "Violence in divorce-prone families."

101. Gelles, *The Violent Home*.

102. Carlson, "Battered women and their assailants."

103. Dobash and Dobash, *Violence Against Wives*; Gayford, "Wife battering: a preliminary survey of 100 cases."

104. Star et al., "Psychosocial aspects of wife battering."

105. Dobash and Dobash, *Violence Against Wives*; Eisenberg and Micklow, "The assaulted wife: 'Catch-22' revisited"; Star et al., "Psychosocial aspects of wife battering."

106. Walker, *The Battered Woman*.

107. Dobash and Dobash, *Violence Against Wives*; Roy, "A current survey of 150 cases."

108. Star et al., "Psychosocial aspects of wife battering."

109. Gaquin, "Spouse abuse: data from the National Crime Survey."

110. Boudouris, "Homicide and the family."

111. Eisenberg and Micklow, "The assaulted wife: 'Catch-22' revisited"; Roy, "A current survey of 150 cases."

112. Dobash and Dobash, *Violence Against Wives*.

113. Rounsaville, "Battered wives: barriers to identification and treatment."

114. Serum, "Battered women and batterers"; Walker, *The Battered Woman*.

115. Gayford, "Wife battering: a preliminary survey of 100 cases."

116. Eisenberg and Micklow, "The assaulted wife: 'Catch-22' revisited."

117. Bard and Zacker, "The prevention of family violence: dilemmas of community intervention"; Carlson, "Battered women and their assailants"; Dobash and Dobash, *Violence Against Wives;* "A current survey of 150 cases."

118. Carlson, "Battered women and their assailants"; Dobash and Dobash, *Violence Against Wives*; Prescot and Letko, "Battered women: a social psychological perspective"; Roy, "A current survey of 150 cases."

119. Carlson, "Battered women and their assailants"; Dobash and Dobash, *Violence Against Wives*; Roy, "A current survey of 150 cases."

120. Carlson, "Battered women and their assailants."

121. Roy, "A current survey of 150 cases."

122. Prescott and Letko, "Battered women: a social psychological perspective"; Star et al., "Psychosocial aspects of wife battering"; Walker, *The Battered Woman*.

123. Eisenberg and Micklow, "The assaulted wife: 'Catch-22' revisited"; Gayford, "Wife battering: a preliminary survey of 100 cases"; Rounsaville, "Battered wives: barriers to identification and treatment."

124. Gelles, *The Violent Home*; Whitehurst, "Violently jealous husbands"; O'Brien, "Violence in divorce-prone families."

125. Gelles, *The Violent Home*.

126. Dobash and Dobash, *Violence Against Wives*; Eisenberg and Micklow, "The assaulted wife: 'Catch-22' revisited"; Gayford, "Wife battering: a preliminary survey of 100 cases"; Prescot and Letko, "Battered women: a social psychological perspective".

127. Eisenberg and Micklow, "The assaulted wife: 'Catch-22' revisited"; Gelles, *The Violent Home*.

128. Eisenberg and Micklow, "The assaulted wife: 'Catch-22' revisited"; Prescott and Letko, "Battered women: a social psychological perspective"; Gayford, "Wife battering: a preliminary survey of 100 cases."

129. Dobash and Dobash, *Violence Against Wives*; Eisenberg and Micklow, "The assaulted wife: 'Catch-22' revisited"; Gayford, "Wife battering: a preliminary survey of 100 cases."

130. Straus, Gelles, and Steinmetz, *Behind Closed Doors*.

131. Wolfgang, cited in "Wife-beating: facts and figures," Fields; Mowat, *Morbid Jealousy and Murder*; Straus, "A sociological perspective on the prevention and treatment of wife-beating."

132. Dobash and Dobash, *Violence Against Wives*; Gayford, "Wife battering: a preliminary survey of 100 cases."

133. Dobash and Dobash, *Violence Against Wives*; Gayford, "Wife battering: a preliminary survey of 100 cases"; Walker, *The Battered Woman*; Langley and Levy, *Wife-beating: the Silent Crisis*.

134. Dobash and Dobash, *Violence Against Wives*.

135. Carlson, "Battered women and their assailants"; Dobash and Dobash, *Violence Against Wives*; Prescott and Letko, "Battered women: a social psychological perspective"; Pagelow, *Woman-battering: Victims and Their Experiences*; Gaquin, "Spouse abuse: data from the National Crime Survey."

136. Gaquin, "Spouse abuse: data from the National Crime Survey."

137. Carlson, "Battered women and their assailants."

138. Albert Bandura, *Aggression—A Social Learning Analysis* (Englewood Cliffs, NJ: Prentice-Hall, 1973); Gelles, *The Violent Home*.

139. Dobash and Dobash, *Violence Against Wives*; Gayford, "Wife battering: a preliminary survey of 100 cases."

140. Gayford, "Wife battering: a preliminary survey of 100 cases"; Gelles, *The Violent Home*; Gelles, "Violence and pregnancy."

141. Gelles, *The Violent Home*; Gelles, "Violence and pregnancy."

142. Carlson, "Battered women and their assailants"; Eisenberg and Micklow, "The assaulted wife: 'Catch-22' revisited"; Flynn, "Recent findings related to wife abuse"; Gelles, *The Violent Home*; Gelles, "Violence and pregnancy"; Rounsaville, "Battered wives: barriers to identification and treatment."

143. Gelles, *The Violent Home*; Gelles, "Violence and pregnancy."

144. Gelles, "Violence and pregnancy."

145. Gayford, "Wife battering: a preliminary survey of 100 cases"; Star et al., "Psychosocial aspects of wife battering."

146. Gelles, "Violence and pregnancy."

147. Gelles, "Violence and pregnancy."

148. Gelles, "Violence and pregnancy"; Eisenberg and Micklow, "The assaulted wife: 'Catch-22' revisited."

149. Gelles, "Violence and pregnancy."

150. "New State Laws Show America Taking Sexual Violence Seriously," *Ann Arbor News*, 10 May 1984, B-1.

151. Star et al., "Psychosocial aspects of wife battering."

152. Gelles, "Power, sex, and violence: the case of marital rape."

153. Walker, *The Battered Woman*.

154. Hilberman and Munson, "Sixty battered women."

155. Prescott and Letko, "Battered women: a social psychological perspective."

156. Pauline Bart, cited in "Violence and pregnancy," Gelles; Susan Brownmiller, *Against Our Will: Men, Women, and Rape.*

157. Dobash and Dobash, *Violence Against Wives*, 182.

158. Ibid, 141.

159. Walker, *The Battered Woman*; Chapman and Gates, eds., *The Victimization of Women.*

160. Walker, *The Battered Woman.*

161. Karin Meiselman, *Incest* (San Francisco: Jossey-Bass, 1978).

162. Judith Lewis Herman with Lisa Hirschman, *Father-Daughter Incest* (Cambridge, MA: Harvard University Press, 1981).

163. M. Faulk, "Sexual factors in marital violence," *Medical Aspects of Human Sexuality* 11, No. 10 (1976):30-43; Walker, *The Battered Woman.*

163½. Walker, *The Battered Woman.*

164. Faulk, "Sexual factors in marital violence."

165. Mowat, *Morbid Jealousy and Murder.*

166. Field and Field, "Marital violence and the criminal process: neither justice nor peace"; Martin, *Battered Wives*; Whitehurst, "Violently jealous husbands."

167. Whitehurst, "Violently jealous husbands."

168. Faulk, "Sexual factors in marital violence"; Fields, "Wife-beating: facts and figures."

169. Gelles, *The Violent Home.*

170. Martin, *Battered Wives*, 169: "The legal definition of condonation is 'full and free forgiveness, expressed or implied, of an antecedent matrimonial offense on condition that it shall not be repeated. . .' . . .'Condonation is automatically implied' from just one act of sexual intercourse."

171. Dobash and Dobash, *Violence Against Wives*; Eisenberg and Micklow, "The assaulted wife: 'Catch-22' revisited"; Flynn, "Recent findings related to wife abuse"; Gayford, "Wife battering: a preliminary survey of 100 cases"; Hilberman and Munson, "Sixty battered women."

172. Gayford, "Wife battering: a preliminary survey of 100 cases"; Dobash and Dobash, *Violence Against Wives.*

173. Gayford, "Wife battering: a preliminary survey of 100 cases."

174. Roy, "A current survey of 150 cases."

175. Hilberman and Munson, "Sixty battered women"; Roy, "A current survey of 150 cases."

176. Pagelow, *Woman-battering: Victims and Their Experiences.*

177. Eisenberg and Micklow, "The assaulted wife: 'Catch-22' revisited."

178. Serum, "Battered women and batterers."

179. Walker, *The Battered Woman.*

180. Hilberman and Munson, "Sixty battered women."

181. Dobash and Dobash, *Violence Against Wives*, 144.

182. Levinger, "Sources of marital dissatisfaction among applicants for divorce"; Straus, Gelles, and Steinmetz, *Behind Closed Doors*; Gaquin, "Spouse abuse: data from the National Crime Survey."

183. Gelles, "Abused wives: why do they stay?"

184. Gelles, *The Violent Home*; Gelles, "Abused wives: why do they stay?"

185. Carlson, "Battered women and their assailants."

186. Walker, *The Battered Woman.*

187. Gelles, *The Violent Home.*

188. Dobash and Dobash, *Violence Against Wives.*

189. Gayford, "Wife battering: a preliminary survey of 100 cases."

190. Carlson, "Battered women and their assailants"; Eisenberg and Micklow, "The assaulted wife: 'Catch-22' revisited"; Flynn, "Recent findings related to wife abuse."

191. Eisenberg and Micklow, "The assaulted wife: 'Catch-22' revisited."

192. Gelles, *The Violent Home.*

193. Straus, personal communication, July 12, 1979.

194. Gelles, *The Violent Home*; Gayford, "Wife battering: a preliminary survey of 100 cases"; Carlson, "Battered women and their assailants"; Eisenberg and Micklow, "The assaulted wife: 'Catch-22' revisited."

195. Roy, "A current survey of 150 cases."

196. Carlson, "Battered women and their assailants"; Gayford, "Wife-battering: a preliminary survey of 100 cases."

197. Wolfgang, cited in *The Violent Home*, Gelles.

198. Eisenberg and Micklow, "The assaulted wife: 'Catch-22' revisited."

199. Bard and Zacker, "Assaultiveness and alcohol use in family disputes."

200. Gelles, *The Violent Home.*

201. Dobash and Dobash, *Violence Against Wives*; Hilberman and Munson, "Sixty battered women"; Martin, *Battered Wives*; Roy, "A current survey of 150 cases."

202. Hilberman and Munson, "Sixty battered women."

203. Straus, Gelles, and Steinmetz, *Behind Closed Doors.*

204. Steinmetz, "The use of force for resolving family conflict: the training ground for abuse."

205. Carlson, "Battered women and their assailants"; Flynn, "Recent findings related to wife abuse"; Gayford, "Wife battering: a preliminary survey of 100 cases"; Roy, "A current survey of 150 cases"; Dobash and Dobash, *Violence Against Wives.*

206. Gayford, "Wife battering: a preliminary survey of 100 cases."

207. Pfouts, "Violent families: coping responses of abused wives."

208. Hilberman and Munson, "Sixty battered women"; Prescott and Letko, "Battered women: a social psychological perspective."

209. Prescott and Letko, "Battered women: a social psychological perspective."

210. Hilberman and Munson, "Sixty battered women"; Walker, *The Battered Woman*; Meiselman, *Incest*; Herman and Hirschman, *Father-Daughter Incest.*

211. Eisenberg and Micklow, "The assaulted wife: 'Catch-22' revisited"; Gayford, "Wife battering: a preliminary survey of 100 cases"; Gelles, *The Violent Home*; Roy, "A current survey of 150 cases"; Star et al., "Psychosocial aspects of wife battering"; Carlson, "Battered women and their assailants."

212. Parker and Schumacher, "The battered wife syndrome and violence in the nuclear family of origin"; Prescott and Letko, "Battered women: a social psychological perspective."

213. Pagelow, *Woman-battering: Victims and Their Experiences.*

214. Parker and Schumacher, "The battered wife syndrome and violence in the nuclear family of origin."

215. Carlson, "Battered women and their assailants"; Eisenberg and Micklow, "The assaulted wife: 'Catch-22' revisited"; Pagelow, *Woman-battering: Victims and*

Their Experiences; Gayford, "Wife battering: a preliminary survey of 100 cases"; Flynn, "Recent findings related to wife abuse."

216. Parker and Schumacher, "The battered wife syndrome and violence in the nuclear family of origin"; Prescott and Letko, "Battered women: a social psychological perspective"; Star et al., "Psychosocial aspects of wife battering"; Walker, *The Battered Woman.*

217. Parker and Schumacher, "The battered wife syndrome and violence in the nuclear family of origin."

218. Prescott and Letko, "Battered women: a social psychological perspective."

219. Pagelow, *Woman-battering: Victims and Their Experiences.*

220. Dobash and Dobash, *Violence Against Wives.*

221. Roy, "A current survey of 150 cases."

222. Ganley and Harris, "Domestic violence: issues in designing and implementing programs for batterers."

223. Hilberman and Munson, "Sixty battered women."

224. Dobash and Dobash, *Violence Against Wives.*

225. Gelles, *The Violent Home.*

226. Carroll, "The intergenerational transmission of family violence."

227. Straus, Gelles, and Steinmetz, *Behind Closed Doors.*

228. Ibid.

229. Ibid.

230. Ibid.

231. Ibid.

232. Ibid.

233. O'Brien, "Violence in divorce-prone families."

234. Straus, "Leveling, civility and violence in the family."

235. Straus, Gelles, and Steinmetz, *Behind Closed Doors.*

236. Ibid.

237. Judson T. Landis, "Social correlates of divorce or nondivorce among the unhappily married", *Marriage and Family Living* 25:178-180.

238. Gelles, *The Violent Home.*

239. Straus, Gelles, and Steinmetz, *Behind Closed Doors.*

240. Star et al., "Psychosocial aspects of wife battering."

241. Dobash and Dobash, *Violence Against Wives.*

242. Gayford, "Wife battering: a preliminary survey of 100 cases."

243. Star et al., "Psychosocial aspects of wife battering."

244. Walker, *The Battered Woman.*

245. Mowat, *Morbid Jealousy and Murder*; Palmer, *The Violent Society.*

246. Serum, "Battered women and batterers"; Serum, "The effects of violent victimization in the family."

247. Dobash and Dobash, *Violence Against Wives*; Elbow, "Theoretical considerations of violent marriages"; John R. Lion, "Clinical aspects of wife-beating," in *Battered Women*, ed. Maria Roy:126-136; Serum, "Battered women and batterers"; Walker, *The Battered Woman.*

248. Hilberman and Munson, "Sixty battered women"; Martin, *Battered Wives*; Natalie Shainess, "Psychological aspects of wife-battering," in *Battered Women*, ed. Maria Roy; Walker, *The Battered Woman.*

249. Davidson, *Conjugal Crime*; Dobash and Dobash, *Violence Against Wives*;

Hilberman and Munson, "Sixty battered women"; Serum, "Battered women and batterers."

250. Elbow, "Theoretical considerations of violent marriages"; Ganley and Harris, "Domestic violence: issues in designing and implementing programs for batterers"; Hilberman and Munson, "Sixty battered women"; Lion, "Clinical aspects of wife beating"; Serum, "Battered women and batterers"; Walker, *The Battered Woman*.

251. Serum, "Battered women and batterers"; Walker, *The Battered Woman*.

252. Davidson, *Conjugal Crime*; Elbow, "Theoretical considerations of violent marriages"; Serum, "Battered women and batterers"; Walker, *The Battered Woman*.

253. Elbow, "Theoretical considerations of violent marriages"; Walker, *The Battered Woman*; Serum, "Battered women and batterers."

254. Davidson, *Conjugal Crime*; Ganley and Harris, "Domestic violence: issues in designing and implementing programs for batterers"; Geller, "Reaching the battering husband"; Saunders, "Marital violence: dimensions of the problem and modes of intervention"; Walker, *The Battered Woman*.

255. Dobash and Dobash, *Violence Against Wives*; Serum, "Battered women and batterers"; Walker, *The Battered Woman*.

256. Dobash and Dobash, *Violence Against Wives*; Walker, *The Battered Woman*.

257. Elbow, "Theoretical considerations of violent marriages"; Walker, *The Battered Woman*; Pagelow, *Woman-battering: Victims and Their Experiences*.

258. Elbow, "Theoretical considerations of violent marriages"; Martin, *Battered Wives*; Walker, *The Battered Woman*.

259. Ganley and Harris, "Domestic violence: issues in designing and implementing programs for batterers"; Gayford, "Wife battering: a preliminary survey of 100 cases"; Hilberman and Munson, "Sixty battered women"; Star et al., "Psychosocial aspects of wife battering."

260. Gayford, "Wife battering: a preliminary survey of 100 cases"; Hilberman and Munson, "Sixty battered women"; Walker, *The Battered Woman*.

261. Serum, "Battered women and batterers."

262. Dobash and Dobash, *Violence Against Wives*; Gayford, "Wife battering: a preliminary survey of 100 cases"; Hilberman and Munson, "Sixty battered women"; Serum, "Battered women and batterers"; Walker, *The Battered Woman*.

263. Dobash and Dobash, *Violence Against Wives*.

264. Dobash and Dobash, *Violence Against Wives*; Elbow, "Theoretical considerations of violent marriages"; Ganley and Harris, "Domestic violence: issues in designing and implementing programs for batterers"; Hilberman and Munson, "Sixty battered women"; Martin, *Battered Wives*; Mowat, *Morbid Jealousy and Murder*; Serum, "Battered women and batterers"; Walker, *The Battered Woman*.

265. Davidson, *Conjugal Crime*; Martin, *Battered Wives*.

266. Camella Serum, "Violent conjugal relationships: new psychological perspectives and treatment of the violent man", (Seminar conducted at the University of Michigan School of Social Work, June 23-24, 1980. Notes in author's possession); see also above discussion of statistical results in this work.

267. Dobash and Dobash, *Violence Against Wives*; Elbow, "Theoretical considerations of violent marriages"; Hilberman and Munson, "Sixty battered women"; Mowat, *Morbid Jealousy and Murder*; Serum, "Battered women and batterers"; Serum, "Violent victimization"; Walker, *The Battered Woman*.

268. Elbow, "Theoretical considerations of violent marriages"; Ganley and Harris,

"Domestic violence: issues in designing and implementing programs for batterers"; Lion, "Clinical aspects of wife-beating."

269. Ganley and Harris, "Domestic violence: issues in designing and implementing programs for batterers"; Martin, *Battered Wives*; Walker, *The Battered Woman*.

270. Martin, *Battered Wives*; Michigan Women's Commission, *Wife Assault in Michigan*; Walker, *The Battered Woman*.

271. Gelles, *The Violent Home*; Michigan Women's Commission, *Wife Assault in Michigan*; Walker, *The Battered Woman*.

272. Elbow, "Theoretical considerations of violent marriages"; Hilberman and Munson, "Sixty battered women."

273. Walker, *The Battered Woman*.

274. Walker, *The Battered Woman*.

275. Dobash and Dobash, *Violence Against Wives*; Eisenberg and Micklow, "The assaulted wife: 'Catch-22' revisited"; Elbow, "Theoretical considerations of violent marriages"; Hilberman and Munson, "Sixty battered women"; Martin, *Battered Wives*; Walker, *The Battered Woman*.

276. Martin, *Battered Wives*; Michigan Women's Commission, *Wife Assault in Michigan*; Walker, *The Battered Woman*.

277. Dobash and Dobash, *Violence Against Wives*; Eisenberg and Micklow, "The assaulted wife: 'Catch-22' revisited": Martin, *Battered Wives*.

278. Elbow, "Theoretical considerations of violent marriages"; Ganley and Harris, "Domestic violence: issues in designing and implementing programs for batterers"; Geller, "Reaching the battering husband"; Serum, "Battered women and batterers"; Walker, *The Battered Woman*.

279. Davidson, *Conjugal Crime*; Elbow, "Theoretical considerations of violent marriages"; Serum, "Battered women and batterers"; Walker, *The Battered Woman*.

280. Hilberman and Munson, "Sixty battered women"; Walker, *The Battered Woman*.

280½. Serum, "Battered women and batterers"; Martin, *Battered Wives*; Walker, *The Battered Woman*.

281. Eisenberg and Micklow, "The assaulted wife: 'Catch-22' revisited"; Serum, "Battered women and batterers"; Walker, *The Battered Woman*.

282. Eisenberg and Micklow, "The assaulted wife: 'Catch-22' revisited."

283. Michigan Women's Commission, *Wife Assault in Michigan*; Serum, "Battered women and batterers"; Walker, *The Battered Woman*.

284. Elbow, "Theoretical considerations of violent marriages"; Gelles, *The Violent Home*; Hilberman and Munson, "Sixty battered women"; Martin, *Battered Wives*; Serum, "Battered women and batterers"; Walker, *The Battered Woman*.

285. Walker, *The Battered Woman*, 87.

286. Walker, *The Battered Woman*.

287. Serum, "Battered women and batterers"; Walker, *The Battered Woman*.

288. Wolfgang, cited in *Violence Against Wives*, Dobash and Dobash, and in *The Battered Woman*, Walker.

289. Walker, *The Battered Woman*.

290. Dobash and Dobash, *Violence Against Wives*; Lion, "Clinical aspects of wife-beating"; Pfouts, "Violent families: coping responses of abused wives"; Serum, "Battered women and batterers"; Walker, *The Battered Woman*.

291. Dobash and Dobash, *Violence Against Wives*; Eisenberg and Micklow, "The assaulted wife: 'Catch-22' revisited"; Hilberman and Munson, "Sixty battered women."

292. Michigan Women's Commission, *Wife Assault in Michigan*.

293. Dobash and Dobash, *Violence Against Wives*; Eisenberg and Micklow, "The assaulted wife: 'Catch-22' revisited"; Hilberman and Munson, "Sixty battered women"; Martin, *Battered Wives*; Pfouts, "Violent families: coping responses of abused wives"; Serum, "Battered women and batterers"; Walker, *The Battered Woman*.

294. Hilberman and Munson, "Sixty battered women"; Martin, *Battered Wives*; Pfouts, "Violent families: coping responses of abused wives."

295. Michigan Women's Commission, *Wife Assault in Michigan*.

296. Ibid.

297. Hilberman and Munson, "Sixty battered women"; Serum, "Battered women and batterers"; Walker, *The Battered Woman*.

298. Martin, *Battered Wives*; Serum, "Battered women and batterers"; Walker, *The Battered Woman*.

299. Serum, "Battered women and batterers"; Walker, *The Battered Woman*.

300. Dobash and Dobash, *Violence Against Wives*; Martin, *Battered Wives*; Serum, "Battered women and batterers"; Walker, *The Battered Woman*.

301. Serum, "Battered women and batterers"; Serum, "The effects of violent victimization in the family."

302. Hilberman and Munson, "Sixty battered women"; Walker, *The Battered Woman*.

303. Gayford, "Wife battering: a preliminary survey of 100 cases"; Hilberman and Munson, "Sixty battered women"; Michigan Women's Commission, *Wife Assault in Michigan*.

304. Margaret Kovac and Celine [no last name], "Building on battered women's strengths," *Aegis*, No. 36 (Autumn 1982):27.

305. Schechter, *Women and Male Violence: The Visions and Struggles of the Battered Women's Movement* (Boston: South End Press, 1982), 232.

306. Elizabeth A. Waites, "Female masochism and the enforced restriction of choice," *Victimology* 2, Nos. 3-4:535-544.

307. Walker, *The Battered Woman*.

308. Walker, *The Battered Woman*, 59.

309. Walker, *The Battered Woman*, 65.

310. Walker, *The Battered Woman*, 69.

311. Walker, *The Battered Woman*.

312. Dobash and Dobash, *Violence Against Wives*, 137.

313. Dobash and Dobash, *Violence Against Wives*, 138.

314. Dobash and Dobash, *Violence Against Wives*; Serum, "Battered women and batterers"; Serum, "Violent conjugal relationships."

315. Dobash and Dobash, *Violence Against Wives*; Martin, *Battered Wives*; Roy, "A current survey of 150 cases"; Walker, *The Battered Woman*.

CHAPTER 4

1. Richard J. Gelles and Murray A. Straus, "Determinants of violence in the family: toward a theoretical integration", in *Contemporary Theories About the Family*, ed. Burr, Hill, Nye, and Reiss (New York: Free Press, 1979).

2. Helene Deutsch, *The Psychology of Women* (New York: Grune and Stratton, 1944-1945); Sigmund Freud, *New Introductory Lectures on Psychoanalysis*, trans. and ed. James Strachey (New York: Norton, 1965), Lecture 33: "Femininity."

3. Snell et al., "The wife-beater's wife."

4. Schultz, "The wife assaulter."

5. Anthony Storr, cited in *Violence Against Wives*, Dobash and Dobash, 134.

5½. Shainess, "Psychological aspects of wife-battering," 115-116.

6. Deutsch, *The Psychology of Women*; Freud, *New Introductory Lectures on Psychoanalysis*, Chapter 33.

7. Karen Horney, *New Ways in Psychoanalysis* (New York: W. W. Norton and Co., 1939).

8. Karen Horney, *New Ways in Psychoanalysis*.

9. Waites, "Female masochism and the enforced restriction of choice."

10. Boudouris, "Homicide in the family"; Martin, *Battered Wives*; Gaquin, "Spouse abuse: data from the National Crime Survey"; Walker, *The Battered Woman*.

11. Serum, "Battered women and batterers."

12. Waites, "Female masochism and the enforced restriction of choice."

13. Singer, "The nature of coercive control."

14. Serum, "Battered women and batterers."

15. Gayford, "Wife battering: a preliminary survey of 100 cases"; Serum, "Battered women and batterers"; Walker, *The Battered Woman*.

16. Martin, *Battered Wives*; Walker, *The Battered Woman*; Pagelow, *Woman-battering: Victims and Their Experiences*.

17. Saunders, "Marital violence: dimensions of the problem and modes of intervention"; Serum, "Battered women and batterers."

18. Saunders, "Marital violence: dimensions of the problem and modes of intervention."

19. Gelles, *The Violent Home*; Steinmetz and Straus, eds., *Violence in the Family*; Straus, "A sociological perspective on the prevention and treatment of wife-beating."

20. Serum, "Battered women and batterers"; Walker, *The Battered Woman*.

21. Albert Bandura, *Aggression—A Social Learning Analysis*; Albert Bandura, Ross, and Ross, "Transmission of aggression through imitation of aggressive models," *Journal of Abnormal and Social Psychology* 63, No. 3:575f.; Albert Bandura, Ross, and Ross, "Vicarious reinforcement and imitation learning", *Journal of Abnormal and Social Psychology* 67 (1963):601-607.

22. Bandura, *Aggression—A Social Learning Analysis*.

23. Walker, "Battered women and learned helplessness"; Walker, *The Battered Woman*.

24. Walker, "Battered women and learned helplessness," 526-527.

25. Walker, "Battered women and learned helplessness."

26. Walker, "Battered women and learned helplessness," 528-529.

27. Hilberman and Munson, "Sixty battered women"; Walker, *The Battered Woman*.

28. Walker, "Battered women and learned helplessness."

29. Serum, "Battered women and batterers."

30. Walker, *The Battered Woman*.

31. Walker, "Battered women and learned helplessness"; Walker, *The Battered Woman*.

32. Pagelow, *Woman-battering: Victims and Their Experiences*, 46.

33. Pagelow, *Woman-battering: Victims and Their Experiences*, 40.

34. Pagelow, *Woman-battering: Victims and Their Experiences*, Chapter 2, 35-40.

35. Singer, "The nature of coercive control."

36. Serum, "Battered women and batterers"; Serum, "The effects of violent victimization in the family"; Singer, "The nature of coercive control."

37. Bruno Bettelheim, *Surviving and Other Essays* (New York: Vintage Books, 1980); Edgar Schein, Inger Schneier, and Curtis Baker, *Coercive Persuasion* (New York: W. W. Norton, 1961); Singer, "The nature of coercive control."

38. Serum, "Battered women and batterers"; Singer, "The nature of coercive control."

39. Steinmetz, *The Cycle of Violence*, 19 (Frontmatter).

40. Steven Morgan, *Conjugal Terrorism: A Psychological and Community Treatment Model of Wife Abuse* (Palo Alto, CA: R & E Research Associates, 1982), 30.

41. Serum, "Battered women and batterers."

42. Singer, "The nature of coercive control."

43. Serum, "Violent conjugal relationships."

44. Bettelheim, *Surviving and Other Essays*; Serum, "Battered women and batterers"; Serum, "Violent victimization."

45. Serum, "Battered women and batterers"; Serum, "Violent victimization."

46. Schein et al., *Coercive Persuasion*; Serum, "Battered women and batterers"; Serum, "Violent victimization."

47. Serum, "Battered women and batterers"; Serum, "Violent victimization."

48. Gelles and Straus, "Determinants of violence in the family"; Steinmetz and Straus, eds., *Violence in the Family*; Straus, "A general systems theory approach to the development of a theory of violence between family members"; Straus, "Wife-beating: how common and why?"; Pagelow, *Woman-battering: Victims and Their Experiences*.

49. Martin, *Battered Wives*; Walker, *The Battered Woman*.

50. Ann W. Burgess and Linda L. Holmstrom, "Rape trauma syndrome," *American Journal of Psychiatry* 131, No. 9:981-986; Martin, *Battered Wives*; Straus, "A sociological perspective on the prevention and treatment of wife-beating."

51. Bettelheim, *Surviving and Other Essays*; Serum, "Battered women and batterers"; Serum, "Violent conjugal relationships."

52. Georg Simmel, *Conflict and the Web of Group Affiliations* (New York: The Free Press, 1955).

53. Gelles, *The Violent Home*; Jetse Sprey, "On the management of conflict in families", in *Violence in the Family*, ed. Suzanne Steinmetz and Murray Straus; Steinmetz and Straus, eds., *Violence in the Family*, editors' introduction; Straus, "Wife-beating: how common and why?"

54. Gelles, *The Violent Home*; Steinmetz and Straus, eds., *Violence in the Family*; Goode, "Force and violence"; Goode, "Violence between intimates."

55. Goode, "Force and violence."

56. O'Brien, "Violence in divorce-prone families."

57. Gelles and Straus, "Determinants of violence in the family"; Straus, "A sociological perspective on the prevention and treatment of wife-beating"; Straus, "Cultural and social organizational influence on violence."

58. Murray A. Straus, "Sexuality inequality, cultural norms, and wife-beating", *Victimology* 1:54-76; Straus, "Wife-beating: how common and why?"

59. Yllo and Straus, "Interpersonal violence among married and cohabiting couples."

60. Steinmetz and Straus, eds., *Violence in the Family*; Straus, "Sexual inequality, cultural norms, and wife-beating."

61. Martin, *Battered Wives*; Walker, *The Battered Woman*.

62. Straus, Gelles, and Steinmetz, *Behind Closed Doors*.

63. Eisenberg and Micklow, "The assaulted wife: 'Catch-22' revisited."

64. Steinmetz and Straus, eds., *Violence in the Family*; Straus, "A sociological perspective on the prevention and treatment of wife-beating."

65. Dobash and Dobash, *Violence Against Wives*; Martin, *Battered Wives*.

66. Goode, "Force and violence."

67. Straus, "A sociological perspective on the prevention and treatment of wife-beating."

68. Ibid.

69. Ibid.

70. Gelles and Straus, "Determinants of violence in the family."

71. Ibid.

72. Goode, "Force and violence in the family"; Goode, "Violence between intimates."

73. Gelles and Straus, "Determinants of violence in the family"; Straus, "A sociological perspective on the prevention and treatment of wife-beating."

74. Gelles and Straus, "Determinants of violence in the family."

75. Martin, *Battered Wives*.

76. Straus, "A sociological perspective on the prevention and treatment of wife-beating."

77. Steinmetz and Straus, eds., *Violence in the Family*; Straus, "A sociological perspective on the prevention and treatment of wife-beating."

78. Owens and Straus, "Social structure of violence in childhood and approval of violence as an adult"; Steinmetz and Straus, eds., *Violence in the Family*.

79. Straus, Gelles, and Steinmetz, *Behind Closed Doors*.

80. Gelles, *The Violent Home*; O'Brien, "Violence in divorce-prone families."

81. Straus, "A sociological perspective on the prevention and treatment of wife-beating."

82. Ibid.

83. Ibid.

84. Ibid.

85. Ibid.

86. Ibid.

87. Straus, "A sociological perspective on the prevention and treatment of wife-beating", 214-215.

88. Straus, "A sociological perspective on the prevention and treatment of wife-beating."

89. Richard J. Gelles, "Child abuse as psychopathology: a sociological critique and reformulation," in *Violence in the Family*, ed. Steinmetz and Straus.

90. Ibid.

91. Straus, "A sociological perspective on the prevention and treatment of wife-beating."

92. Straus, "A general systems theory approach to a theory of violence between family members."

93. Ibid.

94. Dobash and Dobash, *Violence Against Wives.*

95. Straus, "A general systems theory approach to a theory of violence between family members."

96. Gelles and Straus, "Determinants of violence in the family"; Straus, "Sexual inequality, cultural norms, and wife-beating."

97. Straus, "A general systems theory approach to a theory of violence between family members."

98. Straus, "A sociological perspective on the prevention and treatment of wife-beating."

99. Straus, "A sociological perspective on the prevention and treatment of wife-beating," 208.

100. Gelles and Straus, "Determinants of violence in the family"; Steinmetz and Straus, eds., *Violence in the Family*; Straus, Gelles, and Steinmetz, *Behind Closed Doors.*

101. Dobash and Dobash, *Violence Against Wives*; Schechter, *Women and Male Violence.*

102. Kathleen Barry, *Female Sexual Slavery* (New York: Avon Books, 1981); Chapman and Gates, eds., *The Victimization of Women*; Martin, *Battered Wives.*

103. Pagelow, *Woman-battering: Victims and Their Experiences*; Walker, *The Battered Woman.*

104. Dobash and Dobash, *Violence Against Wives.*

105. Walker, *The Battered Woman.*

106. Steinmetz, "The battered husband syndrome."

107. Chapman and Gates, eds., *The Victimization of Women*; Martin, *Battered Wives*; Barry, *Female Sexual Slavery.*

108. Brownmiller, *Against Our Will*; Pagelow, *Woman-battering: Victims and Their Experiences*; Barry, *Female Sexual Slavery.*

109. Pagelow, *Woman-battering: Victims and Their Experiences*, Chapter 7.

110. Eisenberg and Micklow, The assaulted wife: 'Catch-22' revisited."

111. Eisenberg and Micklow, "The assaulted wife: 'Catch-22' revisited"; Barry, *Female Sexual Slavery*; Martin, *Battered Wives.*

112. Davidson, *Conjugal Crime*; Dobash and Dobash, *Violence Against Wives*; Martin, *Battered Wives*; Schechter, *Women and Male Violence.*

113. Schultz, "The wife assaulter"; Snell et al., "The wife-beater's wife."

114. The term "scientific paradigm" as used here is taken from Thomas Kuhn, *The Structure of Scientific Revolutions* (The University of Chicago Press, 1970).

115. Martin, *Battered Wives*; Pagelow, *Woman-battering: Victims and Their Experiences*; Schechter, *Women and Male Violence*; Straus, "A sociological perspective on the prevention and treatment of wife-beating"; Walker, *The Battered Woman.*

116. Walker, *The Battered Woman.*

117. Schechter, *Women and Male Violence*, 215-216.

118. Schechter, *Women and Male Violence*, 232.

119. Barry, *Female Sexual Slavery*, 40.

120. Barry, *Female Sexual Slavery*, 166.

121. Barry, *Female Sexual Slavery*, 165.

122. Barry, *Female Sexual Slavery*, 4-5.

123. Ernest Bell, cited in *Female Sexual Slavery*, Barry, 34.

124. Pagelow, *Woman-battering: Victims and Their Experiences*; Walker, *The Battered Woman.*

125. Steinmetz, "The battered husband syndrome."

126. Goode, "Force and violence in the family"; Goode, "Violence betwen intimates."

127. O'Brien, "Violence in divorce-prone families."

128. Carlson, "Battered women and their assailants"; Gelles, "Abused wives: why do they stay?"; Rounsaville, "Battered wives: barriers to identification and treatment."

129. Dobash and Dobash, *Violence Against Wives*; Schechter, *Women and Male Violence.*

130. Straus, Gelles, and Steinmetz, *Behind Closed Doors.*

131. Gelles and Straus, "Determinants of violence in the family."

132. Gelles and Straus, "Determinants of violence in the family"; Steinmetz, "The use of force for resolving family conflict: the training ground for abuse"; Steinmetz and Straus, eds., *Violence in the Family.*

133. Gayford, "Wife battering: a preliminary survey of 100 cases"; Hilberman and Munson, "Sixty battered women"; Steinmetz, "The use of force for resolving family conflict: the training ground for abuse"; Straus, Gelles, and Steinmetz, *Behind Closed Doors.*

134. Laurie McLaughlin, "Children and women first" (Paper presented at the Visions Forum sponsored by the Pennsylvania Coalition Against Domestic Violence, Pottstown, PA, November 6, 1982).

135. Massachusetts Coalition of Battered Women Service Groups, *For Shelter and Beyond*; Dobash and Dobash, *Violence Against Wives.*

136. Straus, "A sociological perspective on the prevention and treatment of wife-beating."

CHAPTER 5

1. Singer, "The nature of coercive control."

2. Schein et al., *Coercive Persuasion.*

3. Barry, *Female Sexual Slavery.*

4. Schein et al., *Coercive Persuasion*; Robert Jay Lifton, *Thought Reform and the Psychology of Totalism* (New York: W. W. Norton, 1961).

5. Walker, *The Battered Woman.*

6. See Pagelow, *Woman-battering: Victims and Their Experiences*, Chapter 7, for especially dramatic case histories involving abduction; also Martin, *Battered Wives*; Walker, *The Battered Woman*; Michigan Women's Commission, *Wife Assault in Michigan.*

6½. Cognitive dissonance is an effect displayed in psychological research, in which subjects induced to express attitudes contrary to their own experience a resultant attitude change in the direction of the opinion they have been induced to express.

7. Schein et al., *Coercive Persuasion.*

8. Author's process notes.

9. Author's process notes.

10. Singer, "The nature of coercive control"; Serum, "Violent victimization."

11. Schein et al., *Coercive Persuasion*, 131.
12. Schein et al., *Coercive Persuasion*, Chapter 4, 117f.
13. Schein et al., *Coercive Persuasion*, 127.
14. Schein et al., *Coercive Persuasion*, 125.
15. Schein et al., *Coercive Persuasion*, 125.
16. Ibid.
17. Eisenberg and Micklow, "The assaulted wife: 'Catch-22' revisited."
18. Author's process notes.
19. Author's process notes.
20. Schein et al., *Coercive Persuasion*, Chapter 4.
21. Ibid.
22. E.g., *Matchbox*, the newspaper of Amnesty International, reports routinely on incidents of sexual abuse of political prisoners as part of its overall mission of reporting on the condition of prisoners of conscience from around the world.
23. Author's process notes.
24. Schein et al., *Coercive Persuasion*, 126.
25. Walker, *The Battered Woman*, Chapter 8.
26. Schein et al., *Coercive Persuasion*, 126-127.
27. Author's process notes. Similar testimony is given by graduates of the EMERGE counseling program in the film "To Have and to Hold," available from EMERGE.
28. Author's process notes.
29. Schein et al., *Coercive Persuasion*, 127.
30. Singer, "The nature of coercive control."
31. Author's process notes.
32. Author's process notes.
33. Schein et al., *Coercive Persuasion*, 127.
34. Ibid.
35. Lifton, *Thought Reform and the Psychology of Totalism*.
36. Serum, "Battered women and batterers"; Serum, "Violent conjugal relationships"; Singer, "The nature of coercive control"; Walker, *The Battered Woman*; Walker, "Battered women and learned helplessness."
37. Walker, "Battered women and learned helplessness."
38. Serum, "Battered women and batterers"; Serum, "Violent conjugal relationships."
39. E.g., Linda Lovelace, *Ordeal* (New York: Berkley Books, 1981).
40. Straus, "Wife-beating: how common and why?", 446; see also Table 1 in the present work for the identical figures.
41. Schein et al., *Coercive Persuasion*, Chapter 5, 140ff.
42. Schein et al., *Coercive Persuasion*, 140.
43. Ibid.
44. Schein et al., *Coercive Persuasion*, 141.
45. Schein et al., *Coercive Persuasion*, 142.
46. Ibid.
47. Schein et al., *Coercive Persuasion*, 142.
48. Ibid.
49. Schein et al., *Coercive Persuasion*, 142-143.
50. Schein et al., *Coercive Persuasion*, 143.

51. Schein et al., *Coercive Persuasion*; Lifton, *Thought Reform and the Psychology of Totalism.*
52. Barry, *Female Sexual Slavery*, 93.
53. Barry, *Female Sexual Slavery*, 94-95.
54. Ibid.
55. Walker, *The Battered Woman.*
56. Lovelace, *Ordeal.*
57. Waites, "Female masochism and the enforced restriction of choice."
58. Barry, *Female Sexual Slavery*, 93.
59. Barry, *Female Sexual Slavery*, 87.
60. Ibid.
61. Barry, *Female Sexual Slavery*, 91.
62. Author's process notes.
63. Singer, "The nature of coercive control."
64. Steinmetz, *The Cycle of Violence*, p. 19 (Frontmatter).
65. Serum, "Battered women and batterers"; Serum, "The effects of violent victimization in the family"; Serum, "Violent conjugal relationships."
66. *Ann Arbor News*, 14 August 1980.
67. Steinmetz and Straus, eds., *Violence in the Family.*
68. Author's process notes.
69. The particulars of the current definition of family are not important to the present discussion. My definition of family under current standards is a group of individuals related by ancestry, marriage, and/or adoption, who generally—but not necessarily— live together or have lived together. Again, other conventional definitions of family apply just as well at this point.

CHAPTER 6

1. Gelles, "Abused wives: why do they stay?"; Carlson, "Battered women and their assailants."
2. Gelles, "Abused wives: why do they stay?"; Straus, Gelles, and Steinmetz, *Behind Closed Doors.*

CHAPTER 7

1. Eisenberg and Micklow, "The assaulted wife: 'Catch-22' revisited"; Gayford, "Wife-battering: a preliminary survey of 100 cases"; Geller, "Reaching the battering husband"; Parker and Schumacher, "The battered wife syndrome and violence in the nuclear family of origin"; Snell et al., "The wife-beater's wife."
2. Eisenberg and Micklow, "The assaulted wife: 'Catch-22' revisited"; Gayford, "Wife battering: a preliminary survey of 100 cases"; Star et al., "Psychosocial aspects of wife-battering."
3. Straus, Gelles, and Steinmetz, *Behind Closed Doors.*
4. U.S. Bureau of the Census, *Current Population Reports*, Series P-20, No. 349 (Washington, DC: U.S. Government Printing Office), 7.
5. Straus, Gelles, and Steinmetz, *Behind Closed Doors.*
6. Gelles, *The Violent Home.*

7. U.S. Bureau of the Census, *Current Population Reports*, Series P-23, No. 77.

8. U.S. Bureau of the Census, *Current Population Reports*, Series P-20, No. 349:1.

9. U.S. Bureau of the Census, *1980 Michigan General Population and Housing Characteristics* (Washington, DC: U.S. Government Printing Office), 24-1 through 24-17.

10. U.S. Bureau of the Census, *Current Population Reports*, Series P-20, No. 366:4.

11. U.S. Bureau of the Census, *Current Population Reports*, Series P-20, No. 334.

12. Straus et al., *Behind Closed Doors*.

13. Gelles, "Violence and pregnancy"; Star et al., "Psychosocial aspects of wife battering"; Gayford, "Wife battering: a preliminary survey of 100 cases."

14. O'Brien "Violence in divorce-prone families"; Straus et al., *Behind Closed Doors*.

15. U.S. Department of Health and Human Services, Public Health Service, "Trends and Differentials in Births to Unmarried Women: United States, 1970-76," *Vital Health Statistics*, Series 21, No. 36 (Washington, DC: U.S. Government Printing Office), 12-13.

16. Eisenberg and Micklow, "The assaulted wife: 'Catch-22' revisited"; Gayford, "Wife battering: a preliminary survey of 100 cases"; Hilberman and Munson, "Sixty battered women"; Prescott and Letko, "Battered women: a social psychological perspective"; Star et al., "Psychosocial aspects of wife battering."

17. David I. Verway, ed., *Michigan Statistical Abstract 1980* (Graduate School of Business Administration, Michigan State University), 140-141; Michigan Employment Security Commission (MESC), *Michigan Labor Market Review* Vol. 33, No. 9 through Vol. 36, No. 12 (9/78-12/81).

18. MESC, *Michigan Labor Market Review* Vol. 33, No. 9 through Vol 35, No. 10 (9/78-10/80).

19. Ibid.

20. MESC, *Michigan Labor Market Review*, Vol. 34, No. 5 through Vol. 36, No. 12 (5/79-12/81).

21. Lenore Walker, *The Battered Woman*.

22. *Michigan Statistical Abstract 1980*, 41, 256; Lawrence Rosen, State Office of the Budget, Michigan Information Center, personal communication.

23. Carlson, "Battered women and their assailants"; Gayford, "Wife battering: a preliminary survey of 100 cases"; Star et al., "Psychosocial aspects of wife battering"; Yllo and Straus, "Interpersonal violence among married and cohabiting couples."

24. U.S. Bureau of the Census, *Current Population Reports*, Series P-20, No. 365.

25. Carlson, "Battered women and their assailants"; Eisenberg and Micklow, "The assaulted wife: 'Catch-22' revisited"; Gayford, "Wife battering: a preliminary survey of 100 cases"; Gelles, *The Violent Home*; Parker and Schumacher, "The battered wife syndrome and violence in the nuclear family of origin"; Prescott and Letko, "Battered women: a social psychological perspective"; Roy, "A current survey of 150 cases"; Star et al., "Psychosocial aspects of wife battering."

26. Murray Straus, "Wife-beating: how common and why?"; Straus et al., *Behind Closed Doors.*

27. Parker and Schumacher, "The battered wife syndrome and violence in the nuclear family of origin."

28. Straus et al., *Behind Closed Doors.*

29. Straus, "Wife-beating: how common and why?"

30. Straus et al., *Behind Closed Doors.*

31. Straus, "Wife-beating: how common and why?"

32. Parker and Schumacher, "The battered wife syndrome and violence in the nuclear family of origin."

33. Straus et al., *Behind Closed Doors.*

34. Gelles, *The Violent Home*; Parker and Schumacher, "The battered wife syndrome and violence in the nuclear family of origin"; Straus et al., *Behind Closed Doors.*

35. *Michigan Statistical Abstract 1980*, 85.

36. Parker and Schumacher, "The battered wife syndrome and violence in the nuclear family of origin."

37. Straus et al., *Behind Closed Doors.*

38. Carlson, "Battered women and their assailants"; Eisenberg and Micklow, "The assaulted wife: 'Catch-22' revisited"; Gayford, "Wife battering: a preliminary survey of 100 cases"; Gelles, *The Violent Home*; Roy, "A curent survey of 150 cases."

39. Barry Kessner, Washtenaw County Council on Alcoholism, personal communication; U.S. Bureau of the Census, 1980 census figures for the Ann Arbor SMSA, available from the Washtenaw County Planning Commission.

40. Murray Straus, personal communication, July 12, 1979.

41. U.S. Bureau of the Census, *Statistical Abstract of the United States 1979*, Table No. 630 (Washington, DC: U.S. Government Printing Office), 381.

CHAPTER 8

1. Davidson, *Conjugal Crime*; Ganley and Harris, "Domestic violence: issues in designing and implementing programs for batterers"; Geller, "Reaching the battering husband"; Saunders, "Marital violence: dimensions of the problem and modes of intervention"; Serum, "Battered women and batterers"; Walker, *The Battered Woman.*

2. Davidson, *Conjugal Crime*; Walker, *The Battered Woman.*

3. Bulcroft and Straus, "Validity of husband, wife, and child reports of conjugal violence and power."

4. Davidson, *Conjugal Crime*; Walker, *The Battered Woman.*

CHAPTER 9

1. Gayford, "Wife battering: a preliminary survey of 100 cases"; Roy, "A current survey of 150 cases"; Pagelow, *Woman-battering: Victims and Their Experiences.*

2. Gelles, "Abused wives: why do they stay?"

3. Dobash and Dobash, *Violence Against Wives*; Snell et al., "The wife-beater's wife."

4. August B. Hollingshead and Frederick C. Redlich, *Social Class and Mental Illness* (New York: John Wiley, 1958).

5. Walker, *The Battered Woman*.

6. Walker, *The Battered Woman*; Hilberman and Munson, "Sixty battered women."

7. Gelles, "Abused wives: why do they stay?"

8. Gelles, "Abused wives: why do they stay?"

9. Pfouts, "Violent families: coping responses of abused wives."

10. Walker, *The Battered Woman*.

11. Gelles, "Abused wives: why do they stay?"

12. Dobash and Dobash, *Violence Against Wives*; Martin, *Battered Wives*; Snell et al., "The wife-beater's wife."

13. Walker, *The Battered Woman*.

CHAPTER 10

1. Straus et al., *Behind Closed Doors*.

2. Boudouris, "Homicide and the family."

3. Carlson, "Battered women and their assailants"; Pagelow, *Woman-battering: Victims and Their Experiences*; Pfouts, "Violent families: coping responses of abused wives."

4. Carroll, "The intergenerational transmission of family violence: the long-term effects of aggressive behavior"; Owens and Straus, "Social structure of violence in childhood and approval of violence as an adult"; Steinmetz, "The use of force for resolving family conflict: the training ground for abuse"; Straus, Gelles, and Steinmetz, *Behind Closed Doors*.

CHAPTER 11

1. Hilberman and Munson, "Sixty battered women"; Walker, *The Battered Woman*.

2. Michigan Women's Commission, *Wife Assault in Michigan*; Martin, *Battered Wives*.

3. Erin Pizzey, *Scream Quietly or the Neighbors Will Hear* (London: Penguin, 1974).

4. Francine Gemmill, "A family approach to the battered woman," *Journal of Psychosocial Nursing and Mental Health Services* 20, No. 9 (September 1982):22-39.

5. Boudouris, "Homicide and the family"; Gaquin, "Spouse abuse: data from the National Crime Survey."

6. Gayford, "Wife battering: a preliminary survey of 100 cases"; Roy, "A current survey of 150 cases."

7. Eisenberg and Micklow, "The assaulted wife: 'Catch-22' revisited."

8. "Study indicates arrest is best deterrent to repeated acts of domestic violence", *Ann Arbor News*, 14 April 1983, D-4; Ellen Goodman, "Arrests could solve domestic violence", *Ann Arbor News*, 19 April 1983, A-9. The findings of the police study apparently indicate that arrest significantly outstripped both mediation and temporary separation in preventing repeated reports of conjugal violence.

BIBLIOGRAPHY _____

Adams, David, and Isidore, Penn. "Men in groups: the socialization and re-socialization of men who batter." Paper presented before the annual meeting of the American Orthopsychiatric Association, April 1, 1981. Copies available from EMERGE, 25 Huntington Avenue #206, Boston, MA 02116.

Aegis: Magazine on Ending Violence Against Women. Washington, DC: Feminist Alliance Against Rape.

Ball, Margaret. "Issues of violence in family casework." *Social Casework* 58, No. 1:3-12.

Bandura, Albert. *Aggression—A Social Learning Analysis*. Englewood Cliffs, NJ: Prentice-Hall, 1973.

Bandura, Albert, Dorothea Ross, and Shiela A. Ross. "Transmission of aggression through imitation of aggressive models." *Journal of Abnormal and Social Psychology* 63, No. 3:575f.

_____. "Vicarious reinforcement and imitation learning." *Journal of Abnormal and Social Psychology* 67 (1963):601-607.

Bard, Morton. "The study and modification of intrafamilial violence." In *Violence in the Family*, edited by Suzanne Steinmetz and Murray Straus. New York: Harper and Row, 1974.

Bard, Morton, and Joseph Zacker. "The prevention of family violence: dilemmas of community intervention." *Journal of Marriage and the Family* 33 (November 1971):677-682.

_____. "Assaultiveness and alcohol use in family disputes." *Criminology* 12, No. 3 (November 1974):283-292.

Barry, Kathleen. *Female Sexual Slavery*. New York: Avon Books, 1981.

Bellak, Leopold, and Maxine Antell. "An intercultural study of aggressive behavior on children's playgrounds." *American Journal of Ortho-psychiatry* 44, No. 4:503-511.

Bettelheim, Bruno. *Surviving and Other Essays*. New York: Vintage Books, 1980.

Boudouris, J. "Homicide and the family." *Journal of Marriage and the Family* 33, No. 11 (November 1971):667-676.

Brownmiller, Susan. *Against Our Will: Men, Women, and Rape*. New York: Simon and Schuster, 1975.

Bulcroft, Richard A., and Murray Straus. "Validity of husband, wife, and child reports of conjugal violence and power." Unpublished paper in author's possession. Copies available from Family Violence Research Project, Dept. of Sociology, University of New Hampshire, Durham, NH.

Burgess, Ann W., and Linda L. Holmstrom. "Rape trauma syndrome." *American Journal of Psychiatry* 131, No. 9:981-986.

Carlson, Bonnie. "Battered women and their assailants." *Social Work* 22, No. 6:455-460.

Carroll, J.C. "The intergenerational transmission of family violence: the long-term effects of aggressive behavior." *Aggressive Behavior* 3:289-299.

Chapman, Jane Roberts, and Margaret Gates, eds. *The Victimization of Women*. Beverly Hills, CA: Sage Publications.

Davidson, Terry. *Conjugal Crime*. New York: Hawthorne Books, 1978.

Deutsch, Morton, and Robert M. Krauss. "The effect of threat upon interpersonal bargaining." *Journal of Abnormal and Social Psychology* 61:181-189.

Dobash, R. Emerson, and Russell Dobash. "Wives: the 'appropriate' victims of marital violence." *Victimology* 2, Nos. 3-4:426-442.

_____. *Violence Against Wives*. New York: The Free Press, 1979.

Dupont, Robert L., Jr., and Henry Grunebaum. "Willing victims: the husbands of paranoid women." *American Journal of Psychiatry* 125: 152-159.

Eisenberg, Sue, and Patricia Micklow. "The assaulted wife: 'Catch-22' revisited." Unpublished paper in the library of the Domestic Violence Project. (Revised and edited version published in *Women's Rights Law Reporter*, Spring/Summer 1977.)

Elbow, Margaret. "Theoretical considerations of violent marriages." *Social Casework* 58, No. 9:515-526.

Elliott, Frank. "The neurology of explosive rage: the dyscontrol syndrome." In *Battered Women*, edited by Maria Roy, 98-109. New York: Van Nostrand Reinhold, 1977.

Faulk, M. "Sexual factors in marital violence." *Medical Aspects of Human Sexuality* 11, No. 10 (1976):30-43.

Field, Martha H., and Field, Henry F. "Marital violence and the criminal process: neither justice nor peace." *Social Service Review* 47:221-239.

Fields, Marjory D. "Wife-beating: facts and figures." *Victimology* 2, Nos. 3-4:643-647.

Flynn, J.P. "Recent findings related to wife abuse." *Social Casework* 58, No. 1:13ff.

For Shelter and Beyond: An Educational Manual for Working With Women Who Are Battered. Massachusetts Coalition of Battered Women Service Groups, 1981.

Ganley, Anne, and Lance Harris. "Domestic violence: issues in designing and implementing programs for batterers." Paper presented to the American Psychological Association, August 29, 1978.

Gaquin, Deirdre A. "Spouse abuse: data from the National Crime Survey." *Victimology* 2, Nos. 3-4:632-643.

Gayford, John J. "Wife battering: a preliminary survey of 100 cases." *British Medical Journal* 1 (1975):194-197.

Geller, Janet. "Reaching the battering husband." *Social Work With Groups* 1, No. 1 (Spring, 1978).

———. "A treatment model for the abused spouse." *Victimology* 2, Nos. 3-4:627-632.

Gelles, Richard J. *The Violent Home.* Beverly Hills, CA: Sage Publications, 1972.

———. "Abused wives: why do they stay?" *Journal of Marriage and the Family* 38, No. 4:659-666.

Gelles, Richard J. "Child abuse as psychopathology: a sociological critique and reformulation." In *Violence in the Family*, edited by Suzanne Steinmetz and Murray Straus. New York: Harper and Row, 1974.

———. "No place to go: the social dynamics of marital violence." In *Battered Women*, edited by Maria Roy, 46-63.

———. "Power, sex, and violence: the case of marital rape." *Family Coordinator* 26, No. 4:339-347.

———. "Violence and Pregnancy." *Family Coordinator* 24, No. 1: 81-86.

———. "The myth of battered husbands." *Ms.* (November 1979).

Gelles, Richard J., and Murray A. Straus. "Determinants of violence in the family: toward a theoretical integration." In *Contemporary Theories About the Family*, edited by Burr, Hill, Nye, and Reiss. New York: Free Press, 1979.

Gemmill, Francine B. "A family approach to the battered woman." *Journal of Psychosocial Nursing and Mental Health Services* 20, No. 9 (September 1982):22-39.

Gillespie, D.L. "Who has the power?: The marital struggle." *Journal of Marriage and the Family* 33:445-458.

Goode, William. "Force and violence in the family." *Journal of Marriage and the Family* 33 (November 1971):624-636.

_____. "Violence between intimates." In *Crimes of Violence*, edited by Donald Mulvihill and Melvin Tumin. Washington, DC: U.S. Government Printing Office, 1969.

Herman, Judith Lewis, with Lisa Hirschman. *Father-Daughter Incest.* Cambridge, MA: Harvard University Press, 1981.

Hilberman, Elaine C. "Overview: 'The Wife-beater's Wife' reconsidered." *American Journal of Psychiatry* 137, No. 11:1336-1347.

Hilberman, Elaine C., and Kit Munson. "Sixty battered women." *Victimology* 2, Nos. 3-4:460-471.

Jones, Ann. *Women Who Kill.* New York: Fawcett Columbine, 1981.

Komarovsky, Mirra. *Blue Collar Marriage.* New York: Random House, 1962.

Kovac, Margaret, and Celine. "Building on battered women's strengths." *Aegis: Magazine on Ending Violence Against Women.* No. 36 (Autumn 1982):27.

Landis, Judson T. "Social correlates of divorce or nondivorce among the unhappily married." *Marriage and Family Living* 25:178-180.

Langley, Roger, and Richard Levy. *Wife-beating: The Silent Crisis.* New York: Dutton, 1977.

Levinger, George. "Sources of marital dissatisfaction among applicants for divorce." *American Journal of Orthopsychiatry* 26:803-807. Reprinted in *Violence in the Family*, edited by Suzanne Steinmetz and Murray Straus.

Lifton, Robert Jay. *Thought Reform and the Psychology of Totalism.* New York: W. W. Norton, 1961.

Lion, John R. "Clinical aspects of wife-beating." In *Battered Women*, edited by Maria Roy, 126-136.

Lovelace, Linda. *Ordeal.* New York: Berkley Books, 1981.

Lystad, Mary. "Violence at home: a review of the literature." *American Journal of Orthopsychiatry* 45, No. 3:328-345.

Martin, Del. *Battered Wives.* San Francisco: Glide Publications, 1976.

_____. *Battered Wives* (updated edition). New York: Pocket Books, 1983.

Martin, Peter. *A Marital Therapy Manual.* New York: Brunner/Mazel, 1976.

Meiselman, Karin. *Incest.* San Francisco: Jossey-Bass, 1978.

Meyers, Laura. "Battered wives, dead husbands." *Student Lawyer* 6, No. 7:46-51.

Michigan Women's Commission. *Wife Assault in Michigan.* Lansing, MI: Michigan Women's Commission, 1977.

Mill, John Stuart. *The Subjection of Women.* New York: D. Appleton and Co., 1870.

Morgan, Steven M. *Conjugal Terrorism: A Psychological and Community*

Treatment Model of Wife Abuse. Palo Alto, CA: R & E Research Associates, Inc., 1982.

Mowat, Ronald R. *Morbid Jealousy and Murder*. London: Tavistock, 1966.

Mowrer, Ernest R., and Harriet R. Mowrer. *Domestic Discord*. Chicago: University of Chicago Press, 1928.

Nichols, Beverly. "The abused wife problem." *Social Casework* 57, No. 1:27-32.

O'Brien, John. "Violence in divorce-prone families." *Journal of Marriage and the Family* 33:692-698. Reprinted in *Violence in the Family*, edited by Suzanne Steinmetz and Murray Straus.

Owens, David, and Murray A. Straus. "Social structure of violence in childhood and approval of violence as an adult." *Aggressive Behavior* 1, No. 3:193-211.

Pagelow, Mildred Daley. *Woman-battering: Victims and Their Experiences*. Beverly Hills, CA: Sage Publications, 1981.

Palmer, Stuart. *A Study of Murder*. New York: Crowell, 1960.

_____. *The Violent Society*. New Haven, CT: College & University Press, 1972.

_____. "Family members as murder victims." In *Violence in the Family*, edited by Suzanne Steinmetz and Murray Straus.

Parker and Schumacher. "The battered wife syndrome and violence in the nuclear family of origin: a controlled pilot study." *American Journal of Public Health* 67, No. 8 (1977):760-761.

Pfouts, Jane. "Violent families: coping responses of abused wives." *Child Welfare* 57, No. 2:101-111.

Pizzey, Erin. *Scream Quietly or the Neighbors Will Hear*. London: Penguin, 1974.

Prescott, Suzanne, and Carolyn Letko. "Battered women: a social psychological perspective." In *Battered Women*, edited by Maria Roy, 72-96.

Response. Washington, DC: Center for Women Policy Studies.

Reynolds, R., and E. Siegle. "A study of casework with sado-masochistic marriage partners." *Social Casework* 40:545-551.

Rounsaville, Bruce J. "Battered wives: barriers to and identification and treatment." *American Journal of Orthopsychiatry* 48, No. 3:487-494.

Roy, Maria. "A current survey of 150 cases." In *Battered Women*, edited by Maria Roy, 25-44.

_____, ed. *Battered Women*. New York: Van Nostrand Reinhold, 1977.

Saunders, Dan. "Marital violence: dimensions of the problem and modes of intervention." *Journal of Marriage and Family Counseling* 3, No. 1: 43-55.

Schechter, Susan. *Women and Male Violence: The Visions and Struggles of the Battered Women's Movement*. Boston: South End Press, 1982.

Schein, Edgar H., Inge Schneier, and Curtis H. Barker. *Coercive Persuasion*. New York: W. W. Norton, 1961.

Schultz, Leroy G. "The wife assaulter: one type observed and treated in a probation agency." *Journal of Social Therapy* 6:103-111.

Serum, Camella S. "Battered women and batterers." (Title possibly incorrect) Lecture presented at Hoyt Conference Center, Eastern Michigan University, Ypsilanti, MI, on May 9, 1979. Tape recording and notes in author's possession.

_____. "The effects of violent victimization in the family." Paper presented to the Michigan Coalition Against Domestic Violence, December 3, 1979. Notes in author's possession.

_____. "Violent conjugal relationships: new psychological perspectives and treatment of the violent man." Seminar conducted at the 1981 Spring-Summer Symposium, Continuing Education Program in the Human Services, University of Michigan School of Social Work, June 23-24, 1980. Notes in author's possession.

Shainess, Natalie. "Psychological aspects of wife-battering." In *Battered Women*, edited by Maria Roy.

Simmel, Georg. *Conflict and the Web of Group Affiliations*. New York: The Free Press, 1955.

Singer, Margaret T. "The nature of coercive control." Paper presented to the Michigan Coalition Against Domestic Violence, December 3, 1979.

Snell, John, Richard Rosenwald, and Ames Robey. "The wife-beater's wife." *Archives of General Psychiatry* 11 (August 1964):107-112.

Sprey, Jetse. "On the management of conflict in families." In *Violence in the Family*, edited by Suzanne Steinmetz and Murray Straus.

Stahly, Geraldine Butts. "A review of select literature of spousal abuse." *Victimology* 2, Nos. 3-4:591-607.

Star, Barbara, Carol G. Clark, Karen M. Goetz, and Linda O'Malia. "Psychosocial aspects of wife-battering." *Social Casework* (1979):479-487.

Stark, Evan, Anne Flitcraft, and William Frazier. "Medicine and patriarchal violence: the social construction of a 'private' event." *International Journal of Health Services* 9, No. 3 (1979):461-493.

Steinmetz, Suzanne. *The Cycle of Violence: Assertive, Aggressive, and Abusive Family Interaction*. 2nd edition. New York: Praeger, 1977.

_____. "The battered husband syndrome." *Victimology* 2, Nos. 3-4:499-509.

_____. "The use of force for resolving family conflict: the training ground for abuse." *Family Coordinator* 26, No. 1:19-26.

_____. "Wife-beating, husband-beating: a comparison of the use of physical violence between spouses to resolve marital fights." In *Battered Women*, edited by Maria Roy, 63-72.

Steinmetz, Suzanne, and Murray A. Straus, eds. *Violence in the Family*. New York: Harper and Row, 1974.

Stephens, Darrel. "Domestic assault: the police response." In *Battered Women*, edited by Maria Roy, 164-172.

Straus, Murray A. "A general systems theory approach to the development of a theory of violence between family members." *Social Science Information* 12 (1973):105-125.

Straus, Murray A. "Cultural and social organizational influence on violence between family members." In *Configurations: Biological and Cultural Factors in Sexuality and Family Life*, edited by Raymond Price and Barrier. Lexington, MA: Lexington Books, D. C. Heath, 1974.

_____." Leveling, civility and violence in the family." *Journal of Marriage and the Family* 36:13-30.

_____. "Sexual inequality, cultural norms, and wife-beating." *Victimology* 1:54-76.

_____. "A sociological perspective on the prevention and treatment of wife-beating." In *Battered Women*, edited by Maria Roy, 194-239.

_____. "Wife-beating: how common and why?" *Victimology* 2, Nos. 3-4: 443-459.

Straus, Murray A., Richard J. Gelles, and Suzanne Steinmetz. *Behind Closed Doors: Violence in the American Family*. Garden City, NY: Anchor/ Doubleday, 1980.

Waites, Elizabeth A. "Female masochism and the enforced restriction of choice." *Victimology* 2, Nos. 3-4:535-544.

Walker, Lenore. "Battered women and learned helplessness." *Victimology* 2, Nos. 3-4:525-534.

_____. *The Battered Woman*. New York: Harper Colophon, Harper and Row, 1979.

Ward, David, Maurice Jackson, and Renee Ward. "Crimes of violence by women." In *Crimes of Violence*, edited by Donald Mulvihill and Melvin Tumin, 843-909. Washington, DC: U. S. Government Printing Office, 1969.

Warrior, Betsy, ed. *Working on Wife Abuse*. Cambridge, MA: Warrior, 1977.

Whitehurst, Robert. "Violence in husband-wife interaction." In *Violence in the Family*, edited by Steinmetz and Straus.

_____. "Violently jealous husbands." In *Sexual Issues in Marriage*, edited by Leonard Gross, 75-85. New York: Spectrum Publications, Inc., 1975.

Yllo, Kersti, and Murray A. Straus. "Interpersonal violence among married and cohabiting couples." Unpublished paper in author's possession. Copies available from Family Violence Research Project, Department of Sociology, University of New Hampshire, Durham, NH.

INDEX